Cambridge Studies in Early Modern British History

THE BLESSED REVOLUTION

Cambridge Studies in Early Modern British History

Series editors

ANTHONY FLETCHER
Professor of Modern History, University of Durham

JOHN GUY
Reader in British History, University of Bristol

and JOHN MORRILL
*Lecturer in History, University of Cambridge, and
Fellow and Tutor of Selwyn College*

This is a series of monographs and studies covering many aspects of the history of the British Isles between the late fifteenth century and the early eighteenth century. It includes the work of established scholars and pioneering work by a new generation of scholars. It includes both reviews and revisions of major topics and books which open up new historical terrain or which reveal startling new perspectives on familiar subjects. All the volumes set detailed research into broader perspectives and the books are intended for the use of students as well as of their teachers.

Titles in the series

THE BLESSED REVOLUTION

English politics and the coming of war, 1621–1624

THOMAS COGSWELL

Assistant Professor of History, University of Kentucky

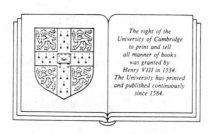

The right of the
University of Cambridge
to print and sell
all manner of books
was granted by
Henry VIII in 1534.
The University has printed
and published continuously
since 1584.

CAMBRIDGE UNIVERSITY PRESS

Cambridge

New York   New Rochelle

Melbourne   Sydney

Published by the Press Syndicate of the University of Cambridge
The Pitt Building, Trumpington Street, Cambridge CB2 1RP
32 East 57th Street, New York, NY 10022, USA
10 Stamford Road, Oakleigh, Melbourne 3166, Australia

First published 1989

Printed in Great Britain at the University Press, Cambridge

British Library cataloguing in publication data
Cogswell, Thomas
The blessed revolution: English politics
and the coming of war, 1621–1624. –
(Cambridge studies in early modern British history).
1. England. Political events, 1603–1625
I. Title
942.06'1

Library of Congress cataloguing in publication data
Cogswell, Thomas, 1952–
The blessed revolution: English politics and the coming of war,
1621–1624 / Thomas Cogswell.
p.   cm. – (Cambridge studies in early Modern British history)
Bibliography.
Includes index.
ISBN 0 521 36078 1
1. Great Britain – Politics and government – 1603–1625. 2. Great
Britain – History – Civil War, 1642–1649 – Causes. I. Title.
II. Series.
DA391.C64 1989
941.06'1 – dc 19 88–28249   CIP

ISBN 0 521 36078 1

WD

For Carole

Such hath bene the mercy of God toward us, that it which seemed the most dolefull accident unto us that hath befallen in this later age of the worlde that is to say, the secret departure of our Prince in Spaine, hath prooved unto us most behooful and beneficiall of anything whatsoever.

Archbishop Abbot to Sir Thomas Roe, 23 June 1624

Oh blessed alteration: oh blessed king: oh blessed Parliament.

[Thomas Scott], *Englands Ioy* (1624)

God bless the worcke . . . the worlde will discover in yt how bravelie he [Buckingham] takes uppon him the hazard of being a publique author of this greate revolution.

Lord Brooke to Sir John Coke, 12 October 1625

If God blesse this Parlement, we may hope to see some blessed revolution in Cristendome.

John Beaulieu to William Trumbull, 5 March 1624

CONTENTS

ACKNOWLEDGMENTS

In completing this study I have incurred many debts which I would now like to acknowledge. For an American simply getting to the archives is a major problem, and I am particularly indebted to the United States–United Kingdom Educational Commission, the American Council of Learned Societies and the Research Committee of the University of Kentucky for very generous assistance in overcoming this obstacle. Likewise the National Endowment for the Humanities underwrote an extended visit to New Haven, and the Graduate School of the University of Kentucky financed the purchase of microfilms. I am also obliged to the Shakespeare Institute of the University of Birmingham and Dr. Susan Brock for providing me with the resources and more importantly the space to begin drafting this book; and to the National Humanities Center where I finished the manuscript.

I would like to thank the many archivists and librarians who assisted this project, and I owe a particular debt to three libraries; the staff of the Berkshire Record Office repeatedly made room for me in tight quarters as did Maija Jansson and Bill Bidwell at the Yale Center for Parliamentary History. At the Public Record Office, in spite of repeated provocations, I never managed to wear out my welcome.

Since portions of this book have appeared elsewhere, I am indebted to two publishers for their kind permission to use some of this material: parts of the Prologue have appeared as "England and the Spanish Match" in *Conflict in Early Stuart England*, edited by Richard Cust and Ann Hughes (Longman, 1989), pp. 106–32; and part of chapter 8 as "Thomas Middleton and the Court 1624: *the Game at Chess* in Context," *Huntington Library Quarterly* XLVII (1984), pp. 273–88.

Early in my career I was fortunate enough to learn that references were an important commodity in an academic free trade zone, and although I fear I have overall been a net importer, I would like to record my thanks to several trading partners. Conrad Russell first introduced me to parliamentary diaries with the extended loan of those of Whitelocke and Grosvenor, while William Bidwell, J. H. Hexter, Maija Jansson, Mark Kennedy, Robert Ruigh and

Christopher Thompson encouraged this growing interest by very generously providing further diaries. I am also grateful to David Hebb for information about the Sterrell letters and to Roger Lockyer for insisting trips to the Berkshire Record Office would not be wasted. To Richard Cust and Christopher Thompson, I owe a particular debt for guiding me in the British Library and in various county record offices.

Advice and criticism is as important as information, and for these benefits I am obliged to Jerry Bowler, the late Joel Hurstfield, Peter Lake, John Nichols, Les Timms and Nicholas Tyacke who allowed far too many conversations to drift into my own concerns in the 1620s. I owe a greater debt to those who read and commented on early drafts of chapters, to Richard Cust, Derek Hirst, J. H. Hexter, Mark Kennedy, Robert Ruigh, Conrad Russell and Christopher Thompson. In this list three scholars deserve particular mention. Derek Hirst guided my first steps in the field as well as my thesis; that I ever finished anything owes much to his wisdom and patience. Richard Cust not only shared his exceptional knowledge of the decade; he also did much to ensure the completion of this study. Conrad Russell likewise has consistently supported my work, and even when it assumed a potentially awkward tack, he never flagged in his encouragement. To all three I am much obliged.

All these debts pale before that I owe to Carole Davis Cogswell who has cheerfully shared her life with an assortment of seventeenth century characters – and with this manuscript – for much longer than I care to admit. This book is dedicated to her in admiration for her talent, her energy and, most importantly, her forbearance.

ABBREVIATIONS

APC	*Acts of the Privy Council*
Beinecke	Beinecke Library, Yale University
BIHR	*Bulletin of the Institute of Historical Research*
BL	British Library
CJ	*The Journals of the House of Commons*
Court and Times	*The Court and Times of James I*, edited by R. F. Williams
CSPD	*Calendar of State Papers Domestic*
CSPV	*Calendar of State Papers Venetian*
Earle	Earle Diary, British Library, Add. MSS 18597
EHR	*English Historical Review*
Gardiner, *Buckingham*	S. R. Gardiner, *England under the Duke of Buckingham and Charles I*
Gardiner, *Prince Charles*	S. R. Gardiner, *Prince Charles and the Spanish Match*
Grosvenor	Grosvenor Diary, Trinity College, Dublin, MSS E.5.17
Hawarde	Hawarde Diary, Wiltshire Record Office, Ailesbury MSS
HHStA	Haus-, Hof und Staatsarchiv, Vienna
HJ	*Historical Journal*
Holles	Holles Diary, British Library, Harleian MSS 6383
Holles Letters	*The Letters of John Holles*, edited by P. R. Seddon
JBS	*Journal of British Studies*
JEH	*Journal of Ecclesiastical History*
Letters	*The Letters of John Chamberlain*, edited by N. E. McClure
LJ	*The Journals of the House of Lords*
Mémoires	J. J. von Rusdorff, *Mémoires et Negotiacions Secrètes*
Nicholas	Nicholas Diary, SP 14/166
NLS	National Library of Scotland
NLW	National Library of Wales

PH	*Parliamentary History*
PP	*Past and Present*
PRO	Public Record Office
Pym	Pym Diary, Northamptonshire Record Office, Finch-Hatton MSS 50
Rich	Rich Diary, British Library, Add. MSS 46191
RO	Record Office
Ruigh	R. E. Ruigh, *The Parliament of 1624*
Russell, Parliaments	C. Russell, *Parliaments and English Politics, 1621–1629*
Russell, "PH"	C. Russell, "Parliamentary History in Perspective," *History* (1976)
SP	State Papers, Public Record Office
Spring	Spring Diary, Houghton Library, Harvard University, Eng. 980
SRO	Somerset Record Office
TCD	Trinity College Dublin
Trumbull MSS	Berkshire Record Office, Downshire Deposit, Alphabetical Series, Trumbull Papers
Trumbull Add. MSS	Berkshire Record Office, Downshire Deposit, Additional Series, Trumbull Papers
Whitelocke	Whitelocke Diary, Cambridge University Library, Dd 12–20, 12–21, and 12–22.

NOTE

All dates are Old Style, except that the beginning of the new year is taken to be 1 January. The original spelling has been retained except in the quotations from the parliamentary diaries, which follow the modernized spelling of the Yale Edition.

Map 1. Europe on the eve of the Thirty Years' War

SCOTLAND
Edinburgh

ENGLAND
London

WALES

FRANCE
Paris
Orleans

North
Sea

SWEDEN

DENMARK
Copenhagen

POLAND

HUNGARY

Hamburg
Bremen
UNITED
PROVINCES
Amsterdam
The Hague

Calais

BRANDENBURG
Berlin

Magdeburg

Leipzig
SAXONY
Dresden

Cologne

HOLY
ROMAN
EMPIRE

LUSATIA
SILESIA
MORAVIA
Prague
BOHEMIA

AUSTRIA
Vienna

STYRIA
CARINTHIA
CARNIOLA
Salzburg

Liège
LUXEMBOURG
SPANISH
Brussels
NETHERLANDS
Trier
Heidelberg
Metz
Strasbourg

LOWER
PALATINATE
UPPER
PALATINATE

BAVARIA
Munich

TYROL

SWISS
CONFEDERATION

FRANCHE
COMTÉ

VALTELINA
MILAN

Lands of the Bohemian Crown.
House of Habsburg (Austrian)
House of Habsburg (Spanish)
Church Lands

100   200 km.
100 miles
0

INTRODUCTION

Radical changes were alien to Jacobean politics and foreign policy, and this stability clearly reflected the wishes of the monarch. Yet in 1624 even James himself could not prevent a shift in policy so fundamental that some contemporaries termed it a "revolution." Remarkable though the "revolution" itself was, equally unusual was the fact that this shift resulted from events in the Empire, not in England. Contemporary Englishmen have often been seen as oblivious to news from London, but at the beginning of the Thirty Years War they avidly followed news of the disasters that overwhelmed Protestants in general and the Palatine household in particular. Early success in translating the Calvinist Elector Palatine and his English wife to the Bohemian throne in 1619 was to prove short-lived. In the following year the Spanish troops acting under an Imperial warrant invaded the Palatinate itself, and Imperial forces financed by Spanish contributions crushed the Bohemian rebellion and sent the son-in-law and daughter of James I into exile. The collapse of the Bohemian uprising, moreover, did not appease Emperor Ferdinand II; thus in 1622 Imperial soldiers stormed Frederick's capital in Heidelberg, and in 1623 Ferdinand transferred Frederick's Electorate to Bavaria. These Catholic successes produced mounting domestic pressure for James to intervene to redress the balance. The eventual result was one of the more dramatic reversals in early Stuart history; in 1624, James abandoned his longstanding entente with the Spanish Habsburgs for a bellicose policy of confrontation, which the following year led to open war. In domestic politics this reversal was equally remarkable. A loose coalition of "Patriots," dedicated to a war on behalf of the Palatine exiles, ousted the "Spanish" faction which had hitherto dominated Whitehall, and the triumph of the "Patriots" was in large part due to their ability to work with Parliament, a task which had hitherto baffled James himself.

The present study analyzes this major shift in politics and diplomacy in late Jacobean England. It is hoped that the results will illuminate some of the murkier aspects of the interplay of foreign and domestic policies, the relationship between Crown and Parliament, and the linkage of "high" Court politics to the "low" politics outside the royal entourage.

In pursuit of these goals, it may appear initially that the appropriation of the term, "revolution," is unwarranted. After all, while the modern political definition of the term was in general use by the 1640s, the case for its extension to the 1620s is much more problematic; quite plainly neither Brooke nor Beaulieu had in mind "the complete overthrow of the established government . . . by those previously subject to it." Yet they seem to have meant the word more generally to describe "a great change in affairs," or as Henry Cockeram defined the word in 1623, "a winding or turning back." That definition certainly fits the situation in 1623–4 when plans for a Spanish war almost immediately replaced plans for an Anglo-Spanish domestic alliance. Furthermore, both men may have employed the word's original astronomical sense of a completed orbit as a metaphor for contemporary events; when Brooke congratulated Buckingham on leading "this greate revolution," he was praising the favorite for leading England back to the heroic days of Elizabeth, back to a Spanish war and Protestant unity.[1] Hence there is little question that both men witnessed in 1623–4 what was in their own terms a political revolution.

While revolutions, however defined, are inherently interesting, their fascination is intensified if they bear on historiographical disputes as directly as the "revolution" of 1623–4 does. The publication in 1979 of Russell's seminal *Parliaments and English Politics, 1621–1629* initially so unsettled the interpretation of early Stuart history that one scholar aptly described the period as a historiographical "minefield" in which those who publish "deserve awards for bravery."[2] Russell's "revisionist" work has done much more than produce a remarkable controversy; it has also emphasized the need for further detailed research. Although the dispute quickly polarized scholars in the field and even generated epithets like Whiggish "Old Guard" and revisionist "antiquarian empiricists," the two sides have never really joined in the promised battle royal.[3] Instead to date Russell has largely won the debate by default. Unfazed by furious theoretical counter-attacks, the revisionists have insisted that their opponents must "answer evidence with evidence,"

---

[1] Henry Cockeram, *The English Dictionarie* (London, 1623), sig. k; and C. Hill, "The Word 'Revolution' in Seventeenth-Century England," *For Veronica Wedgwood These* (London, 1986), pp. 134–51.

[2] Christopher Haigh, Review of Margot Heinemann's *Puritanism and Theatre*, EHR XCVIII (1983), p. 194.

[3] Kevin Sharpe, "An Unwanted Civil War?," *New York Review of Books*, 3 December 1982, p. 45; and Lawrence Stone, "The Revival of Narrative," *PP* LXXXV (1979) p. 20.

and the general failure to meet this challenge has justifiably allowed Russell early in 1987 to conclude that the "revisionists" had "won the debate".[4]

This outcome is particularly unfortunate; Russell's theories deserve a careful assessment, and a field renowned for exacting standards demands such an examination. This present study is in part a belated answer to the call for hard evidence. The essential task of evaluation arguably should be limited in its scope to the early 1620s. The present study began as an analysis of the ill-fated English attempt to intervene in the continental war, and considerable research into the origins of the Mansfelt, Cadiz and Ré expeditions revealed only that all lines of reasoning led back to the early 1620s and especially the Parliament of 1624. It is only a slight exaggeration to suggest that much of the controversy between Charles and his subjects later in the decade stemmed from different impressions about what really happened in the 1624 session. In 1626, for example, Roger Mainwaring sought to remind his countrymen that "the Resolutions of his [Charles's] owne Subiects represented in the high Court of Parliament, caused him to undertake [those wars] and that, with the highest Protestations and fullest Assurances from them, to yield him all those Subsidarie helpes that way, which, the Power, or Love of Subiects, could possibly reach unto." The other side of the coin can be seen in Mr. Newbery's *cri de coeur* of the same year; "when we engaged the king in this war it was not the intention of this House that we should send away our treasure and ships into other countries and pay 50,000l. per mensem to I know not who beyond the sea, but for a war as should be for our good and the weakening of our enemies."[5] Given the intense contemporary confusion over the agreements struck in 1624, a thorough understanding of this earlier Parliament was essential in order to comprehend the later problems.

Methodology also supports this narrow focus on the early 1620s. Generations of historians have struggled to make the often maddeningly ambiguous parliamentary documents speak more eloquently, and Conrad Russell has recently advanced one of the most promising means of gaining a new perspective on the Palace of Westminster. The traditional variety of parliamentary history, he argued, runs the grave risk of becoming so obsessed with legislative minutiae that it ignores the broader political milieu in which peers and MPs operated. And given the nature of Parliaments, a firm understanding of the milieu is indispensable. Since Parliament in one sense was a mirror reflecting events taking place outside Westminster, the best way of clarifying the fuzzy mirror images is to come to a better understanding of the outside

---

[4] Conrad Russell, "The Prisoner of His Documents?," *Times Higher Education Supplement* 9 January 1987, p. 16; Geoffrey Elton, "Two Kinds of History," *Which Road to the Past?* (New Haven, 1983), p. 113, n. 25; and Sharpe, "An Unwanted Civil War?," p. 45.

[5] Roger Maynwaring, *Religion and Allegiance* (London, 1627), pp. 28–9; and 12 June 1626, Whitelocke Diary, Cambridge University Library, MSS DD.12–22, fo. 232.

events.[6] Persuasive though this argument is, its leading advocate ironically cannot be said to have followed it in his book on parliamentary history; the overwhelming number of references and the focus of the volume is on Parliaments, not English politics. Russell himself confessed that by vaulting from session to session across a turbulent decade, an author "risks presenting something like a badly-cut film: a series of shots from a story in which the continuity has been lost."[7] Consequently, the fitful pursuit of his own model has produced a work which sometimes resembles this cinematic nightmare. More importantly, his axioms about parliamentary behavior have yet to be tested against the parliamentary context.

This book proposes to correct this lacuna. Russell rightly cautioned that "no mortal historian is ever likely to become equally familiar with the misdeeds of the saltpetre men at Chipping Sodbury, the fortunes of the Dartmouth fishing industry, the limits of King James I's confidence in the Duke of Buckingham, and the day-to-day fluctuations in Richelieu's relations with Marie de Medici."[8] In keeping with this injunction, the present study has been limited to the period between the Parliaments of 1621 and 1624 and during the latter session; it has also been restricted to *the* topic in this period, the appropriate English reaction to the disintegrating Protestant position on the continent. Such limitations and restrictions allow us to unravel the tangled political skein of diplomacy, Court politics and popular opinion immediately before and after the "revolution" of 1623–4; it also permits us for once to place the parliamentary texts of 1624 within their political milieu.

There is in addition a final reason for focusing on 1622–4. Ample opportunity exists for contextual studies of other parliamentary sessions, but centering on 1621, 1626 or 1628 would not bear as directly on the question of popular and parliamentary enthusiasm for intervention in the continental mêlée. Both Russell and Lockyer have argued that the majority of the political nation was "lukewarm" about military intervention in the first place. The localist perspective of most MPs meant that they were at best only dimly aware of the reasons for English involvement and more importantly that they regarded the costs of warfare as a violation of provincial autonomy. Consequently the ultimate blame for the failure of the war effort must be laid before the House of Commons whose members refused to shoulder the necessary financial and administrative burdens. Admittedly this view has elicited vigorous dissent, but it has also been employed to exculpate the government and in one extreme case to compare the Duke of Buckingham favorably with Sir Robert Walpole.[9] We can arrive at a more considered judgment of this

---

[6] Russell, *Parliaments*, pp. 1–2.
[7] Russell, *Parliaments*, pp. 1–2 and 121.   [8] Russell, *Parliaments*, p. 121.
[9] Roger Lockyer, *Buckingham: The Life and Political Career of George Villiers, First Duke of Buckingham, 1592–1628* (London, 1981), pp. 469–74; and Russell, *Parliaments*, pp. 70–84

question through the close study of England's road to war in the early 1620s. First of all, an investigation into the background of the continental military involvement will clear up some of the confusion that currently exists about the reasons for the press for war and about the strategy Charles and Buckingham sought to pursue. Equally important, a tight focus on the period before the expense of war made some contemporaries think with their purses affords us the opportunity to reconstruct a fairly clear picture of the contemporary response to the German crisis and to James's inaction. This contextual background in turn will illuminate the 1624 parliamentary debates on which Lockyer and Russell have largely constructed their cases. Thus then we will have more substantial grounds on which to come to a decision about the ultimate failure of the war effort.

These justifications, it is hoped, will excuse another work on 1620s, but they cannot excuse the fact that criticism is perhaps more evident than approbation. Unfortunately it is not possible to redress this imbalance without producing an intolerably long work. The students of the period will quickly see how much this book owes to preceding scholars; for others, suffice it to say that such is the achievement of earlier historians that this book at very best can merely hope to supplement their labors; it cannot supplant them.

and *passim*. See also Kevin Sharpe, "The Personal Rule of Charles I," *Before the English Civil War*, pp. 54–8; and J. C. D. Clark, *Revolution and Rebellion* (Cambridge, 1986), pp. 85–6.

Prologue

"The evill time," 1622–1623

CAROLUS REDUX

Late on 5 October 1623 Mr. Wiat, a publican in Godalming, welcomed a group of prominent travellers who had stopped to refresh themselves. The fact that such a distinguished party insisted on riding through the night to London was peculiar, and the visitors' evasive replies to polite enquiries about their travels further aroused suspicion. Eventually these questions were all resolved when they paid the bill – in Spanish coin. In the ensuing excitement, Mrs. Wiat repeatedly kissed the leader of the party while an old woman refused to let go of his hand until he vowed never to return to Spain.[1]

The man was Prince Charles, and the scene at the tavern gave him fair warning of the pandemonium his arrival would cause in the capital. One commentator noted that Mrs. Wiat "had the first kisse the Prince gave"; there were to be many others in the next few hours. Earlier in the day, a salute from the guns of the fleet announced his arrival to the inhabitants around the Solent. Charles, impatient of any delay, left his entourage to disembark at Portsmouth while he and a small party rode to London. Dawn found the party at Lambeth where George Abbot, the Archbishop of Canterbury, greeted Charles and escorted him across the Thames to the Duke of Buckingham's city residence at York House.[2] When the Lord Mayor had learned of the prince's imminent arrival, he ordered the constables to prepare the customary demonstrations of joy. The citizens, however, had already anticipated the command and were in the midst of celebration before Charles crossed the Thames. Peter Heylin recalled that "Publick Societies and Private Families everywhere abounded in all expressions, both of Religious and Civil rejoycing," and John Beaulieu was confident his brother-in-law in Brussels

---

[1] Simonds D'Ewes, *The Diary* (Paris, 1974), pp. 162–3.

[2] *Ibid.*, pp. 162–3; John Finett, *Finetti Philoxenis* (London, 1656), p. 221; Phineas Pett, *The Autobiography* (London, 1918), p. 132; and Chamberlain to Carleton, 11 October 1923, *Letters*, II, p. 515.

could hear the city's "unspeakable joyes and universall acclamation." The bells pealed incessantly, and the "reioycing noyses" of "Ordnance, Musket . . . Drums and Trumpets" filled the air. The ensuing cacophony from "ringing of the Bells and the harmonie of the Mutiche was heard in every street 'pour l'aubade de sa bien venu.' "[3]

In the citizen's display, light was as important as sound. Fireworks "most delightful flew in every way," and the roof of St. Paul's was decorated with "as many burning Linkes as the Prince his Highnes was yeares old." On such a "very fowle and rainie" day, a bonfire required careful attention and considerable fuel. The crowds devoted themselves to the task and erected fires of "almost incredible" size and number: one at Blackheath for example began with fourteen loads of wood, and D'Ewes counted 335 fires between Whitehall and Temple Bar. Once the shops were "emptied" of their stocks of firewood, anything flammable was added; furniture, tubs and fat. In order to keep the blaze roaring, coachmen broke up their coaches, and watermen their boats. In places, "the people were so mad with excess of joy" that rather than drag a cartload of wood to an existing bonfire, they torched the cart and cargo on the spot. Later in the day when Charles hurried out to see his father at Royston, his coach had to turn up Charing Cross Road; it simply could not have proceeded directly through the City because several hundred bonfires blocked the main streets and "seemed to turn the City into one flame."[4]

Conflagrations of such size easily could have ended in tragedy, if, as Secretary Calvert remarked, "the heate" had not been "well allayed with London Liquor." Gentlemen and wealthy citizens distributed drink to the revellers, since Sir Benjamin Rudyerd observed, "So open-hearted men were, as't had been / No point of faith to think excess a sin."[5] "The saluations of joy" convinced Secretary Conway that there could not have been "a sober head between Southampton and . . . "; at first he wrote Royston, then added Cambridge and finally settled on "God knowes where to fynde one." Little wonder then that one poet found in the carnival atmosphere the appropriate image to commemorate the occasion. Just as 5 November lent itself to rhymes about "remember," so too 5 October naturally rhymed with "sober," as in "on the 5th day of October / it will be treason to be sober."[6] The collective result was awesome. "Harke," one popular poet began,

---

[3] Beaulieu to Trumbull, 12 October 1623, Trumbull MSS, VII/104; John Taylor, *Prince Charles His Welcome From Spaine* (London, 1623), p. 102; and Peter Heylin, *Cyprianus Anglicus* (London, 1668), p. 104.

[4] Chamberlain to Carleton, 11 October 1623, *Letters*, II, p. 515; and Taylor, *Prince Charles*, pp. 102 and 105.

[5] Calvert to Conway, 7 October 1623, SP 14/153/22; and "Benj. Rudyerd to the Prince at his Return from Spain," *The Memoirs of Sir Benjamin Rudyerd, Knt.* (London, 1881), Appendix, xliv–xlv.

[6] Conway to Aston, 10 October 1623, SP 94/28/127; and Taylor, *Prince Charles*, p. 102.

> I heare the bells doe ringe,
> Good Lord here the gunnes doe singe . . .
> The Mallincholly drummers doe beat,
> The Bonfires all are in a sweete,
> And melt away themselves in ioy.

Another contemporary recorded a scene of wild exultation: before dawn

an infinitt number of bondfires (and more I thinck then ever was seene before) was made, and that seconded with the noise of bells and drincking his Highnesses health even in the streets, there being many that caused whole peeces of wine and of beere to be brought in to the streets for everyone to take and the people for joy and gladness ran up and down like madde men and none of what condition soever would work upon that day.[7]

Fortunately for seven men and two women, their execution was planned for this day when "Ioy did so transport the soule of the whole Kingdome that death was loth to do his office," and the crowds liberated the prisoners on the way to Tyburn. Even normally staid Privy Councillors found it impossible to conduct business as usual. They attempted to handle the case of a minister who had plunged into affairs of state, but gave up the task "by reason of his Highnesse most happy arrivall here." Instead the councillors sent a letter to James reporting "such is the universall joy at this present and ours in particular . . . as we can better conceive it than express it."[8]

In all the "universal joy," the main attraction remained Charles. While he refreshed himself at York House, a mass of citizens, eager for a glimpse of the prince, immediately surrounded the palace. The throng was so thick that courtiers and officials had trouble getting into the ducal town-house, and when Charles eventually came out, his carriage had to be carried in places through the crowds. The celebration peaked when the coach passed with the duke "bowing to the people" and the prince "waving his hand and smiling." "The Peoples hearts did burn to see him," and the prince "leaned his body out of the Coach, with his hat in his hand and gave thancks to them all for their loves." The crowd in response shouted, "God save your Highness and the Lord of heaven preserve you." Once he had passed, the crowds then cried "We have him . . . We have our prince again."[9] The city, Dr. Ryves reported, "resounded all over with such shouts as is not well possible to express," and Sir Robert Naunton himself proclaimed " GLORY BE TO GOD." Sir Henry

---

[7] "Uppon Prince Charles his arrivall," Beinecke Library, Osborn b197, pp. 63–5; and Woolley to Trumbull, 10 October 1623, Trumbull MSS, XLVIII/104.
[8] *The Ioyfull Returne of the Most Illustrious Prince Charles* (London, 1623), p. 42; and *APC*, XXXIX, p. 95.
[9] Woolley to Trumbull, 10 October 1623, Trumbull MSS, XLVIII/104; Thomas Reeves, *Mephibosheths Hearts Ioy* (London, 1624), p. 31; Heylin, *Cyprianus Anglicus*, p. 104; and D'Ewes, *Diary*, p. 163.

Goodere observed "within the cirkles of myne eye and ear / I nought but ioy desceerne nought els can heere."[10]

Rejoicing quickly spread with the news across the country. In Coventry the bells rang through the night while the city council toasted the prince's return. In Great Yarmouth where the celebration rivaled that of London, old men "with droppes of ioy trickling along their cheekes" insisted "such triumphanting they did never behold." Even in small towns, the festivities were extraordinary: in Manningtree in Essex, when Samuel Ward preached a sermon on the prince's return, he spent much of his time rebuking his congregation for overindulgence. While it was understandable that the community scarcely know "how to express our ioyes enough," Ward reminded his congregation that "cheer of countenance, gestures of the body leaping and dancing are but dumb shewes."[11] After the initial celebration, many other towns held similar solemn thanksgivings with a sermon and a salute by the trained bands. The city of Oxford, for example, laid out almost nine pounds for the thanksgiving ceremonies, the city's largest expenditure for the fiscal year. "The Cantabrigians" on the other hand "will not be so contented" merely with "bondfires and musicke upon the topps of their steeples and such a noise with gunnes and orations in every college besides sermons in Latine and english"; they also dispatched "theire chiefe Doctors" to Royston to tell James "for all the rest" of their joy.[12]

The festivities were not confined to England. In Edinburgh, when news of the prince's return arrived on 13 October, the Scottish Council immediately despatched town criers to announce public celebrations and a sermon later in the day. As in London, official encouragement was scarcely necessary; the news itself prompted "shooting of ordanance, ringing of bells, setting on of bonfires, with the greatest contentment." Likewise the citizens of Aberdeen went out of their way to "expres the joy and gladness of the hartis of the people." Trumpets at the town cross, drummers in every street, and all the city bells summoned the population together to hear a sermon and toast Charles's return. Later the magistrates led the young men armed with muskets in a procession through the town. In the Irish plantations, the lack of bells often forced the English settlers to give their commemoration more overtly martial overtures: there the local militia mustered to practice drill

---

[10] Ryves to Ussher, 8 October 1623, quoted in Anthony à Wood, *The History and Antiquities . . . of Oxford* (Oxford, 1797), p. 351, n. 3; Naunton to Buckingham, 6 November 1623, *Fortescue Papers* (London, 1871), p. 9; and H. Goodere, "Congratulations to the Prince," SP 14/153/112.

[11] *Coventry: Records of Early English Drama* (Toronto, 1981), p. 417; Reeves, *Mephibosheths Hearts Ioy*, p. 37; and Samuel Ward, *A Peace-Offering to God* (London, 1623), pp. 12 and 16.

[12] *Oxford Council Acts, 1583–1626* (Oxford, 1928), pp. 322–3 and 420–1; and Locke to Trumbull, 10 October 1623, Trumbull MSS, XXIX/160.

formations and marksmanship. But whatever form it took, celebrations were held, Stephen Jerome proclaimed, "from Ulster to Connaught, as all in Great Britaine, even from Dan to Beersheba, from Barwicke to Dover, from Edenborough to utmost Orcades."[13]

The joy over the occasion was not soon forgotten, for poems, squibs, sermons, plays and buildings soon immortalized the event. Both universities organized formal ceremonies and issued volumes of Latin verse, and Cambridge printed George Vaughan's Latin oration to commemorate 5 October.[14] Sir Henry Goodere, Edmund Bolton, John Taylor, Sir John Beaumont and Sir Benjamin Rudyerd hastened to produce similar efforts in English while more popular writers brought forth less elegant rhymes, as one did, on "prince Charles his arrivall from Spain."[15] A little later, once "the extemporall dinne of balladry" had died down and "all the country and the Citie-wit, of bels and bonfires and good cheere was spent," Ben Jonson offered his own gloss on Charles's return in a masque, *Neptune's Triumph*. He recycled this masque in the following year as *The Fortunate Isles*. Later in 1624, Thomas Middleton aimed at a more popular audience and achieved a brilliant success in his version of the prince's trip abroad.[16]

For the rest of the decade the return of the prince remained popular material for literary treatment. In later collections in honor of Charles I, a poem on 5 October 1623 was almost de rigueur as it was in popular chronicles: "sodianely," John Vicars recalled, "sweetly to our admiration / He came to us, to our Hearts exultation." Likewise preachers found the topic irresistible. In 1625 Daniel Price intoned, "O let it never be unsavory to remember . . . your Highnesses returne." There was little danger of that: any minister attempting to persuade his congregation to reflect on God's providential care of England would be certain to link 5 October to 5 November and the Protestant Wind. "Shall we not blesse the God of Jacob," Henry King asked in 1628, "who hath brought back the staffe of our Jacob?"[17] The

[13] Stephen Jerome, *Irelands Iubilee* (Dublin 1624), dedication to Henry Wright; David Calderwood, *History of the Church of Scotland* (Edinburgh, 1842), VII, p. 580; and *Extracts from the Council Register of . . . Aberdeene, 1570–1625* (2 vols., Aberdeen, 1848), II, pp. 389–90.

[14] George Vaughan, *Oratio qua auspicatissumum serenissimi Principis Caroli* (Cambridge, 1623); *Carolus Redux* (Oxford, 1623); and *Gratulatio Acadamiae Cantabrigiensis* (Cambridge, 1623).

[15] Edmund Bolton, "Vinden, or the Blame is Spaines," Bodleian Library, Tanner MSS, LXXIII, fos. 420–1; "Poems of Sir John Beaumont," *The Works of the English Poets* (London, 1810), VI, pp. 33–4; Taylor, *Prince Charles; Memoirs of Rudyerd*; SP 14/153/112; and Beinecke Library, Osborn b197, pp. 63–5.

[16] Ben Jonson, *Neptune's Triumph* and *The Fortunate Isles*, printed in *The Complete Masques* (New Haven, 1969), pp. 409–24 and 433–53; and Thomas Middleton, *A Game at Chess* (London, 1966).

[17] John Vicars, *Englands Hallelu-jah* (London, 1631), stanza 55; Daniel Price, *A Heartie Prayer in a Needfull Time* (London, 1625), p. 18; and Henry King, *An Exposition upon the*

appropriate step, several preachers publicly suggested, was to add "one red Letter more . . . to our Calendar" on 5 October. Almanac-makers had no problem with memorializing 5 October, and at least at St. Margaret's, Westminster, church bells continued to toll on that day until the outbreak of the Civil War.[18] Others opted for more lasting memorials. John Packer, the duke's private secretary, erected on his estate in Kent a roadside chapel "ob foelicissimim Caroli Principis ex hispaniis reditum." Likewise the fellows of Exeter College, Oxford, made a conscious decision to dedicate their new chapel on the anniversary of "that very Day which made England most happy and triumphant."[19] Charles and his generation rather obviously were to find it hard to forget that something extraordinary had happened on 5 October.

The response to Charles's return was remarkable indeed. Unprompted and rapturous acclaim for a member of the royal family was a phenomenon with which the early Stuarts had not regularly dealt, at least not in the years immediately preceding 1623. The popular response earlier in the year to another order of public celebration only underscored the extraordinary character of the later festivities: then the citizens attended the bonfires "very thinly, if at all" and allowed them "to burn out without company." The contrast with the later celebration, D'Ewes observed, "twas prettye."[20] The public rejoicing, Naunton maintained, was "the happiest that mine eyes have seen" since James's accession to the English throne. Secretary Conway was less qualified: the "reall and hartie expressions" of joy exceeded those "as ever hath ben known upon anie occasion." Lord Carew concurred; "such ioy [was] expressed by all sorts of people as in the whole course of my life I have not seene it equalled."[21] From courtiers well known for their coolness towards Spain, these judgements are not especially surprising. But that of Bishop Laud is. The celebration on the prince's return clearly stunned this prelate who was certainly not driven by the desire for popularity: he recorded in his diary that on 6 October he witnessed "the greatest expression of joy by all sorts of people that ever I saw." Doubtless other courtiers and officials hardened to popular criticism shared Laud's surprise. Likewise for Charles

---

Lords Prayer (London, 1628), p. 102. On the later recollection of the event, see for example *Anagramma Regis* (London, 1625?).

[18] Westminster City Library, Archives, St. Margaret's Churchwardens' accounts, 1640–1, E23 [pp. 3–4]; Jerome, *Irelands Iubilee*, p. 214; Taylor, *Prince Charles*, p, 102; and *Pond 1629: A New Almanacke* (Cambridge, 1629). I am grateful to Conrad Russell for the first reference.

[19] John Newman, *West Kent and the Weald* (London, 1969), pp. 296–7; and John Prideaux, *A Sermon Preached on the Fifth Day of October 1624* (Oxford, 1625), dedication to G. Hakewell. I owe the first reference to the kindness of James Robertson.

[20] Mead to Stuteville, 5 April 1623, *Court and Times*, II, p. 385; and D'Ewes, *Diary*, p. 162.

[21] Naunton to Buckingham, 6 November 1623, *Fortescue Papers*, p. 9; [Conway] to Trumbull, 9 October 1623, SP 77/16/297; and Carew to Roe, 8 December 1623, TCD, MSS 708, I, fo. 228.

himself, the revelry must have been striking: nothing he had ever done had produced such unmistakable signs of popular satisfaction. Little wonder then that John Taylor proclaimed 5 October "our Royall Charles his second birth."[22]

Few historians would fail to note 5 October 1623 as a major divide in early seventeenth-century history, but fewer would find it easy to explain precisely why the country responded in such an extraordinary fashion. Thomas Scott, the celebrated pamphleteer of the 1620s, argued that the high spirits on 6 October were due to the fact that Charles returned "ALONE – o words of comfort." David Calderwood was even more specific; contemporaries gained the "greatest contentment" from the knowledge that "the Prince was not married upon the daughter of Spaine."[23] Yet while the Spanish match is the primary explanation, it is also one of the most mysterious episodes in early modern English history. While the records for the study of this episode are abundant, no scholar has pursued the line of investigation that S. R. Gardiner began over a century ago. Therefore, given the obscurity surrounding this entire period, any explanation about 5 October must remain tentative. Nonetheless an explanation, however provisional, is essential, for the return of the prince marked more than the final stage of the longstanding Anglo-Spanish entente; it also inaugurated a rapprochement of elements of the Court and the Country which had earlier been antithetical. This chapter will analyze the domestic crisis over the Spanish match in the hopes of making sense of the celebrations in October 1623.

THE SPANISH MATCH AND THE PALATINATE

Both the Spanish match, and the opposition to it, had their origins in the war and the myth that James I inherited from his English cousin in 1603. The former, after almost twenty years of warfare, had not proven an outstanding success. Elizabeth's greatest victory was simply holding her own against Philip II of Spain, and for this limited victory, the old queen paid an almost prohibitive price. Extraordinary parsimony and generous parliamentary subsidies proved unable to underwrite her restricted strategic plans; as a result even the sale of extensive Crown lands could not halt the steady descent into debt. Admittedly she secured the continued independence of the new Dutch Republic and the French monarchy, but her generosity seemed somewhat misplaced in 1598 when Henri IV concluded a separate peace with Philip,

---

[22] Laud's Diary, entry for 6 October 1623, *The Works of . . . William Laud* (7 vols., Oxford, 1853), III, p. 143; and Taylor, *Prince Charles*, p. 102.

[23] [Thomas Scott], *Vox Regis* (London, 1624), pp. 69–70; and Calderwood, *History of the Church of Scotland*, VII, p. 580.

leaving Elizabeth and the Dutch to shift for themselves. The obvious English response was to follow Henri's lead; thus one of the last acts of her Privy Council was to authorize the pursuit of an Anglo-Spanish peace. The new king heartily endorsed this move and presided over the Treaty of London in 1604.[24]

Englishmen soon discovered that in 1603–4 James was responding not so much to particular events as to a general aversion to war. A difficult childhood as a political football which Scottish magnates struggled to control left James with little appreciation for the traditional martial game of princes. "No man gaines by Warre," James insisted, "but hee that hath not wherewith to Live in Peace." Later experience only confirmed the view that the pursuit of a glorious military reputation generally changed little except the prince's financial solvency; "no Countrie," he observed, "can be called Rich wherein there is Warre." All things considered, he could think of more imaginative and enjoyable ways of spending money. One kind of war particularly horrified him. Religious wars, which had become all too common after the Reformation, made life precarious for prince and peasant alike. Confessional rivalries, more importantly, not only started many conflicts, they also threatened to eradicate the one James was bound to defend. Since Catholics substantially outnumbered the various reformed creeds and ruled the two largest European states, a general religious war was likely to make things quite uncomfortable for the reformed churches. Consequently, for James, a much wiser, if less glorious, alternative to religious confrontation was to avoid reviving "that bloody saint" of the "Bartholomey business," which had racked the late sixteenth century.[25]

James's devotion to the maxim, *beati pacifici*, should not overshadow the vital fact that his celebrated policy did not exclude the use of force. While a ruler should deal with "other Princes as your brethren, honestly and kindely," he should never forget that "warres upon just quarrels are lawful." James told his first English Parliament that "a secure and honourable warre must be preferred to an unsecure and dishonourable Peace." The operative word for James was "honourable"; he had warned Prince Henry, "let not the wrong cause be on your side." Thus James's parliamentary address on the conclusion of the Elizabethan wars neatly summarized his position on war: "I shall never give the first occasion of the breach thereof neither shall I ever be

[24] R. B. Wernham, *The Making of Elizabethan Foreign Policy, 1558–1603* (Berkeley, 1980), pp. 45–95; and Simon Adams, "The Protestant Cause: Religious Alliance with the West European Calvinist Communities as a Political Issue in England, 1585–1630" (D.Phil. thesis, University of Oxford, 1973), pp. 146–60.

[25] James I, *Flores Regis* (London, 1627), pp. 7–9; and James to Edmondes, 27 August 1612, *The Letters of King James VI and I*, ed. G. P. V. Akrigg (Berkeley, 1984), p. 324. See also D. H. Willson, *King James VI and I* (New York, 1967), pp. 13–57.

moved for any particular or private passion of mind to interrupt your publique Peace." But in a just, honorable cause, he would take up arms.[26]

Fortunately James reached the English throne at a moment when two decades of warfare had exhausted the major powers. In such a climate, James and his chief minister Salisbury found it comparatively easy to resist the pressure for a confrontational foreign policy and to adopt a position of friendly neutrality with both of the major dynasties, the Bourbons and the Habsburgs. From this position of safety the new king and a host of divines lectured the nation on the blessings of peace. "How did the Poets," John Denison asked in 1611, "sing of the Spiders making their webs in harnesse in the days of Numa Pompilius? And how doe stories ring of the shutting up of Janus Temple dore and keeping warre under locke and key, in the dayes of Augustus Caesar?" The same could be said for "these blessed daies of Peace" under King James.[27] His success in dealing with the Elizabethan war ironically meant that he had less luck with the other legacy from the old queen. Well before she died, the history of Elizabeth had begun to merge with the Golden Legend of Eliza. And as the memory of incessant warfare and grinding taxes faded, so too a recollection of Elizabeth's Spanish war grew rosier. Although the main thrust of her efforts had been on the continent, not in the Atlantic, it was the memory of the "sea-dogs" that tended to dominate all else. Since popular poets and writers rather than strategists were responsible for the articulation of this myth, it is scarcely surprising that dashing tales of larceny on the high seas overwhelmed more tedious accounts of garrison duty in Zealand and campaigns in Irish bogs. Thus the reign of Rex Pacificus ironically witnessed the florishing of a romanticized vision of naval action against Spain. John Webster, for instance, was only appealing to this popular sentiment when he interrupted a Lord Mayor's pageant to present "these seaven worthy Captaines who have made England so famous in the remotest partes of the world." Richard Hakluyt had obviously prepared the audience well with his extensive account of *The Principiall Navigations . . . of the English Nation.*[28]

As long as foreign neutrality could be maintained, the Elizabethan myth represented no danger to the Jacobean regime. Yet in the early years of his reign, peace owed much less to James's rhetoric than it did to Henri IV whose eagerness to challenge the Habsburgs allowed James to play France and Spain off one another. In one stroke in 1610, however, Ravaillac rendered James's

---

[26] James I, *Basilikon Doron* and "Address to Parliament, 19 March 1603," printed in *The Political Works of James I*, ed. C. H. McIlwain (Cambridge, Mass., 1918), pp. 88 and 270.

[27] John Denison, "The Blessedness of the Peace-maker," *Foure Sermons* (London, 1620), A2 and p. 33; and Adams, "The Protestant Cause," pp. 160–7.

[28] John Webster, *Monuments of Honour* (London, 1624), p. 2; and Richard Hakluyt, *The Principiall Navigations* (London, 1598).

foreign policy untenable. The assassination of the bellicose French monarch left France in the hands of Marie de Médicis and her thoroughly Catholic son, Louis XIII. Far from confronting the Habsburgs, Marie presided over a double marriage binding the two rival dynasties together.[29] Afterwards James could no longer assume that the Bourbons would check any aggressive moves by the House of Austria. Furthermore this dynastic reconciliation greatly increased the likelihood of any conflict degenerating into a general war along confessional lines. Consequently, whether or not James welcomed the role, he was increasingly to be expected to act his part as the Defender of the Faithful. The clearest indication of the rapidly altering continental situation came in 1612 when his daughter, Elizabeth, married the leading Calvinist in the Empire, Frederick V of the Palatinate. For years German Calvinists had pressed for closer English ties, and their efforts had long been seconded by a group of English peers, including the Earl of Southampton and the young Earl of Pembroke. Once the Habsburg–Bourbon marriages clinched their argument about the importance of confessional solidarity, James eventually agreed to the Palatine marriage.[30]

Although some contemporaries celebrated the match as the union of England and the continental Protestants, James had no intention of giving himself entirely to denominational politics. Closer ties to the foreign brethren offered excellent ammunition for those cool to the Protestant cause, to courtiers like the earls of Northampton, Suffolk and Somerset, and to envoys like Diego Sarmiento de Acuna, later the Conde de Gondomar. A godly foreign policy would not only increase the risk of a general religious war, but it would also force James into a humiliating dependence on Parliament. While members of Parliament may well have had no intention of seizing power from the Crown, opponents of the tilt towards Heidelberg were not concerned with such niceties. Instead they constantly stressed that down that road lay religious war and an impotent, impoverished monarch. The alternative to this bleak scenario was for James to re-establish the balance of power, and so ensure continued peace, through another marriage alliance with either of the great Catholic powers.[31]

These arguments guided James for much of the 1610s when he searched somewhat languidly for either a Habsburg or a Bourbon daughter-in-law. Haste was not noticeable in these negotiations, which one diplomat characterized as "relaxed" and another as subject to "many variations and changes." After Prince Henry's death in 1613, James was in no hurry,

---

[29] Roland Mousnier, *L'Assassinat d'Henri IV, 14 mai 1610* (Paris, 1964); and Maurice Lee, Jr., *James I and Henri IV* (Urbana, 1970), pp. 168–85.
[30] Adams, "The Protestant Cause," pp. 168–222.
[31] Adams, "The Protestant Cause," pp. 244–72.

particularly when delay forced the French and the Spanish into a bidding war for the adolescent Prince Charles. Of the two sides, James inclined to the Habsburgs. With a Spanish marriage to complement the Palatine one, the Stuarts would bind together the leading families of both religious camps and so serve as an insurance policy against another confessional bloodbath. In addition, the Spanish willingness to offer a dowry considerably in excess of the proposed French one, and indeed of the annual royal income, had a good deal to do with James's preference. The Parliament of 1614 inadvertently reinforced his inclination; while the persons responsible for addling this session remain unclear, the thought of a generous Spanish dowry allowed James to contemplate life without parliamentary subsidies. When the Privy Council in the following year suggested a new Parliament as the only certain financial cure for the indebted regime, James ignored the advice; he would rather talk with Gondomar about the charms of the Infanta Maria.[32]

For several years the discussion continued at this pace, at times apparently more as a basis for further Anglo-Spanish cooperation rather than as a realistic goal. But over the winter of 1617–18 all hopes of a Spanish match nearly vanished when James at last resolved to press Madrid for a final agreement. His resolution succeeded only in laying bare the vexatious issue which both sides had hitherto avoided; the Spaniards insisted on a full toleration for the English Catholics, while James refused to consider anything more than toleration for the princess's household and a royal promise of a "mild hand upon the papists." Over this vexatious issue the discussions doubtless would have foundered – if the Bohemian crisis had not intervened.[33]

Until 1618 those alarmed by the negotiations with Spain had difficulty finding substantial grounds for their apprehensions. They were much better supplied after James's daughter and son-in-law attempted to alter the continental balance of power. If the Bohemian Estates succeeded in replacing their Catholic monarch, Ferdinand II, with a Protestant, Frederick V of the Palatinate, a majority of the Imperial Electors would for once be Protestant. In addition, a Bohemian success would set a tantalizing precedent for other Habsburg lands with substantial Protestant populations as in Austria proper and Hungary. Some contemporaries in their excitement heralded the accession of Frederick to the Bohemian throne as the dawn of a new age, in which the Habsburgs would at last be humbled; one fictitious conference on the Bohemian crisis concluded with one Spaniard urging another to "look not

---

[32] Foscarini to the Doge and Senate, 30 September 1614, *CSPV*, XIV, p. 38; Contarini's Relation, [1618], *ibid.*, XV, p. 422; and *The Letters and the Life of Francis Bacon*, ed. J. Spedding (London, 1869), V, pp. 194–207.
[33] James to Buckingham, [1619–20], *The Letters of James VI and I*, p. 373; and S. R. Gardiner, *History of England* (London, 1883), II, pp. 249–58, 364–98 and III, pp. 37–71, 102–5.

sadlie on thy friend / But lets with Spanish patience wait the end."[34] The Habsburgs in fact were much less fatalistic, and as open conflict became imminent in 1619–20, Bohemian and German Protestants appealed to their English brethren for assistance. Their appeal agitated many of James's subjects, who revelled in the apocalyptic aspects of the furore: "God hath set up this Prince," Archbishop Abbot maintained, "to propagate the Gospel and to protect the oppressed." By the revolution in central Europe, Catholic rulers "shall leave the Whore [of Babylon] and make her desolate." In such an emotional atmosphere, many Englishmen doubtless found much more than a catchy tune to recommend the contemporary ballad, "Gallants, to Bohemia."[35]

These glittering prospects, far from exciting James, terrified him. The validity of the Bohemians' right to eject Ferdinand and to install Frederick remained most uncertain to him. A sober assessment of Frederick's military position only further disposed James to caution. Notwithstanding the chiliastic frenzies of some Protestants, a quick calculation revealed which side had the larger and more experienced battalions, and in a central European conflict, James could do little to tip the balance unless, as one contemporary quipped, "his greate Fleete could flie thether over land." In the circumstances, James saw little reason to ask awkward favors of the Lord. "God doth not in these dayes," one German prince reportedly warned Frederick, "send Prophets more to the Protestants then to others, to warrant them to drawe their Swords against Nations . . . [and] to engage them into unnecessarie Warres and combustion with theire Neighbours."[36] James could scarcely have expressed his own sentiments better. Overshadowing all other considerations, however, was the feeling that a wrong move would simply revive the "Bartholomey business"; not only could he do little to assist Frederick in Bohemia, but he was afraid that any military intervention "would be like to stir up the other Catholic princes" in a "mere quarrel of religion." James could not, Buckingham explained, "foresee what a war would lead to in these

[34] *Prosopopeia, or the Conference held at Angelo Castle* (n.p., [1620?]), p. 6. See also Frances Yates, *The Rosicrucian Enlightenment* (London, 1972), pp. 1–30; and Geoffrey Parker, *The Thirty Years War* (London, 1984), pp. 47–61.

[35] Abbot to Naunton, [1619?], John Rushworth, *Historical Collections* (8 vols., London 1659–1701), I, p. 12; and *Gallants to Bohemia* (n.p., [1620?]). H. E. Rollins dates this ballad twelve years later, but this seems unlikely since it refers to Christian IV, not Gustavus Adolphus, and since there are references to it in 1623. See *A Pepysian Garland*, ed. H. E. Rollins (Cambridge, Mass., 1922), p. 410; and Mead to Stuteville, 20 September 1623, BL Harleian 389, fo. 360.

[36] "The Relation of Sir Balthasar Gerbier," BL Add. 4181, fos. 14–16. I owe the last reference to Isaac D'Israeli, *Curiosities of Literature* (New York, 1865), III, p. 101.

days . . . [and] this consideration causes his Majesty more thought than any-thing else."[37]

In the face of the rapidly worsening foreign situation, the only hope for James's pacific foreign policy increasingly appeared to be the Spanish match. While James consistently pressed for a return to the status quo *ante bellum*, he had little leverage with the Emperor. But he was much better placed with Ferdinand's Spanish cousins, who supplied much of the Imperial army and revenue. Thanks to the extended marriage negotiations, diplomatic channels between Madrid and London were open and well-trodden. Moreover, the prospect of an English fleet in the Atlantic seeking to equal Elizabethan naval exploits would produce more anxiety in Madrid than it did in Vienna. Thus from 1619 to 1621 James sought at once to frighten and to appease the Spaniards in hopes that Philip III, and indirectly Ferdinand II, would seek to resolve the crisis by diplomacy rather than by main force. To display his power, he sent a naval expedition against Algerian pirates, who had defied the Spanish for generations, and dispatched a force of volunteers to guard the Palatinate. And to exhibit his fundamental desire for a peaceful accommo-dation, he revived the marriage negotiations. Rather obviously the Spaniards warmly applauded his initiative, which was a splendid opportunity "to divert him from taking any action" in Central Europe. Consequently, envoys travelled between London and Madrid with increasing frequency, while James testified to his new willingness to accommodate Catholic sensibilities by releasing some imprisoned priests.[38]

The Bohemian crisis, mercifully for James, was soon over; late in 1620 at White Mountain, Imperial troops smashed the rebel army and forced Frederick and Elizabeth into a hasty withdrawal from Prague. Unfortunately, by that time the Habsburgs had already precipitated another crisis, one which James could not ignore so easily. In August 1620, while English ambassadors were negotiating a cease-fire and while an English squadron was searching for Moorish pirates off the coast of Spain, Spinola acting on Imperial warrants led the Spanish Army of Flanders in an invasion of the Palatinate. For many of James's subjects, Spinola's assault was prima facie evidence of Spanish deceit and ample grounds for war. Indeed James himself recognized that this action drastically altered the situation; Buckingham explained to Gondomar that, whatever Frederick's errors in Bohemia, James's "grandchildren were the legitimate heirs [of the Palatinate] and it was neither just nor reasonable

---

[37] Anon. to [Carlisle?], 16 September 1619, *Court and Times*, II, p. 189; and Lando to the Doge and Senate, 13 March 1620, *CSPV*, XVI, p. 198.

[38] Gritti to the Doge and Senate, Madrid, 6 September 1618, *CSPV*, XV, p. 306; S. R. Gardiner, *A History of England, 1603–1642* (10 vols., London, 1884), III, pp. 261–396; and S. L. Adams, "Foreign Policy and the Parliaments of 1621 and 1624," in *Faction and Parliament*, ed. Kevin Sharpe (Oxford, 1978), pp. 139–52.

to deprive them of their inheritance when they were no wise guilty, especially considering the uniformly correct attitude of their grandfather." While James was at last convinced that justice was on the side of his family, there still seemed to be little that he could do aside from embarking on a potentially suicidal holy war; Imperial troops were energetically crushing Central European resistance, while Louis XIII was much more interested in harrying his own Protestants than in challenging his fellow Catholics. Thus, the Venetian ambassador noted, since "the whole weight of the recovery of the Palatinate will rest upon his shoulders alone," James rejected any forthright military response; "if he was cold before [to intervention], he now seems ice."[39]

The Palatine furore served only to wed James even more firmly to the idea of a Spanish match, which seemed the only means of peacefully resolving the crisis. With the Spanish invasion, he simply added the restoration of his grandchildrens' inheritance to the Infanta's dowry. Saber-rattling would continue to complement these negotiations, but this time he brandished the noisiest weapon in the royal armory – a bellicose Parliament. MPs in 1621 proved ready enough to play the part James cast for them. They broke with precedent, promptly voting James two subsidies before passing any other bills. When James unexpectedly adjourned the session, they found solace in publicly vowing to assist James in a war on behalf of Frederick and Elizabeth. Likewise when James summoned the Parliament-men for an emergency session in November, they quickly agreed to underwrite the defense of the Palatinate over the winter. Throughout both sessions, MPs had carefully avoided the delicate question of the Spanish match itself, but their true feelings became apparent on 29 November when James apparently encouraged criticism of the marriage. The result was a forthright petition begging James to make war on the king of Spain, not marry into his family. Disaster then unexpectedly engulfed the session. Since James in fact was not willing to tolerate any public attacks on the projected marriage, the Commons' petition produced a bitter wrangle between the king and the Commons over freedom of speech and eventually a rancorous dissolution.[40]

Gondomar pronounced the dissolution the best news in a century. Although James may well have felt considerable satisfaction in demonstrating his authority over the MPs, he paid a high price for this exercise of his prerogative, because the acrimonious conclusion of the second session delivered him entirely into the Spaniards' hands. Early in 1622, Sir Robert Crane felt no need to explain to Trumbull in Brussels "howe the Parlement

---

[39] Buckingham to Gondomar, [October 1620], *CSPV*, XVI, p. 461; and Lando to the same, 30 April 1621, *ibid.*, XVII, p. 36.

[40] Robert Zaller, *The Parliament of 1621* (Berkeley, 1971); and Conrad Russell, "The Foreign Policy Debate in the House of Commons in 1621," *HJ*, XX (1977), pp. 289–309.

ended and what buysnesses are now begune." In fact without parliamentary assistance, James had only one business he could begin: he had no other choice than to continue marriage negotiations. For their part, the Spaniards were at once eager to discuss these matters and loathe to conclude them. And as threats were no longer in season, the trickle of concessions became a flood in 1622. James curtailed the supply of volunteers to Frederick while in April he allowed two Catholic peers, Lord Vaux and the Earl of Argyll, to raise regiments for the army of Flanders, which had invaded the Palatinate two years earlier. He stood by hopelessly while the army of the Catholic League reduced the last of Frederick's strongholds in the Palatinate and in the process massacred Sir Gerard Herbert and other English defenders of Heidelberg. And he ordered a *de facto* toleration of the English Catholics in August.[41] Gondomar thus had ample reason for his delight at the end of 1621.

Sir Balthasar Gerbier, one of Buckingham's diplomatic agents, later recalled that "James was constrayned to treate" with the Spaniards. Nevertheless he conceded James's logic eluded most of his subjects, and the popular incomprehension of royal goals in 1619–23 in turn led to "the cooling of theire affections towards theire Souveraigne."[42] In order to appreciate fully why a courtier like Laud was so struck by the cheers in early October 1623, it is essential to understand exactly how cool popular affections had become in 1622–3.

THE *ARCANA IMPERII* AND THE PAUL'S WALKERS

While the news of defeat after defeat announced the rapid erosion of the Protestant position in central Europe, a battle of sorts raged in England between the king and many of his subjects. Officially the population was to trust the king's judgment in "causes of States and Secrets of Empire" and to await the outcome of any given affair with patience. But there were abundant signs that a growing number of James's subjects gave only lip-service to the theory of *arcana imperii*. A proclamation issued late in 1620 against "excess of lavish and licentious speech in matter of State" noted that "there is at this time a more licentious passage of lavish discourse and bold censure in matters of State then hath been heretofore." Eight months later a second proclamation remarked "the inordinate libertie of unreverent speech ... doth dayly more and more increase."[43]

---

[41] Crane to Trumbull, 19 February 1622, Trumbull Add. MSS, XIV/unfoliated; and Gardiner, *History of England*, IV, pp. 272–402. On the diplomatic background to these years, see A. W. White, "Suspension of Arms" (Ph.D. thesis, Tulane University, 1978).
[42] Gerbier's Relation, BL Add. 4181, fos. 11 and 17–17v.
[43] *Stuart Royal Proclamations*, ed. F. Larkin and P. Hughes (Oxford, 1973), I, pp. 495–6 and 519–21.

In theory "unreverent speech" should have been easy to suppress. All publications from news-sheets to sermons had to be licensed, and those bold enough to defy these restrictions were apt to find themselves before either the Star Chamber or the Privy Council. Such stern measures, however, were generally effective. "The Councill-table and Star-chamber," Arthur Wilson observed, "are such terrifiers that (as one said) none durst run riot but keep at the stirrop at excellent command." Indeed, the list of a mother's warnings to her fond son included an admonition that "with Kings and Great men tis ill making sport / For the Star Chamber is a dangerous court."[44] Consequently, whatever James's financial and diplomatic problems, his control of the press was the envy of many continental rulers. English envoys often discovered this fact in their pursuit of those who published offensive material abroad; as a somewhat embarrassed Cardinal Richelieu explained to English representatives, "wee were in a place where theyr owne Kinge is not free from libellers."[45] The implication is clear; in James's realm "licentious speech in matter of state" was a dangerous pastime.

There were, however, ways around these restrictions. While overtly political tracts on controversial subjects could not hope to be published, sermons which alluded to them sometimes could, and at times, as will be seen, some printed sermons were remarkably critical of royal policy. Furthermore political tracts, sermons and verse, which had no hope of receiving a license, could find a wide circulation in the unofficial market for news. Lack of access to a printing press was not a crippling blow; all that was necessary to get around this restriction was curiosity and a method for gathering the curious together to compare notes, both of which Jacobean England possessed before the Bohemian crisis.

Early in James's reign, Joseph Hall maintained that one of the vices of England was that of the "busie-body." Unlike his modern counterpart, the Jacobean busy-body was fascinated with the affairs of his nation and the world rather than those of his neighbors. "What everie man ventures in Guiana voyage and what they gained he knowes to a haire. Whether Holland will have peace he knowes and on what conditions." Tireless and brazen in the collection of information, "no post can pass him without question." Indeed, "if he see but two men talke and read a letter in the street he runnes to them and ask if hee may not be partner of that secret relation." John Davies transformed Hall's "busie-body" into "the intelligencer" who loved

---

[44] Arthur Wilson, *The History of Great Britain* (London, 1653), p. 145; and Nicholas Breton, *A Mother's Blessing* (London, 1621), [sig. C2v].

[45] Holland and Carleton to Conway, 23 January 1626, SP 78/77/55. For one of the more dramatic pursuits of a foreign libeller, see William Trumbull's arrest of the printer of *Corona Regis*; Woolley to Trumbull, 28 March and 4 and 12 April 1624, Trumbull MSS, XLVII/116–18.

> to prate
> Of nothing but great Matters of estate:
> He can anatomize France, Flanders, Spaine,
> And where their life-blood lies, well knowes the Veine,
> In State-craft he still his betters braving.[46]

His information was in wide demand from the university scholar who "earnestly enquires after the weekely Currantoes" and the London waterman who made it his business that "hee knowes all newes" to the humble citizen who learned his scuttlebutt from "sitting in a Barbers chaire."[47] These characterizations initially appear too sharply drawn until one considers contemporaries like John Castle whose passion for trawling the anterooms of Whitehall for tid-bits of news equalled that of Hall's busy-body and Dr. Joseph Mede who subscribed to private newsletters as well as corrantoes.

An item of information on its own was of limited value unless it could be compared against other reports and assessed. In taverns, cross-roads, markets, at dinner tables and even in one Northamptonshire parish, meetings of the church-wardens – the greeting, "what's the news?" offered ample occasion for exchange and discussion of the latest information. In London, the market had become more sophisticated; "quid novi" was the salutation among the connoisseurs of news who gathered in Lincoln Inn's Fields, Moorfields, and the Exchange.[48] The center of the network was St. Paul's Cathedral, from which the newsmongers took their name, "the Paules walkers." Where could you find a courtier when he was not at Court? The answer, Sir Thomas Overbury quipped, was obvious; "in Paules with a pick-tooth in his Hat." Admittedly during some weeks, visitors could only mix with "our round headed citizens," who predictably could only offer "dull and unworthy" news. But at others, particularly during term-time, the aisles were filled with attorneys, country gentlemen, merchants, courtiers, and the ever-present curious eager to eavesdrop on conversations.[49] One contemporary whimsically described them: "Paules is their walke . . . where the whole discipline designes, projects, and exploits of the States, Netherlands, Poland, Switzer and all are within the Compasse of one Quadrangle walke most

---

[46] Joseph Hall, *Characters of Vertues and Vices* (London, 1608), pp. 80–1; and John Davies, *The Scourge of Folly* (London, 1611), p. 3. See also F. J. Levy, "How Information Spread Among the Gentry," *JBS*, XXI (1982), pp. 1–24; and particularly R. P. Cust, "News and Politics in Early Seventeenth-Century England," *PP* (1986), pp. 60–90.

[47] Wye Saltonstall, *Picturae Loquentes* (London, 1635), numbers 10 and 15; and S.R. [Samuel Rowlands], *Good Newes and Bad Newes* (London, 1622), p. 6.

[48] Saltonstall, *Picturae Loquentes*, number 35; and Northamptonshire RO, 344P/501. I am grateful to Richard Cust for the last reference.

[49] Sir Thomas Overbury, *A Wife now the Widow* (London, 1614), "A"; J. Gaudle[?] to Castle, [24 August 1624], Trumbull MSS, XVIII/130; and Rowlands, *Good Newes and Bad Newes*, p. 6.

judiciously and punctually discovered." Another with equal derision described Paul's walk as "the eares Brothel." Since this "Synod of all pates politicke" produced "a strange humming or buzze mixt of walking, tongues and feet," some came to identify the cathedral's steeple with the tower of Babel.[50] In fact, the Paul's walkers even produced their own idiom: since most gathered at noon to exchange information, those more eager for a stroll than lunch were said "to dine with Duke Humphrey," the late medieval nobleman, renowned for his hospitality, who was honored in St. Paul's. Thus one poet would hail the "Poets of Paules those of Duke Humfryes messe." A few of the habitués of St. Paul's such as Thomas Gainsford and John Pory made their living reporting news either in printed corantos or in manuscript news-letters. Others like John Beaulieu, John Meddus, Thomas Locke and the celebrated John Chamberlain simply reported their gleanings to friends abroad, "lest," as one noted, "their Countrey freind should bee deprived of the benefits of so rich a prize." The growing contemporary interest in these "prizes" of reportage can be seen in the inclusion in a 1616 gentleman's primer of a section on the composition of letters "Nuncupatorie, or Letters of Newes."[51]

The importance of "Duke Humphreyes servants" in the politics of the 1620s cannot be emphasized enough; they provided the members of the political nation, whom the government generally sought to leave "in the Suds," with the information necessary to arrive at an independent judgment. To be sure, some items that Ralph Starkey, the distinguished antiquary, offered his customers were little better than soft-core porn with a dash of anti-Catholicism; once he eagerly retailed a copy of a lease in which an Abbot required his tenant to provide him "a Virgine to purge his Raynes at certaine monthyes in the yeare." Yet he also provided his clients with copies of controversial tracts which were too hot to sell over the counter, and he pro-vided what was political gold-dust for a budding Parliament-man, journals of the Commons "wherein everie speece [*sic*] and proceedinge in that house is expressed at large." It is worth always remembering that contemporaries out-side a tiny circle at Court were generally woefully deficient in the details of major events; in 1626, for example, MPs were so ill informed of the particu-lars of the duke's foreign policy that they considered impeaching him for farting in the presence of the King of Spain.[52] In this situation, the key to all

---

[50] [Richard Brathwaite], *Whimzies* (London, 1631), pp. 17–19; John Earle, *Micro-cosmographie* (London, 1628), no. 53.

[51] T. Gainsford, *The Secretaries Studie* (London, 1616); and *The Poems of Richard Corbett* (Oxford, 1955), pp. 78 and 148. See also S. L. Adams, "Captain Thomas Gainsford, the *Vox Spiritus* and the *Vox Populi*," *BIHR* XLIV (1976), pp. 141–4; and W. S. Powell, *John Pory, 1572–1636* (Chapel Hill, 1977).

[52] Starkey to Scudamore, 11 February 1626 and May 1627, PRO C115/N4/8575 and 8578; and Mende to Richelieu, [April] 1626, PRO 31/3/63, fo. 61.

"opposition" to royal policies was accurate information, and that the Paul's walkers, more likely than not, were able to provide.

The official response to the development of the market for news was mockery. The carefully considered judgments of the Paul's walkers, which Hall pronounced "ever far-fetcht," led Ben Jonson to suggest a new London street-cry: "Ripe statesmen, ripe; They grow in every street." Elsewhere he characterized the discussion which took place "in Pauls . . . and in all the taverns" as "a Babel of wild humours."[53] Any success, however, in checking the popular appetite for news vanished with the first reports of the Bohemian crisis: nothing focused public attention so closely and so long as the first decade of the Thirty Years War. "The World is now all eare and tongue," Robert Harris noted in 1622, "the most given . . . to little else then to heare and tell newes." Two years earlier, John Taylor maintained he "cannot pass the streets but I am continually stayed by one or other, to know what newes, so that sometimes I am foure hours before I can goe the length of two paires of Buts." By 1624, the greeting "what's the best news abroad" had become as enshrined as "the Garb . . . the grand salute and common preface to all our Talk," that one preacher delivered a popular Easter sermon by suggesting how the Paul's walkers would have covered the resurrection.[54]

Unfortunately for James, "the grand salute" in the early 1620s often led to increasingly bitter and slanderous critiques of his foreign policy, and even more troubling, thanks to Jonson's "ripe statesman," these slanders quickly spread across the country. Sir Robert Ayton neatly explained the situation. James's pursuit of justice led him to the point where "with unwater'd undew'd cheeks [thou] canst see / Throwne out of house and home thy progenye." While Ayton conceded "this way perhapps a iust Kinge thou mayest seeme," he warned James "men a cruell father will thee deeme." Another commentator openly pronounced as madness James's policy

> to guard the Spanish coasts from Pyrats feare,
> The whilst the Catholique King might force combine
> Both Holland, Beame [Bohemia], and Paltz to undermine.[55]

In reporting the criticism from London alehouses, *Tom Tell-Troath* further developed the theme of the "cruell father" who abandoned his children and England's honor. There one mocked "your word, Great Britaine, and offer to

---

[53] Ben Jonson, *Poems* (Oxford, 1975), pp. 48–9; and *Time Vindicated*, in *Complete Masques*, pp. 398. See also Sara Pearl, "Sounding to Present Occasions: Jonson's Masques of 1620–25," *The Court Masque* (Manchester, 1984), pp. 60–77.

[54] Robert Harris, *Peters Enlargement* (London, 1624), "To the reader"; John Taylor, *Taylors Travels to Prague* (London, [1620]), p. 90; and Thomas Lushington, *The Resurrection of our Saviour Vindicated* (London, 1741), p. 1.

[55] Sir Robert Ayton, *The English and Latin Poems* (Edinburgh, 1963), pp. 58 and 241; and *The Interpreter* (n.p., 1622), p. 4.

prove, that it is a great deal less then Little England was wont to be." Another, after reviewing his many concessions to the recusants, acknowledged James to be the Head of the Church, only to ask "of *what* church they would gladly know." All joined in a plea that James avenge Frederick and Elizabeth: since Philip IV palpably was "the greatest cheater in christendom . . . there is no way to recover your losses and vindicate your honour, but with fighting with him that hath cozened you." With such sentiments circulating in the taverns, Lord Treasurer Cranfield clearly was not overreacting when he ordered the circuit judges in the summer of 1621 to do all they could to "preserve a good and reverent opinion in the people concerning his Majesty, his government, and his meaning in the present businesses and affaires of state."[56]

The muttering in the alehouses was not unique; some of the literati were also restive in 1622. In fact the second part of Michael Drayton's *Poly-Olbion* stands as a monument to what the poet dubbed "the evill time" of Jacobean neutrality. After the first part of his epic work had met with "barbarous Ignorance and base detraction," a sequel, Drayton confessed, scarcely seemed in order. Yet he pressed on in part because he felt his "Heroick Rymes" about the glories of the Elizabethan sea-dogs were essential reading in a period when

> we are inforc'd to prie
> And search the darke Leaves of Antiquitie
> For some good name.

And although most of the second part was a prosaic topographical description, William Browne in the preface promised Drayton's public more stirring stuff once James resolved on a more honorable course abroad; "durst we act, he durst to write."[57] Drayton's bitter discontent with royal inaction can be seen even more clearly in the private poems he wrote in "the evill time." Direct discussion of current events he politely avoided; "I feare, as I doe Stabbing," he maintained,

> this word, State,
> I dare not speake of the Palatinate,
> Although some men make it their hourly theame
> And talke what's done in Austria and Beame [Bohemia].

Nevertheless, his contempt for James's cowardice emerges in his portrait of "that dull Sot"

> who n'er thing yet worthy man durst doe,
> Never durst looke upon his countreys foe,

---

[56] *Tom Tell-Truth*, printed in the *Somers Tracts*, II, pp. 471 and 473; and Mead to Stuteville, 30 June 1621, *Court and Times*, II, p. 264.

[57] Michael Drayton, *The Works* (Oxford, 1961), IV, pp. 391, 393 and 395. I am indebted to Dr. Les Timms for many discussions on Drayton and his circle.

> Nor durst attempt that action which might get
> Him fame with men.

Consequently emigration to Virginia was preferable to continued residence among the "drones" at home who were bored with "brave numbers" of martial poetry which had earlier been "to our men at armes / 'Gainst pikes and muskets were most powerfull charmes." Thus as he explained to one emigrant, the news from "our wofull England" in the early 1620s was particularly bleak. Given James's resolute insistence on negotiations with the enemy, it was impossible to believe that "Our King James to Rome shall surely goe / And from his chaire the Pope shall overthrowe."[58]

Nor was the London stage oblivious to the Palatine crisis. Admittedly playwrights were not able to turn an entire production into a commentary on current events as Middleton was later able to do in 1624. But Massinger proved in *The Maid of Honour* that they could get away with a scene or two. Only by intricate reasoning can the main action of the play be linked to the Thirty Years War. Yet no contemporary would have required a code to decipher the message in the opening acts. Ferdinand, Duke of Urbino, like Frederick of the Palatine, admitted

> Hee too late is conscious
> That his ambition to incroach upon
> His neighbours territories, with the danger of
> His liberty, nay his life, hath brought into question
> His owne inheritance.

Consequently, Siena, like Heidelberg, was besieged by a famous general who

> admits no parley,
> Our flags of truce hung out in vaine, nor will hee
> Lend an eare to composition.

Yet Roberto, the king of Sicily, like James, refused his ally's desperate pleas for immediate military assistance "since without our counsell, or allowance / He hath armed." Furthermore Roberto/James was not the sort of ruler who would force his subjects to

> change
> Their plough-shares into swords, or force them from
> The secure shade of their owne vines to be
> Scorch'd with the flames of warre, or for our sport
> Expose their lives to ruine.

James's pacifism, however, found an eloquent opponent in Bertoldo, a Sicilian/English nobleman; "this peace (the nurse of drones, and cowards)" was actually not "Our health, but a disease." Sicily, like England, was not a

---

[58] Michael Drayton, *The Works*, III, pp. 206–10 and 238–41.

rich country like "France / Spaine, Germany, Portugall." Rather "Nature did
/ Designe us to be warriors." Furthermore, given the recent population
increase, "we must starve / Or eat up another" without a foreign adventure
to trim back the excess. Therefore Bertoldo urged Roberto to follow the
example of Elizabeth of England:

> When did she [England] florish so, as when she was
> The Mistress of the Ocean, her navies
> Putting a girdle round the World
> When the Iberian quak'd.

Thus he begged the king to "Rowze us, Sir, from the sleepe / Of idlenesse, and
redeeme our morgag'd honours!" Bertoldo's oration led other courtiers to cry
out, "warre, warre, my Soveraigne!"[59] Although the plot soon veered back to
defense of a woman's virtue, the first act clearly presented the audience with
a remarkably clear portrait of the tensions which the Palatine crisis created
within the English Court.

The most troubling and persistent criticism came neither from the theater
nor the taverns; rather it came from the pulpits. It could be expected that
there would be some drunken muttering about the *arcana imperii* or that
some bold author would glance at a controversial foreign policy. But it was
both extraordinary and disquieting to find ministers doing so in the middle of
Sunday services. It was "the Pulpits," Wilson recalled, that "were the most
bold Opposers." Many of the more celebrated sermons, unfortunately for
historians, were never printed, and we know only that in 1622 a procession
of clergymen, John Everard, Thomas Young, Thomas Winniffe, Mr. Clayton,
Richard Randes and Samuel Ward were reprimanded for dealing in various
ways with Spain and the Palatinate.[60] Enough, however, has survived to
convey a clear sense of the skirmishing that took place every Sunday in 1622.

One of the brisker engagements centered around the Protestant martyrs in
Bohemia and the Palatinate whom James sought to claim for his policy of
neutrality. The king himself sketched out the royal line on this issue in his
final rancorous address to the 1621 Parliament: in response to the petition
from the Commons for a Spanish war, James remarked "we rather expected
you should have given us thanks for the so long maintaining a setled Peace in
all our Dominions, when as all our Neighbours about are in miserable
combusion of War." He concluded by reminding MPs of the old adage,
"dulce bellum inexpertis." The keynote having been struck, a series of
preachers at Paul's Cross, the most celebrated forum in the capital, elabor-

---

[59] Philip Massinger, *The Maid of Honour*, printed in *The Plays and Poems* (Oxford, 1976), I,
    pp. 125–9.
[60] D. H. Wilson, *James VI and I* (New York, 1961), p. 151; and Kenneth Fincham and Peter
    Lake, "The Ecclesiastical Policy of James I," *JBS*, XXIV (1985), pp. 171–2.

ated on the blessings of peace and horrors of war. Samuel Buggs contrasted the Bohemian Protestants who "groane under a heavie and intolerable burden" with "Happy Britaines" who "sit under our own Vines and our own Fig-trees." For him the lesson was obvious: England must repent of its sins, particularly that of disobedience, lest it join in "the sighes" of the distressed abroad.[61] Daniel Donne repeated the same theme with only a more graphic reference to "other Nations" which "doe ride even up unto their horsebridles in blood." Lest his fellow countrymen failed to appreciate the benefits of living in the Jacobean "cittie of peace," Thomas Adams reminded his listeners that none of the continental horrors "come neare us. There is no rifling of houses, no flying to refuges . . . no Rapes of Virgines, no dashing of Babes against the stones, nor casting them as they droppe from their mothers wombs into theire mothers flame."[62]

Graphic though these arguments were, they all paled before more sensational ones. Robert Harris urged his listeners "in our peace" to "consider their warres." To aid in this grim contemplation he presented a rendition of "their scriching [sic]": "O Husband, o wife, o my child, my child, o mother, mother, mother, my father is slaine, my brother is torne, my legge is off, my guts be out, halfe dead, halfe alive, worse then either because neither." His sermon, however, was not a call to arms, but rather one to obedience: "woe be to the Heathen's armie when all will be Captaines and none Souldiers." Equally lurid was Samuel Purchas who maintained Englishmen would not "long for Warre, if wee would but present to our imagination the miseries of Warre." He exhorted his auditors to "think what it is to see thy house fired; thy Goods seized; thy servants fled; thy Wife ravished before your face and then hung up by the heels (modestie forbids the rest); thy Daughter crying to thee for helpe in one corner while thy little Sonne is tost on anothers Pike and the Sword at thine own throat." Having rivetted his audience, Purchas reminded them of James's adage, *dulce bellum inexpertis*, and begged them to repent: "none of the least of sinnes," he concluded, was "to bee censorious of those whom God hath called Gods."[63]

Such arguments, however, ignored that "daily reports of our brethren in foraine parts, either assaulted or distressed or surprized by Popish forces," could lead to an entirely different interpretation. In *A Sparke Toward the Kindling Of Sorrow For Sion*, Thomas Gataker readily agreed that the spectacle of suffering abroad should prompt a general repentance in England.

---

61 James I's answer, 11 December 1621, printed in Rushworth, *Historical Collections*, I, p. 48; and Samuel Buggs, *Davids Straits* (London, 1622), p. 57.
62 Daniel Donne, *A Sub-poena from the Star-chamber of Heaven* (London, 1623), p. 41; and Thomas Adams, *Eirenpolis* (London, 1622), pp. 171–2.
63 Robert Harris, *Gods Goodness and Mercy* (London, 1622), pp. 8 and 16; and Samuel Purchas, *The Kings Towre* (London, 1622), pp. 101–2.

But he did not stop there: England must as well "helpe and releeve" the foreign Protestants. If England evaded this clear obligation, God would find "other meanes" to relieve Bohemia and the Palatinate, and Gataker warned, "the Curse of Meroz may light upon us; we and ours may be destroyed; the destruction threatened them may be inflicted on us."[64]

This chilling threat turned the plight of continental Protestants into a clarion call for intervention which other "sonnes of thunder" sounded in the early 1620s. The sufferings of the foreign brethren led Thomas Jackson to ask "why doth the Church of God suffer so much evill?" The answer doubtless discomforted some in Whitehall: "because Gods faithful servants give way and doe not stand in the breach for her." Jackson then reminded his congregation of "a curse, yea a bitter curse, laid upon the inhabitants of Meroz," and lest they think this a Biblical oddity, he pointed out "no lesse curse doth lie on the Inhabitants of any Place and Country" that failed to assist the godly. John Rawlinson reached the same conclusions and insisted on the immediate application of *lex talionis*. The Emperor and the Pope, who were responsible for Frederick's tribulations, were acting like Adonidezek who mutilated the thumbs and toes of captive monarchs. In this situation James and Charles would only be following the example of Judah and Simeon in waging a holy war of retribution; "yea, it is a duty charged upon the Publicke Magistrate," Rawlinson argued, " ... Thine eye shall have no compassion, but life for Life, hand for hand, foot for foot, like as here in my Text, God requireth thumb for thumb, and toe for toe." The horrors of war therefore could be used to encourage as well as to stifle criticism of royal policy. It is now hard to judge which interpretation carried the most weight with contemporaries, but Jackson at least was quite pleased that by 1622 "by word and writing from pulpit and presse" the critics seemed to carry the field, not those who cried "peace, peace when there is no peace."[65]

Questions about dissent and obedience quickly gave way to fears of rebellion, and another of the hotly debated topics in the period centered on who represented more of a threat to the realm – Catholics or Puritans. During James's reign it had become commonplace for English divines to identify the Catholic Church as antichristian and the Pope as the Whore of Babylon. A tract like Thomas Thompson's *Antichrist Arraigned* was fairly mundane when it was printed in 1618; and as late as 1621, no less than the Vice-Chancellor of Oxford, Dr. Prideaux, could confidently boast that his university audience would scarcely "make a doubt, whether the Pope be Antichrist,

---

[64] Thomas Gataker, *A Sparke toward the Kindling of Sorrow for Sion* (London, 1621), pp. 32 and 37–8.

[65] Thomas Jackson [of Canterbury], *Judah Must Into Captivitie* (London, 1622), pp. 41, 60, and 84–5; and J[ohn] R[awlinson], *Lex Talionis* (London, 1621), pp. 21–2.

or no, seeing hornes and markes are so apparently discovered."[66] But in Whitehall, such attacks on Rome produced embarrassment, if not actual doubt, once James began serious negotiations with Spanish Catholics and eventually the Pope himself. Moreover, as James began to relax and eventually to suspend the penal laws, the commonplace became inflammatory attacks on royal policy. Some preachers such as Thomas Clarke simply dwelt on the Catholic threat in *The Popes Deadly Wound* and left the direct application of the sermon to his listeners. Others were more pointed: Thomas Taylor in *A Mappe of Rome* recounted the Catholic conspiracies against Elizabeth and James which proved "how insatiable she [Rome] hath alwaies beene of blood, and English blood." There was, however, another message in Taylor's tract. After a recapitulation of Rome's implacable hatred of English Protestantism, "I cannot thinke we can be so inconsiderate as to dreame of any toleration." More explicit was Thomas Jackson: while he generally praised James for his care of the Church, he publicly queried in 1622, "Have we not too many Chemarians [*sic*], Seminarians, Priests and Iesuits sacrificing to Baal? . . . Is not the number of Idolatious Recusants gratly increased?" England's deliverance could only come from repression, and he exhorted "all godly Magistrates . . . to suppresse and beate downe" the English Catholics.[67]

Such criticism could be interpreted as treasonous; Richard Gardiner, for instance, leapt to the defense of James against the "brainsicke undisciplin'd Disciplinarians." John Denison for his part launched a full-scale *Checke to Curiousitie*, based appropriately on Christ's rebuke to Peter, "what is that to thee?" Not only was curiosity the root-cause of every heresy from Anabaptism to Arminianism, it was also rampant in the "evill time" of the early 1620s. "There is scare so meane a Mechanicke or silly rusticke," Denison observed, "but is ready to censure the Church, the King, the State." And yet he asked adapting Christ's query to James's day, "what have they to do with matters and mysteries of State?" Robert Aylett sought a more practical rationale against curiosity; the more immediate result of an obsession with "mysteries of State" was poverty, not heresy. Thus he announced "I meddle not with newes of Parliament / Court Favorites or Kingdomes government." Instead he exhorted his readers to "let gods, who have the charge to all, beare sway / That Muses must not censure, but obay."[68] Likewise Robert Harris in

---

[66] Thomas Thompson, *Antichrist Arraigned* (London, 1618); and John Prideaux, *Epheseus Backsliding* (London, 1621), p. 36. See also Paul Christianson, *Reformers and Babylon* (Toronto, 1978); and Peter Lake, "The Significance of the Elizabethan Identification of the Pope as Antichrist," *JEH*, XXI (1980), pp. 161–78.

[67] Thomas Taylor, *A Mappe of Rome* (London, 1620), p. 2; T[homas] C[larke], *The Popes Deadly Wound* (London, 1621); and Jackson, *Judah Must Into Captivitie*, pp. 41 and 96.

[68] Richard Gardiner, *A Sermon Preached at St. Marys, Oxford* (London, 1622), p. 23; John Denison, *A Checke to Curiousitie*, printed in *The Christians Care* (London, 1624), pp. 86 and 90–1; and Robert Aylett, *Thrifts Equipage* (London, 1622), preface.

another sermon in 1622 sought to soothe popular anxieties about royal policy and to forestall further criticism; he blamed the current obsession for news and urged his listeners to speak "to God, rather than to, and of, man." Second-guessing the king could lead only to sin, and "instead of others pratling and enterdealing in State businesse, doe thou pray, pray for thy Souvereigne." Foreign affairs, Harris repeated, must be left to James, for "it is not for us to sit uppon Crownes and Thrones and to turne Statemen." These attempts to rebuke the godly for their overly zealous approach to the European crisis in turn generated further controversy. Timothy Rogers argued that the efforts to label Puritans as seditious "is that which the cunning Papists do desire and reioyce to see." Instead he pressed for a united Protestant front and a joint assault with "all our forces againse these our common adversaries the Papists."[69] Notwithstanding Rogers's plea for unity, unity was most conspicuous in its absence from the Church of England in 1622.

Although defenders of royal policy regularly described their opponents as advocates of rebellion, there were no calls for insurrection. Yet in a notorious case, John Knight, a young Oxford scholar, provided the intellectual basis for revolt. He began a sermon in April 1622 by asking "whether subjects se defendendo in case of Religion might take up arms against their Sovereign?"; both the writings of David Pareus and the example of James's assistance to the Huguenots led Knight to take the affirmative. Given the persistent rumors that James was about to become a Catholic, Knight's conclusion was far from academic. Certainly the sermon elicited a swift royal response. Although Knight promptly recanted, James confined him to the Fleet prison, where he was to stay for almost two years. The king also ordered all copies of Pareus's work be publicly burned. In addition, all divinity students thereafter walked past "in every hall" the royal command that they should concentrate on Scripture and the Church Fathers, and avoid all modern authors who "live in Churches and States which are not so settled as . . . these are within this Kingdome."[70]

Knight's open promulgation of resistance theory rendered the open dissent in the alehouses and St. Paul's and the thinly veiled criticism from the pulpits more ominous, and as a remarkable royal poem, "The wiper of the Peoples teares," clearly shows, James himself was becoming alarmed by the situation. The piece was centered on the question, "purblinde people why doe yow prate / Too shallowe for the deepe of state," and the next 170 lines sought to relieve popular apprehensions. James's dogged defense of the *arcana imperii* was essential for national defense, otherwise "to noe use were Council tables

[69] Timothy Rogers, *The Roman Catharist* (London, 1621), pp. 41–2; and Robert Harris, *Peters Enlargement,* "To the Reader" and p. 22.

[70] Anthony à Wood, *The History and Antiquities,* pp. 341–5; and *APC,* XXXVII, pp. 232, 234 and 237.

/ If state affaires were publique bables." Likewise he explained that impassioned objections to "our princely match" would only "mar or patch" but not prevent the Anglo-Spanish match. In conclusion he pleaded with his subjects to stop alarming one another with false reports and to "hold your pratling spare your penn / Bee honest and obedient men." Yet the sound of many of his subjects crying "as Babes doe" over his policies did not weaken James's resolve to proceed on the same course. "Come councell me when I shall call," but if they presumed to offer advice unbidden, he warned, "bewarr what may befall." Although he had already issued two proclamations against "lavish and licentious speech of matters of State," James vowed "if proclamations will not serve / I must do more . . . to keepe all in obedience."[71]

By the summer of 1622, James had lost patience and resolved to "do more" to silence domestic dissent. In early August 1622 he issued "Directions concerning Preaching." Bishops and deans alone were allowed free rein in their sermons – and then only on special feast-days. The rest of the clergy in all morning sermons must avoid any mention of predestination, "bitter invectives and indecent railing speeches" against the Catholic Church, and all "matters of State." Instead James suggested they deliver "homilies of Obedience" together with general comments on "faith and good life." The restrictions on afternoon sermons were even more severe; indeed they practically prohibited preaching altogether. If ministers did not relish the prospect of reading out one of the set sermons in the *Book of Homilies*, James advised them to "spend the Afternoons exercise in the examination of Children in their Catechisme." Finally, to close any potential loopholes, James ordered the first reprinting of the *Book of Homilies* in thirty years, and several catechisms quickly came out to guide apprehensive parsons in administering ecclesiastical *Milke for Babes*.[72]

The severity of James's response, which struck at the taproot of the evangelical faith, vividly illustrates the depth of his concern about the steady criticism from the pulpits. Severe it was; as soon as the Anglo-Spanish entente began to disintegrate late in 1623, the city of Norwich petitioned for the revocation of the Directions, and the memory of these restrictions continued to rankle the godly in later years. The immediate response to the Directions was another wave of rumors about James's imminent conversion. Yet even John Donne's eloquent and repeated defenses of the restrictions could not greatly relieve popular apprehensions about their real intent, because two

---

[71] *The Poems of King James VI* (Edinburgh, 1958), pp. 182–91.
[72] "Directions concerning Preachers," 4 August 1622, printed in Thomas Fuller, *The Church History of Britain* (London, 1655), pp. 109–10. See also *Certaine Sermons or Homilies* (London, 1623); *The Second Tome of Homelyes* (London, 1623); and William Crashaw, *Milke for Babes, or A North-Country Catechisme* (London, 1622).

days before they were issued, James ordered the formal suspension of the penal laws.[73] Archbishop Abbot's involvement in the scheme plainly embarrassed him. At great length he pleaded with his friend William Trumbull not to "give an ill construction to that which may receive a faire interpretation" if only Trumbull would "not take them up upon report but do punctually consider the tenure of the word." The Primate's justification, however, could not dispell the widespread fear that the Directions and the suspension of the recusancy laws was part of a broader plan; "Papists shall have a toleration here in England," Walter Yonge grimly recorded in his diary, "and the Protestant ministers shall preach but once a Sabbath."[74]

Strategic error though the Directions may have been, they were nonetheless a tactical success. Before their introduction, there had commonly been "rude indecent raylings" against the Catholics, and the "ignorant medling with Civell matters" represented "a Shooting up of those idle fancies which in this blessed time of so long a peace do boyle in the brains of unadvised people."[75] Afterwards there was certainly less "medling," "rayling" and "shooting up". To be sure, some ministers opposed to royal policy made their point by simply drawing attention to the fact that they were being muzzled. The Directions, for example, led John Everard, the controversial lecturer at St. Martins in the Fields, to adopt two stage sermons; after carefully dividing the discussion of a text into spiritual and political halves, he would analyze the spiritual section; then he announced that on the following Sunday he would discuss the more provocative half, vowing in "brave termes" that "he would feare no mans . . . anger whilst he should handle the discourse of it." The result of such a procedure was obvious; without having said a word against royal policy, Everard provoked the Council into arresting him and so confirming his popular image as a Protestant martyr. Another minister defied a warning from Bishop Montaigne and preached on St. Paul's attack on apostates. After a general discussion of the text, the sermon concluded abruptly; although the congregation "might expect some application," the minister declared that "he was not ambitious of lying in prison, and so ended." *Tom Tell-Troath* observed that "though there be orders given to preach nothing but court divinitie, a man may easily perceive by the very choice of their texts and

---

[73] John T. Evans, *Seventeenth Century Norwich* (Oxford, 1979), p. 86; and The Lord Keeper's letter to the Circuit Judges, 2 August 1622. This last letter is almost omnipresent in surviving gentry collections; for two examples of its wide distribution, see *The Buller Papers* [from Cornwall], (n.p., 1899), pp. 9–10; and Chester RO, 63/2/10, fo. 28v. On the later recollections of the Directions and toleration, see Henry Burton, *For God and King* (n.p., 1636), pp. 111–14; Nehemiah Wallington, *Historical Notes* (London, 1869), I, p. 3; and Paul Seaver, *Wallington's World* (Stanford, 1985), p. 157.

[74] Abbot to Trumbull, 4 September 1622, Trumbull MSS, I/46; and *The Diary of Walter Yonge* (London, 1848), p. 64.

[75] Abbot to Trumbull, 22 September 1622, Trumbull MSS, I/46.

the very tears in their eyes, that if they durst, they would speak their consciences."[76] The Directions, however, denied them this liberty.

Having gagged the ministers and released the Catholics, James moved to break up the centers of secular dissent in London. In November 1622 a royal proclamation commanded "Noblemen, knights and gentlemen of quality" to retire to their rural estates. Few were convinced by the official reason for the order, the need for hospitality in the countryside: rather the proclamation seemed aimed at the gentry, who in London "being together and often [*sic*] meeting . . . one revealing their discontents to another and soe in time grow to some head." Although 7,000 people reportedly left the city, some ignored the proclamation. James, "sensible of their contempt," ordered a "diligent survey" of the metropolitan area for remaining nobles and gentry and announced in March 1623 his intention to begin prosecutions. So resolute was James in the matter that Salvetti judged "very fewe will venter the kings displeasure at this tyme." Given James's success in depopulating the capital, one of the more remarkable aspects of the celebration on 6 October 1623 was that it took place without the assistance of many of the city's elite whom James had driven into rural exile.[77]

Whatever muttering James's action provoked, few could deny at the end of 1622 that James had reasserted control and had ridden out a particularly alarming storm of popular criticism. Some ministers continued to overstep the bounds of the royal Directions, but, as Buckingham boasted to Gondomar, "no man can sooner now mutter a word in the Pulpit, though indirectly, but he is presently catched and set in straight prison." More importantly, the Directions also appear to have tightened royal control on the press: as will be seen, after August 1622 very little even implicit criticism of royal policy slipped into print. In late September Dr. Donne, whose sermons in 1622 often hammered home the theme of obedience, remarked "the people are flat": they had at last learned to "trust in God and the King's Way."[78]

Nonetheless, the resolute pursuit of such an unpopular goal was not without psychological costs, the most embarrassing of which were the rumors of James's imminent conversion to Catholicism. These reports angered James; in "The Wiper," he asked

> You that know me all soe well
> Why doe you pushe me downe to hell
> By making me an Infidell?

[76] Castle to Trumbull, 9 August 1622, Trumbull MSS, XVIII/79; Mead to Stuteville, 28 September 1622, *Court and Times*, II, pp. 334–5; and *Tom Tell-Troath*, printed in *Somers Tracts*, II, p. 472.

[77] Salvetti to Scudamore, 21 December 1622, PRO C115/N8485; *Stuart Royal Proclamations*, I, p. 561–2; APC, XXXVII, p. 413; D'Ewes, *Diary*, pp. 122 and 162.

[78] Donne to Goodere, 24 September [1622], *The Life and Letters of John Donne* (London, 1899), II, p. 168; and [Buckingham] to Gondomar, [late 1622], *Cabala* (London, 1654), p. 242.

Persistent rumors about the future of the Church of England prompted Abbot to send out a second circular letter in September assuring ministers that James had no intention to "make a breach to ignorance and superstition," two nouns customarily used to describe the old faith. James himself in a letter to the Scottish Privy Council roundly denied that his recent actions represented the "begunning of a further purpois in us to tollerat or graunt libertie or conscience." Rather the Directions and the suspension of the penal laws were "groundit upon goode and approvable ressonis of state in the deepe and misterie quhair of every man is not to dive and wyde."[79] Several preachers also came to James's defense, and they all stressed his commitment to Protestantism. Thomas Myriell asked the crowd before Paul's Cross, "should we nowe feare a defection? . . . certainly wee should be very disloyal to his Majesty if we should needlesse feare [and] perplexe our selves with that wherein wee ought to beleeve him most firme and constant." John Donne similarly urged the audience at St. Paul's not to believe the worst of James. Rumors of his conversion came from Catholics engaging in wishful thinking and from "libellous and seditious" Puritans convinced "the King and the Prince were declining from that Religion." In fact James "is in his heart, as farre from submitting us to that Idolatry, and superstition, which did heretofore op?resse us, as his immediate Predecessor [Elizabeth]." Yet in spite of these passionate efforts, the rumors continued unabated; during Twelfth Night services at St. Paul's, Dr. Francis White led the congregation in a prayer that God "preserve the King and Prince from any that should go about to withdraw them from their first love and zeale to religion."[80]

The tension from maintaining the drive for an Anglo-Spanish entente and some shred of belief in his faith affected James in other ways. John Buchanan, the formidable Calvinist divine who had been James's tutor, reportedly began to trouble James's sleep in the autumn of 1622. But the best illustration of the mental costs of the Spanish match came late one night over the Christmas holidays. A group of students at the Inns of Court concluded an evening's revelry by passing a sword around and swearing "to live and die" in the service of Elizabeth of Bohemia. They then touched off some small cannon, and the report sounded across the city. When James heard the noise, he started out of bed crying, "treason, treason."

---

[79] James to the Scottish Council, 31 October 1622, *Registers of the Privy Council of Scotland* (Edinburgh, 1877–), XIII, pp. 80–1; Abbot's circular letter, 4 September 1622, *Documentary Annals of the Reformed Church* (Oxford, 1845), II, p. 203; and *The Poems of King James VI*, pp. 182–91.

[80] Thomas Myriell, *The Christians Comfort* (London, 1623), p. 50; John Donne, "A Sermon upon the fifth of November 1622," *The Sermons of John Donne* (Berkeley, 1959), IV, pp. 253–4 and 256; Chamberlain to Carleton, 25 January 1623, *Letters*, II, p. 473.

AWAITING THE BRIDE, 1623

When two Dutch envoys left London early in 1623, John Chamberlain, one of the inveterate denizens of St. Paul's and the Exchange, confessed that he was no longer "greatly inquistive after that or any other news." Admittedly at his age he found it awkward to get around, but he also attributed his lack of interest to "the continual bad tidings" which "hath taken away my taste." The continual bad tidings of 1622, however, would soon pale before those of the first three-quarters of 1623.[81] The German conflict which had hitherto gone badly for Frederick V came in 1623 to a complete halt. In Bohemia Imperial troops supervised the conversion of the entire population, while in the Palatinate, the situation was only marginally better; and from both states came refugees with heart-rending tales of persecution. Frederick himself had been forced to flee the Empire and had joined his family in exile in The Hague. Frederick's last hopes centered on Christian of Brunswick who raised another motley army in the spring. Unfortunately this force also had to race for sanctuary in the Dutch Republic, and only a few miles from safety, Imperial troops massacred Christian's troops. With this defeat, all further opposition to the Emperor ceased. Little wonder then that many Protestants felt the millennium was at hand in "this latter age of the world." Gataker, for example, interpreted the string of Protestant reverses as firm evidence that "the last houre is now running. And we are those on whom the end of the world are fallen."[82]

Further confirmation of this belief came in February 1623 when Prince Charles and the royal favorite, Buckingham, slipped out of England in disguise and rode for Spain. Why they went to Madrid remains a perplexing question, one which will be examined in the following chapter, but at the time most English Protestants had trouble finding any good coming out of the journey. When D'Ewes first heard the news, he refused to believe it, and once the realization sunk in, practically no one was pleased. Beaulieu reported Charles's action "hath left a great amazement among the people who are much perplext," and the Earl of Kellie wrote to a Scottish friend that "you can not beleive sutche a deade dumpe it did streake in moste mens mynds heir."[83] The same Spanish talent for spinning out negotiations, which had forestalled

---

[81] Chamberlain to Carleton, 25 January 1623, *Letters*, II, p. 475. On the end of continental hostilities, see Geoffrey Parker, *The Thirty Years War* (London, 1985), pp. 66–70.

[82] Gataker, dedication to Thomas Crewe; and *A Gagge for the Pope . . . or the Arraignment and Execution of Antichrist* (London, 1624). On millenarian expectations, see, for example, *A Prophesie of the Judgement Day* (London, 1620); Nehemiah Rogers, *A Strange Vineyard in Palaestrina* (London, 1623), pp. 211–14; and John Brinsley, *The Fourth Part of the True Watch* (London, 1624), pp. 61 and 112.

[83] Kellie to Mar, 13 March, *HMC Mar and Kellie*, II, p. 155; Beaulieu to Trumbull, 21 February 1623, Trumbull MSS, VII/98; and D'Ewes, *Diary*, p. 121.

any English intervention on behalf of Frederick V, had also promised a distant wedding date – at least until Charles took horse for Madrid. Consequently the only question early in 1623 was not when the match would be concluded but rather at what cost. It required only a fleeting knowledge of *realpolitik* to understand that with the prince in Spain the English bargaining position would be weak indeed. Thanks to Elizabeth and her children, the Spaniards would go to great lengths to see that no harm befell the prince. On the other hand, Charles's sister could not ensure that her brother could leave Madrid at will. One contemporary noted, "whiles our Prince is in Spaine, the Spaniarde gett what they wist from us," and another exclaimed "alas our hands are now bound by the absence of our most precious jewel." Consequently Englishmen spent much of the year in grim speculation on the terms the Spaniards would "extort." "If I was with you," Beaulieu wrote to his brother-in-law, "I could tell you such things as would make your haires stand at an end. God have mercie upon us for we are in a deplorable condition."[84]

An almanac for 1623 had predicted that "this yeare shall Religion be scoft at," and if the religion was understood to be Protestant, the prophecy was painfully accurate. While godly ministers remained checked by the Directions, Catholics openly flourished since there were no longer prosecutions for recusancy. In London and the provinces, Catholic clerics and especially Jesuits began to appear openly as did the Bishop of Chalcedon who led processions around the Midlands in full episcopal attire. In fact, the toleration provided Richard Montague with his formal excuse for plunging into a theological controversy which was to split the English Church: in that year he had to struggle with Catholic priests for the souls of his parishioners.[85]

Notwithstanding Montague's best efforts, the Catholics garnered a rich harvest almost daily both within and without the Court. Buckingham's mother announced her conversion; his Catholic father-in-law, the Earl of Rutland, moved into a more prominent role at Court, ultimately serving as admiral; and a "Catholic" group of peers, Lords Windsor, Morley and Vaux among others, even began to operate openly. Englishmen in the provinces did not have to read of the Catholic revival in the metropolis; they could see it in their localities. In Kent, for example, "a greate many Papists . . . have declared themselves," not the least of whom was Lord Wotton, a former Lord-Lieutenant. Quite rightly, John Vicars in his popular chronicle of the decade

---

[84] Beaulieu to Trumbull, 19 April 1623, Trumbull MSS, VII/106; and Mead to Stuteville, 14 March 1623, *Court and Times*, II, p. 374.

[85] Jacke Dawe, *Vox Graculi* (London, 1623), p. 42; and Montague to Cosin, 12 December 1624, *The Correspondence of John Cosin* (Durham, 1869), I, pp. 32–3. On the Catholic revival, see Hugh Aveling, *Northern Catholics, 1558–1790* (London, 1966), p. 222; and John Gee, *The Foot out of the Snare* (London, 1624), p. 34.

labeled 1623 as the year "the Romish Foxes came out of their Holes."[86] What
made the Catholic resurgence even more offensive to many Protestants was
the tendency of some Catholics to gloat over the fact that tables might soon
be turned if James or, more likely, Charles should convert. Even a warm
advocate of the Spanish match had to confess that many Englishmen found
the marriage odious, thanks to the efforts of some "impetuous, unbounded,
unlimited" Catholics who broadcast "dangerous and fearefull positions,
insolently intimating what a golden time they now shall have."[87]

A trend that was distressing in England was positively alarming in Ireland,
from where disturbing reports regularly issued throughout 1623. "Out of the
confidence of the match," the Catholic majority became unbridled. A mob of
women disrupted a Protestant funeral with impunity, and bands of priests
roamed the major cities brandishing safe conduct passes reputedly from the
Privy Council. In Cavan, the only thing that stopped a Catholic reoccupation
of the parish church was Capt. Forbes's vow that, in spite of any warrant
from London, "he should make the antiphonie of their mass be sung with
sound of musket." Any less dramatic attempt to check the resurgent majority
was pointless, given the widespread violation of laws against Catholics in
municipal office. Such boldness seemed in order when rumors swept through
the country, like the one proclaimed at the Kells fair that Charles and
Buckingham had converted to the old faith. These reports account for one
Catholic's confident offer to a Protestant of 20 to 1 odds that "he could pull
him to mass within a twelve month by the hair of his head." When the
Protestant retorted that James would never permit such an alteration, the
Catholic pointed out that "you have a king, but we have a prince." In fact the
situation in Ireland deteriorated so dramatically that by the end of 1623 the
Lord Deputy did not dare employ a secretary when reporting the Catholic
excesses to London.[88]

Equally unsettling for loyal adherents of the Church of England was the
discovery within their ranks of "Hollow Hearts" who "swamme with the
tide." The imminent *rapprochement* with Catholic Spain led a few oppor-
tunists to promote a more ecumenical stance for the English Church. John
Donne praised Spanish theologians for their vigor and industry, although he
stopped short of praising their conclusions, and Francis Bacon began com-

---

[86] Peter Clark, *English Provincial Society . . . Kent, 1500–1640* (Hassocks, Sussex, 1977),
      p. 325; Peter Clark, "Thomas Scott and the Growth of Urban Opposition to the Early
      Stuart Regime," *HJ* XXI (1978), p. 12; and Vicars, *England's Hallelu-jah*, stanza 40. On the
      "Popish" party, see Castle to Trumbull, 20 June 1623, Trumbull MSS, XVIII/98, and
      D'Ewes, *Diary*, pp. 131 and 138.

[87] Edmund Garrard, *The Countrie Gentleman Moderator* (London, 1624), p. 54. For an
      example of this tendency, see Nottingham to Abbot, 20 May 1623, SP 14/145/22.

[88] *Calendar of State Papers, Ireland*, XVI, pp. 421, 429, 432, 433, 455 and 460.

posing a treatise urging all Christian states to exchange their doctrinal differences for a common holy war against the Turks.[89] While Bacon never completed the tract, his theme was common in 1623: Michael DuVal sought to reconcile Catholics and Protestants in a new crusade as did John Stradling in a long poem, *Beati Pacifici*. For Stradling, rival theologians on both sides were simply careerists seeking to feather their own nests by obscuring the common points of agreement. Typical of his talent for resolving century-old theological disputes in couplets was his solution to the question of good works: "Tis safest to doe well, yet claime no hire / But waivering Merit, Mercy to desire." The essential point for him was "w'are Christians all," and some bloodletting in the Near East could only lead to wider acceptance of this point.[90]

In terms of controversy generated, however, the printed works of Stradling and DuVal could not equal a manuscript poem of Sir Henry Goodere on the journey of the "Admirable Prince." If fanatics on both sides could be silenced, it could easily be proven, Goodere argued, Rome and Geneva "are not directly opposite / As North and South Poles." The fanatics who particularly interested him, however, were those of Geneva, those opposed to the Spanish match "through transported zeal" about the "daunger to the Churches weale": he pleaded with them to

> Retaine more charity then to presume
> Soe farr to say the present Church of Rome
> Is not part of Gods church or to denie
> A way to heaven to all that therein die.

Doctrinal niceties plainly bored him, and he praised instead "waxen hearts with pure and simple zeale / They soften and they fit them for heavens weale." Finally, for those who persisted in regarding the Catholic Church as antichristian, Goodere offered up a prayer: "Father forgive they know not what they doe."[91]

Such works were hard to dismiss as literary oddities given the nature of the discussions within the Privy Council over the summer. During one of the many debates over the terms of the match, Lord Keeper Williams reportedly "wished that a waye might be thought on howe that walle of difference Religion might not give impediment to the Marriage." In the end Archbishop Abbot carried the day with the argument that "it were better lett that walle

---

[89] Donne to Buckingham, [March–May 1623], *The Life and Letters of John Donne*, II, p. 176; "Advertisement touching an Holy Warre," *The Works of Francis Bacon* (London, 1861), VII, pp. 1–36; and Vicars, *England's Hallelu-jah*, stanza 40.

[90] Sir John Stradling, *Beati Pacifici* (London, 1623), pp. 20 and 22; and Michael DuVal, *Rosa Hispani-Anglica* (n.p., [1623?]), p. 73.

[91] Sir Henry Goodere, "Admirable Prince," SP 14/145/12A. For an unfavorable reaction to this poem, see Carleton to Chamberlain, 11 July 1623, SP 84/113/32.

alone than adventure to alter or breake it downe." Nevertheless it was clear
that there was considerable interest in high quarters in 1623 in making "the
walle of difference" more malleable. In light of this public quest for a *via
media* between Rome and Canterbury, both the violence of Richard
Sheldon's public attack on "our Luke-warm Laodiceanizers . . . gaping after
preferments" and the swiftness of the official response becomes readily
comprehensible. At Paul's Cross he denounced "Neutralists . . . such as dare
secretly mutter . . . Rome and the Reformed Churches agree in the substance
of Religion; that there is no fundamental difference betwixt them and us."
For his pains Sheldon, hitherto a favorite of the king, lost all royal patronage
and was haled before the church courts. He had quite clearly exposed a
sensitive nerve; "a cardinal's hat," a contemporary remarked, would "make
many a scholar in England beat his braines to reconcile the Church of Rome
and England."[92]

While some Englishmen eagerly sought to meet Rome half-way, others
prepared for the worst as it became increasingly apparent that "true
Religion's buried in the Dust / The popes Bulls breath and crosses be
adorned." The ordinary function of a godly minister was to chastise his congregation for their shortcomings and to exhort them to lead a good life, but
in 1623 Gataker felt they had "more need of cheering up." Admittedly "in
times of grief" and "in such a time especially when so much cause of sorrow,"
it was hard to avoid being downcast. Nevertheless, he urged his listeners to
maintain their composure; otherwise the spectacle of their public dejection
would "hearten" the Catholics and "giveth them occasion of triumph when
they see God's Children hang the head."[93] Thomas Jackson likewise urged his
listeners to "see the good" of the recent disasters which led many to repent
their sins. Besides John Wing pointed out, "how ill doth sorrow or feare . . .
become a Saint?" Instead the godly should reply to those who taunt them
with the recent Catholic victories that "I will not change states with thee . . .
all thou canst doe, cannot make me so bad as thy self."[94] On the other
extreme, Dr. DuMoulin in *A Preparation to Suffer for the Gospel* attempted
to steel his congregation to undergo the trials their continental brethren were
already suffering; and Simonds D'Ewes in April received a divine message "to
arme my selfe for preparation against worser times."[95] Godly Englishmen

92 Chaworth to Trumbull, 27 June 1623, Trumbull Add. MSS, XV/67; Richard Sheldon, *A
    Sermon Preached at Paules Crosse* (London, 1625), pp. 30 and 49; and [Anon.] to Mead,
    25 April 1623, *Court and Times*, II, p. 391.
93 Thomas Gataker, *The Ioy of the Iust* (London, 1623), pp. 1 and 28; and a poem on the
    Spanish trip, Folger Library, V.a.275, pp. 11–12.
94 John Wing, *The Saints Advantage* (London, 1623), "To the Christian reader" and p. 76; and
    Thomas Jackson [of Canterbury], *The Raging Tempest Stilled* (London, 1623), p. 128.
95 Pierre DuMoulin, *A Preparation to Suffer for the Gospel* (London, 1623); and D'Ewes,
    Diary, p. 130.

quite understandably found the *rapprochement* with Spain and Rome uncomfortable. In September John Winthrop confided to his wife that although he hoped for the best "yet we have cause to feare the worst, in regarde of that all things are so farre out of order." In Dorset some Puritans did more than lament; following the lead of their minister John White and prominent MPs such as Sir Walter Erle, they took the first steps towards wholesale emigration to New England. However drastic these reactions to the Anglo-Spanish entente may seem in retrospect, they were for some contemporaries the only logical response to take in a year in which, as one popular prophecy insisted, "sure much alteration / Shall happen in religion."[96] Even those who did not number themselves among the saints could not regard the Spanish match with complete equanimity. The sudden appearance of Anglo-Spanish grammars and dictionaries in London book-shops during 1623 heralded the imminent conclusion of the long-standing negotiation. The marriage alliance with Spain promised more than a new language for the aspiring courtier to learn: the English vision of the past also would have to change. Plainly the popular tales about hammering the Dons during the long Elizabethan war would be due for modification, if not retire-ment. In fact, as early as 1621, one clergyman had been imprisoned for merely producing a print in honor of divine intervention which had saved the realm in 1588 and 1605.[97] Goodere urged his countrymen "to comprehend the change of time and state." England had outgrown the earlier Hispanophobia just as it had "outworne the French and Scottish hates." DuVal similarly argued Spain was not the bugbear of English legend. The invasion attempt in 1588, for example, was actually "provoked by Grievous and Intolerable Iniuries," the most heinous of which was Elizabeth's aid "to the Rebellious Hollanders." DuVal's slighting reference to the Dutch Republic also illus-trated another important change to which Englishmen would have to get accustomed. For almost half a century, the English had regarded the Dutch as loyal, if tetchy, allies and fellow Protestants. With a new Spanish alliance, however, all this would have to change; one commentator strongly in favor of the match delighted in the thought that now "the Dutchmen must pay."[98]

The impending alterations were equally monumental in domestic policy, and in particular the marriage was not a favorable augury for the future of

[96] J. Winthrop to Winthrop, 27 September 1623, Massachusetts Historical Society, Winthrop Papers, I, fo. 193; Frances Rose-Troup, *John White: The Patriarch of Dorchester* (New York, 1930), pp. 58–61; and "A Prophecy," Beinecke Library, Osborn b197, p. 189.

[97] On Samuel Ward's print, see Chamberlain to Carleton, 10 March 1621, *Letters*, II, p. 349; and on the Anglo-Spanish publications, see John Minsheu, *Pleasant and Delightful Dialogues in Spanish and English* (London, 1623); Richard Perceval, *A Dictionnaire in Spanish and English* (London, 1623); and same, *A Spanish Grammar* (London, 1623).

[98] "Hope do mee noe harme," Beinecke Library, Osborn b197, pp. 110–11; Goodere, "Admirable Prince," SP 14/145/21A; and DuVal, *Rosa Hispani-Anglica*, p. 54.

Parliaments. Spaniards had no reason to revere an institution which had customarily been the forum for attacks on their religion and country; they certainly had no sympathy for the claims of some MPs about Parliament's importance. DuVal, for example, ridiculed Parliament's aversion to a strong monarch; instead of a "Royal Cedar" or "Palmes of Caesars," MPs longed for a "Hedge-Bramble" as their sovereign. Thus Robert Tisdale was selecting his words with care when he used the phrase, "goe Parliament," to describe the actions of royal critics. Moreover, given the massive dowry which would provide, as one song went, more gold "than London can hold / Were the walls built as high as heaven," Parliament could well be as redundant as the Anglo-Dutch entente. The prognosis for English liberties in short did not appear promising: while "each Nation hath . . . their own rules," the Spaniard, Scott explained, "labors to take from humane societie and prescribe Lawes to all Christendome."[99]

The supporters of the match, both within and without the government, were well aware of the apprehensions that flourished in England, and by continuing the stress on the benefits of peace, they hoped, as Edmund Garrard did, that "people might not so much expostulate of our Princes Royal Match and the affaires of state as now they doe." At Paul's Cross, Elias Petley reminded the crowd of the "priveledge we enjoy by our Rex shalem"; and Thomas Myriell was deeply troubled by the fact that although "a happy peace" was "indeede the greatest mercy Heaven can communicate to earth," "may we not heare some weary of ease and wishing for Warre?" He pleaded "take heed, be not weary of peace."[100] Similarly, DuVal praised James for using the prince's marriage to secure peace "for the dismembred and dis-joynted Bodie of Christendome;" while Stradling argued against the "the raylings of some hot-spurs" that "Sweet is Warre" only "to him that Warre yet never knew." Sir John Hayward again sounded the leitmotif of royal policy. The application of his meditation on Christ's prayer, "Father, forgive them, for they know not what they doe," was certainly timely in 1623: after his example, "let me not esteeme," Hayward prayed, "the iniuries intoler-able, which any man shall doe unto mee, let me be no lesse unwilling to revenge the one then I would be to bee punished for the other." For Hayward it was obvious that James's handling of the German crisis followed the doctrine of Christ, "a perfect peace-maker." Those who failed to appreciate the divine blueprint behind James's foreign policy continued to be labeled as seditious Puritans who posed as great a threat to the realm as the Jesuits them-

---

[99] Robert Tisdale, *Pax Vobis* (London, 1623), p. 8; [Thomas Scott], *The Belgick Pismire* (London, 1622), "To the half-hearted English Spanish reader"; DuVal, "To James"; and Beinecke Library, Osborn b197, pp. 110–11.
[100] Elias Petley, *The Royal Receipt* (London, 1623), p. 42; Myriell, *Christians Comfort*, pp. 57–8; and Garrard, "To the Reader".

selves. Thus, George Warburton could only pray for "certaine scrupulous brethren of our owne, inflam'd with a precipitate zeale" who could not understand that James was engaged in "a worke well becoming a King of Righteousness" – "a general Peace of the Catholique Church."[101]

In this controversy over war or peace, Robert Tisdale weighed in with an extended poetic defense of royal policy. *Pax Vobis* was aimed directly at "Sir Politicke Woodbe," "Furtivo Tacticus" and "Curio Coxcombe." These "Criticke Satyrs" opposed to James's desire to "be liberall and free / To foraigne States" longed to

> call out for warre
> Say the Times rust, and that we trust too farre
> These piping dayes of Peace, whilst Lullaby
> Sings us asleepe with chaunting melody.

In reply, Tisdale paraphrased James's adage, *dulce bellum inexpertis*, to chide their "unexperienced folly" which longed "to breake open Janus Temple Gates." Given the somber results of such an action, which he spelled out in detail, Tisdale asked "Why then you brain-sick wits, with whispering Charmes, / Seeke you to stirre our Prince of Peace to Armes?" Their criticism, moreover, was a direct assault on royal authority, and Tisdale belabored "Sir Politicke" and his fellows for their presumption. While monarchs had to "rule and guide / The ship of State," "our place is to obey and serve / Not to direct." Besides, he argued,

> Secrets of State
> Are depths, by us not fadom'd, but relate
> To the Prime Motor, who full well doth know
> This Art to governe, yet to forebeare to show
> To us his reason.

Therefore he warned those "that thinke you can great Phoebus Chariot guide" to "beware! forbeare! long since you have beene taught / Aspiring Lucifers doe come to naught." All Englishmen needed to know was that Charles had gone to Madrid in the name of "Love and Peace," and the duty of James's subjects was to await the outcome with patience and, most importantly, in silence.[102]

James himself again attempted to comfort his subjects over the departure of "Jacke and Thom," which "hath darkt of late / The glorye of th'Arcadian state." After sketching the grief that "afflicts Arcadia soe," James chided the "Kinde Sheappeardes" for doubting his wisdom – "bee not soe rashe, in

---

[101] Sir John Hayward, *Christs Prayer Upon the Crosse* (London, 1623), pp. 113 and 117–18; George Warburton, *Melchizedech* (London, 1623), pp. 35–7 and 51; DuVal, *Rosa Hispani–Anglica*, p. 13; and Stradling, *Beati Pacifici*, p. 3.

[102] Tisdale, *Pax Vobis*, pp. 8–10.

Censuring wronge" – and urged them to trust him; "remitt the Care to Royall Pan / Of Jacke his sonne and Tom his man."[103] In normal circumstances, few of James's subjects would have had trouble following this admonition, but in a crisis such as that of 1623, some simply could not hold their peace. For example, immediately after Charles's departure, Bishop Montaigne of London sought to head off excessive lamentations by ordering all his clergy to offer brief prayers for the prince's safety "and no more"; one minister reappeared before his diocesan for leading his congregation in prayers for Charles's return "and no more." In another celebrated incident, when a preacher began to wander into the *arcana imperii*, the more cautious parson ordered "the clerke to sing him downe with a psalme before he was half don." In general, however, it seems that the parson, not the preacher, prevailed during the height of the Anglo-Spanish negotiations in 1623; James had become far too resolute in this matter for any local ministers to risk his wrath. Consequently, much of the open clerical opposition in 1623 came from preachers at Court who had powerful patrons to save them from serious harm when they stepped into the *arcana imperii*. Furthermore, the privileged positions of Court divines made them feel more keenly the need to testify for their faith; it is essential, Joseph Hall maintained, that "the world can see in what stile we speak at the Court."[104] And they also knew that while they could not publish these controversial sermons, the Paul's walkers would make sure that many outside the Court would learn of their willingness to risk martyrdom.

The two best documented cases are those of Drs. Whiting and Hall. When the prince was in transit from Madrid without the Infanta, Whiting scandalized Hispanophiles by taking as his text, the exhortation, "remember Lot's wife." Before the assembled courtiers, he prayed "with much zeale" that since the recusants remained as dangerous as they had ever been, "the powder treason and 88 might never be forgotten." The height of his audacity was his public lament over the recent Catholic toleration; "would any man have thought to have lived to see these times," he asked the doubtless squirming courtiers, "in a Country wher the Gospell is preached?" For his pains, Whiting was immediately arrested and imprisoned, but the tale of martyrdom quickly spread across the kingdom, and many endorsed Thomas Locke's observation that "we have a good preacher here put to silence."[105] Joseph Hall, not to be outdone, was equally sensational. His text, "buy the truth and sell it not," was obviously uncomfortable to royal officials who had rational-

---

[103] "Off Jacke and Tom," *The Poems of King James VI*, pp. 192–3.
[104] Chamberlain to Carleton, 21 March 1623, *Letters*, II, p. 486; Mead to Stuteville, 29 March 1623, *Court and Times*, II, p. 381; and Joseph Hall, *The Best Bargaine*, printed in his *Works* (London, 1634), pp. 476–7.
[105] Locke to Trumbull, 10 October 1623, Trumbull MSS, XXIX/160.

ized swapping Catholic toleration for continued peace. Hall proclaimed that there were those who had forgotten this Biblical adage and would now trade "their liberty, their country, the life of their Soveraigne" for the "ill bargains of mis-religion." Admittedly some justified such a bargain in the name of peace, and Hall conceded that "if anything in the world may seeme a due price of truth, it is Peace." Yet, even if the other option was war, "when all is done . . . we may not offer to sell Truth for Peace," and he went on to rebuke those about him who "should truck for the Truth of God as if it were some Cheap-side, or some Smith-field Commoditie."[106] Hall promptly shared Whiting's fate – imprisonment and popular glorification.

Those Englishmen who applauded the boldness of the ministers unfortunately could not read the sermons, for the censors became particularly discriminating during this most delicate stage of Anglo-Spanish negotiations. A few tracts, however, managed to slip into print, and none equalled the audacity of Nehemiah Rogers in *A Strange Vineyard in Palaestrina*. He began modestly enough, renouncing "the controverted points of Predestination" for a plain discussion of "Faith and the Good Life." After having quoted James's Directions, Rogers proceeded to ignore them. The Catholic revival of 1622–3 remained one of the great taboo subjects for public discourse, yet Rogers pleaded with the magistrates to enforce the penal laws ruthlessly and begged them "let neither young nor old bee spared." Next Rogers calmly advanced into the *arcana imperii*. "It is lawfull," he pointed out, "for Catholic Princes to make leagues with Protestants only for their owne advantage." The example he offered was far from academic in the early 1620s: "to dispatch some businesses which hinder them from falling upon the Protestants with all their forces." The perfidy of this policy led him to ask "whether it be safe then to suffer such [in treaties] . . . as is their doctrine such is their practice . . . making leagues only for their own ends; breaking their promises, oathes, vowes, at their pleasure."[107]

Few authors slipped such direct criticism into print in 1623. Yet the government's particularly tight control of the press in this period did not forestall similar efforts; it simply forced them into the channels that newsletter-writers had developed for circulating their manuscripts. At least three items strongly opposed to the match moved by hand from St. Pauls and the Exchange to the provinces. Two of them were letters. One, an emotional plea from Thomas Alured to Buckingham, reviewed all the Tudor Anglo-Spanish marriages in order to illustrate "how little God hath blest [them], the successe shewes." Not surprisingly, Alured concluded that the latest proposed match was neither "safe for the Kings person nor good for his Church and Common-

---

[106] Hall, *The Best Bargaine*, pp. 476–7.
[107] Rogers, *A Strange Vineyard in Palaestrina*, dedication and pp. 116–18.

wealth." The other dispatch, a spurious one from Archbishop Abbot to James, dismissed all diplomatic or historical nicety and instead rebuked the king for his attempt "to set up that most damnable and heretical Doctrine, the Whore of Babylon." The last of the three was Simonds D'Ewes's first literary work, a highly dramatic account of the ceremony on 20 July when James and the Privy Council swore to abide by the marriage treaty: the terms were so harsh, D'Ewes maintained, that James began to shake uncontrollably when he heard them, and afterwards High Holborn, where the Spanish ambassadors resided, "was the only merry street of so spacious a cittye."[108]

Notwithstanding the passion of these efforts, the most violent, and certainly the most scurrilous, exchanges over the Spanish match took place in poetry, not prose. DuVal was appalled by the "most Bitter and Virulent Satyrs and Invectives" that "the busie State-Smatterers" produced. D'Ewes for his part noted "daylie moor and moore libels weere dispersed," and while many of them shocked him, they all testified to "the miserie of a discontented and almost daring people."[109] James himself had contributed to the battle of the couplets with his own upbeat piece on Jack's pursuit of the "golden fleece." In less skillful hands, *double entendre* often gave way to more graphic descriptions; while one poet politely ended with Charles and Maria closing the drapes of the bridal bed, another could scarcely contain his delight with the thought that "our north pole shall bee put in the hole / Of the Southerne Inferior beare."[110] Likewise the death of Mr. Washington, one of Charles's attendants whom Catholic clerics had hounded in his final hours and ultimately denied burial, was the subject of no less than three poems all denouncing Spain and Catholicism; one asked the readers not to inquire about "his disease or paine / He died of nothing else but Spaine," and another concluded it must be "counted a greate mishappe / To see Spaine anywhere but in a mapp." The point of these and other poems written during Charles's absence was summarized in one poet's prayer that "Come thou [Charles] awaye and leave Medea there."[111]

Perhaps the best indication of the violence of the dispute between the "pot-poets" was the reception of Richard Corbett's courtly praise for Buckingham's role in the trip to Madrid. Corbett, the Dean of Christ Church, wished that his patron could return from Spain in order to walk in disguise through

---

[108] "A shorte viewe," Longleat House, Whitelocke Papers, II, fos. 101–102v; D'Ewes, *Diary*, pp. 147–8; Alured to Buckingham, [1623], printed in Rushworth, *Historical Collections*, I, pp. 91–4; and [Abbot] to James, [August 1623], Beinecke Library, Osborn fb 57, p. 125.

[109] DuVal, *Rosa Hispani–Anglica*, p. 52; and D'Ewes, *Diary*, p. 135.

[110] "On the Princes goeing to Spain," Folger Library, V.a.418, fo. 48v; *The Poems of King James VI*, pp. 192–3; and "Hope do me no harme," Beinecke Library, b197, pp. 110–11.

[111] "On Mr Washington," Folger Library, V.b.43, fo. 3; "An Elegie," Beinecke Library, Osborn b197, pp. 190–2; and "Illium deplores," Folger Library, V.a.275, pp. 11–12.

"Paules" to witness "the Flouds" of rumors which "run in the middle Ile" of the cathedral; one of Corbett's favorites was the report that the Spaniards were reportedly starving the prince into submission and isolating him from his Protestant chaplains. For his witty portrait of the Paul's walkers, the Dean quickly received two savage counter-attacks. One attributed Corbett's recent ecclesiastical elevation to his "ballads more then his merits" and his ability to "draw downe white canary and sherry." Another from "a Catholique gentleman" threw the book at the "unlearned uncivill and unchast unholy . . . mad vainglorious" Dean who was "a Parasite, a Sycophant, [and] a foist." It concluded with the chilling vow that before the poet would join Corbett and "bee a Protestant, I will turne Turke."[112]

As the poems became more abusive, so too their focus narrowed on Buckingham. The purported letter from Abbot had warned that even if Charles returned unharmed, "the drawers of him to that action . . . wil not passe unquestioned and unpunished," and the leading candidate for chief "drawer" was the duke. Thus one poem maintained Buckingham and Sir Francis Cottington "used there best tricks with Catholicks / To bring our Prince to Spaine," only to find once in Madrid that the Spaniards actually did not want the match. The squib ended with a prayer that many doubtless repeated in 1623: "God send our Charles well home againe / And lett his Worshippe [Buckingham] tarry." The extraordinary degree to which Buckingham became identified with the Spanish alliance certainly accounts for the violent abuse that one contemporary used to prove – "they get the divell and all / That swive the kindred [of the Villiers]." Buckingham's mother, a convert to Catholicism in 1623 who supported her new faith at Court, was a close friend of the Lord Keeper, Bishop John Williams, one of the mainstays of the "Spanish" party and the royal official who ordered the relaxation of the penal laws in 1622. For the author of the poem, friendship was simply a euphemistic term for their relationship:

> Old beldame Buckinghame
> With her lord keeper
> Shee loves the fucking game
> Hee's her cunt creeper.

The author then placed cuckhold's horns on Lord Treasurer Middlesex, another of Buckingham's in-laws and another prominent advocate of the Spanish match: thanks to the careful attention of the Earl of Arundel, yet another Hispanophile, to the Countess of Middlesex, the Lord Treasurer could

---

[112] "A Letter," *The Poems of Richard Corbett*, pp. 76–9; "Reply," Folger Library, V.a.345, pp. 133–4; and "An other," Northamptonshire RO, Isham of Langport MSS, IL 4278. I am grateful to Les Timms for assistance in interpreting this last poem.

Keep the money
Which he can better keepe
Then his wife's cunny.

After working through "the kindred" who were full of drunkards, idiots and
adulterers, the poet offered his supreme insult to the duke and his family – a
graphic description of Sir Anthony Ashley sodomizing Philippa Sheldon's
"blackarse hole." And throughout this systematic villification of the Villiers
echoed the refrain,

These be thee, goe soe gay
In Court and citty
Yett no man cares for them
Is not this [a] pitty.

These and other squibs clearly stung, for late in 1622 the favorite offered a
£1000 reward for information on the author of one "song."[113] Buckingham,
like any other royal favorite, had to accept the lack of popular applause for
his rise; yet the remarkable level of abuse in these poems of 1622–3 was
clearly due much more to the policies he advocated than to the speed of his
elevation.

Evidence of mounting opposition to the Spanish match can also be found
in the streets of London. Booksellers who attempted to move DuVal's *English
Spanish Rose* found that customers vied with one another for the wittiest
explanation for the frontispiece which depicted Christ bringing Charles and
the Infanta together; one quipped "I am glad that Christ is betweene them;
for then sure he will never suffer them to ioyne together," and another maintained the match was "impossible! For if Christ meant any such matter, he
would have dispatcht it before now." The mood was apt to get much uglier
when live Spaniards appeared. In the summer of 1621, Londoners greeted the
Spanish envoys and their servants with "many Insolencies of rude and savage
barbarisme" which clearly revealed the "wicked and devlish humor of those
base people." Moreover, local magistrates were loathe to interrupt the hail of
catcalls and stones. Eventually James himself had to intervene in order to
instill some sense of "respect and civillity" into the urban population. In
1623, however, there was another wave of "insolencies," and the ambassadors formally complained that they were "beseeged" in Exeter House and
that they "dares scarce goe abroade" because "the people throwes stones at
them and abuseth them in their Coaches." After an investigation, Secretary
Calvert could only conclude, "I feare the people are extreame unruly and

---

[113] "All the newes," Beinecke Library, Osborn b197, pp. 222–3; D'Ewes, *Diary*, pp. 122–13;
and "Heaven bless King James," BL Add. 5832, fo. 206v and Beinecke Library, Osborn
b197, pp. 186–8.

rude."[114] The running battles along the Strand finally resulted in a fatality in September 1623 when a brawl in Drury Lane left one English baker dead. At this point, when faced with the prospect of "the peoples revenge" for this martyr, the Privy Council intervened ordering a close guard around the embassy. Popular hispanophobia nonetheless remained high: a highwayman went to the gallows a folk hero for his insistence that hatred of the Spanish match, not avarice, had driven him to rob a Spanish courier.[115]

The crisis began to abate somewhat a few weeks before 6 October as it became increasingly likely that Charles would return home alone. Simonds D'Ewes had chosen an appropriate occasion for his first tract: 20 July, when James and the Council formally accepted the Spanish terms, marked the end of the extended negotiations. As Beaulieu noted with considerable uneasiness, "we account him as good as married." Indeed after the espousal, "he may lye if he please with his Mistres." Well might the English Catholics "not expresse small exultations" – and one country gentleman remarked, "I pray God all be well."[116] D'Ewes spent the next few days on his knees "praying for and hoping the best," and an answer to his prayer came from an unlikely quarter: while Philip and James had agreed to the terms, the Pope "will not alowe / King James to bee her dady." Even better news quickly followed. Charles, exasperated with the delays, refused to wait in Madrid while Catholic theologians haggled over details. He remained espoused to the Infanta, and he left his proxy behind. Further, the Spaniards spoke eagerly of sending over the new Princess of Wales in the spring.[117] Nonetheless it was clear that the best chance to conclude the match had slipped past in the summer of 1623. By September the situation in July was reversed: now "the publicke love . . . doth ring lowed" while the recusants "are silent and much dasht in their countenance." After having closely followed the seemingly inexorable progress of the Spanish match, John Castle was delighted with the sudden change of fortune: the "gloria patri" of the recusants would shortly become "sicut erat in principia." Even the long list of gifts Charles left behind with Spanish grandees failed to dampen Castle's joy: "so wee have him safe, lett our honour doe what it will; in bringing no Mistres wee have an incomparable recompense for our losse." Longing for the prince's arrival

---

114 [Thomas Scott], *Boarneges* (Edinburgh, 1624), p. 30; *Stuart Royal Proclamations*, I, pp. 508–11; and Calvert to Conway, 2 September 1623, SP 14/152/4.

115 Locke to Carleton, 14 September 1623, SP 14/152/40; Castle to Trumbull, 8 August 1623, Trumbull MSS, XVIII/101; and Conway to Aston, 18 May 1623, BL Add. 36,446, fos. 104–104v.

116 Waterhouse to Taylor, 24 July [1623], Northamptonshire RO, Fitzwilliam (Milton) Correspondence, 249; and Beaulieu to Trumbull, 18 and 25 July 1623, Trumbull MSS, VII/120 and 121.

117 "All the newes," Beinecke Library, Osborn b197, pp. 186–8; D'Ewes, *Diary*, p. 148; and Lockyer, *Buckingham*, pp. 156–62.

became so intense in September that several false reports of his landing plunged London and other towns into premature celebration – and sent Lord Montagu galloping to Northampton with the good news.[118]

ENGLISHMEN AND SPANIARDS

For both James and his subjects, the pursuit of a Spanish match had been an ordeal. Never before in James's reign had a single political issue so deeply divided the kingdom: the repeated royal stress on obedience had only drawn attention to the widening fissures within the state. In the tense atmosphere of 1622–3, several foreign diplomats understandably perceived a nation on the verge of rebellion.[119] Foreign visitors of course often tended to reach extreme verdicts, but several natives also concurred: Thomas Alured, together with *Tom Tell-Troath* and a Kentish gentleman, Thomas Scott, pointed ominously to the marriage of Mary and Philip II, "which was so discontenting to the people that it caused Wyatt's Rebellion."[120] Advocates of the match certainly were eager, as DuVal was, to label their opponents as those who sought "to raise sedition in the Commonwealth," and their success in portraying a realm swarming with traitors can be seen in the suspicion that first came to James on waking to the sound of cannonfire early in 1623. By that time, Thomas Scott the pamphleteer, one of the earliest and most forceful opponents of the match, had become alarmed over the possibility that charges of treason might soon begin to stick. The real traitors, he argued, were the Spanish sympathizers who "labor to breed jelousies betwixt Him and His . . . which may estrange and alienate the heart of the Prince from his people." On the other hand, critics of the match were like vigilant ants attempting to rouse a sleeping lion around whom "the Hunters were pitching Toyles." Far from rebellion, a verse from the Psalms actually expressed Scott's pious and loyal wish: "let the King hear us when we call." Charles's return from Madrid without a bride marked the near collapse of a policy for which James had strained every nerve in the body politic. Under the circumstances when the people called out on 6 October, it was almost impossible that the king and his ministers did not hear them. Indeed, after the silence of the preceding two years, the noise must have been deafening. Hence D'Ewes excused the "great excess and drunkennes" on 6 October because the wild display of "the

---

[118] Castle to Trumbull, 12 and 18 September 1623, Trumbull MSS, XVIII/103 and 104; Whiteway Diary, BL Egerton 784, fo. 67; and D'Ewes, *Diary*, p. 158.

[119] Tillières, the French Ambassador, and Van Male, the Flemish Agent, quoted in *Stuart Royal Proclamations*, I, p. 495, n. 1 and p. 562, n. 2; Valaresso to the Doge and Senate, 26 August 1623, *CSPV*, XVII, p. 397.

[120] Alured to Buckingham, [1623], printed in Rushworth, *Historical Collections*, I, p. 92; *Tom Tell-troath*, printed in *Somers Tracts*, II, p. 474; and Peter Clark, *Thomas Scott*, p. 7. I am grateful to Richard Cust for drawing my attention to this topic.

abundant and true love of his people to himselfe" rebutted "the forged popish perswasion . . . that subjects loved not him nor his sonn."[121]

An examination of 1662–3 obviously does not suggest that the Civil War nearly broke out two decades early. It does, however, reveal a domestic crisis of considerable proportions, one which casts a new light on events later in the decade and century. Until recently, the willingness of seventeenth-century Englishmen to believe tales of Catholic plots had not generally struck a sympathetic chord among modern historians. With the exception of the Gunpowder Plot, the reports seem either flimsy or fabricated, and their veracity is scarcely improved by the eagerness of some contemporaries to retail these allegations. Furthermore, as Robin Clifton noted, the fact that the anti-Catholic hysterias occurred "only once in a generation" points to the collective neuroses of English Protestants as the explanation rather than any actual Catholic provocation. Caroline Hibbard, however, has shown recently that the reports of Popish plots which John Pym employed so effectively in the Long Parliament rested on a solid foundation of fact. Admittedly the situation twenty years earlier had not deteriorated as markedly as it had in the late 1630s when Arminian bishops harrassing the godly and Papal agents at Charles's elbow seemed part of a larger plan. Nevertheless, there were enough trends in the early 1620s to have seriously alarmed committed Protestants: Archbishop Laud never restricted the activities of his clergy as drastically as James I did with the 1622 Directions, and George Con had to be satisfied with the lax execution of the penal laws, not their total suspension. Likewise Henriette Marie's brother was simply the Most Christian, not the Most Catholic. Therefore, if we elevate the opposition to the Spanish match to the status of a serious outbreak of anti-Catholicism roughly equal to those of 1605 and 1638–42, Englishmen of Pym's generation would have reckoned Laud and Con as the third attempt in their lifetime to subvert the Church of England. Moreover, anti-Catholicism, which Clifton pronounced "not particularly helpful" as a cause of the Civil War, becomes much more plausible.[122]

Gerbier's observation about the "cooling" of popular "affections" during the Spanish match is also useful in explaining the course of events later in the decade. Previous scholars working on the 1620s have tended to examine either parliamentary affairs or individual courtiers. Their concentration is eminently sensible, but it has meant that they are likely to miss the full significance of the domestic turmoil over the Spanish match. Thus, for D. H.

---

[121] [Thomas Scott], *The Belgick Pismire*, "To the truehearted British readers" and p. 100; DuVal, *Rosa Hispani–Anglica*, p. 68; and D'Ewes, *Diary*, pp. 163–4. I am indebted to Peter Lake for many discussions on Scott's work.

[122] Robin Clifton, "Fear of Popery," *Origins of the English Civil War* (London, 1973), p. 157; and Caroline Hibbard, *Charles I and the Popish Plot* (Chapel Hill, 1982).

Willson, James's response of "treason, treason" to the celebration at the Inns of Court early in 1623 was simply another manifestation of his "timidity," and it owed nothing to the popular dissent and James's crack-down in the preceding year. Likewise Robert Ruigh observed that at the beginning of the 1624 session, "the Puritans had seized the initiative" and played "on the religious fervor of the majority." He did not, however, consider how profoundly the events of the preceding year had terrified Puritans and consequently how inflamed religious fervor was in 1624. Yet it was precisely this religious fervor and the memory of the fears under which the nation had earlier labored that accounts largely for the organization of the "patriot" coalition and its success in the 1624 Parliament. In the dark days of 1622, Thomas Scott urged those who shared his apprehensions to wait patiently for the time when "the Lion may awake"; then James's "best and truest subjects" could reveal their devotion to England and to the king. After 6 October 1623, the royal lion, it seemed, had begun to stir, and the time for national unity and cooperation had at last arrived.[123] Thus many Englishmen who had been deeply suspicious of elements at Court which they found unsavory would be disposed to work with anyone, even a royal favorite like Buckingham, in order to thwart the Spaniards, at home and abroad. This willingness, as will be seen, was to be the bedrock on which the "patriots" built.

The foundation unfortunately proved unable to support the load, and this fact too owed much to the domestic crisis before Charles's return. Charles in later years was clearly surprised and offended with the rapidity with which parliamentary applause in 1624 turned into truculence in subsequent sessions. Historians as well have puzzled over the reversal: Conrad Russell has questioned the country's basic commitment to the war effort and Roger Lockyer has stressed the "neurotic" motives behind the volte-face.[124] But if we accord the crisis in 1622–3 its full contemporary importance, the celerity with which the consensus on the war disintegrated becomes less surprising and certainly less neurotic. In the early 1620s many had come to doubt the wisdom of royal policies and even the religion of the royal family. Likewise, Buckingham, before his remarkable metamorphosis into the architect of a Spanish war, had been reviled as a Spanish stooge and crypto-Catholic. Even for those most eager to form a broad anti-Spanish consensus after the prince's return, these sentiments were too powerful to be erased quickly. Therefore, it was almost predictable that initial difficulties in the conduct of the war would revive the earlier suspicious view of the duke and the government. In short, the era of good feeling from October 1623 to the summer of 1625 would

---

[123] Ruigh, p. 160; and D. H. Willson, *James VI and I* (London, 1956), p. 425; and [Scott], *The Belgick Pismire*, "To the true-hearted British readers."

[124] Lockyer, *Buckingham*, p. 474; and Russell, *Parliaments*, pp. 70–83.

prove the exception to the general pattern of the decade, not the domestic opposition to the war in 1626–8.

Somber thoughts about a renewal of sharp divisions within the realm, however, were far from everyone's thoughts on 6 October 1623. All that could be deduced was that Charles against all expectations had returned a bachelor. Although the Catholic Habsburgs had handily won the first round of the European conflict, they had inexplicably fumbled Charles's marriage, the action which would have concluded the entire game in their favor. Now that Charles had returned alone, there was suddenly a chance for a second round, which might reverse the outcome of the first. Late in 1623 many in the political nation were eager to try their luck. A tract from this period describes how a former MP and a courtier resolved their differences in order to form a common anti-Spanish front; in the end the gentleman made a vow which succinctly expressed the mood on Charles's return: "though we be constrayned to play an after game, yet by the assistance of god and by the wise orderings of our affayres, we shall quickly make him [James] see as well our injury as his own errour."[125] Rather than accept a Spanish match with all its fearful implications for England and the brethren abroad, he would wager all double or nothing in an "after game." And it was this willingness to accept long odds that does much to account for the "Blessed Revolution" later in 1624.

---

[125] "A Discourse . . . betweene a Counsellor of State and a Country Gentleman," Somerset RO, Phelips MSS 277/16. I owe the loan of this important document to the kindness of Derek Hirst.

Part I

THE COURT,
OCTOBER 1623–FEBRUARY 1624

1

"A sharp edge": the rationale and strategy of a Spanish war

Over the noise on 6 October several contemporaries heard a song, "now let us to the warres againe." Given the popularity of this tune on that day, the rejoicing would indeed have become frenzied if it had been known that the prospective bridegroom and the newly created duke endorsed the song's sentiment. Without question they did. Secretary Conway perhaps best explained their reasoning; "when knots cannot be untied by fingers, a sharp edge must be applied." To clarify his meaning, he added "when justice, wisdom and courtesy cannot prevail, courage, resolution and force must be brought to the proof." For him the prince's journey was far more than an amorous junket; it was also a personal embassy to resolve the Palatine crisis by "justice, wisdom and courtesy." And since by autumn 1623 diplomacy and reason had clearly failed, the time had come to try "courage, resolution and force"; "a sharp edge must be applied."[1]

The simple statement that Charles and Buckingham decided to replace diplomatic "fingers" with "a sharp edge" raises complex questions. Why had they adopted the cause of war? If they returned advocates of war, what had they been six months earlier? Their strategy was at least as mysterious as their motivation; exactly how did they propose to resolve the German question by arms? What allies did they suggest to James, and what strategy did they advance – military operations on the continent or naval ones in the Atlantic? These questions baffled contemporaries, and generations of historians have done little to resolve the confusion. It must be emphasized again that pending a thorough study of the Spanish match, any answers must be considered tentative. Nonetheless, even at this preliminary stage, several important points appear quite clearly.

---

[1] Conway to Buckingham, 15 June 1623, Geoffrey Goodman, *The Court of King James the First* (London, 1839), II, p. 293. On the presence of the song, see above, p. 17, n. 35.

THE PRESS FOR WAR

When confronted with the mounting criticism over his handling of the Palatine crisis, James adopted the guise of the modern Odysseus oblivious to popular sirens. Yet in the ears of his son and favorite, the wax had been poorly fitted, and neither of them endured the events of 1618–23 with James's sang-froid. Padre Maestro, a Spanish diplomatic agent, discovered this when he suggested that Charles might like to peruse a justification of Ferdinand's claim to the Bohemian crown; "nothing occupies my mind more," Charles replied, " . . . than the affaires of the Bohemians and of my brother-in-law," and he added that he had hitherto found Frederick's position "well-founded." With the invasion of the Palatinate in 1620, the prince's sentiments emerged even more clearly; "you must know," he explained to Gondomar, "that at bottom this concerns my sister." By the opening of the 1621 session, he was notable for being "deeply interested in the present events of the world, but more for his sister and religion than for other reasons."[2] As for the favorite, it is worth remembering that Buckingham's first major clashes with James came in 1619 over his enthusiasm for the Palatine cause. He reminded James "to remember the honour of the nation" and voiced his desire to lead the fleet in action. The Spaniards had sought, with some success, to immobilize him by playing up Frederick and Elizabeth as potential rivals to his influence, but with the Palatine invasion, he suddenly became "more enthusiastic" about intervention "than any of the others" at Court.[3] Later in the 1621 Parliament, it was Buckingham's creature, Sir George Goring, who proposed the controversial ultimatum, Spanish neutrality or war.[4] And in the following year prince and favorite became noticeably restive. When the news of the fall of Heidelberg and the massacre of Col. Herbert arrived in London in late September 1622, the report sorely taxed the obedience of many Englishmen. Sir Robert Crane insisted "this courte hath not a man that is Spanish any longer, all ressent the iniurie wee have suffered." He promised Trumbull details of an imminent resolution "worthy of our antient honor," and his confidence stemmed from the fact that Charles "desseignes himselfe to some brave Enterprise abroade, to recover at least what we have lost." Charles's "brave enterprise" called for an

---

[2] Lando to the Doge and Senate, 30 January and 11 October 1620 and 15 January 1621; *CSPV*, XVI, pp. 151, 433 and 524.

[3] Same to same, 16 May, 11 June, 25 September, and 11 October 1620, *ibid.*, pp. 256, 275, 418 and 431; Lockyer, *Buckingham*, p. 83; and Adams, "The Protestant Cause," p. 297.

[4] Robert Zaller, *The Parliament of 1621* (Berkeley, 1971), pp. 151–2; and Russell, "The Foreign Policy Debates in the House of Commons in 1621," *HJ*, XX (1977), pp. 302–9. My interpretation of Goring's motion differs from that of Russell; I hope to explore this variance elsewhere.

army of 20,000 foot and 3,000 horse to operate in conjunction with the Dutch and the remnants of the Protestant forces under Count Mansfelt. Charles himself begged James for the command, and Buckingham pleaded merely to serve in the force. To underwrite the expedition, a new Parliament was planned, and rumors of the imminent dispatch of election writs continued almost to the end of the year. The prince was not easily diverted from this plan; although James quickly left the Privy Council to work out the details, Charles "stayes behind to steere the Resolution of the Councell and to bringe this busynes to an Issue."[5]

The bellicosity of the heir apparent and the royal favorite does not seem to have been feigned for Spanish consumption. The marquis at least spent time in 1622 at the drillyard learning to trail a pike, and his closest associate was Sir Edward Conway, an Elizabethan veteran who "doth advise much and often with him" about possible military options.[6] To be sure, Charles and Buckingham did not object to a diplomatic resolution through an Anglo-Spanish dynastic alliance; "so that we may have satisfaction concerning the Pallatinat," Charles wrote late in 1623, "I will be content to forget all ill usage and be hartie frends." Yet while he and Buckingham clearly hoped that "that happie match will settle the stirrs in Germanie," the possibility that the Spaniards were using the negotiations to immobilize England alarmed them; when the marquis announced his desire to take arms in September 1622, he maintained "the affairs are now come too near a period to admit of any dissimulation."[7] These young men naturally felt that if England was to be dishonored, the blow should be received on the battlefield rather than at the negotiating table. Their careful plans unfortunately overlooked James and Lord Treasurer Middlesex, who possessed considerably more patience than they did. Thus when the rumblings from London led to new Spanish promises about a prompt marriage and a Palatine restoration, James shelved his son's alternative plans. Furthermore, opposition to a new session crystallized around Cranfield who, as Giles Mompesson reported, "hath proposed som other meanes for monye." These arguments ultimately forced Charles to yield. Nevertheless, the prospect of endless negotiations still concerned him; "I see," the Earl of Kellie noted, "the Prince wilbe at a point quicklye."[8] A few months after the crisis over Heidelberg, Charles and Buckingham suddenly left for Madrid.

[5] Crane to Trumbull, 5 October 1622, Trumbull Add MSS, XIV/unfoliated; and Kellie to Mar, 9 October 1622, *Mar and Kellie*, II, p. 138–9.

[6] Nethersole to Elizabeth, SP 84/109/106–8, quoted in Lockyer, p. 165; D'Ewes, *Diary*, p. 88; and Chamberlain to Carleton, 12 October 1622, *Letters*, II, p. 457.

[7] Charles to Aston, 8 October 1623, SP 94/28/138; [Conway] to Trumbull, 9 October 1623, SP 77/16/297; and Nethersole to Elizabeth, SP 84/109/106–8.

[8] Mompesson to Trumbull, 7 November 1622, Trumbull Add. MSS, XIV/unfoliated; and Kellie to Mar, 25 September 1622, *Mar and Kellie*, II, p. 138.

Their impatience with the pace of the negotiations and their willingness to fight cast another light on the trip to Madrid; the fate of Charles's sister and her children as much as Charles's eagerness for a bride led him to slip out of the country early in 1623. The prince, Conway maintained, "hath his ayme upon the business of the Pallatinat equally upon his own and principally intended the reducinge that of the Pallatinat to a short conclusion." Likewise Buckingham told Gerbier the principal reason for the journey "was to put the Spaniards to it once for all to knowe what satisfaction they were like to have in the businesse of the Palatinate."[9] Charles himself wrote his sister that "the chiefe cause of his Journey" was "to cutt of delayes." Indeed the king acknowledged this goal; the "business of Christendome" lured Charles to Spain as much as, in James's salty phrase, "the cod-piece point." Most Englishmen were too terrified of the possible risks to appreciate this logic, but at least one European prince did. Charles Emanuel, the Duke of Savoy, applauded the wisdom of the design as well as the valor of the execution; "there was no other way to come speedily out of the Labirinth of Treatyes in which his Majestie did stand" than to press for an answer. And as uncle of Philip IV, he spoke from experience.[10]

While the trip has often been described as a failure, it did have one spectacular success which historians have often overlooked – it cut through years of diplomatic nicety and brought the negotiations to a swift conclusion. The English were painfully ready to meet the Spaniards more than halfway; Charles displayed his faltering Spanish, and Buckingham spent £13 learning the local dance steps. More importantly they agreed under protest to additional concessions in the marriage treaty.[11] Yet their willingness to accommodate themselves to their host's wishes in all things save personal conversion to Catholicism produced little fruit; in place of a clear Spanish assurance of diplomatic and, if need be, military assistance in the Palatinate's recovery, the best Spanish offer was a blank paper from Philip IV on which James could set his own terms. As Elizabeth protested, "they have given us blancs inough with nothing in them as I think this will be the same." Nevertheless, every penny of the small fortune spent in Madrid was well spent; only in Spain had Charles and Buckingham been able to see the bottom of the Spaniards' bag, and the importance of that glimpse cannot be emphasized

[9] Conway to Edmondes, 24 March 1624, BL Stowe 176, fo. 246; and "The Relation of . . . Gerbier," BL Add. 4181, fos. 17v–18.

[10] Carleton to Roe, 26 May 1623, TCD MSS 708, I, fos. 186–186v; James to Charles and Buckingham, 31 July 1623, *Letters of King James*, p. 420; and Wake to Conway, 11 March 1623, SP 92/10/57.

[11] "Crowes Booke of Accomptes," BL Add. 12,528, fo. 9; and Lockyer, *Buckingham*, p. 135. On events in Madrid, see J. H. Elliott, *Olivares* (New Haven, 1986), pp. 203–14.

enough. Earlier in 1623 Elizabeth had complained that "my father will never leave treating though with it he hath lost all."[12] A few months later, her lament was unnecessary; the end of incessant treating had at last arrived.

The discovery of the Spanish refusal to link the Anglo-Spanish marriage to the Palatine restoration was no exit visa. In order to extricate themselves from their hosts, Charles and Buckingham agreed to a revised marriage treaty. But their fundamental regard for the new treaty can be seen in Charles's parting message to Sir Walter Aston, the resident ambassador in Madrid. As the treaty required, Charles followed the terms and left behind his proxy, which the ambassador was to deliver within ten days of the arrival of the papal dispensation. Privately, however, Charles ordered Aston not to deliver the proxy until further word from the prince. The finality of his resolution becomes plain in his response to the envoy bearing Elizabeth's greetings and gifts to her new sister-in-law; Charles turned him around. Buckingham explained his action to Elizabeth: "he for whose cause you sent them . . . hath thought it nott fitt . . . to putt it in their powers to answere your kindness with scornes." For a twenty-three-year-old man frustrated with bachelorhood, the decision had not been an easy one, but in the end he could not abandon his sister. "What an unnatural brother you have," Buckingham wrote, "who when he had most caus of confidence in the good succes of his mariage protested he would not be ingaged till he might gudge what would become of your business."[13]

Once we understand that Charles was testing the Spanish resolutions on the Palatinate as well as fetching the Infanta, the Spanish journey indeed resembles, in Charles Emanuel's metaphor, a bold cavalry charge. Roger Lockyer in his study of the duke maintained that in Madrid Buckingham "had been made forcibly aware of the very real dangers that the expansion of Habsburg power offered to the western world."[14] But given the goals of the trip, Buckingham had very real fears about Spanish designs *before* he went to Madrid. Charles's sudden appearance at Philip's Court represented a tacit ultimatum; as James himself conceded, "if my baby's credit in Spain mend not these things [the Palatine question], I will bid farewell to peace in Christendom." What Charles and Buckingham found in Madrid was not startling new information about the "universal monarchy," but rather *prima facie* evidence of these ambitions. They returned convinced, as the duke told

---

[12] Elizabeth to Roe, 19 May 1623, TCD MSS 708, I, fos. 174–174v; and Elizabeth to Conway, 6 September [1623], SP 81/29/120.
[13] Buckingham to Aston [outlining Charles's earlier order to Aston], [January 1624], SP 94/30/66v–69; and [Buckingham] to [Elizabeth], [September 1623], BL Harleian 6987, fos. 151–2.
[14] [Wake] to [Conway], [March 1623], SP 92/10/84; and Lockyer, *Buckingham*, p. 168.

the French ambassador, that Philip's ministers had been publicly leading James "par le nez."[15]

Lofty public reasons for a Spanish war of course did not preclude less dignified ones. Later in the decade the Earl of Bristol charged that picque alone caused the abrupt transformation of the eager bridegroom into the committed hispanophobe, and modern scholars have tended to adopt this explanation. Admittedly neither Charles nor Buckingham cared for their "drye entertainment" in Spain, and admittedly Gerbier went to the other extreme when he argued that Charles's press for war later in 1623 "had no other ground butt his firme constant and generous disposition to the Interest of his Royall Sister and Familly."[16] But to ascribe their passionate bellicosity largely to picque is to overlook their earlier interest in a more martial response to the German crisis and to ignore the role of Elizabeth's plight in the Spanish trip. Even the duke's tiffs with Olivares and his elephantine memory for snubs cannot account for his vigorous support for the war effort. Plainly motives went much deeper than mere revenge for the humiliation in Madrid.

It is hard to separate the young prince from the cause of peace, which his father advocated for half a century and which Charles after 1629 was to adopt as his own. Indeed the Rubens ceiling of the Banqueting House, which Charles later commissioned, apparently testified to the consistent response of the dynasty to the lure of continental wars. We would do well, however, to remember that father and son arrived at the same place by radically different routes. While James followed the maxim, "beati pacifici," out of preference, Charles did so after 1629 out of necessity. Even in the halcyon days of peace in the 1630s, Charles's preferred image of himself was that of a martial king in full armor on horseback.[17] Loyal son though he was, Charles was in some ways the mirror opposite rather than the carbon copy of his father. He abhorred the disorder and profanity of his father's Court, and he disliked his father's willingness to swallow his pride in the interest of peace, both foreign and domestic.[18] Indeed one of the most striking aspects of Charles's personality was his rejection of his father's policy of muddling through crises; instead he was inclined to dig in his heels over a point of honor, coolly oblivious of the potential dangers of rigidity. It is not surprising therefore that his capacity for intransigence, which was to cost him his kingdom and his

---

[15] James to Charles and Buckingham, 11 March 1623, *Letters of King James*, p. 394; and Tillières to Puysieux, 12 October 1623, PRO 31/3/57, fo. 257.

[16] Charles to Aston, 8 October 1623, SP 94/28/138; and "The Relation of . . . Gerbier," BL Add. 4181, fos. 19–19v. See also Adams, "Spain or the Netherlands," p. 89.

[17] Roy Strong, *Van Dyck: Charles I on Horseback* (New York, 1972), pp. 45–57.

[18] On Charles's reformation of Court manners, see Beaulieu to Trumbull, and Woolley to same, 8 April 1625, Trumbull MSS, VII/177 and XLVII/164.

head, first became apparent in his championship of that most honorable cause, the vindication of his sister's honor.

The decision to adopt the Palatine cause was one which a host of his father's subjects had been urging him to make. Heirs apparent customarily receive lavish praise, but since the Bohemian crisis the encomiums for Prince Charles had a distinct martial tone. One poem presented a select list of Charles's ancestors for his edification, and the virtues that Rollo of Normandy, "great Richard," the Black Prince and Henry V shared were not domestic legislation and peace. This litany was to serve at once as constant "reproches to your Princely blood" and as examples which, if followed, would make Charles "the best and greatest Prince on Earth." This final transformation was essential, for in the current foreign situation, "we must have Charles the Great." Other authors were less wide-ranging; the 1619 *Mirror of Maiestie* urged Charles to equal the fame of the Black Prince and to reflect that "those high-borne acts which from his valour flue / With new additions are impress't in you."[19] Another likened Charles to Joshua, and a third predicted that Charles would personally lead a Protestant army over the Alps to punish the Papacy.[20] Without question those eager for continental intervention pinned their hopes on Charles. In 1622 Francis Markham's dedication of his book on military exercises reminded the prince that "Your Highness is an Heare of many Kingdomes and may iustly have occasion to command many swords, either to recover your rights in foraine parts or relieve your frends." Valaresso, the Venetian envoy, noted after the prince's return that Charles "desires by every means to win general popularity among the people."[21] In pursuing this task, Charles needed no soothsayer to predict that widespread applause would greet open advocacy of a Spanish war.

A Spanish conflict would allow Charles to make a reputation for himself in defense of an eminently honorable cause and to gain both domestic and foreign praise. "Never man," Bishop Goodman recalled, "did desire wars more than King Charles." By the end of the decade, frustrated by foreign disasters and domestic turmoil, Charles was to come to a new appreciation of his father's critical attitude to warfare. Consequently, the Rubens ceiling can perhaps best be seen as belated homage to his father and as penance for his youthful military passion. If we completely ignore his earlier interest in war and emphasize only picque, we can make little sense of his frustration in later

---

[19] "To my Deare and Greate Master Prince Charles," Bodleian Library, Dodsworth MSS 79, fos. 165–165v; and H.G., *The Mirror of Majestie* (London, 1619), "To the Prince."

[20] Thomas Taylor, "An Everlasting Record," *Two Sermons* (London, 1624), p. 23; and "A Weeke After" [continuation of *Prospopeia*], [1621], Northamptonshire RO, Cokayne Papers, C2480, p. 5.

[21] Francis Markham, *Five Decades of Epistles of Warre* (London, 1622), "To the Prince"; and Valaresso to the Doge and Senate, 31 January 1624, *CSPV*, XVIII, p. 211.

years and of Rubens's flamboyant depiction of the blessings of peace in the Banqueting House. In short, the middle-aged monarch praised for his love of "sweet calm of civil concord," should not obscure the younger man eager to win fame as Charles the Great by force of arms. When Lord Carew predicted late in 1623 that the prince "will exceed most of all the proceedinge Plantagenets as well in Judgement as Vallor," he could not have stated Charles's ambition more succinctly.[22]

The heir apparent's resolution to oppose the reigning monarch was unusual but not unprecedented. What was unique was the royal favorite's decision to join the enterprise. Early quarrels notwithstanding, Charles and Buckingham had grown to be close friends and indeed half-brothers since James regarded Buckingham as his "bastard brat." The adventure of the Smith "brothers" in Spain only solidified the alliance; on their return the two "never goe asunder but arme in arme."[23] Buckingham as a result was probably the only man who ever broke through Charles's cool exterior; when for example sexual relations temporarily ceased between Charles and his new bride in 1625, the frustrated husband turned to the duke for advice. The duke certainly was the only one who gained enough familiarity to close a letter with the salutation, "babie charles, I kiss thie wartie hands." The Spaniards had good reason to complain that Buckingham was apt to "call the Prince by ridiculous names."[24] This relationship permitted Buckingham to help Charles implement, if not to form, the "correct" English response to the continental crisis. Correspondence between the two men is particularly scant, but a letter to Conway in 1625 offers a glimpse of Buckingham's familiar advice: "if his Majestie hould up him self and speake bould language," all would go well.[25] His was a reassuring hand to a shy, anxious young man who lacked nothing for greatness save a little gumption, and the duke would be glad to help him overcome this deficiency.

The duke's exhortations to follow the honorable course unfortunately did not spring from entirely honorable motives. While Buckingham was concerned about the ignominy of James's foreign policy, he cannot have been unmindful of other considerations. In less than ten years, a second son by a

[22] Goodman, *The Court of King James*, I, p. 382; Sir William Davenant, *Salmacida Spolia* (1640), quoted in Strong, *Van Dyck*, p. 86; and Carew to Roe, 8 December 1623, TCD MSS 708, I, fo. 228.

[23] James to Charles and Buckingham, 11 March 1623, *Letters of King James*, p. 394; Sir Richard Wynne, "A Brief Relation," [1623], printed in *The Autobiography and Correspondence of Simonds D'Ewes* (London, 1845), II, p. 442; and Chaworth to Trumbull, 16 January 1624, Trumbull Add. MSS, XVII/unfoliated.

[24] Comte de Tillières, *Mémoires Inédits* (Paris, 1862), p. 100; Buckingham to James, [Spring 1624], NLS 33.1.7 [Denmilne Papers, vol. XXII], no. 77; and [anon.] to James, [Spring 1624], *Cabala*, pp. 217–22.

[25] Buckingham to Conway, October 1625, SP 84/129/211.

second marriage of a minor Leicestershire knight had been transformed into a duke with broad acres, the hand of an aristocratic heiress, and the ear of the king. This metamorphosis certainly made George Villiers one of the spectacular specimens of that early Stuart genus, the "Court Mushroom." By 1623, however, while his honors continued to rise, his influence had not. The royal patronage secretary had the vexatious task of distributing positions and honors among Court factions. Men who claimed Buckingham as their "angel" or, as the aged Lord Brooke did, their "grandfather," had significant advantages, but they were far from consistent winners.[26] Quite simply, James listened closely to Buckingham's advice, but felt no compulsion to follow it. For Buckingham, therefore, the concerted attempt to maneuver James out of his humiliating dependence on Spain had an additional allure; it would also increase his own influence.

Increased power meant increased amounts of patronage, money and fame. A general purge of hispanophiles from the administration would naturally produce the patronage bonanza of the early seventeenth century. There would probably be openings for a new Lord Treasurer, Lord Keeper, Vice Chamberlain, Secretary of State, Master of the Court of Wards, Master of the Mint, and possibly Chancellor of the Exchequer. Furthermore, Buckingham's triumph would allow him to pack the administration with his "creatures." Eager candidates in turn would provide their "angel" with gifts of cash, artworks and particularly spouses to help expand the connection of the Villiers clan. The office of Lord Admiral, which entitled Buckingham to a tenth of all prizes, promised even more handsome returns. Precisely how lucrative this prerogative would be depended on the fortunes of war, but the preceding Lord Admiral, the Earl of Nottingham, had pocketed a considerable fortune in tenths during the Elizabethan war.[27] Finally it should not be forgotten that the task of leading England into a righteous conflict would earn Buckingham considerable acclaim. Feelings of profound insecurity are perhaps characteristics of all powerful political favorites, whose fall was likely to be as meteoric as their rise, and certainly the extraordinary tale of Robert Carr, Earl of Somerset, can only have underscored for Buckingham the fundamental precariousness of a Jacobean favorite. Buckingham's attempt to legitimate his position clearly accounts for his heavy outlay of cash and time in the development of a major art collection. Nevertheless, the acquisition of a few Titians and Caravaggios could scarcely compare with the acquisition of widespread popularity. This consideration was not lost on the

[26] Greville to Villiers, [1617?], Scottish Record Office, GD 24/1/825 [Abercairny Papers], no. 88e; and R. Rebholz, *The Life of Fulke Greville* (Oxford, 1971), p. 275.
[27] R. W. Kenny, *Elizabeth's Admiral* (Baltimore, 1970), pp. 63–87. On the role of gifts among prospective Villiers clients, see J. H. Barcroft, "Carleton and Buckingham: The Quest for Office," *Early Stuart Studies* (Minneapolis, 1970), pp. 122–36 and esp. 128–30.

duke; when he spoke of his desire to take the fleet to sea, his passion to win "more fame" was also linked to his almost pathetic eagerness to earn "more . . . popularity among the people and sailors than he could obtain any other way."[28] In the absence of his personal papers, it is now impossible to discover the duke's exact ranking of these priorities. But it seems that while the vindication of English honor was foremost in his mind, he cannot have forgotten the ancillary benefits of such a policy.

While ulterior motives may well have been behind the bellicosity of Charles and Buckingham, it does not necessarily follow that personal ambition alone drove them on; no evidence suggests that their concern about Habsburg expansion was insincere. Indeed if their public rhetoric is set against the continental situation, much of the mystery disappears about their clamor to take up arms. What initially appears as opportunistic posing becomes an eminently logical response to a deteriorating foreign situation. Few surprises in early modern Europe were more complete than the swift disintegration of the anti-Habsburg camp at the opening of the Thirty Years War. Modern scholars who know all too well that the first decade would prove an unrelieved Protestant disaster have difficulty recapturing the contemporary amazement. They can only smile at the widespread expectations like that of the German print of 1620 which revelled in the prospect of Bethlen Gabor personally castrating the Jesuits.[29] Nonetheless, the initial elation and the subsequent shock reveals that Charles and Buckingham's urgent press for intervention had much more to do with the radically altered balance of power than it did with their shabby treatment in Madrid. Two English tracts reporting spurious debates in papal councils capture the initial confidence. The Curia was reportedly terrified that Frederick, the new Julius Caesar,

> will
> Adventure ore the Alpes to us and fill
> The world with tumult, and Italy feare.

Since this bold expedition would unite all Protestant rulers, the Pope himself noted with dismay

> Aye, me, in fourscore yeres how they are growne
> . . . The number of their Princes, Dukes and Countes
> With their free Lords and States, ours farre surmounts.

Consequently, nightmares tormented the Pontiff in which "the northern nations come down the mountains / As did the Gothes and Vandalls." Prince Charles led the English contingent who arrived brandishing their copies of

---

[28] Lando to the Doge and Senate, 16 May 1620, *CSPV*, XVI, p. 256. On Buckingham's art collection, see Lockyer, *Buckingham*, pp. 408–12.

[29] "Transylvanian Wares," [1620], printed in *Propaganda in Germany during the Thirty Years War*, ed. E. A. Beller (Princeton, 1940), pp. 21–3.

"Fox and Brightman" which gave them "certaine expectation / Of my destruction and Romes desolation." Meanwhile the props of the old faith fell away one by one. Emperor Ferdinand II "cries out for helpe and can no longer stand" against the rebellion which had spread to the Austrians who "are infected with Luthers heresie" and "with their fellow Lutherans combine." The Spaniards were unable to assist their cousins in Vienna because "the waie by sea and land are blockt"; fear of the Dutch kept the Army of Flanders at home; internal wrangles paralyzed the Catholic League of the Empire; and no help could be expected from the eldest son of the Church, Louis XIII, for "if he sawe us down, hee'd sing and dance."[30] These extravagant predictions make one contemporary's interpretation of Halley's comet in 1618 quite plausible; the star clearly indicated that "the House of Austria cannot continue above the yeare 1623" and Rome 1646.[31]

Astrology notwithstanding, 1623 actually found the House of Austria in its strongest position in decades, and its opponents in their worst. The seizure of the Valteline passes enabled the Spaniards to move troops and funds from Milan to Vienna; Spinola's army in fact launched a lightning campaign in the Palatinate; and the Catholic League, far from self-destructing, fielded a formidable army under Count Tilly. The perils of disunity, which the Protestants eagerly predicted for the Habsburgs, were visited instead on themselves. The Protestant Union, not the Catholic League, quickly dissolved amid mutual recriminations, and without a solid military alliance, the numerous Lutheran and Calvinist princes became a liability rather than an asset. Furthermore, the invasion of the new Goths and Vandals was not forthcoming. Catholics later quipped that Christian IV, the Dutch Republic and James were each rushing 100,000 to the aid of Frederick – Christian 100,000 herring, the Dutch 100,000 cheeses, and James the same number of ambassadors. In the event, the vaunted new Caesar had to flee Prague in midwinter with his pregnant English wife, and the subsequent fate of the abandoned Protestants of Central Europe at the hands of the Counter-Reformation moved even James to protests.[32]

By 1623 much more than the honor of a jilted bridegroom was at stake. For decades the possibility of Habsburg domination of the continent, and indeed the world, had haunted Europeans, and during the Bohemian revolt these apprehensions were very much alive. One Englishman's description of the

[30] *Prosopopeia, or a Conference held at Angelo Castle* (London, 1620?); and "A Week After" [continuation of *Prosopopeia*] [1620], Northamptonshire RO, Cockayne Papers, C2480, pp. 2–5.

[31] "A Recitall of the Celestiall Apparitions," Inner Temple Library, Petyt MSS 538, fo. 33v.

[32] Howell to Howell, 10 June 1622, *Epistolae Ho-elianae* (London, 1840), p. 130; and James to the Infanta Isabella, 11 October 1623, SP 77/16/297. See also Geoffrey Parker, *The Thirty Years War*, pp. 48–70.

brave new Spanish world illustrates this fear; Philip IV "will quickly lead all Europe in triumph, make the Pope himselfe become his Chaplaine, turne all Kingdoms into his Provinces, and Plant them with colonies of Moores or Indians, all Princes to be petty Officers of his House, and send the meane people to dig in his Mines or to fish Him some Pearles in America."[33] During Charles's journey to Madrid, the Habsburgs appeared on the verge of exercising firm control over the autonomous German states, and this fact bid fair to rearrange completely the face of international politics. Ferdinand's insistence on punishing his opponents sent several princes into exile with the Palatine family and Frederick's Electorate to Maximilian of Bavaria. Imperial vengeance together with the collapse of the Protestant Union left no German prince in a mood to defy the Emperor, and without any German support, neither Christian IV of Denmark nor Gustavus Adolphus of Sweden could be expected to intervene. The Imperial victory left little time to mourn for German liberties and for the Reformation, because it called the continued existence of the United Provinces into question. If Tilly's army joined the Army of Flanders and if the Hanse towns came under Imperial control and their fleets seconded those of Dunkirk, the reduction of the "disobedient" provinces would be only a matter of time. The fall of the Dutch Republic would in turn signal the end of English independence; once the maritime power of Holland and Zealand was added to that of Flanders, Hamburg and Bremen, any English challenge to the Habsburgs would be suicidal. "If we suffer the Flemings to be ruined," St. Albans observed, "they are our outwork, and we shall remain naked and dismantled." Sir Thomas Fairfax predicted that when Englishmen heard the bells sounding the Habsburg victory over the Dutch, they would be hearing "our funerall peales before our deaths." Thus Sir Benjamin Rudyerd's anxiety about the Dutch Republic was well-founded: "believe it," he assured his fellow Parliament-men in March 1624, "the day of the loss of the Low Country will be no eve of a holiday to us."[34]

Such an interpretation of events was not without serious flaws. It overestimated the monolithic nature of the Austrian family. Moreover, the self-induced crisis mentality, which perceived political liberty and the Reformation in grave danger, violated the maxim Talleyrand would later popularize, "pas de passion." Consequently, as Charles and Buckingham were to discover, this mentality left its advocates vulnerable to deception by allies who did not share the same bleak outlook. It was nevertheless precisely

---

[33] Paolo Sarpi, *The History of the Quarrels of Pope Paul V* (London, 1625), translator's introduction.

[34] 1 March 1624, Pym Diary, fo. 11; T. Fairfax, "The High Way to Hedelburgh," BL Add. 28,326, p. 46; and "Considerations Touching a War," *Letters and Life*, VII, p. 480. I am grateful to Simon Adams for the Fairfax reference.

the view to which Charles and Buckingham subscribed, and it clearly accounts for their unwillingness to accept any other option than immediate intervention in the continental mêlée. Time and again Conway was to explain the impatience of the prince and the duke. "In this Chrisis of the affaires of Christendome," Conway maintained, there was "nothing soe daungerous . . . as the suspention of councells and the want of resolution, what must be expedited and what done." In one letter the Secretary insisted that "there is nothing can be of so evil consequence as admittance of delay"; and in another that since "it is the winning of tyme that will serve theire turnes and ends and disadvantage ours, answeres in any other figures then yea or noe are not safe for us to meddle with."[35] The importance of this doctrine of immediate action in the plans of Charles and the duke cannot be emphasized enough; it explains why they wanted war, and it also explains, at least in part, why their strategic plans often went awry.

Tangled though their motives may have been, their reasons for advocating war can be reconstructed. The policy of "a sharp edge" would allow Charles to gain a martial reputation and Buckingham to expand his influence over the administration and the Court. But these personal ambitions were clearly set in motion and kept in train by the desire to save Europe and England from Habsburg domination and the Protestant religion from the Counter-Reformation. For them, it was in fact a war of revenge, but not the revenge that seems all too obvious to some historians. Charles and Buckingham sought to avenge not so much their "drye entertainment" in Madrid as they did White Mountain, Wimpfen, Hochst, Stadtlohn, and particularly Heidelburg.

CONWAY'S THREE-YEAR PLAN

Strident rhetoric was not a detailed plan of action, and in the case of war with Spain, one without the other would not go very far. Well entrenched at Whitehall was a powerful group of pro-Spanish officials and courtiers who could ensure a searching examination for any proposal to terminate the Anglo-Spanish entente. Given the number of calamities that could befall armed confrontation with the most powerful dynasty in Europe, critics would hammer on the feasibility as well as the justice of a Spanish war. Thus for Charles and Buckingham, a well-developed strategy was a necessity, and they had worked out the details of their plan by the end of the year when the duke presented to the Venetian and French ambassadors a plan promising

---

[35] Conway to Aston, 30 December 1623 and 27 June 1624, SP 94/29/190v and 94/31/71; and Conway to Buckingham, 15 June 1623, Goodman, *The Court of King James*, II, p. 293.

victory in three years.[36] Fortunately for later scholars, a treatise has survived in which Conway elaborated on aspects of the strategic plan. Hence, the exact policy of Charles and Buckingham, which has baffled historians, can be reconstructed in some detail.[37]

In Conway's call to arms, the vindication of sullied honor figured prominently. Nevertheless, the loss of Elizabeth's dowerlands and the Spanish manipulation of the marriage treaty was not the primary justification for war; *raison d'état* was. So fundamentally had the Bohemian war altered international relations that effective counter-measures were necessary before it was too late; "while the rest of the world is in contemplation, the ioynt monarchall forces [of Spain and the Empire] goe actually on." In fact the recent Habsburg successes made the earlier crisis of 1588 compare unfavorably with that of 1623. The recitation of the recent Habsburg triumphs made this point: in 1610, the Cleves-Julich inheritance, in 1620 Bohemia, Moravia, Silesia, and the vital Valteline passes over the Alps, 1622 the Palatinate and Baden, and in 1623 Hesse. More ominous than the list itself was the likelihood of further additions in the near future. According to the seventeenth-century equivalent of the "domino theory," the fall of Prague and Heidelberg represented the first major pieces in a chain that led inexorably to the United Provinces and England. The Dutch Republic was the key to the entire situation: "if the Kinge of Spaine become Master of those Harbours, that Shippinge, the order, industrie and skill of that Nation," Conway maintained, "it is not visible what are the Impediments betweene him [Philip IV] and his [universal] monarchie."

His analysis carefully avoided millenarian terms. Conway did not propose an overtly religious conflict between the godly and the Habsburg Antichrist. He advanced instead a strictly legal operation to check the high-handed actions of one dynasty. It was to be "a warr for the stoppinge of that threateninge monarchie, for the generall and intire peace of Germanie, for the recoverie of the Pallatinatt and for the perpetuall sueritie of his [James's] friends and Allies." The goal of the war could be expressed even more succinctly; "we are all marching towards the same purpose," James later maintained, "to confine them within theire own frontiers."[38] Such strict definition would also permit the formation of the broadest possible anti-

---

[36] Pesaro to the Doge and Senate, 2 January 1624, *CSPVB*, XVIII, p. 191; and Tillières to Puysieux, 1 February 1624, PRO 31/3/58, fo. 21.

[37] "A Discourse Concerning the Precedent and Present State of the Low Countries," [winter 1623–4], SP 103/42/unfoliated. Although the author is not clearly stated, this document is written in the hand of one of Conway's secretaries and composed in Conway's "military style." I am grateful to Professor S. J. Stearns for drawing my attention to this class of documents.

[38] Pesaro to the Doge and Senate, 1 January 1625, *CSPV*, XVIII, p. 536.

Habsburg "confederacy," cutting across religious lines to unite Venice, Savoy and France with Denmark, Sweden, the United Provinces and England. The paramount problem was that England alone could take the lead. "Unlesse they see action," the German and Scandinavian princes "have lesse power and more fresh and neerer feares and will not dare to declare upon promises, hopes or probabilities;" and Louis XIII "will temporize and proceede coldly, which in case of this nature may hazard the cause." Ironically, only *Rex Pacificus* could save Europe. But once James raised his standard, all else would fall into place, "for the remedies being easie and sure, if the Princes will but stirr up their owne virtues, industrie and power." Christian IV after considering his brother-in-law's lead "might have time and reason to put forth his industrie and ayde"; the German princes would begin to stir in support of the "common cause" as would the Venetians and Savoyards; and Louis XIII "it is like will find good cause to make a diversion for the quarrell of the Valteline."

The advantage of a broad confederation appeared clearly when Conway sketched out his military plans. The bleak fact of the matter was that an isolated attack on such a powerful "empire" would be at best inconclusive and at worst self-destructive. Yet if the confederates shared the risk of confrontation and struck the House of Austria in several places, the allies would be able to exploit the Habsburgs' Achilles heel – distance. While a single attack would allow the Habsburgs to prepare an overwhelming military response, multiple attacks would force them to divide their troops and to give their opponents a fighting chance. As another English contemporary shrewdly observed, the proud boast that "the sunne doth every hower in the fower and twenty shyne upon one or other of his countries" did nothing to ease the near impossible task of defending a far flung "empire."[39] This fundamental principle informed Conway's plan. The French, Savoyards and Venetians would strike the Valteline passes to vital to Habsburg lines of communication and, if all went well, attack Milan and Naples. The Danes and various German princes would operate on the other side of the Alps. Meanwhile the English and the Dutch would concentrate on naval diversions. Admittedly James had to "stir up" the continental powers; subsidizing Mansfelt's army would permit the German "Princes that are willinge to save themselves" to "gather head" and remove the immediate danger to the Dutch Republic. Beyond these limited operations, the Secretary adamantly opposed any further continental ventures; if the war went well, James "may" then think of either "a diversive warr upon flanders" or a direct march on Heidelberg. But the difficulty of these projects "renders the worke impossible or at least improbable, which by the other wayes in lesse than three yeares will

[39] Fairfax, "The High Way to Hedelburgh," BL Add. 28,326, p. 35.

easely bee affected." The "other wayes" were naval raids; James "might bee pleased ... to wast the Kinge of Spaines Shipping upon his coast, interrupt the retornes of his Plate and share as deeply with him as occasion and fortune will give leave." Eventually Anglo-Dutch squadrons would strike across the Atlantic in an effort "to supplant him in the West Indies." These three simultaneous campaigns would bring the Habsburgs to heel "in lesse than three yeares."

The most remarkable aspect of this plan, aside from its breath-taking confidence, was the adroit resolution of the sharp strategic disagreements among Englishmen. James, with hair-splitting precision that many Englishmen simply could not comprehend, limited his enemies to Maximilian of Bavaria, the Catholic League, and Emperor Ferdinand II, and he confined any military action to the Palatinate. This logic bewildered Sir Edward Giles; "we must fight the Spanyards in the Pallatinate and be friends with them Every where elce." A host of MPs in the 1621 Parliament shared his uneasiness. An expeditionary force operating inside the Empire would be perilously exposed and financially ruinous; little wonder Sir Richard Grosvenor wryly observed that "to have an armie maintayned in the Palatinate is the desire of the enemie."[40] More easily accessible targets lay closer at hand in Flanders and in the West Indies if only James cared to notice the Spanish gold which financed the Emperor and the Spanish troops who had first attacked the Palatinate. Thus Thomas Crewe pleaded with James "not to fight with a concealed enemy but with the King of Spain and not with the Duke of Bavaria." Instead he hoped that "we might march with the protestant princes." Another MP even openly prayed that James "would rather thinke of Queene Elizabeths course and the West Indies."[41] James nonetheless clung fast to his views, and the differences over strategy, which became more apparent as the session progressed, eventually contributed to the final dissolution.

It must be conceded that James's position was not simply that of a timorous old sybarite whom one contemporary dubbed "Queen James." Although his views may well have disguised a basic aversion to war, they remain eminently valid objections from a veteran statesman with few illusions about international realities. The Protestant cause plainly would unnecessarily reduce the already limited number of potential allies and automatically increase the list of opponents. Admittedly when confronted with a diplomatic and strategic tangle, the simple clarity of the elect nations against the minions of the Antichrist had an undeniable appeal. Yet any comfort in Protestant solidarity would soon prove exceedingly cold when a confessional league

[40]   26 and 27 November, Commons' Debates 1621, ed. Wallace Notestein (New Haven, 1935), IV, p. 438, and V, p. 216.
[41]   26 November 1621, ibid., II, p. 451, and IV, p. 438.

forced France, Venice and Savoy into alliance with the Habsburgs. Several years later the Countess of Buckingham conjured up James's memory in order to dissuade her son from driving Louis XIII into the arms of Philip IV; after denouncing the Ré expedition, she added, "you knowe the worthy king your maister never liked that waye."[42] Indeed as far as James was concerned, the faithful were to await Armageddon patiently, not precipitate it with a war of religion.

James also had reservations about the company he would keep in a confessional league; the rhetoric of a north European alliance of the godly could not mask the reality of a league with the Dutch Republic as England's principal ally. James had found their High Mightinesses of the Estates General exceptionally troublesome. To be sure, he had started off on the wrong foot with the separate Anglo-Spanish peace of 1604, which the Dutch still recalled with bitterness twenty years later. A host of subsequent commercial disputes only further exacerbated Anglo-Dutch tensions and allowed the Dutch to exhibit their considerable talent for tetchiness and James to display his most imperious manner. In addition, thanks to the grave financial problems of the Republic, James scoffed at the idea of asking "the beggarly Dutch" for assistance in the Palatinate; it was much more likely that he would have to assist them. War for an old and unbloodied king, James insisted, was "a new world," one which he would not willingly explore with the "Mynheers" as his guides.[43]

Equally unsettling was the maritime emphasis of a Protestant league. A vigorous Anglo-Dutch naval campaign might well divert the flow of Spanish silver from Seville to London and so force Philip to restore the Palatinate. On the other hand, the Elizabethan experience suggested that a more likely outcome would be a long, inconclusive and expensive conflict. Exciting though many Englishmen found the prospect of larceny on the high seas, James was interested in it only as a means of recovering the Palatinate; and towards that end, naval operations on their own were not particularly promising. Even an advocate of a "blue water" policy had to confess that a strictly naval war promised "much may be for the Commonwealth, but nothing for the Church in Germany."[44] Therefore James's refusal to initiate an extended naval conflict can scarcely be termed cowardice.

---

[42] "Dr Plume's Notebook," *Essex Review*, XIV (1905), p. 163; and Countess of Buckingham to Buckingham, 1 October [1627], Warwick County Record Office, CR 2017, C1/22. I am indebted to Conrad Russell for this last reference.
[43] G. Edmundson, *Anglo-Dutch Rivalry during the First Half of the Seventeenth Century* (Oxford, 1911), pp. 11–81; and esp. J. C. Grayson, "From Protectorate to Partnership: Anglo-Dutch Relations, 1598–1625" (Ph.D thesis, University of London, 1978).
[44] BL Egerton 2651, fos. 78v–79.

The sharp debate over strategy makes the attraction of the "common cause" obvious; it provided a *via media* down which king and interventionists might jog. The "common cause" overcame James's objections to a confessional league, and it still remained appealing to those eager to assist the battered continental churches. Intervention could scarcely become a war of religion if the Defender of the Faith fought beside, not against, the Eldest Son of the Roman Church; indeed by operating with Catholic princes, Protestants could at last hope to separate the interests of the house of Austria from those of the Catholic Church. A broad coalition also moved the recovery of the Palatinate from the realm of the unlikely to that of the possible; the common cause with its additional theater of operations in northern Italy would unquestionably stretch the Habsburg resources much more than a confessional league would, and only by pressing the enemy hard on several fronts could the coalition hope for success. Furthermore, an Anglo-Dutch league need no longer trouble James since it would be circumscribed within a much broader league. The ideals of Conway's plans would have been equally hard for James to reject out of hand. Instead of avenging insults to the reformed religion and the Stuart dynasty, the common cause defended nothing less than the sovereignty of all independent states, Protestant and Catholic alike, from what one contemporary termed "the swellinge pride of this Mightie Monarch still thristinge after new conquests." It was an appeal well-wrought to rouse a sovereign who had always resented the Habsburgs' high-handed actions; for example the Imperial subjugation of Hesse prompted James to exclaim "they would shortly (if these things be suffered) attaque himself also and take his Jerkin from his back." Little wonder then that James found the idea of "boundinge . . . every man with in his owne" much harder to reject than the confessional alternative.[45]

The altered situation late in 1623 further disposed him to examine the "common cause" more carefully. First, once the English garrisons on the Rhine had been withdrawn or overrun, the English now had the leisure to consider responses which had earlier been dismissed as too slow to relieve Colonels Vere, Herbert and Burroughs. The English military experts unquestionably preferred a diversionary war to a major expedition into the Empire. In fact, one expert concluded that since the Palatinate itself "cannot in a long tyme be recovered without infinit expenses of men and money," England was "better [to] be without it then to buy itt at so deare a price." With the reduction of the last Palatine strongholds early in 1623, these arguments against a direct assault down the Rhine became overwhelming while the merits of a naval war appeared more clearly. In short, it was then very hard to ignore

---

[45] Castle to Trumbull, 20 November 1623, Trumbull MSS, XVIII/111; Fairfax, "High Way to Hedelburgh," BL Add. 28,326, p. 18; and Conway to Carleton, 9 January 1624, SP 84/16/15.

Gainsford's call for a naval war in which England would seize "treasure by hatt fulls, by hart fulls, by house fulls" and Fairfax's advice "to seeke the Palatinate in America."[46] The other important development in 1623 was that Louis XIII was no longer ignoring the German conflict while he concentrated on crushing the Huguenots. In 1621, when the faithful were harried in France and in the Empire, a Protestant version of the Catholic League made some sense; in 1623, however, when Louis was at peace with his Calvinist subjects and interested in checking the Austrians, it also made sense to work with the Catholic anti-Habsburg states and to shelve plans for a confessional league. Moreover, the goals of the "common cause" must have reassured those apprehensive about compromising religious solidarity in return for some Catholic regiments; the officially non-denominational league was attempting to restore the Valtelina and the Palatinate to Protestant control. Thus the Earl of Pembroke was to agree to a broad war against the Habsburgs rather than "a warr for religion" because "I know in the consequencie these cannot be severed."[47] The alarming course of events in the early 1620s had blurred the once pronounced differences between militant Englishmen and their king, and ensured a sympathetic royal audience for the "common cause."

The audience who most concerned Charles and Buckingham was in the royal box, but they were not unmindful of humbler groups in the pit. Notwithstanding its rejection of confessional politics, the "common cause" called for close military cooperation between England and other Protestant states. Cooperation would also be in order with Catholic states, but a generation raised on Elizabethan tales should have been able to tolerate such a compromise. After all, one of her greatest achievements had been the salvation of Catholic France and its renegade Huguenot sovereign, Henry IV, from Habsburg domination. "Did she not," one minister reminded his congregation in the 1620s, "relieve France . . . and astonish the world?"[48] If a contemporary could overcome apprehensions about James's taste in allies, there was much to excite him in the actual operational role of English troops and vessels in the "common cause." Both Conway's rejection of a direct attack down the Rhine and his call for limited assistance to "stir up" continental allies were based on earlier parliamentary proposals and Elizabethan precedents. After all, the key to naval success, Fairfax argued, was "first the kinge of Spaine and the Emperor must be imployed on land by the kinges of Fraunce and Denmarke and the Princes of the Union." The bulk of the English war-chest, however, Conway reserved for the fleet. Conway

---

[46] "In What Lamentable Estate," [1621–2], and [T. Gainsford], "Vox Spiritus," Folger Library, V.a.24, p. 34, and V.a.223, fo. 6; and Fairfax, "High Way to Hedelburgh," BL Add. 28,326, p. 36.
[47] Pembroke to Carleton, 10 December [1624], SP 14/176/34.
[48] William Worship, *Three Sermons* (London, 1625), p. 17.

obviously was in step with those calling for a revival of the Elizabethan model of warfare. The major difference was that Conway was more conservative in his timetable for victory; his confident prediction of success in three years appears fantastic until it is set against the prescriptions of Sir Dudley Digges and Sir Thomas Fairfax, which guaranteed results in two years.[49] Finally, by 1623 those who remained suspicious about either the allies or the strategy were probably not in the mood to quibble. Three years earlier, one Englishman had drawn up an elaborate outline of James's possible military options, and although the author favored an assault on Spain or Flanders, he concluded with an observation that could have doubled as a prayer: "any-where is better than no where."[50] It seems unlikely that after having watched as the realm drifted closer to Spain in 1621–3 the author would have changed his mind about the desirability of *any* war.

Fortunately the author of this tract did not have to stand by his word. Charles and Buckingham had taken great pains to draft a plan to overcome James's objections and to attract the broadest possible support. Full details of their plan became publicly available only in early 1624, and until then there was considerable speculation about James's next move. Fairfax, for example, responded to the prince's return by composing an extended military tract on the question, "What is to be done?"[51] He would have been delighted to know that the prince and the duke had anticipated his query and had already produced a well-reasoned justification for the application of "a sharp edge." For them, the problem late in 1623 was not what was to be done; it was how they could organize a domestic coalition in support of their plan.

---

[49] 26 November, *Commons Debates 1621*, II, p. 451; and Fairfax, "High Way to Hedelburgh," BL 28,326, pp. 46 and 48. On the Elizabethan war, see R. B. Wernham, *The Making of Elizabethan Foreign Policy, 1558–1603* (Berkeley, 1980), and esp. Wernham, *After the Armada* (Oxford, 1984).

[50] BL Egerton 2651, fos. 78v–79. Since this document is found among the Barrington Papers, it is tempting to ascribe it to one of the Barringtons. There is, however, no clear indication of the author.

[51] Fairfax, "High Way to Hedelburgh," BL 28,326, p. 30.

2

"The English match": the organization of the "Patriot" coalition

Excitement over the prince's return soon gave way to apprehension about the new foreign policy. In the confusion those who sought enlightenment at their local bookseller were not disappointed; there browsers could find the ghost of the Elizabethan Earl of Essex eager to offer guidance. Since the noted controversialist Thomas Scott had coached the earl on current events, it is scarcely surprising to learn that Essex denounced the Anglo-Spanish negotiations as "perfidious and dangerous." He ended his advice, however, with an unusual flourish; Englishmen should exhort James to terminate these negotiations immediately and "in lieu of the Spanish match, to promote the English match."[1] The advice from Elysium was not entirely fanciful; in fact perceptive contemporaries noted a remarkable *rapprochement* of normally antithetical elements of Court and Country over the winter of 1623–4. This major re-alignment of Court factions represented nothing less than the preliminaries of the English match.

Leading members of James's household had never before sedulously courted popular favor. Their success can be see in the fact that never before and never again in early Stuart England would the gap between the "political" Court and Country narrow as much as it did in 1624. To be sure, the architects of this grand *rapprochement* were far from disinterested; they sought allies in the struggle with the Spanish ambassadors for James's ear much more than they wanted intimate friends among the "popular" lords. Nevertheless, their success in organizing a domestic coalition against Spain was remarkable. The alliance was to prove transitory, but to dismiss the coalition for this reason would be to miss the importance of the *rapprochement* and to misread the history of the later decade. For those who had customarily kept their distance from the center of the Jacobean Court, the close and fairly harmonious relationship between government and people in 1624 confirmed that the system could work if the government wanted; it also illustrated the fundamental necessity of parliamentary supply to a government

---

[1] [Thomas Scott], *Robert, Earle of Essex His Ghost* (Paradise, 1624), p. 14.

contemplating war. Likewise, Charles formed potent memories of the events of 1624, memories which certainly accounted for much of his later frustration with parliaments and his people. When Thomas Carew in 1632 praised Charles's patience with "this obdurate land," he was in part sympathizing with Charles's extended struggle to make his obdurate people honor the agreements struck in 1624.[2]

Later chapters will analyze how the coalition operated; the present one will examine the espousals of the English match between Charles and the political nation. It will discuss first the duke's inner circle of clients, then the appeal for broader support against the Spaniards, and finally the success in recruiting domestic allies.

THE DUKE'S CREATURES

The adoption of the "common cause" presented monumental problems. In order to change the course of English foreign policy, Charles and Buckingham had to seize control of the administration and to make an unparalleled plunge into popular politics. The fact that the number of their loyal supporters late in 1623 could be counted on one hand only made their undertaking even more daunting. The limiting factor was Buckingham, not Charles; while many courtiers and bureaucrats would readily defer to the heir apparent, a much smaller percentage were eager to work in close conjunction with the favorite. This phenomenon would soon disappear, but even when new recruits abounded, the men at the center of the "Blessed Revolution" were the old "creatures" of Buckingham. Given their importance, the inner circle of ducal supporters deserves an introduction.

Buckingham's most distinguished adviser was James Hay, Earl of Carlisle. A parvenu Scot, Hay had come south with the new monarch in 1603, and after James gave Hay free rein in the Wardrobe, conspicuous consumption became the norm for both James and Hay. His administration, prodigal even by Jacobean standards, eventually fell afoul of the financial reforms of Lionel Cranfield, to whom Hay resigned his most lucrative offices in 1618. With the royal household no longer a safe haven for spendthrifts, Hay shifted his attention to diplomacy where the Bohemian crisis allowed him ample opportunity to establish a reputation as Ambassador Extraordinary. Predictably, his services abroad were expensive; when James complained in later Parliaments about the high price of diplomacy, he was largely talking about the high cost of retaining Carlisle. His reputation would cause the French considerable anxiety in 1624; while they would warmly greet a francophile such as Carlisle

---

[2] "In an answer . . . upon the death of the King of Sweden," *The Poems of Thomas Carew* (Oxford, 1949), p. 75.

in Paris, they found the cost of defraying a notoriously lavish envoy daunting. In the end, Carlisle demonstrated his goodwill by agreeing to limit his expenditures.[3]

Carlisle's *nouveau riche* taste for opulence should not obscure his intelligence, a talent much rarer among Jacobean courtiers than the ability to spend money. He had a good weather-eye for domestic politics; for example, he had the sense to work with rather than against Buckingham, and he readily appreciated the importance of royal concessions in a harmonious Parliament.[4] His speciality, however, was foreign affairs and the Protestant cause. Given his long-standing opposition to the idea of a Spanish match, it was only natural in 1619 that the Spaniards should accuse him of organizing a public celebration in Liège to honor Frederick's election to the Bohemian throne. Whether or not he actually did so is irrelevant; what is important is that he was considered quite capable of such a provocative act. By 1623 the Scotsman had come to represent the mirror image of Bristol, the leading advocate of Anglo-Spanish cooperation. Not surprisingly, when Carlisle followed Charles to Madrid, Olivares singled him out for a cool reception; his public enthusiasm for all things Castilian could not obscure the fact that he had "no devotion to Compostella."[5] He was partly responsible for advancing the idea of using the "common cause" to split the Catholic states. Of course a non-confessional league against the House of Austria had a distinguished pedigree, but during the reign of James I, the memory had faded. In 1623 Sir Dudley Carleton, the ambassador in The Hague, lamented that "that word [the common cause] be [an] all most forgotten cause amongst us."[6] Carlisle was one of the few who remembered, and from this fact stems his importance in the great reversal of policy in 1623–4.

Carlisle was also adept at talent-spotting, and two of the prominent "revolutionaries" of 1624 had earlier been protégés of the Scotsman. Neither Henry Rich, Lord Kensington, later Earl of Holland, and Sir George Goring, later Lord Goring and Earl of Norwich, were particularly good at formulating policy; indeed Kensington's budding diplomatic career ended in 1626 precisely because he often became hazy on the finer points of strategy. Yet both men florished in the hothouse environment at Court where they found an appreciative audience for their charm and wit. As befitted the handsome

---

[3] Conway to James, [Spring 1624], SP 78/72/91. On his background, see Roy Schreiber, *The First Carlisle* (Philadelphia, 1984), pp. 5–54 and 144–51; and Menna Prestwich, *Cranfield* (Oxford, 1966), pp. 158–62 and 228–32.

[4] Carlisle to James, 14 February 1624, BL Harleian 1580, fos. 193–6; and Ruigh, pp. 151–2.

[5] Nethersole to Carleton, 8 January 1619, *Letters and Other Documents . . . between England and Germany*, ed. S. R. Gardiner (London, 1868), II, p. 133; Lionello to the Doge and Senate, 11 May 1617, *CSPV*, XIV, p. 503; and Castle to Trumbull, [summer 1623], Trumbull MSS, XVIII/94a.

[6] Carleton to Conway, 23 September 1623, SP 84/114/137.

Captain of the Royal Guard, Kensington was a past master of discreet liaisons and intrigues. This talent served him well during his Parisian embassy of 1624–5 when he scored a brilliant success with the Court ladies.[7] Goring for his part was amusing and gay; typical of his activities was the organization of an assembly of "the fellowes and frends, maides, wifes, widowes and gossups of what sort soever" to while away the hours at The Hague. Charter members like Elizabeth's ladies delighted in Goring's antics like the "ballet" he danced "uppon a broome with my Lady Nethersoles chambermaide."[8] Little wonder then that reports of their deaths on the way to Madrid sent the Court into mourning. Both men, one observer lamented, were "the two blazing starres of this Curt," whose brilliance can be seen in the memorial service one wit proposed for them; he summoned forth

> Your churchales and your moresses
> with hobby-horse advancinge
> Your Round-games with some fine sam and sis
> about the May-pool dauncinge.[9]

Underneath the gaiety and bright conversation, both men were invaluable go-betweens in the delicate matters of reconciliation and patronage. As the pressure on the duke's time increased, so too did the need for intermediaries between the favorite and suitors; Goring and Kensington filled this role admirably. Goring for all his playful exterior was a shrewd analyst of the Court, and when his "court eyes" assessed the situation, he was rarely far off the mark.[10] Kensington brought to the war coalition a surprisingly broad range of contacts; even after the 1626 session had marked him as one of "the Dukes friends or our kingdomes worst Foes," he continued to advise "popular" peers like the Earl of Essex on Court advancement.[11] Therefore Goring and Kensington were vital in implementing policy.

Buckingham's most valuable associate was Sir Edward Conway, later Lord Conway, Viscount Killultagh of Ireland and Viscount Conway of England. The formation of the "common cause" owed much to him, and as Secretary of State he was at the center of the attempt to wrest control of the administration. His influence like that of Carlisle would fade by the middle of the decade as the duke came to rely on other councillors. Until that time, how-

[7] Tillières, *Mémoires*, p. 122; Roy E. Schreiber, *The First Carlisle: Sir James Hay, First Earl of Carlisle as Courtier, Diplomat and Entrepreneur, 1580–1636* (Philadelphia, 1984), p. 14.

[8] "The assemblie" to "George" [Goring], [winter 1624 to 1625], SP 84/121/181.

[9] [L. Whitaker], "Upon the Report of the Death of the Earle of Kensington and Sir George Goring," Beinecke Library, Osborn b197, pp. 130–1; and Castle to Trumbull, 25 April 1623, Trumbull MSS, XVII/92.

[10] Goring to Carleton, 8 September 1625, SP 16/5/35.

[11] Clyve to Newdegate, 16 June 1626, Warwick County RO, Newdegate of Arbury MSS, CR 126/b108, fo. 1v; Holland to Essex, [1627], BL Loan 23, fo. 176. I owe the material in Loan 23 to the kindness of Christopher Thompson who drew this class to my attention.

ever, he was the indispensable righthand man of Charles and Buckingham. As one contemporary explained, "the Prince referrs all to the Duke of Buckingham who hath head and hand full and he trusts no man but one" – Edward Conway.[12]

Conway's importance initially appears unlikely, given his unimposing and somewhat comical character. When Carleton praised him for *not* being "plaine pen-man," he was attempting to set a favorable construction on Mr. Secretary's most embarrassing failure – his handwriting; Buckingham once begged him to dictate his letters to a scribe and "then I shall be verie glad to see them often." His wobbly latin prompted James to protest that the duke had given him a secretary who could neither read nor write.[13] Equally incongruous was his overly ceremonious style. Contemporaries were at first alarmed at Conway's attempt to accord the duke the title of "Your Excellency," which was customarily given to independent princes, but they soon learned that it was hard to take such praise seriously when it effortlessly reached ludicrous heights. To the English resident in Madrid, Conway insisted that the royal Secretary was simply "a little shrubb" compared to Buckingham's "cedar"; and in another instance he stunned one country gentleman with his prolix compliments to a servant of the man's wife.[14] Carlisle was not exaggerating when he begged Conway to eschew the salutation, "the humble servant of your humblest slave." Hence the pun that his subordinates used behind his back, "your great wordy frend," becomes understandable.[15] Conway's uneasiness with diplomatic conventions only enhanced his bumbling air. His decidedly "military style" was often unintentionally abrasive. In December 1624, a wrangle over a procedural point between Conway and a French envoy troubled the conclusion of the Anglo-French marriage treaty; James assured the Frenchman that the incident arose more from "his [Conway's] ignorance then out of malice."[16] Likewise the Secretary once plunged the Court into premature mourning when he interpreted a letter from Christian V as a discreet announcement of Christian IV's death. More experienced hands soon explained the Danish

---

[12] Carleton the younger to Carleton, 18 December 1624, SP 14/176/67.
[13] Carleton to Conway, 2 December 1623, SP 84/115/85; and Buckingham to Conway, [July–August 1623], BL Harleian 6987, fo. 175. Conway himself made light of his "especiall hand", which formed one of the running jokes of his administration; see for example, Conway to Carleton, 19 March 1623, SP 84/111/201.
[14] Chamberlain to Carleton, 25 January 1623, *Letters*, II, p. 474; Conway to Aston, 7 April 1624, BL Add. 33,447, fo. 72v; and J. Oglander, *A Royalist's Notebook* (New York, 1971), p. 143.
[15] Carlisle to Buckingham, 6 August 1624, SP 78/73/1; and "P. Ronsarde" [Castle] to Trumbull, 31 December 1624, Trumbull MSS, XVIII/140.
[16] Woolk to Trumbull, 31 December 1624, Trumbull MSS, XLVIII/157; and Carleton the younger to Carleton, 3 May 1623, SP 84/112/103.

custom of according the regal style to the heir apparent when the sovereign left the country as Christian IV just had. Tillières rightly judged that Conway was a better soldier than diplomat.[17]

These shortcomings, however, do not necessarily validate Gardiner's judgment of the man. "It was soon understood at Court," Gardiner maintained, "that he had in reality no opinions of his own. His thoughts as well as his words were at the bidding of the great favorite . . . he was impressed by nature with the profoundest admiration for any feather-brained courtier who happened to enjoy the favour of the King."[18] On the other hand, the mere fact that Buckingham advanced someone should not be taken as proof of witless sycophancy. Even with the most suspect category of clients, those who married into the Villiers clan, scholars must proceed with caution lest they dismiss Sir Edward Coke with Sir John Sheldon. Generally a client had to display some talent, especially before the duke achieved his greatest power in 1625. Buckingham simply could not afford to have a dithering old man as one of his first "creatures" in great office. It seems that Gardiner overlooked one vital fact; from Conway's office issued the stream of memoranda and treatises directing the campaign against Spain. Some of these owed much to his staff, especially William Chesterman and John Devic, and to Buckingham and other pro-war councillors. Nevertheless, all these documents bore the distinctive stamp of "military style" of Edward Conway, the chief strategist of the early war effort. Quite clearly, among the re-appraisals of early modern history, Edward Conway deserves some mention.

First and foremost, Conway was the duke's "Martial Secretarie." A recent biographer of Sir Richard Weston has observed that "Conway was a brusque man with little talent for the niceties of diplomacy, and Weston would doubtless have made a more effective Secretary."[19] This remark, however, ignores that politesse and penmanship were the least of Buckingham's concerns. Indeed the old Governor of Brill readily confessed, "I am not verie good att complements and Courtly observances . . . my breeding hath beene a souldier which gives me a tast of rudenes then finenes." The duke himself was more than content with these limitations and proclaimed Conway "the best companie that may be."[20] Late in 1622 the best company tended to military discourses; Conway for example entertained the favorite with a detailed analysis and maps of the seige of Bergen-op-zoom. Admittedly his analysis of

[17] Christian V to Charles, 31 May 1625, SP 75/6/67; Mead to Stuteville, 25 June 1625, BL Harleian 389, fo. 466; and Tillières to Puysieux, 11 December 1623, PRO 31/3/57, fo. 271.

[18] S. R. Gardiner, *Prince Charles*, II, pp. 294–6.

[19] Wotton to Portland, *Cabala*, pp. 198–9; and Michael Alexander, *Charles I's Lord Treasurer* (New York, 1975), p. 28.

[20] Conway to Trumbull, 23 August 1623, SP 77/16/255; and Chamberlain to Carleton, 12 October 1622, *Letters*, II, p. 458.

the continental situation lacked the polish of experienced diplomats like Sir Dudley Carleton and Sir Isaac Wake. Yet he more than compensated for this defect when the conversation turned to military options, and that was precisely what Buckingham wanted in 1623. Consequently Carleton's choice of a gift for the new Secretary was eminently appropriate; a brace of fine pistols personally designed by Prince Maurice, the celebrated Dutch general, was the only logical present when James "had a soldier to his Secretarie."[21]

Each of these four men had their own limitations which were often severe. But as a group they did much to supply each other's deficiencies: Carlisle and Conway did admirable service as the brain trust, and Kensington and Goring as intermediaries in the task of reconciling Buckingham and various "popular" lords. They also possessed other qualities; since each was associated with certain positions in domestic and foreign policy, their prominence near the prince and the duke only confirmed the popular impression of the new war coalition. These positions can best be examined in a broader discussion of the early image of the coalition.

THE APPEAL OF THE "PATRIOTS"

Immediately after Charles's return, the Earl of Kellie detected unusual activity up and down the backstairs at Court; "certenlye their is," he accurately noted in mid-October, "great emulations and banding in this Court." The return of Charles empty-handed initiated an open season on the pro-Spanish faction, and it signalled the beginning of a major factional re-alignment which left many courtiers, among them Kellie, out in the cold. As Chaworth reported in October, there was "nowe more busynes" pending "then was these manie yeares." At the center of the maelstrom of Court cabals and bureaucratic infighting were the prince and the duke who were convinced that only a major shake-up at Whitehall would permit a diplomatic revolution in foreign policy. In the circumstances it was only logical to expect, as Lord Haughton did, that on the prince's return, "the cards" would be "new shuffled, and we may expect a new play."[22]

In the new game the first important move was broadening the network of Charles and Buckingham. The duke was attempting nothing less than changing factions in mid-stream, and a number of the "popular lords" who had consistently advocated intervention would not welcome being tarnished by close association with the brazen parvenu. Eventually the prince's prestige

---

[21] Conway to Buckingham, 10 November 1622, Bodleian Library, Add. D111, fo. 225; and Carleton to Conway, 14 July 1623, SP 84/113/33.
[22] Kellie to Mar, 18 October 1623, *Mar and Kellie*, II, p. 182; Chaworth to Trumbull, 18 October 1623, Trumbull Add. MSS, XV/114; and Haughton to Somerset, 16 September 1623, *Holles Letters*, II, p. 283.

and the prospect of an aggressive foreign policy overcame, at least temporarily, any fastidiousness about Buckingham, and a broad pro-war coalition emerged over the winter. That such a coalition developed is easier to state than it is to explain. Abundant evidence chronicles the courtship of prominent courtiers and documents suggestive contacts between the duke's creatures and various "popular" lords. Yet the actual negotiations and arrangements remain so obscure that it is tempting to believe, as some later did, in Buckingham's "magique thralldome" over his followers.[23] Nevertheless, much of the mystery about the duke's magic vanishes once we examine several aspects of Buckingham and his associates which do much to explain the broad appeal of the war coalition.

The coalition was first and foremost one of patriots, and the importance of the use of that term cannot be overestimated. The term generally applied to critics of the status quo, and historians have used the term to describe those defenders of traditional liberties who were appalled by greed and incompetence within the Jacobean government. One poet felt that Felton's assassination of Buckingham in 1628 "wonne / The prize of Patriots to a British sonne."[24] By definition therefore "Patriot" was not a label regularly granted to Buckingham and his creatures; nor would they have been eager to adopt it. Nonetheless, the term has a surprising history in the 1620s. Earlier, when the Spanish match divided the nation, the word inevitably described someone opposed to corruption at home and neutrality abroad. Thus in 1621 Frederick V privately appealed to the Marquis of Hamilton for the support of "les autres bon patriots," and another contemporary in 1621 listed Southampton, Oxford, Warwick and Saye as "Noble Patriots."[25] By the end of the decade, however, George Wither made it clear that something unusual had happened in the mid-1620s to the use of the word;

> Those pers'nages, whose words were heretofore
> As Oracles; are credited no more
> Then Cheaters are.

The persons Wither was particularly bitter about were those who

> make themselves appeare unto the State
> Good Patriots, who being sifted well
> Are scarce so honest men as go to hell.

In another passage he denounced "Hypocrites" whose "Double-hearts,"

---

[23] "An encouragement to the Noble Lieutenant," NLS 33.1.7, vol. 4 [Denmilne MSS 26], number 44.

[24] *Ibid.*; and for a perfect example of the term "patriot" used to describe the "opposition", see Alexander Brown, *English Politics in Early Virginia History* (Boston, 1901), p. 250.

[25] Frederick to Hamilton, 8 May 1621, Scottish RO, GD 406/1/9344; and Wilson, *History*, p. 163.

"counterfeited Graces," and "honest-seeming Faces" allowed them to "passe for Statesmen" and more importantly "for a Patriot."[26]

Wither's "false Patriots" were the key to the grand rapprochement of 1623–4. The "popular lords" did not have to abandon long held positions in order to join Buckingham; rather the duke joined them in the guise of a patriot. Buckingham's adoption of an "opposition" term understandably aroused suspicion, but given the alternative, continued Anglo-Spanish negotiations, few were in the mood to do anything except rejoice over the unusual transformation of a royal favorite into a "Patriot." Sir Dudley Carleton perhaps best explained the metamorphosis. In February 1624 he mourned the unexpected death of the Duke of Richmond and Lennox, "a good patriot and in a high degree of favor with the King, which conditions meete seldom in a courtier." Carleton then added a significant sentence; "yet now they concurre in others, for the Duke of Buckingham is happie in both." The term moreover was not simply used to describe the duke and his supporters. Rather it was one they themselves employed; Secretary Conway regularly used "the Patriots" as a convenient label for those who supported the coalition.[27] Immense advantage attended the description of a war coalition as a *patriot* coalition; in the duke's effort to cooperate with "popular" peers, the term "Patriot" cast the fairest possible name on their alliance. The duke's assumption of the term apparently signalled that the wide fissures then dividing the "political" Court and Country would finally be closed.

Among the Patriots' anti-Spanish, pro-Dutch and pro-Palatine sentiments, their hispanophobia was most evident. The campaign against Madrid began, not on the continent, but rather in the drawing rooms of Royston and the corridors of Whitehall with cold shoulders and open contempt for the Spanish envoys and pro-Spanish courtiers. John Beaulieu reported in October that the duke "doth not spare to discharge his mind a bouche ouverte both against the nation and the Countrie"; and three months later, Mr. Bonham confidently maintained "the Spanish parte have no Stoake at Court nor [are] well-looked on."[28] Buckingham's sentiments became public knowledge when the Spanish ambassadors welcomed Charles on his return; the audience, John Woolley reported, was "not after the wonted kind." On arrival at Royston, "not one noble man met them;" Charles was "colder and more stranger;" and "by my Lord Admirall specially," Beaulieu noted, "they found themselves neglected who never turned his lookes towards them but kept himself

---

[26] George Wither, *Britain's Remembrancer* (London, 1628), fos. 135 [153], 221v and 222v.
[27] Carleton to Roe, 1 March 1624, TCD MSS 708, II, fos. 265–6v; and Conway to Carleton, 16 April 1624, SP 84/117/58.
[28] Beaulieu to Trumbull, 24 October 1623, and Bonham to same, 22 January 1624, Trumbull MSS, VII/133 and Trumbull Add. MSS, XV/13.

a loofe with some noblemen in a corner of the Chamber att the time of their Audience. And when they came unto him to complement with him he gave them such assurance as made them plainly see that his hart was ulcerated."[29] The dramatic impact of the duke unmasking his batteries can be seen in the case of Sir George Chaworth. Frustrated over the delays in securing the viscountcy James had promised a year earlier for diplomatic service at Brussels, Chaworth naturally looked to the Spanish ambassadors for assistance in prodding the king's memory. As Coloma and Inijosa prepared to meet the newly reunited royal family, Chaworth coached them on how to handle "the great duke." Yet to his dismay, the envoys were "confident all will be well and crye pocas dias and puff at his power" which Chaworth added, "I believe will puff all theyrs awaye." On their return from Court the crestfallen diplomats confessed Chaworth had been right and "nowe says playnely they must alter theyr saile and seeke to Buckingham in my busynes as in others."[30]

Unfortunately for the envoys, greater attention to the favorite did not improve matters, and within a few weeks the ambassadors had begun to complain to James about Buckingham's conduct. Their protests resulted only in "much heate and contestation betweene them." When they objected to Buckingham's invariable presence during their royal audiences, he insisted he had learned the trick from Olivares; and when they complained about the difficulty in seeing James, the English replied that the envoys had had "in a few dayes Eleven Audiences."[31] The breach between the ambassadors and Buckingham became so pronounced that in mid-November James attempted to reconcile the three men with a masque in their honor at the duke's London townhouse. The masque itself, however, undercut this purpose, for it depicted "des Espangoliz representées avec des actions dignes de risée."[32] A week later, the duke returned to the offensive; at a dinner party Carlisle had given in honor of a delegation from Brussels, Buckingham singled out the Walloons in the group and in a loud voice expressed surprise that "si brave cavaliers obeissant a des gens si vils, infames et si perfides ques les Espagnols."[33] The clients quickly followed their patron's lead. In December

[29] Woolley to Trumbull, 17 October 1623, and Beaulieu to same, 24 October 1623, Trumbull MSS, XLVIII/105 and VII/133.

[30] Chaworth to Trumbull, 18 October 1623, Trumbull Add. MSS, XV/114. On the background to his claim, see *The Loseley Manuscripts*, ed. A. Kempe (London, 1835). With the discovery of a rich cache of Chaworth letters in the Trumbull Add. MSS, I plan to write an article on Chaworth in the early 1620s.

[31] James to Bristol and Aston, [early January 1624], SP 94/30/72; and Tillières to Puysieux, 17 January 1624, PRO 31/3/58, fo. 15.

[32] Tillières to Puysieux, 16 November 1623, PRO 31/3/57, fo. 264. See also Chamberlain to Carleton, 21 November 1623, *Letters*, II, pp. 526–8; and Castle to Trumbull, 17 November 1623, Trumbull MSS, XVIII/108.

[33] Tillières to Puysieux, 28 November 1623, PRO 31/3/57, fo. 268; and *The Loseley Manuscripts*, p. 476.

a Flemish envoy derisively ascribed James's refusal to grant the diplomat naval protection across the Channel to abject fear of the Dutch fleet; Secretary Conway sharply replied that his master "neither feared to displease the Hollanders nor those who called themselves their Masters [i.e. the Spaniards]." Likewise the oath that Goring swore to illustrate his commitment to Elizabeth does not seem to have been coincidental; rather than abandon her, he would allow "the hottest spaniard surfeited uppon raw bulls fleshe and garlicke spit in my face."[34]

The scope of the anti-Spanish offensive also included those still committed to the match. With good reason, the Spaniards began to protest that "frends to the peace and correspondency betwixt the crownes were nowe under a kind of persecution." The Earl of Bristol continued to press for the marriage, and for his pains it became apparent that he "suffereth under the Ecclipse."[35] As his nephew, Simon Digby, discovered when he sued for a Court appointment, royal favor which the Digbys once enjoyed had abruptly ended; the duke rejected Digby's suit with such warmth that, as one observer noted, "it were a miracle if the Duke brake not his necke." Public notice had been served; the future rewards for the ambassador and his kinsmen "wilbe small as long as the Duke can helpe it." At the same time Chaworth deduced that for himself and "anye that wished [to be] endifferent to that syde, . . . we shold not prosper with sunne shyne from that court."[36] Quite understandably there was little contemporary surprise in December when James recalled Bristol. The humiliation of the Digbys prompted other prominent hispanophiles to discover the merits of obscurity. Amid rumors late in 1623 of his imminent imprisonment, the Earl of Arundel wisely resolved "not to come so frequentlie to the Councell of late as he did." In fact important letters requiring his signature had to be sent out to his villa at Highgate.[37] The luxury of internal exile was not available either to the Lord Treasurer, the Earl of Middlesex, or to the Chancellor of the Exchequer, Sir Richard Weston; instead both maintained a low profile in the weeks following the prince's return. What all three most feared was the loss of their offices, and such apprehensions can only have been aroused by reports late in the year that Lord Mandeville would soon replace Bishop Williams as Lord Keeper. Need-

---

[34] Goring to Carleton, 31 October 1623, SP 14/153/111; and an anonymous newsletter, [late December 1623], Trumbull Add. MSS, XV/149a.

[35] Castle to Trumbull, November 1623, Trumbull MSS, XVIII/106; and Aston to Buckingham, 5 December 1623, SP 94/29/122v. For details of Bristol's negotiations after Charles's departure, see below, pp. 107–13.

[36] *The Loseley Manuscripts*, p. 476; Castle to Trumbull, 17 November 1623, and Woolley to same, 14 November 1623, Trumbull MSS XVIII/109 and XLVIII/109.

[37] Locke to Trumbull, 26 December 1623, Trumbull MSS, XXIX/162; and Kevin Sharpe, "The Earl of Arundel, His Circle and the Opposition to the Duke of Buckingham, 1618–1628," *Faction and Parliament*, pp. 220–2.

less to say, in such a political climate the hispanophiles who once flocked to the Spanish embassy left it deserted "without scarce any coache all the day longe at their doores or any noyce in their House."[38]

Inobtrusiveness, however, was merely a temporary defense as Secretary Calvert was to learn. The institution of two Secretaries of State with vaguely defined purviews was inherently unstable, and in 1623 Calvert and Conway who reportedly "do nothing but kicke and winse at one another" publicly displayed the potential for acrimony.[39] Theoretically Calvert, the Senior Secretary, handled all diplomatic correspondence into which Conway could intervene in an emergency. The journey to Madrid, however, altered the standard procedure. Charles and Buckingham, much to Calvert's chagrin, directed all their letters to Conway. Indeed, when the duke soothed the "angrie" secretary with the observation, "its no matter, theres manie more," Conway relayed the message. Admittedly Calvert continued to receive Bristol's dutiful letters, but the devotion of a hispanophile already marked for disgrace can only have been cold comfort.[40] A similar transition took place with the other ambassadors. Conway's direct correspondence with Carleton in The Hague began over special matters and always included apologies to Calvert for having "convayed my sickle to farre into another man's harvest." The scope of Conway's special assignments, however, quickly expanded to include almost all Anglo-Dutch and Anglo-Palatine affairs. Meanwhile Carleton's weekly letter to Calvert grew increasingly perfunctory. In fact he wrote more detailed letters to his friend, John Chamberlain, than he did to his superior.[41] News of the shift in power soon reached other envoys; in January 1624, Sir Edward Herbert in Paris offered without apparent prompting to write to Conway as well as Calvert. A few weeks earlier, friends at Court warned William Trumbull, the agent in Brussels and a perennial candidate for promotion, that any further reliance on Calvert was pointless; the superceded Secretary of State was powerless.[42]

---

[38] Beaulieu to Trumbull, 9 January 1624, Trumbull MSS, VII/142; and an anonymous newsletter, [late December 1623], Trumbull Add. MSS, XV/149a. See also Prestwich, *Cranfield*, pp. 424–31; and Alexander, *Lord Treasurer*, pp. 50–2.

[39] Carleton the younger to Carleton, 21 August 1623, SP 84/113/205. See also G. E. Aylmer, *The King's Servants* (London, 1961), pp. 25–6; and F. M. G. Evans, *The Principal Secretaries of State* (Manchester, 1926), pp. 61–82.

[40] Buckingham to [Conway], [September 1623], BL Harleian 6987, fo. 175; and Conway to Buckingham, 20 December 1623, SP 14/155/65. For a more detailed analysis of the Conway–Carleton affair, see R. E. Bonner, "Administration and Public Service under the Early Stuarts: Edward Viscount Conway as Secretary of State, 1623–1628" (Ph.D. thesis, University of Minnesota, 1968), pp. 31–71.

[41] [Conway] to [Carleton], 6 May 1623, SP 84/112/115. Compare Carleton's letters of 19–21 December 1623 with Conway (SP 84/115/125), Calvert (SP 84/115/135) and Chamberlain (SP 84/115/142).

[42] Herbert to Conway, 19 January 1624, SP 78/72/13; and Castle to Trumbull, 17 November 1623, Trumbull MSS, XVIII/109.

The campaign against Calvert was not without its costs; Conway, whose health was never excellent, temporarily had to do the work of two secretaries. Nevertheless, the game was worth the candle. In Calvert's progressive isolation lay a clear augury for all to read about the future course of England: a prominent Spanish sympathizer had been edged out of a sensitive position from which he could, as he had done in the past, simply palm diplomatic messages he disliked. Notwithstanding these maneuvers, Calvert retained his office until early in 1625. Yet it was soon clear a replacement would be in order; candidates then began to jockey for position, and Buckingham privately promised Calvert's office to Sir Albertus Morton.[43]

Hand-in-hand with the aversion to all things Spanish went a pronounced affection for the Dutch Republic. Indeed given that "Spaine and the United Provinces are at this present [1623] the two most diametrically opposite and hostile countreys in the whole world," the two prejudices were in fact inseparable. Thus the logical consequence of the duke's loud complaints against Spain was an Anglo-Dutch entente. Furthermore, the powerful allure of the Elizabethan model of warfare meant that English strategists naturally regarded a firm Anglo-Dutch entente as the fundamental basis for all other plans. In addition an opening to the Dutch was sure to meet with considerable support among godly Englishmen. *The Interpreter* of 1622 neatly described a loyal Protestant's polarized view towards the Dutch Republic:

> if the States friend, none can be his foe,
> But if the States foe, bee hee what hee will
> ... hee counts him ill.

Thus it was only natural that the first foreigners to hear the coalition's proposals were Dutchmen, whom Goring visited in December 1623. While his actual brief remained unknown, his general purpose was clear enough to the Paul's walkers; "nowe we are laboring," John Beaulieu remarked, "to close againe and to assure ourselves of our old friends."[44]

Goring's mission only confirmed the pro-Dutch bias of the coalition whose charter members were often distinguished by their close ties to the Dutch state. Kensington, like many other Englishmen, had learned to trail a pike in the English regiments of the Dutch army, and his younger brother, Sir Charles Rich, devoted his entire life to these units. Where Kensington spent years, Conway spent decades. He even married a Dutch women, Katherine

---

[43] On Calvert's successor, see P. Morton to W. Morton, 19 July [1625], BL Add. 33,395, fos. 83–4; and on his interception of orders, see Carleton the younger to Carleton, 3 May 1623, SP 84/112/103, and Conway to Carleton, 15 May 1623, SP 84/112/124.

[44] Beaulieu to Trumbull, 9 January 1624, Trumbull MSS, VII/142; *The Interpreter* (n.p., 1622), p. 5; and Carleton to Chamberlain, 21 March 1623, SP 84/111/204. See also J. Polisensky, *The Thirty Years War* (London, 1971), pp. 11–12; and especially Simon Adams, "Spain or the Netherlands?," *Before the English Civil War*, pp. 79–101.

Hueriblock, and named his celebrated daughter Brilliana after the Dutch cautionary town he had commanded for many years. As Secretary of State, the most appalling strategic nightmare he could imagine was an Anglo-Dutch war, which would sever the intimate links between the countries that Conway himself embodied. His official correspondence regularly included recollections of "the ancient acquaintance I have had with those Countries, wherein I have eaten much bread had manie children with dayes of comfort and contentment continuing in affection manie yeares."[45] Conway's "ancient acquaintance" made it perfectly understandable that some suspected secret Dutch funds of having actually purchased his office for him; it also explains why the Spanish ambassadors deeply resented his presence near James. Conway, in short, was living proof of the coalition's firm Dutch bias. It had earlier been feared that the drift towards Spain would lead at best to an Anglo-Dutch estrangement and at worst to a joint Anglo-Spanish assault on the Dutch. Hence Thomas Scott's tracts consistently stressed the importance of the old Anglo-Dutch alliance, and one popular poet warned that "while English and Dutch doe brawle / The Spaniard watcheth and advantage catcheth." In a "needlesse fray" between old allies, "you both become a preay."[46] In the circumstances those apprehensive about Anglo-Dutch relations can only have been heartened to see a friend of the Republic like Edward Conway at James's elbow.

Staunch supporters of the Dutch were also generally devoted Protestants. Much more than economics and history bound both states together; Conway pointed to "the Unitie, or at least correspondencie in religion" which meant that "the safetie of the Church" depended on Anglo-Dutch cooperation.[47] It followed that the "Patriots" would also stress their devotion to the Reformed creed, and this godly aspect accounts for much of the coalition's popularity. During the trip to Madrid, a chilling nightmare haunted Englishmen; Buckingham might follow his mother's path to Rome and take Charles with him. Not surprisingly contemporaries at the end of 1623 revelled in the public piety of Charles, Buckingham and their clients.

With the prince's return, "our courtiers and others that were in Spain," Chamberlain noted, abandoned their earlier secrecy and "begin now to open their mouths and speak liberally of the coarse usage and entertainment." Their stories often dealt with religion; one related Charles's refusal to bow to the blessed Sacrament, another to the duke's contempt for the Junta of

[45] Conway to Carleton, 15 May 1623, SP 84/112/124; Schreiber, *Naunton*, p. 56. See also "Charles Rich," *DNB*.

[46] "Uppon the English Quarrell with the Dutchmen," Beinecke Library, Osborn b197, p. 220; [Thomas Scott], *The Belgick Pismire* and Valaresso to the Doge and Senate, 3 February and 8 September 1623, *CSPV*, XVII, p. 558 and XVIII, p. 106.

[47] Conway to Carleton, 15 May 1623, SP 84/112/124.

Divines and a third of Sir Edward Verney's physical assault on a priest attempting to convert a dying Englishman.[48] Even Archie Armstrong, the royal jester, earned applause; he refused to acknowledge Christ's presence in the host, quipping to Philip IV himself that "christ was so ill used when he was on earth that he thought he had no mind to come among them again." All these tales reiterated the Spanish failure at conversion, a failure which Charles illustrated by publicly receiving communion at St. Paul's in late October.[49] The contemporary response to these tales and actions was warm indeed. Chamberlain generally praised "the goode yt the trip hath don in religion by layeng open their grosse ignorance and superstition": and Beaulieu could not restrain his delight over Charles's public communion; the prince, "God be thancked, hath brought home this happie blessing with him that he came home al sound and stronger rather in the roote of his religion than he was before."[50] Later in the decade Charles still earned praise for his earlier constancy; "his fiery trial in Spain," Sir John Finch proclaimed in 1628, " . . . gave us then assurance that your faith is built on the rock against which the gates of hell shall never prevail." No wonder then that the engraver depicting the royal family in 1624 placed the Prince of Wales leaning on the Bible.[51] Even Buckingham suddenly found, as his sister reported, that "you have gained your selfe much honor in being so constant to your religion." The Countess of Bedford, never an admirer of the favorite, praised him for bringing "light out of darkness" and recovering "much of what he had lost." Thus it was not the sedulous courtier speaking when Viscount St. Albans announced, "I am glad his Grace is comen home with so fair a reputation of a sound Protestant."[52]

The coalition's piety also found less overt expression. The elevation of Conway, a man who "will fight a good fight and overcome the mortal enemies of the Spirit" reportedly led "to the general reioycing of all religious hearts." The new secretary attempted to save the classis of English ministers in the United Provinces, and its vice president, Thomas Scott, from ruin, and he regularly supported continental ministers in their English exile. He also

---

[48] Chamberlain to Carleton, 25 October 1623, *Letters*, II, p. 519; Howell to North, 15 August 1623, *Epistolae Ho-Elianae*, p. 171; and Mead to Stuteville, 21 June and [anon.] to Mead, *Court and Times*, II, pp. 406 and 435.

[49] 4 May 1626, Grosvenor Diary, TCD MSS E.5.17, p. 42; and Woolley to Trumbull, 1 November 1623, Trumbull MSS, XLVIII/107.

[50] Beaulieu to Trumbull, 31 October 1623, Trumbull MSS, VII/134; and Chamberlain to Carleton, 25 October 1623, *Letters*, II, p. 519.

[51] 19 March, *Commons Debates 1628*, I, p. 15; and W. Van de Passe, engraver, "Triumphus Jacobi" (1624), printed in R. T. Godfrey, *Printmaking in Britain* (New York, 1978), plate 7.

[52] Countess of Denbigh to Buckingham, [July–September 1623], BL Harleian 6987, fo. 156; Countess of Bedford to Lady Cornwallis, 28 November [1623], *The Private Correspondence*, pp. 84–6; and "Minute for an Advice to . . . Buckingham," *Life and Letters*, VII, p. 441.

secured Dr. Preston the right to lecture in Cambridge and prevented the zealous Bishop Montaigne of London from examining London preachers too closely. This last action earned Conway the lavish encomiums of John Davenport, who promised in 1623 always "to blesse the fountaine of all good for ioyning such a head with such a heart and honouring such a person with such a place." "Both Church and commonwealth," the future Separatist continued, were fortunate to have "such a friend." Another clergyman concurred; the Secretary was well-known for "your fervent zeale to the reformed religion and pietie, which so attend and guard your person that you can hardly be severed or abstracted from them."[53] An equally prominent patron of godly preachers was the dapper Lord Kensington who maintained as his chaplain, John Everard, one of the most controversial preachers in the early 1620s. In Everard's extended public campaign against "the great sin of matching with Idolaters," Kensington ensured that his prison stays were so brief as to earn him the sobriquet of "Dr. Ever-out."[54]

Rather improbably the most important "saint" among the "patriots" was Buckingham himself. Given his boundless ambition, his sincere religious views must remain a mystery; as John Selden was to remark in 1628, "what his religion is I know not." Compounding the uncertainty was his friendship with such theologically diverse friends as Bishop Laud and Dr. Preston. Nevertheless, the duke's enthusiasm for ecclesiastical fencesitting should not obscure the fact that late in 1623 he apparently decided to favor Preston and the godly.[55] Laud's continued access to the favorite would seem to argue against any tilt toward the godly, and Matthew Wren's tenure as Charles's chaplain in Madrid convinced him of the prince's inherent anti-Calvinism. Yet it must be remembered the Laudian success was clearly apparent only in 1626 when Charles and Buckingham publicly supported the Arminians and when Laud finally left his isolated Welsh bishopric. Richard Montague, the divine who opened the conflict over predestination, plainly had none of Wren's confidence. With good reason, Montague responded to the news of Charles's accession with profound dismay; the father, not the son, had encouraged his controversial publications. Thus Laud's influence over the duke in 1623–4 was in fact more limited than the bishop understandably

[53] Davenport to Conway, 17 October 1623, *Letters of John Davenport* (London, 1937), pp. 13–15; John Gerard, *The Conquest of Jerusalem* (London, 1623), dedication to Conway; and Ferdinando Texada, *Texada Retextus* (London, 1623), dedication to Conway. See also Conway to the Bishop of Ely, 6 May 1624, SP 14/164/39; and Paul Seaver, *The Puritan Lectureships* (Stanford, 1970), p. 65.

[54] John Everard, *The Gospel-Treasury Opened* (London, 1657), "To the Reader"; and Irwonwy Morgan, *Prince Charles's Puritan Chaplain* (London, 1957), p. 54.

[55] 11 June, *Commons Debates 1628*, IV, p. 248. Set against this, Russell, *Parliaments*, pp. 9–10.

liked to acknowledge: indeed the difference between Laud's promises of advancement and reality led Montague to conclude, "I smell a ratt."[56]

Much more than any Arminian renaissance, what was visible in 1623–4 was Buckingham's "godly fit." These years witnessed no repetitions of the scene in 1622 when one of the favorite's chaplains preached a sermon "totally for Arminianism."[57] A tilt towards the Puritans made political sense in a struggle to root out Spanish influence at Court, and St. Albans wisely pressed the duke to lend credence to his newfound piety by being "the author of some counsel to the Prince that tasteth of religion and virtue." The result in 1624 was to be a mild persecution of Catholics, lavish favor to the more traditional English Protestants, and a remarkable popularity for the royal favorite who "was cryed up by all the Godly Party in the kingdome."[58] It is worth remembering that the trip to Madrid provided Buckingham as well as Charles with a stock of impressive tales about his Protestantism which were later marshalled in his defense. In the 1626 Parliament, Sir John Hippesley countered the attempt to label Buckingham as a Papist with the recollection of events in Madrid three years earlier; when Hippesley had in his confusion knelt before a religious procession, Buckingham had immediately pulled him to his feet with the admonition, "arise thou great ass, must thou be so mad to kneel with others?" In the 1628 session, as criticism of the favorite's religion became particularly intense, his creatures pointed to Buckingham's support for Preston, Ussher and other "preachers of great esteem." What was only marginally persuasive in 1628 was much more convincing in 1624. Then under his aegis the gap between the godly and the government narrowed to the point where John Davenport could safely swear "an hearty detestation" for those "that secretly encourageth men in opposition to the present government." By choosing his words with care even a firebrand like Davenport could safely support "the present government" when it was dominated by pious "Patriots."[59]

Abhorence of Spain and devotion to the godly at home and abroad was of course nothing new. The Protestant cause has a distinguished Elizabethan history, and it was onto this venerable pedigree that Buckingham sought to

---

[56] *Parentalia, or Memoirs of the Family of Wren*, ed. S. Wren (London, 1760), pp. 45–7; and Montagu to Cosin, 30 October [1624] and 28 March [1625], *The Correspondence of John Cosin* (Durham, 1869), I, pp. 23–4 and 67–8. See also Patrick Collinson, *The Religion of Protestants* (Oxford, 1979), pp. 6–7.

[57] Roger Coke, *The Detection of England* (London, 1719), p. 139; Morgan, *Puritan Chaplain*, pp. 59–62; and Mead to Stuteville, 6 July 1622, *Court and Times*, II, pp. 319–20.

[58] "Notes for a Conference with Buckingham," 2 January 1624, *Letters and Life*, VII, p. 444; and Thomas Ball, *The Life of the Renowned Doctor Preston* (Oxford, 1885), p. 65.

[59] 4 May 1626, Grosvenor Diary, TCD MSS E.5.17, p. 40; 11 June, *Commons Debates 1628*, IV, pp. 249, 254 and 256; and Davenport to Conway, 17 October 1624, *Letters of John Davenport*, pp. 13–15.

graft the "Patriots". This conscious similarity in fact accounts for the Spanish attempt to tar Buckingham with the same brush as had been employed against the Earl of Leicester a generation earlier; in Brussels late in 1624 a tract circulated entitled *Buckingham's Commonwealth*, which was clearly modelled on the celebrated *Leicester's Commonwealth*.[60] The parallel was apt. Supporters of the Protestant Cause in the 1620s found both a heroine and a link wht past Protestant glories in the name of Elizabeth, and with the Queen and Bohemia and the former Queen of England, the "Patriots" could claim a special relationship. Conway's vow that he would gladly do the "blessed Queene advantagious service even with my life" was no idle compliment. Among Englishmen, Frederick's claim to the Bohemian throne was more likely to produce confused discussions of central European constitutional theories than a domestic consensus on the war.[61] A much more clear-cut matter was the plight of a pregnant English princess and her small children driven out of her dower lands along the Rhine and into exile with her husband's family. Kinship made these indignities even more intolerable; after all until her brother produced offspring, Elizabeth stood second in line to the British Crown. Chivalry therefore combined with religious solidarity and *realpolitik* to transform Elizabeth of Bohemia into a living *casus belli*.

In her distress Elizabeth sought the broadest possible support in England; nonetheless she could not have helped recognizing that some responded more readily than others. The flight from Prague in 1620 bound the young queen and Conway together; four years later she insisted "I will never be unthankful to you." She acquired a taste for Lady Conway's lamprey pies and felt close enough to the Secretary of State to make fun of his handwriting and his choice of Killultagh for the title of an Irish peerage; "you have got the maddest name that can be, it will spoile anie good mouth to pronounce it right."[62] If familiarity is any indication of affection, her nickname for Carlisle, "old Camel-face," suggests that the two had become friends during his earlier embassies on her behalf. Carlisle furthermore kept close tabs on the Palatine household through Sir Francis Nethersole, a talented secretary whom Carlisle had seconded to Elizabeth's service. The degree of frank intimacy between Nethersole and Carlisle's new secretary, John Woodford, can be seen in Nethersole's anxiety on Woodford's death; only after Carlisle had burnt all

---

[60] Trumbull to Conway, 3 October 1624, SP 77/17/355; *Leicester's Commonwealth* (Athens, Ohio, 1985); and S. L. Adams, "The Protestant Cause: Religious Alliance with the West European Calvinist Communities as a Political Issue in England, 1585–1630" (D.Phil. dissertation, University of Oxford, 1973).

[61] Conway to Carleton, 25 August 1623, SP 84/113/75. For examples of the treatises, see Somerset RO, DD/Ph 221/44 and 211/ fos. 157–157v and 160–163v.

[62] Eizabeth to Conway, 16 February 1624 and 22 May [1627], SP 84/116/41 and 81/34/193; Thomas Conway, 21 October 1623, SP 84/114/259; and SP 14/163/47.

of Nethersole's letters in Woodford's cabinet would he "sleepe somewhat more soundly."[63]

Comforting though the support of Carlisle and Conway doubtless was, Elizabeth pinned her hopes on her brother and the favorite. Charles consistently sought to assist his sister; in October 1622, for example, "upon his knees and with tears" Charles begged his father "to take pity upon his poor distressed sister." Elizabeth certainly appreciated his good intentions; even in the dark days of the trip to Madrid she noted that "my brother is still loving to me. I would others had as good nature."[64] The question was whether Charles would ever defy his father and act on his principles; when he eventually did so late in 1623 her delight was boundless. She reported to Roe early in the following year that there was "so much good newes to write." Since Charles's return, "all is changed from being Spanish." Her praise extended to the duke who was "most nobly and faithfully for me." Elizabeth and her husband, Carleton informed Buckingham, were "no lesse confident of your affection then they are of your sincerity." She could not, however, say enough about her brother; Charles "does shewe me so much love to me in all things as I cannot tell you how much I am glade."[65] Therefore, the rapidly narrowing gap between Elizabeth and Charles allowed support for the "Patriots" to become support for Elizabeth. Early in the 1624 session, Sir Thomas Crewe, the Speaker of the House, privately told Nethersole of his desire to assist Elizabeth; in reply, she thanked Crewe for his "respect and affection" and told him to follow the lead of her brother. The newly united front of James's children can find no better illustration than the jewelry Elizabeth began to wear after November; then the exiled princess began wearing an ornament whose centerpiece was a lock of Charles's hair.[66]

The mystique surrounding Elizabeth of Bohemia, however, was not entirely of her own making. Her reputation gained much support from the inevitable confusion between herself and her namesake, the formidable sixteenth-century queen; this confusion was in part deliberate. Earlier in his reign James had quickly grasped the propaganda potential in the skillful use of his predecessor's memory; thus the official medal struck to commemorate the marriage of Elizabeth and Frederick billed James's daughter as "Elizabeth Altera." The advent of the German war, however, ended this practice. Those

[63] Nethersole to [Carlisle], 11 September 1625, SP 81/33/188; same to Trumbull, 4 October 1624, Trumbull MSS, XXXIII/139; and Schrieber, *Carlisle*, p. 25.

[64] Mead to Stuteville, 19 October 1622, *Court and Times*, II, p. 344; and Elizabeth to Roe, 19 May 1623, TCD MSS 708, I, fo. 174v.

[65] Carleton to Buckingham, 1 December 1623, SP 84/115/73; and Elizabeth to Roe, February 1624, TCD MSS 708, I, fos. 262–3 (damaged) and a full nineteenth-century transcript printed in M. E. Green, *Lives of the Princesses of England* (6 vols., London, 1852), V, p. 432.

[66] Nethersole to Carleton, 20 March 1624, SP 81/30/88; Carleton to [Nethersole], SP 84/117/22; and Morosini to the Doge and Senate, 24 November 1623, *CSPV*, XVIII, p. 163.

dejected by James's inaction turned to "Saint" Elizabeth and to "Blessed Eliza," in whose reign they found the bellicose response they desired. "Did we in those days," one contemporary asked, "ever meet the Spanyards but to their disadvantage?" and variants on this theme were legion in the early 1620s.[67] Given this nostalgic mood, Palatine adherents eagerly claimed the Elizabethan mantle for their mistress. During the 1624 Parliament one poet confidently predicted that "Astrea that swore to see earth no more / Shall visit us once more," and John Reynolds, one of the more vigorous pro-war pamphleteers, had no doubt about the identity of the reincarnated Elizabeth; the Electress Palatine had "inherited the Name and Vertues, the Majestie and generositie of our Immortal Queene Elizabeth." The remarkable success of these propagandists of the Palatine cause can be best seen in the murder of Thomas Scott in 1626. Under torture, the assassin confessed his motive; convinced that the "spirit" of "the late Queene of England . . . transmigrated into her Majesty the Queen of Bohemia," he killed the man who he believed blocked the advancement with "his Mistris."[68] Quite clearly John Lambert, the murderer, had not been a stranger at the local bookseller's shop.

At first glance it seems that the Patriots would have insurmountable problems recruiting the memory of the old queen. In the Parliaments of the 1620s, the mention of Elizabeth's name, Sir John Eliot recalled, was to the royal officials and courtiers "like as Basalisks to their eyes." The popular vision of Elizabeth, codified in William Camden's *Annales*, represented, Dr. Haigh has recently argued, an "implied condemnation of Jacobean domestic policy" and an "implied criticism of the Stuarts' supine foreign policy." In addition, "for those who needed pictures to point the difference in foreign policy," the frontispiece of the *Annales* depicted raids on Cadiz and Porto Rico as well as the victory over the Armada in 1588.[69] In short, for a member and retainers of the Stuart dynasty to have endorsed this Elizabethan legacy would apparently have been for them to have embraced their nemesis.

A single fact, however, reveals the vital flaw in this line of reasoning. Various episcopal chaplains generally assumed the task of licensing books for the press, but on 20 March 1624 the Duke of Buckingham personally licensed the first English translation of Camden's *Annales*; it was the only occasion

---

[67] T. Fairfax, "The High Way to Hedelburgh," BL Add. 28,326, p. 41; and E. Hawkins, *Medallic Illustrations of the History of Great Britain* (London, 1885), p. 204. The cycle of poems to "Saint" Elizabeth badly requires serious scholarly analysis; for a selection of these poems, see [untitled], SP 14/80/107; "To Blessed Eliza," Bodleian Library, Malone MSS 23, pp. 28–45; and "A Gracious Answere," Chester RO, 63/2/19, fos. 31v–33.

[68] [Untitled], SP 14/163/130; [John Reynolds], *Votivae Angliae* (Utrecht, 1624), dedication to Charles; and *A Briefe and True Relation of the Murther of Mr Thomas Scott* (London, 1628).

[69] Sir John Eliot, *Negotium Posterorum* (London, 1881), II, p. 26; and C. Haigh, Introduction, *The Reign of Elizabeth I*, pp. 8–9.

that Buckingham ever did so. His intervention is not at all difficult to explain. Criticism of Jacobean foreign policy indeed abounds in the book, criticism that the Patriots echoed. Moreover, we do not have to accord the duke functional literacy. He need not have read the text to have revelled in the *Annales*; the pictures alone would have delighted him, pictures which illustrated the dreams that fired the imaginations of the young prince and the Lord Admiral. As we have seen, their strategic proposals were revivals of the Elizabethan model of warfare. Little wonder the exploits of Elizabeth's sailors and the allure of the West Indies plainly fascinated Charles and Buckingham; the duke installed at Newhall a mural depicting Drake at sea, and one of the three books that Charles purchased in Spain dealt with Spain's Caribbean empire.[70] The glories of Elizabethan England in short were the ideals to which both men aspired.

The administration of the nascent war effort illustrates the reverence for the earlier heroic age. The *sine qua non* for senior staff and field commands was military service under the old queen. Since the Council of War was comprised exclusively of Elizabethan veterans, its first meeting in the spring of 1624 had the air of a reunion of the surviving Elizabethan war-heroes; Vere and Ogle from the Dutch conflict sat next to Belfast, Carew and Grandison from the Irish campaigns. Conway's rise to power was in part due to his memory of the wars of the 1590s; his knighthood dated from the Earl of Essex's delight with the sack of Cadiz, and even after honors had fallen thick and fast on the old soldier in the 1620s, his gravestone gave prominence to his youthful service under Gloriana.[71] Once the war began, disputes between colonels and captains over strategy and tactics were peppered with references to hallowed Elizabethan precedents, and the duke generally sided with those who could muster the most number of phrases like "as they did in Queen Elizabeths time" and "as Queene Elizabeths time did trulie shewe." Thus the Earl of Kellie's prediction late in 1623 that "the young folks shall have their world" must be reckoned as dramatic but nonetheless incorrect; "young folks" were far from dominating the world of Charles and Buckingham.[72] In fact their fondness of staffing senior posts with superannuated Elizabethans may have contributed to the later difficulties in the conduct of the war. In any event, it becomes quite clear why Charles and Buckingham would later have grown restive over the mention of Elizabeth's name in

---

[70] *A Transcript of the Registers of the Company of Stationers* (London, 1877), IV, p. 76; Charles's expenses in Madrid, NLS, MSS 1879, p. 5; and *The Diary of John Evelyn* (Oxford, 1959), p. 372.

[71] Memorial Brass to First Viscount Conway, Arrow Parish Church, Warwickshire.

[72] Kellie to Mar, 4 November 1623, *Mar and Kellie*, II, p. 183. For a good illustration of the role of Elizabethan precedents in military debates, see Capt. Gifford, "An Advice" and "Proposition," [(1626), SP 16/54/5 and 10.

Parliament; her's was the achievement they had hoped to equal, and against this yardstick, they had failed dismally. In the optimism and naïveté of 1623–4, however, the Patriots embraced the Golden Legend of Gloriana as avidly as they did Elizabeth of Bohemia.

There was also a domestic component to the Elizabethan legacy, one that emphasized reform and retrenchment and that had considerable popular appeal. Doubtless these goals did not naturally spring to the mind of those like Buckingham who had voraciously battened down on the royal treasury. Nevertheless, in the 1624 session the Patriots advanced an exceptionally attractive program of domestic reform in which the Earl of Middlesex served as the scapegoat for the Court's sins. And the centerpiece of their domestic policy was an institution for which Charles and Buckingham easily matched Elizabeth I's enthusiasm – Parliament. The day Charles returned from Spain contemporaries predicted that "wee shall shortlye have a Parliament." Given Charles's desire for a major, and expensive, foreign conflict, his press for a Parliament was constitutionally correct; "the Kings of England," Conway explained, "having noe other sure or good wayes to ayde themselves must doe it by Parliament." Whatever the government's motives, the vast majority of Englishmen welcomed a new Parliament. There had been no additions to the statute book in over a decade, and until Charles and Buckingham had suddenly exhibited an interest in the institution, the figure seemed bound to go higher; as St. Albans remarked in 1624 the conclusion of the last session made it unlikely "a Parliament would have been so soon."[73] The "Patriot" interest in Parliament was arguably the most popular single plank of their platform; it represented a substantial downpayment on a return to the Elizabethan ideal of harmony at home and war against Spain abroad. This prospect certainly must have done much to relieve any anxiety about working closely with Buckingham.

On closer examination it becomes apparent that the applause that contemporaries continued to lavish on Charles and Buckingham transcended the popular delight over the collapse of the Anglo-Spanish entente. Within a few weeks of Charles's return, the major elements of the English match were already available for all to see. By then the heir apparent and the royal favorite had adopted the patriotic garb that critics of James's regime had worn for years. They suggested a revival of the Elizabethan war would restore Elizabeth to the Palatinate and firm support for the Dutch Republic and the godly at home. And to implement these policies Charles and Buckingham sought an early parliamentary session.

---

[73] Lulls[?] to Newdegate, 7 October 1623, Warwick County RO, Newdegate of Arbury MSS, CR 136/ B266; Conway to Aston, 30 December 1623, SP 94/29/19v; and St Albans to Southampton, 31 January 1624, *Letters and Life*, VII, p. 454.

Overall they constructed an eminently pleasing alternative to James's inaction abroad and to infrequent, acrid parliamentary sessions. Charles, Valaresso noted, "desires by every means to win general popularity among the people," and his success can be seen in the almost universally adulatory references to the prince. John Beaulieu thought Charles "not a little improved by his journey," although he confessed the prince's new beard did much for his image. The Countess of Bedford concurred; "the Prince is the most improved man that ever I saw." And in her approbation she even included Buckingham who "recovers much of what he had lost."[74] Little wonder that "the people here [in London] flocke in infinite numbers to beholde his Highnesse, who pressed in such multitudes about him last night that his servants had much adoe to serve him at table." Simonds D'Ewes was among the multitudes, and his deep affection for the prince survived being personally ejected from the room by Charles.[75] Even the duke shared in the applause. Admittedly the earlier resentment did not vanish overnight; one poet mourning the demise of the Duke of Lennox early in 1624 asked Death if he "could finde no other Duke to ceize upon?" His query was quite pointed; there was only one other, Buckingham. Yet aside from this less than flattering reference, most other responses were much more positive. Another poet, clearly suspicious of Buckingham's motives, finally confessed "I have enquir'd and found you did in Spaine / A noble Englishe . . . height mayntayne."[76] Opponents of the match could do nothing but rally around Buckingham. Thus in December there was considerable popular concern when he attended a large wedding in the city of London; Catholics, it was feared, would seize on the occasion to assassinate "the onely ennemy and hinderer of their so much desired match." Others offered Buckingham more tangible tribute. His expense book normally records a fairly dismal string of gambling losses. There is, however, one remarkable exception to this general pattern. The day before he landed at Portsmouth, he won £119; the day he rode through London in triumph, he netted £155; and the following day £165.[77] Luck may account for such fantastic hands. A more likely explanation, however, is that his opponents were much more interested in listening to how he maintained his "noble Englishe . . . height" than they were in their own cards.

Twenty-seven years later a contemporary looking back over Charles's life

[74] Valaresso to the Doge and Senate, 31 January 1624, *CSPV*, XVIII, p. 211; Beaulieu to Trumbull, 7 November 1623, Trumbull MSS, VII/134a; and Countess of Bedford to Lady Cornwallis, 28 November 1623, *The Private Correspondence*, pp. 84–6.

[75] Castle to Trumbull, 31 October 1623, Trumbull MSS, XVIII/105; and D'Ewes, *Diary*, p. 170.

[76] "On the death of . . . Lennox," Folger Library, V.a.345, p. 307; and "Upon the Dukes first Coming out of Spain," SP 14/153/114.

[77] Anonymous newsletter, [December 1623], Trumbull Add. MSS, XV/149a; and BL Add. 12,528, fo. 7.

remarked that the dead king had been "the Tennis-Ball of Fate."[78] Without question his strongest serve came in 1623–4, and it is worth remembering that his personal charm and continued bachelorhood cannot account for this powerful volley.

ARISTOCRATIC RECRUITS

The policies Charles and Buckingham advocated do much to explain the re-alignment of the Court over the winter. Admittedly some courtiers would not willingly collaborate with the upstart on anything other than his perma-nent retirement. Yet the issues he supported and the company he kept softened some of the harsher resentment. Indeed some who had grave reser-vations about Buckingham found it well nigh impossible to rebuff him once he and his clients had begun to trumpet these sentiments at Court. The duke and the prince may well have harbored these sentiments earlier in the decade, but once they made a public confession of these views, it appeared that they had finally joined the opposition. And with such a formidable increase in political leverage, the opposition would not remain in the wilderness much longer, provided all agreed to work together.

Among the first to succumb to this argument were four earls who had a common desire for military command; the Earls of Southampton, Essex and Oxford had each served in the English regiments of the Dutch field army, while the Earl of Warwick had more exclusively maritime ambitions. None of them had been able to sit through the Parliament of 1621 in silence, and all supported the Palatine cause. The belligerence of Southampton and Oxford in the first session earned them a short stay in the Tower and a royal suggestion that they avoid the second session.[79] His conformity notwith-standing, Oxford returned to the Tower in April 1622 for having slandered the royal favorite, and he was still there when Charles returned. While these men clearly had little love for Buckingham, they had even less for Spain. In fact, their fervent opposition to Spain was one of the few things all four men had in common; Warwick and Southampton for example had spent the early part of the decade at loggerheads over the future of Virginia and Bermuda. Yet their hispanophobia easily overcame any squeamishness about potential allies. As Oxford confessed to James in 1622, all he really wanted was per-mission to join his cousin Horace Vere in the defence of the Palatinate where

---

[78] Samuel Sheppard, *The Faerie King* (Salzburg, 1984), p. 46.
[79] Zaller, *The Parliament of 1621*, pp. 139–41 and 163; A. L. Rowse, *Shakespeare's Southampton* (New York, 1965), pp. 263–89; and Chamberlain to Carleton, 27 April 1622, *Letters*, II, p. 433.

he could obtain "the haite of his desire by ending my life in your service."[80]
While James ignored his request, Charles and Buckingham late in 1623 were
much more accommodating.

Early in November Charles and Buckingham reportedly discussed at
Whitehall "the great worke of a Parliament and to consulte of the means to
sweeten the peoples affection and to open so happy a way to it." And one of
the proposed sweeteners was "to bestowe some beames of grace upon the
chiefe of them that were in displeasure upon the rupture of the last Parliament." The two names of Southampton and Oxford cropped up repeatedly.
The former appears to have made his peace fairly quickly, perhaps because he
was not on record as having reviled the duke. In any event, by 2 November
Buckingham felt confident enough of Southampton's loyalty to leave him the
delicate task of chaperoning James lest the Spanish ambassadors unexpectedly visit. A few days later James, Buckingham and Southampton held a
public show of reconciliation which was "very loving."[81] Oxford was next in
line, and his rehabilitation was a sentimental favorite since his imprisonment
delayed his marriage to one of the beauties of the age, Lady Diana Cecil.
Kensington and Goring assumed the case and relayed Conway's offer to
arrange a reconciliation. By 6 November Goring reported Oxford's delight
that "a person of soe much iudgement honor and honesty hath the survey and
contriving of the path wherein he is to walk for . . . the recovery of his former
favor." To the duke, Oxford vowed he would be "both thankfull faythfull
and usefull to his grace."[82] Consequently Conway personally drafted
Oxford's letter of submission to the Council. James, however, proved
unexpectedly averse to the scheme, and his diffidence delayed the earl's
release until 30 December. Then Kensington personally escorted him from the
Tower to meet "his New yeares gift," Lady Cecil, "the goddesse of
Chastitie," whom he married two days later. The emotional climax of the
wedding was not when the bride and groom kissed; Buckingham upstaged
this traditional scene when he appeared to congratulate the couple.[83] The two
men exhibited "a grete deal of external love and frendship"; as Salvetti concluded, "alls well that ends well." Oxford plainly subscribed to this view; he

---

[80] Oxford to James, [1622], NLS, MSS 33.1.7, no. 61. On the quarrels over Virginia and
      Bermuda, see *The Rich Papers: Letters from Bermuda, 1615–1646* (Toronto, 1984),
      pp. 391, 397.
[81] Castle to Trumbull, 7 and 14 November 1623, Trumbull MSS, XVIII/106 and 110; and
      Chamberlain to Carleton, 8 November 1623, *Letters*, II, p. 522.
[82] Goring to Conway, 6 November 1623, SP 14/154/13; and Chamberlain to Carleton,
      19 April 1623, *Letters*, II, p. 492.
[83] Beaulieu to Trumbull, 2 January 1624, Trumbull MSS, VII/143; Conway's draft, SP
      14/154/103 and 104; and Chamberlain to Carleton, 3 January 1624, *Letters*, II, pp. 537–8.

assured Buckingham that "your Lordships Noble and free beginning to place your favours upon me, bynds me in a perpetuall acknowledgement."[84]

The obligation was mutual, particularly after the 1624 session. Thus the later rivalry between the two earls for the command of the English expeditionary force was a painfully awkward problem for Buckingham. Since "they are two noblemen I so much respect," the duke ordered Conway "to walke betweene them" in hopes of sorting out a solution. Buckingham found Oxford's case the stronger of the two, but he was equally concerned that he not slight Southampton since "I understand there are som in court busi to do him il ofices with his Majesty." In the end, the compromise between Oxford and Southampton owed much to Buckingham's desire to embarrass neither man.[85] His sensitivity, however, was a novel phenomenon dating from the *rapprochement* late in 1623.

The evidence on Warwick and Essex unfortunately is much more fragmentary. The former's opposition to Spain accounts for his support for Nehemiah Roger's pointed attack on Catholic toleration early in 1623. But later in the year Warwick scarcely figures in the series of reconciliations; his obscurity may well be related to his wife's illness and eventual death in December. Yet immediate access to the favorite was never a problem for someone whose brother was Lord Kensington; when Warwick bitterly lashed out at all those who ignored him during his defense of the Essex coast in 1625–6, he carefully excluded his brother.[86] This close linkage suggests that Kensington arranged his brother's *rapprochement* with Buckingham. While their understanding cannot be dated, it certainly existed; two years later, for example, he prefaced a plea to the duke by requesting the "Continuance of your particular favor in those thaings that concerne myselfe." Furthermore, contemporaries were well aware of Warwick's relationship to the duke; one even considered the earl to be the duke's likely successor as Lord Warden of the Cinque Ports.[87] Essex appears to have often moved in tandem with his Rich cousins, and almost inevitably he proceeded down the broad path that they had beaten to the duke. He certainly had reason enough to do so; in his early years haunted by his father's treason, he exchanged the intense political broils of Jacobean England for military service and the Palatine cause; no wonder Christian of Brunswick, the celebrated paladin of Elizabeth,

[84] Salvetti to Scudamore, 3 January 1624, PRO C115/N1/8484; and Oxford to Buckingham, January 1624, SP 14/158/74.

[85] Buckingham to Conway, [13?] June 1624, SP 14/167/58. On the rivalry and eventual compromise, see below pp. 276–7.

[86] Warwick to Conway, 29 September 1625, Bodleian Library, Firth MSS C4, fo. 179; Carleton to Chamberlain, 21 November 1623, *Letters*, II, p. 527; and Rogers, *A Strange Vineyard*, dedication to Warwick.

[87] Warwick to Buckingham, [September 1625], Bodleian Library, Firth MSS C4, fo. 175v; and Woolley to Trumbull, 5 November 1625, Trumbull MSS, XLVIII/149.

referred to Essex as one of his "premier amys." Among his other intimate friends, however, he never numbered Buckingham. Yet he cooperated enough with the "Patriots" to have earned a signal mark of favor later in 1625; given that the duke was incapable of a disinterested appointment, then his selection of Essex as vice-admiral of the Cadiz fleet would seem solid evidence of a functioning relationship between the two men.[88]

These four "military" earls represented a critically important expansion of the war coalition. Each brought with them their considerable popular prestige as well as their own personal talents; Southampton and Oxford, for example, were virtual martyrs for the Protestant cause. In addition, each had clients and friends in the Commons who in the cases of Warwick and Southampton included some particularly influential MPs. Yet for all this, they could provide only psychological support for Charles and Buckingham in the crucial impending battles in the Privy Council and the Bedchamber. If the prince and Buckingham were to hope for any success, they had to persuade the "grandees" of the Protestant cause, the Duke of Richmond and Lennox, the Marquis of Hamilton, and the Earls of Pembroke and Belfast, of the merits of the "Patriot" coalition.

This task was exceptionally difficult. These prominent courtiers found James's extended courtship of Spain in the midst of the German crisis decidedly uncomfortable; the logic of an Anglo-Spanish entente eluded them, and yet they could not risk losing direct access to the king by strenuously supporting the Protestant cause. As one contemporary recalled, Lennox "opposed to farre as he might to [sic] the Spanish Matche." Nevertheless, even they could not maintain complete control of their emotions; rather than sign the Spanish marriage treaty, Pembroke took to bed feigning illness, while Hamilton spent 1622–3 in repeated quarrels with Middlesex and Bristol which left all three "on evill terms."[89] Such closet opponents of Spain should have welcomed assistance in their struggle from any quarter. But they were also the leading peers of the realm, and Richmond and Hamilton royal kinsmen. They more than anyone in the kingdom deeply resented the favorite who had assumed influence and honors that they felt should rightly be theirs. To be sure, relations between these nobles and the favorite were always at least outwardly friendly; Buckingham in fact helped Hamilton assume a more prominent position in Scottish politics. His assistance, however, only under-

---

[88] Christian of Brunswick to Essex, 13 June 1624, and Buckingham to Essex, 12 September 1625, BL Add. 46,188, fos. 24 and 73. On the relationship between Essex and the Rich brothers, see C. Rich to Essex, 8 January [1627], BL Add. 46,188, fo. 95; Holland to Essex, [late December 1727], BL Loan 23, fo. 170; and Carleton to Conway, 16 August 1623, SP 84/113/174.

[89] Calderwood, *History of the Church of Scotland*, VII, p. 595; Melros to Mar, 10 April 1622, NLS, MSS 3134, no. 99; and Beaulieu to Trumbull, 25 July 1623, Trumbull MSS, VII/121.

scored Hamilton's dependence on the favorite. In the circumstances they would not readily embrace a man whose tomb eventually contained "one duke and twenty places."[90] Understandably, their abhorence of the new duke led them during the trip to Madrid to explore a temporary alliance with pro-Spanish courtiers to destroy the royal mignon. Apparently a little ideological inconsistency was worth Buckingham's disgrace. Likewise a violent quarrel between Pembroke and Carlisle, which ultimately came to blows, indicated their regard for Buckingham and his creatures. Pembroke's half-hearted apologies did not fool observers who noted "the ill impressions remayneth and will againe breake forth upon occasion."[91]

Fortunately for the coalition the "grandees" could not insult and cabal against the prince with equal ease. Charles himself persuaded them to over-look their personal animosity for the greater good of the Palatine cause, and with some misgivings they agreed. The result in mid-November was the public reconciliation of Pembroke and Buckingham. Likewise Buckingham's tips to Hamilton's coachman over the winter suggest a working relationship, which the duke's use of the marquis in delicate overtures to the French in December confirms.[92] As for Lennox, Sir George Chaworth observed that Buckingham bitterly mourned Lennox's death in February 1624, for Lennox "was of our Great Dukes opinion touching the dishonor the Prince under-went" in Madrid. More importantly, he followed the advice "his Grace propounded." This is not to say that the grandees ever became close personal friends with Buckingham, but under the prince's aegis, they did accept a business relationship. And that was more than enough for Charles and Buckingham. Once the grandees fell into line, all advocates of the Palatine cause at Court presented a united front. The expanded coalition could now look on a new parliamentary session with some confidence; as John Castle noted after Buckingham's reconciliation with Southampton and Pembroke, "if they be directed to become Instuments to smoothe a way out to a Parliament, I think the tooles very proper for the worke as persons deerly beloved of the people."[93]

The English match, which the ghost of the Earl of Essex had advanced, still had major obstacles before it, not the least of whom was the bridegroom's father. Nevertheless, over the winter the bridal party had been formed. The

[90] [Untitled], Bodleian Library, Malone MSS 23, fo. 145; and Maurice Lee, Jr., *Government by Pen* (Urbana, 1980), pp. 181, 196, and 213.

[91] Alured to Coke, 14 June 1623, *HMC Cowper*, I, p. 142; Tillières to Puysieux, 3 October 1623, PRO 31/3/57, fo. 252; and Castle to Trumbull, 18 July 1623, Trumbull MSS, XVIII/100.

[92] "Crowes Booke of Accomptes," BL Add. 12,528, fos. 12 and 13; and Tillières to Puysieux, 8 January 1624, PRo 31/3/58, fo. 9.

[93] Chaworth to Trumbull, 14 November 1623, Trumbull Add. MSS, XVII/unfoliated; and Castle to Trumbull, 14 November 1623, Trumbull MSS, XVIII/110.

coalition, as its name implies, was never a tightly organized and disciplined political group; as Charles and Buckingham were to discover, the Patriots were as apt to fight amongst themselves as they were with the Spaniards. Yet this loose organization might be enough to persuade James to bless the match and to bring Charles and the political nation to the altar.

3

"The clock doth now stand": the frustrated campaign against Spain

With major changes in royal policy imminent late in 1623, all those away from Court pressed their friends for the latest news. Lord Zouche, Lord Warden of the Cinque Ports and a firm Protestant, was no different, and from Theobalds on 11 November Richard Yonge offered his considered opinion that "the clock doth now stand and goeth nether forward nor backward." It followed that "what is time I know not." Yonge's analysis, if not his metaphor, was far from unique. The signals from Court were so contradictory that John Beaulieu placed the government "in a woode and in a Cloud." He added that "I cannot, nor I suppose any man els, tell you where we are; I meane what waye we stand in or tend unto our great Business." The scene at Court John Chamberlain likened to the slow dance, the Spanish pavan, in which James and his courtiers moved "backward and forward." As a result, "we knowe not what to judge of the match."[1]

Caution over the future was well in order. The resounding success of Charles and Buckingham with the people was not repeated with the numerous courtiers and officials who were unwilling to abandon the Anglo-Spanish entente without a murmur; hence resistance from the bureaucracy and the Court was to stymie progress towards "the blessed revolution." For the prince and favorite, therefore, the fact that "the clock doth now stand" represented a decidedly mixed blessing. Although they were to have victories in these months, the *coup de grâce* they could never deliver. Spanish propagandists chose an apt image when they began to spread the rumor that Charles was unable to consummate the marriage; political impotence in fact was often a major public problem for the prince and Buckingham who were far from in control of events over the winter. Early modern Parliaments have recently been judged to have been "powerless," yet it was this moribund, weak institution that offered Charles and Buckingham the only means,

---

[1] Yonge to Zouche, 11 November 1623, SP 14/154/25; Beaulieu to Trumbull, 14 November 1623, Trumbull MSS, VII/135; and Chamberlain to Carleton, 15 November 1623, *Letters*, II, p. 525.

barring the death of James, of seizing the initiative and of starting the clocks again.[2]

The present chapter will examine the frustrations of the prince and the duke on the eve of the Parliament. It will deal with their attempts to cool Anglo-Spanish relations, to recruit foreign allies, and to hold the coalition together.

THE COLLAPSE OF NEGOTIATIONS

Impressive domestic allies and elaborate military plans were all beside the point until James was convinced that the Spaniards had never been serious about an Anglo-Spanish marriage alliance. Charles and Buckingham set about this vital task immediately after their return. While the exact discussion between James and the "deare boyes" on their reunion must remain unclear, the basic outline can be deduced. The tale of adventure and romance returned again and again to Spanish perfidy and duplicity. Extraordinary concessions to Catholic sensibilities had failed to link the Palatinate to the marriage. Earlier in March James had admitted that if Charles's embassy failed to resolve the German crisis, then "I will bid farewell to peace in Christendom." Yet holding James to this view was another matter. Not surprisingly the noises that eavesdropping courtiers overheard were confused: "sometimes they laught and sometimes they chafed."[3] Charles and the duke, however, did secure significant and immediate changes in policy and personnel.

James's decision on 8 October to shuffle his envoys represented a subtle but nonetheless major shift in policy. Although two English diplomats were in Madrid, Sir Walter Aston and the Earl of Bristol, the earl alone had responsibility for the marriage negotiations. More importantly, the finalized marriage treaty gave him alone Charles's proxy and the authority to deliver it. Plainly Charles was not thrilled with this arrangement, but he could not personally abrogate an arrangement that his father and the Privy Council had sanctioned. And until James fully appreciated flaws in the treaty, Bristol might well marry Charles to the Infanta. Yet while Bristol was unlikely to heed an informal request to drag his feet, Aston would be more attentive. His ambition and his close connection to Buckingham and his Warwickshire neighbor, Secretary Conway, counterbalanced his embarrassing Catholic sympathies and ensured that he would recollect a word in his ear from the heir apparent. Before leaving Madrid, Charles informed Aston of "his care and resolution not [to] ingage himself into the marriage without good conditions

---

[2] Russell, "Parliamentary History," p. 3.
[3] John Hacket, *Scrinia Reserata* (London, 1692), I, p. 165; and James to Charles and Buckingham, 11 March 1623, *Letters of King James*, p. 394.

for the Palatinate." Thus when James on 8 October ordered Bristol to accept Aston as a co-negotiator, he was clearly checking Bristol's discretionary powers.[4] The same dispatch had an even more dramatic impact on the marriage treaty, which both sides had earlier approved. James blithely ignored the detailed timetable called for the wedding promptly after Bristol delivered Charles's proxy, which he was to do within ten days after the dispensation arrived; instead he unilaterally deferred the wedding date until Bristol and Aston could extract a "punctual answer" on the Palatinate. Philip would surely appreciate a father's reluctance to "give joy to our only son" and "a portion of tears" to Elizabeth. Admittedly James did not formally link the marriage to the resolution of the German issue. In a private letter to Bristol Charles vaguely instructed the earl "to try what the King of Spain will do concerning the business of the Palatinate before I be contracted." Yet with the new ambassador extraordinary, the prince made the linkage quite explicit; Aston was "not to deliver the proxie untill we know certainlie what the king of spain will doe."[5]

S. R. Gardiner's judgment on these dispatches was severe. James in his "utter bewilderment" had given a "personal insult" to Philip IV by ignoring the agreed time schedule and by reviving the discussion of the Palatinate. In fact these alterations could very well ruin years of negotiations. Yet Gardiner overlooked the possibility that James might have known exactly what he was doing. Contemporary observers thought he did; "the King speakes roundly about the Palatinate and it semes the Prince doth lykewyse think fit that both businesses goe on paru passu."[6] Although this judgment overstated the case since there was no direct linkage, the dispatches nevertheless represented an important step towards testing Spanish sincerity. Philip's ministers had always exhibited their finest legerdemain when the English raised the question of the Palatinate whose return Philip vowed to arrange after the Infanta's marriage. Unfortunately persistent English efforts and even Charles's personal plea failed to uncover anything other than these confident but distressingly vague promises of restoration. Several months in Madrid convinced Charles and Buckingham that these promises lacked any substance; hence the request for a "punctual answer' would expose Olivares's juggling.

---

[4] James to Bristol, 8 October 1623, SP 94/28/136; and Buckingham to Aston, [late December 1623], SP 94/30/66v. On the Warwickshire connection between Conway and Aston, see SP 94/28/148v and 94/29/191v.

[5] James to Bristol, 8 October 1623, SP 94/28/136v–137; Charles to Bristol, 8 October 1623, HMC 8th Report, Appendix 1, p. 215; and same to Aston, 8 October 1623, SP 94/28/138.

[6] Dickenson to Trumbull, 21 [October] 1623, Trumbull MSS, XXII/101; and Gardiner, Prince Charles, II, pp. 428–9.

8 October witnessed another important departure from earlier patterns. James then asked Frederick to consider marrying his heir, Frederick Henry, to the Emperor's daughter and permitting the young couple to reside in Vienna. For Frederick and Elizabeth, the relegation of their eldest son to life as an Imperial hostage and as a likely Catholic convert was an ignominious price for returning to Heidelberg. But in stark contrast to earlier proposals, James did not extort Frederick's approval; he simply asked his son-in-law's opinion.[7] Just as unusual as the tone of James's letter was the manner of its delivery. Sir James Ramsey, the gentleman of the bedchamber who carried the dispatch to The Hague, also bore a packet from Charles to his sister. The prince, who wanted to take no chances with Frederick's response, sent word that "if she like not the ouverture contained in his Maiesties last letters, the answear should be deferred til he [Charles] be heard from again." Elizabeth had good reason late in 1623 to be delighted with her brother who had at last begun to conduct an independent foreign policy. In the circumstances, Frederick's reply was predictably uncompromising; his son could take an Imperial bride provided Frederick himself, and not as the Spaniards proposed, another member of the Palatine family, first received "pleine et entière restitution" of his territories.[8] Since neither Philip IV nor Ferdinand II could accept these conditions, James's son and son-in-law had managed to insert a large monkey-wrench into the diplomatic machinery for a peaceful restitution.

Having lodged the question in Madrid that the Spaniards had always avoided, and having dispatched Ramsey, the royal entourage devoted itself exclusively to the business of reunion and reconciliation; on 20 October Yonge reported that "wellcome home is (as yet) the only busenes in agitation." At the end of the month Charles returned to London where with bells ringing the citizens welcomed him back. After relieving apprehensions about his faith with communion at St. Paul's, the prince convened a debate in the select committee of the Council, which after a full report from Madrid debated on the fate of the Anglo-Spanish treaties. A few days later, James himself, though hobbled by gout, arrived to preside over the debate.[9] The issue promised to be controversial. Controversy, however, soon gave way to crisis as new dispatches arrived from Madrid which made November 1623 one of the most uncomfortable periods in Charles's life. Charles had left Bristol with his proxy and Aston with the order to ignore the formally ratified

[7] James to Frederick, 8 October 1623, SP 81/29/216.
[8] Carleton the younger to Carleton, 15 October 1623, SP 84/114/224; and Frederick to James, 20 October 1623, SP 81/29/234.
[9] Yonge to Zouche, 20 October 1623, SP 14/153/81; Westminster City Library, Archives, St Margaret's Churchwardens Accounts, entry for 30 October 1623, E13, p. 37; and Woolley to Trumbull, 7 November 1623, Trumbull MSS, XLVIII/105.

marriage treaty. Since James's dispatch of 8 October only deepened the confusion, Bristol rightly requested immediate clarification: must a satisfactory answer about the Palatinate precede the execution of the marriage treaty? Pending James's reply, the earl announced that he presumed the original treaty was still in effect and so would deliver the proxy once the dispensation arrived. Alarming as this news was, Charles could still find comfort in the Curia's reservations about the marriage, which suggested an early wedding date was unlikely. But on 1 November Bristol announced the destruction of the reluctant bridegroom's last refuge; the dispensation was expected hourly, and in fact it arrived the following day. The Spaniards, eager to honor their new relative, planned the wedding for Charles's birthday, 20 November. But the envoys succeeded in pushing the date back to the 29th.[10]

Bristol was swept up in the excitement – and Aston plunged into despair. The envoys had to decide between the marriage treaty, which James had yet to qualify, and Charles's clear personal wish to delay the ceremony. Aston begged the duke to appreciate "the perplexitie I was in finding my self in such a Dilema that one way I was subject to a check and the other way to a hanging." Since Aston alone had received Charles's emphatic messages, he would have had to stand "singly against it," and his sole warrant for wrecking the marriage treaty would be "what I conceaved of his Highnes intentions by his Letters and without any other direction or commands." To complicate the matter further, Olivares had responded that he counted the Palatine restoration as good as done, but for the sake of decency, Philip could put nothing in writing. His answer, although far from satisfactory, did not offer ample grounds to violate the marriage treaty. In the end, Aston decided it was neither "fitt for me nor safe to opose myself in anything for which I had not precise order."[11] Bristol for his part had no qualms about deciding between the prince's reservations and the end of his long, torturous negotiations. With an apparent straight face, he congratulated Buckingham about "this happy conclusion of the Prince his marriadge" in which "your Grace hath taken so much paynes . . . and passed so manye destasts and misunderstandings." To James, he promised "a merrye Christmas;" the spring would bring "Ioye . . . unto his Sonn and to his daughter" and "a happye ende of this miserable business of the Palatinate."[12]

Bristol's delight was not widely shared. Having declared themselves against Spain, Charles and Buckingham saw Bristol anxious to preside over the nup-

[10] Bristol to James, 24 October 1623, *Cabala*, II, pp. 137–41; Bristol to Calvert, 1, 3 and 5 November 1623, SP 94/29/6, 27–27v, and 45; and Ruigh, p. 25.

[11] Aston to Buckingham, 29 November 1623, SP 94/29/94; same to Conway, 27 November 1623, SP 94/29/91; and Bristol and Aston to Calvert, 23 November, SP 94/29/80.

[12] Bristol to Buckingham, 23 November 1623, SP 94/29/68v; and Bristol to Conway, 23 November 1623, SP 94/29/84.

tials. In light of the ambassador's actions in October and November, the bitter resentment of Charles and Buckingham for the earl becomes more readily comprehensible; his errors before and during the prince's visit were nothing compared with those in the weeks after Charles's departure. Bristol's actions of course were perfectly correct. Even Charles later confessed that there really was no legal case against the envoy who had conducted himself "so judiciously that you can be taxed for nothing in public court, but can justifie yourself... and so free yourself." Yet his scrupulous adherence to the letter of James's commands willfully ignored the spirit of the heir apparent's wishes. When Aston eventually plumped for the marriage treaty, he at least professed embarrassment over his decision; Bristol on the other hand seemed thrilled by it. As Kenelm Digby reported Charles's view, "between him and you, he doubted not but your Lordship will acknowledge you were too forward and confident" in pursuit of the Spanish match.[13] Whatever the reason for the envoys' decision, their resolution had an electrifying effect on the Junta; according to Buckingham, the select committee's first reaction was to revoke both men. James's formal response was almost as dramatic as a revocation. For weeks, the prince and the favorite had argued for the formal linkage of the marriage to the restoration; on 13 November James at last agreed. Since he simply could not "receave one daughter in ioy and contentment and leave another in teares and sighes," the ambassadors must labor for "punctuall answeares" to the German question "with as much earnestness as may stand with modestie, discretion and good manners." If the Spanish ministers returned no answer in fifteen days, then Bristol was to present an ultimatum; "an exact answer in five days" or the ambassador would return to England.[14]

Charles himself left Bristol no room for misinterpretation. Belatedly he realized that Aston was far too weak to stand up to Bristol; as the duke later chided Aston, "you may thinke how straunge it was to the prince and how much I was troubled" to learn "how you had concurred with the Earl of Bristol to ingage his Highness . . . without making certaine the restitution of the Palatinate." In another letter, Buckingham added "by none of your letters have I perceaved that you have or will have understood the Prince." The only option now was to deliver utterly unambiguous commands directly to Bristol. "The false interpretation of the King's and my directions concerning the not delivering my proxie" prompted the prince on the 13th to order the envoy "not to deliver my proxie untill you heare further frome the king and my

---

[13] K. Digby to Bristol, 27 May 1625, *HMC 8th Report*, Appendix 1, p. 217.
[14] James to Bristol, 13 November 1623, SP 94/29/10; and Conway to Bristol, 13 November 1623, SP 94/29/24–24v; and Buckingham to Aston, [late December 1623], SP 94/30/67.

selfe." Lest Bristol overlook this direct command, Charles repeated it; "I command you as you answer it upon your perrill, not to deliver my proxie till you heare further." His frustration with Bristol was vividly illustrated in his closing prayer that "you will obey this command punctuallie." Not content with one letter, he penned another the following day because "I see you have need of paraphrase upon the text." The text was predictable; since "ther can neither be marriag nor frendshippe" without the Palatinate, "ye must not deliver the proxie." And to make doubly sure, Charles told Aston of his order to Bristol and commanded him to see that the earl obeyed.[15]

Repetition of this command, moreover, was not insurance against a mishap on the road or a tardy courier, and a delay inevitably meant that Charles would soon find himself the brother-in-law of Philip IV. Thus with the dispatches of 13–14 November Charles and the duke took no chances. Since an express courier might reach Madrid in two weeks and since the wedding was planned for the 29th, there was almost no room for error. Therefore they dispatched four messengers with duplicate packets and the promise of a £4,000 reward to the fastest. In the circumstances, the couriers understandably pushed themselves to the limit, and one of the four, Edward Clerke, arrived in Madrid "soe unfitt to undertake a jornie for England that a race of a hundred yards is more than I could well performe."[16] Clerke's sharpest pain was doubtless that Mr. Wood had arrived before him. News of Wood's feat three days before the wedding prompted renewed celebrations. "You cannot conceive," Castle wrote to Trumbull, "what exceeding great demonstrances of joye are made both at the Courtes of the King and his Highness and generally in this Cittie, where the hope that this interruption will be the seede to begett an utter falling from the Match."[17]

The seed produced fruit very quickly. Just as Bristol had predicted, the introduction of the Palatine question brought the negotiations to a swift conclusion. The last minute change of plans deeply offended the Spaniards who began to suspect the worst, and confirmation came with the news of "the smale encouragement . . . given of late to the well-wishers of the match, and grace and employment to those of the Contrarie partie." As a result the Spaniards began to prepare for war, not marriage. The idea of formally linking the Palatinate to the marriage Olivares received sarcastically; Philip would be glad to do so if James tied the marriage to the restoration of the

---

[15] Charles to Bristol, 14 and 15 December 1623, *HMC 8th Report*, Appendix 1, p. 216; same to Aston, 14 November 1623, SP 94/29/34.

[16] Clarke to Buckingham, 4 December 1623, SP 94/29/120; and Chandler to Trumbull, 16 December 1623, Trumbull MSS, XIX/151. See also Woods's petition from 1635, *CSPD*, IX, pp. 424–5. I owe the last reference to the kindness of Conrad Russell.

[17] Bristol to Calvert, 6 December 1623, SP 94/29/126; and Castle to Trumbull, 12 December 1623, Trumbull MSS, XVIII/112.

disobedient Dutch provinces to Spanish control.[18] In Philip's actual "punctual answer" of 9 December, his anger over the prospect of a linkage was much more apparent than details of the restitution itself. Philip's response nonetheless provided James with all he wanted to know; after reading it, "wee doe not a little mervaile," James wrote to Bristol, "that you take our affaires to have bin in a good condition." Since Conway had already told Buckingham that "you will ever have more Chaffe then Corne thence, whilest you have that Winnower [Bristol] there", Philip's answer led to the ambassador's recall on 30 December. The sharp response in both Madrid and London amply confirmed Aston's observation that "if the king our masters and his Highness intentions [in their letters of 13 November] be to come to a breach with this king, leaving but things alone as they are they will soone see that desire affected."[19]

An open breach was plainly not James's desire, who reportedly denounced the advocates of a new Parliament as "traitors" and dismissed the duke's more extravagant military plans as those of "une jeune homme." In more maudlin moments he begged for "le repos ou bien le cercueil" and found solace in an endless cycle of cardgames and long naps moving, as Conway explained, "from bedd to board and from board to bedd without anytime to business." Nevertheless, these scenes should not overshadow the important fact that his basic approach to the European conflict and to Spain was rapidly changing; his preceding dispatches reveal a man exasperated with Spanish excuses and evasions. Pressure from any source, counciliar or popular, he continued to find abhorent. Yet once his son and his favorite joined the mass of Englishmen inside and outside Whitehall, he could no longer ignore the fact that his continental policy had proved a spectacular failure. Early in November the French ambassador reported that James longed for "sa vie accoustumée," but "ayant la raison qui combat entierement contre luy, l'affection de son favory, les remonstrances de son fils et les souhaits de son peuple, il y a apparence que tant de choses pourront faire qualque impression en son âme . . . elle pourra se tourner à la fin, en rage et desespoir."[20] Rage and despair perhaps best account for his decision to conclude high-level negotiations in Madrid. If the Spaniards wished to avoid a more provocative English response to the Palatine problem, they could come to London.

---

[18] Aston to Buckingham, 5 December 1623, SP 94/29/122; and Bristol to Calvert, 6 December 1623, SP 94/29/133; and Philip to James, 9 December 1623, SP 94/29/148.
[19] James to Bristol, 30 December 1623, SP 94/29/193; Conway to Buckingham, 20 December 1623, SP 14/155/65; and Aston to Buckingham, 29 November 1623, SP 94/29/94v.
[20] Tillières to Puysieux, 4 November and 9 December 1623, PRO 31/3/57, fos. 261 and 280; Woolley to Trumbull, 7 November 1623, Trumbull MSS, XLVIII/108; and [Conway] to Calvert, 19 December 1623, SP 14/159/7.

THE OPENING TO THE DUTCH

After some admittedly hair-raising weeks in November, Charles and Buckingham had apparently managed to get the clock moving again. Bristol's recall coincided with the summoning of a new Parliament, a decision which, in S. R. Gardiner's celebrated judgment, opened the reign of King George. Once the election writs went out, Buckingham "was the ruler of England"; "if Buckingham had told the commons, 'I am the King,' he could not have expressed himself better."[21] While, as will be seen, Gardiner overstated the case, the fact remains that something unusual happened to the control of power. Far from abdicating, James simply admitted the failure of his mediatory foreign policy. Bereft of alternatives, he allowed his son and favorite to try their hand. But he imposed one crippling limitation: he denied official credence to their efforts to revive the "common cause." This limited delegation of power would permit the two optimistic young men to confront the baffling complexities surrounding the Palatine restoration. Moreover, a little saber-rattling from Charles and the duke, while James himself remained scrupulously neutral, might bring on new Spanish proposals. Confining though the arrangement was, Charles and Buckingham accepted it, and to their credit they got some fitful movement out of the minute hand of Yonge's clock. Yet as they were to discover, the mechanism would not function properly without parliamentary assistance.

The resolutions taken in mid-November signalled the first attempt to recruit foreign allies to the "common cause" as well as the end of the Anglo-Spanish marriage negotiations. Reports then ran through the Court and St. Paul's of a major diplomatic offensive; Kensington reportedly would soon be sent to France, Sir Isaac Wake to Turin and Venice and Sir Robert Anstruther to north Germany and Denmark. In the event, however, only Kensington left merely "to hunt with the King without anie other publick errand or qualitie."[22] The heralded diplomatic initiative foundered for reasons that Sir George Goring discovered in The Hague in late November.

Officially Goring was merely standing in for Buckingham and Lennox at the christening of the latest addition to the Palatine nursery; they could not attend, Lennox explained, because "this business of the prince his marriage is yet unsettled and the king will not have us to bee away at this occasion." But given that Carlisle's secretary dubbed Goring's journey as "the greatest newes the time hath yet produced," the visit of the duke's client was not exclusively

---

[21] Gardiner, *Prince Charles*, II, p. 453; and *England under Buckingham*, I, p. 14. Set against Gardiner, Ruigh, pp. 385–7.

[22] Beaulieu to Trumbull, 19 December 1623, Trumbull MSS, VII/140.

ceremonial.[23] In fact he had two missions, one with Frederick and Elizabeth and the other with the Prince of Orange. To the former Goring carried a letter from James, who for the first time offered his son-in-law a real choice. All the cards were laid on the table before Frederick "afin que vous puissiés avoir recours à vostre prudence et apres meure deliberation faire une choix convenable à la providence honneur et seureté de Vostre Estat." Quite significantly James was serious, for he ordered Carleton to forebear the whips. Again a peaceful settlement would be based on an Imperial–Palatine marriage, only this time Frederick Henry would be raised in London in the Infanta's household. The young man would immediately receive the bulk of the estates and the Electoral title on the death of Maximilian of Bavaria. These details quickly led to a royal lecture on the benefits of compromise and the quiet life on the Neckar. Yet if Frederick wanted to try "une hazardeuse longe attente à d'autres voyes incertaines," then James asked for "moyens probables et faisables" to restore the Elector by main force. The plan was to be detailed and include "nos forces, celles de nos Alliéz et celles que nous pourrons asseurer ou espère."[24]

James's letter was most remarkable for its novel interest in Frederick's military options. Frederick's response was quite logically of paramount importance for Charles and Buckingham. In recent weeks their own military plans had occasioned James's mirth, but not his outright rejection. As evidenced in his letter to Frederick, James wanted to hear more. Hence, it was essential that Frederick's answer, which would doubtless plump for military intervention, roughly second the strategy of the common cause. The private diplomacy of Charles and Buckingham began in earnest with Goring's mission and paid its first dividends in Frederick's reply. His letter began with an impassioned, if predictable, call to arms. Once James brought himself "de lever le masque de beau semblant et malice cachée des Espagnols," he would find powerful foreign supporters. The non-Habsburg German princes only required "l'appuy d'un grand Potentat, pour les supporter contre la puissance de la Maison d'Autriche" and awaited "la premiere bonne occasion que se presentera pour la liberté d'Allemagne." They currently had their eyes on Christian IV of Denmark, but Christian, "plein de circumspection ne voulant pas entrer seul en ieu," had "a les siens sur Votre Majesté." Likewise the Dutch would "hazard de vie et biens vers le service de Vostre Majesté fondée sur l'experience du passé." James's greatest asset, however, was his three war-like kingdoms. "Nul prince du monde" was better loved and revered, and his

---

[23] Lennox to Elizabeth, 19 October 1623, SP 84/114/235; and Woodford to Nethersole, 8 November 1623, SP 81/29/259.

[24] James to Frederick, 20 November 1623, SP 81/29/277; and Conway to Frederick, 20 November 1623, SP 84/115/42.

subjects' voluntary contributions to the Palatine cause clearly indicated the broad support James could expect from his people in a war for the Palatinate. The strategy that Frederick proposed called for the Danes, the Dutch and the Germans to occupy the Austrian Habsburgs while England shepherded her resources for a joint Anglo-Dutch naval assault on the Indies. In the dispatch Frederick suffered no rivals in his enthusiasm for a blue water policy which was "le seul et unique moyen pour faire tomber en terre la puissance effroyable d'Espagne."[25]

From the pen of a landlocked central European prince, a passion for English naval operations must have sounded a little strange. On other occasions Frederick showed considerably more enthusiasm for military assistance on the continent; in 1625, when Charles was about to launch 10,000 men against the Habsburgs, Frederick begged his brother-in-law to strike at Hamburg, not Cadiz. If the reply of 20 December did not sound like vintage Frederick, it did have remarkable similarities to the plans of Conway and Buckingham. Thus Frederick's eloquent advocacy of the English navy signalled his willingness to work with Charles and Buckingham in the task of convincing *Rex Pacificus* of the merits of war. If successful, Frederick and Charles would inevitably have different ideas about strategy. But late in 1623, when all other support was rapidly vanishing, the Elector was delighted to do what he could for his brother-in-law. In any event, a future wrangle was infinitely preferable to being pressed every few months with ever stranger plans for Frederick Henry's education. Frederick understandably welcomed Goring's advice, especially since it came from a rapidly expanding group of Palatine supporters. The reason for Elizabeth's high spirits immediately after Goring's visit did not elude contemporaries; since she had spent most of the year attempting to restrain her despair, "all conclude there is good news out of England."[26]

Goring had less success with the Dutch. He had come to suggest that Dutch envoys should come to London to discuss an Anglo-Dutch league. For the "Patriots" who clung to Elizabethan precedents, a close relationship with the Dutch Republic was a vital prerequisite for any military action. Admittedly the inability of senior English military leaders to think in any other terms was partly due to the fact that all of them had served in the Dutch army. Nonetheless, they could not imagine a strategy in which the Dutch did not play a major role. In December 1623 Rusdorff, the Palatine envoy, emphasized to Conway the importance of immediate assistance to Transylvania, but his eloquence

[25] Frederick to James, 20 December 1623, SP 81/29/311.
[26] Carleton to Conway, 24 January 1624, SP 84/116/56; and see above, pp. 69–76. On the Palatine plan for Hamburg in 1625, see Mémoire [from Rusdorff to Charles], 29 October 1625, SP 81/33/198.

did not cause the Secretary to alter his priorities; "il falloit auparavant," Conway explained, "faire l'alliance avec les Etats, après on puroit plus aisément persuader le Roi à une correspondence avec le dit Prince [Bethlen Gabor] . . . mais sans que le premier soit parfait, on ne pouvoit venir commodement au second."[27] The extent to which many Englishmen felt the Dutch to be junior partners is a little surprising. The mercantile tension which was to disrupt Anglo-Dutch relations thirty years later was already clearly present in the 1620s. But most Englishmen dwelt much more on the common heritage than commercial problems. Exceedingly tight-fisted and phlegmatic, the Dutch were nonetheless a thoroughly known quantity. Therefore the crucial first step in any English return to continental warfare was the clarification of the Dutch position.

Goring's best efforts brought forth only evasive, albeit friendly replies from Prince Maurice and no Dutch ambassadors. Carleton, the ambassador in The Hague, explained the "shye and circumspect" response to Buckingham. When Maurice sounded some influential members of the Estates General about the possible revival of the Elizabethan protectorate, they unanimously replied, "nothing would be more agreeable." Yet they were keenly aware that they were no longer dealing with Elizabeth; as Maurice pointedly informed Carleton, "when the King woulde be to this State as Queen Elizabeth was, this State would be to him as it was to Queen Elizabeth." The passage of time obviously had done nothing to dull the memory of the separate Anglo-Spanish peace in 1604; Maurice insisted on assurances that "when they putt themselves wholy under his Majesties wings his Majesty will not flye from them and make his peace with out them." In other words, James could best demonstrate his good intentions by formally concluding the Anglo-Spanish marriage discussions. Furthermore, the recently concluded Franco-Dutch defensive agreement contributed to the diffident response; the Dutch were understandably "loth to adventure the exchange of a substance for what appeares . . . no better than a shadow." The ambassador regretfully concluded "there needes more then a bare signification that his Majesties eares are open this way for we must know that his hart is not onely well inclined but thoroughly resolved."[28]

Goring returned home with singularly unpleasant news. Although Frederick enthusiastically embraced the "Patriots," his cooperation was worthless without the Dutch. The sting of this failure, however, was softened by a greater potential disaster which threatened to engulf Charles and Buckingham. Maurice, Frederick and all martial plans were ultimately beside

---

[27] Rusdorff to Frederick, 11 December 1623, *Mémoires et Négotiacions*, I, pp. 151–5.
[28] Carleton to Buckingham, 9 [draft] and 18 December 1623, and same to Conway, SP 84/115/102 and 151 and 84/116/41.

the point if James decided to plunge back into negotiations for a peaceful restitution. And that was exactly what a Capuchin friar convinced James to do late in November. The king's hopes for a negotiated settlement had not vanished with his ultimatum of 13 November. There still remained many other ways of reaching that end – as Francesco de la Rota told James. Ambiguity surrounded the man; he offered the good offices of the Nuncio in Brussels and the Archbishop-Elector of Mainz to mediate an arrangement with Maximilian of Bavaria, but he came without credentials. His remarkable proposal inclined James to overlook the irregularities surrounding it. Frederick Henry again was the centerpiece; this time he would marry Maximilian's niece and reside in Munich. The Upper Palatinate and the Lower Palatinate east of the Rhine, currently occupied by Bavarian troops, would be immediately transferred to the young prince, while Maximilian and the Pope would intercede with Ferdinand II for the rest of his inheritance. Rota's proposal bypassed the Habsburgs entirely through a direct settlement with the power occupying the bulk of Frederick's estates. Furthermore, given that the Catholic League, dominated by Bavaria, had provided most of the Emperor's military muscle in the Bohemian conflict, an Anglo-Bavarian settlement raised the tantalizing prospect of separating Bavaria from the Habsburgs. James's response was predictable; although Charles and Buckingham joined with Philip's ambassadors in denouncing Rota, the king listened. "I thincke," Beaulieu sighed, "though we never come to conclude, yet we will never leave treating."[29]

The sequence of events was to become all too common. Charles and Buckingham patiently shepherded James towards one policy only to witness him suddenly jump out of their carefully constructed path. Although they might return to fetch James, his periodic backsliding represented more than a personal setback; it also rendered a consistent English foreign policy well-nigh impossible in the last years of James's life. For all their recently acquired, and expanding, authority within the state, Charles and Buckingham were powerless to restrain James when he really wanted to do something: it was after all his prerogative. Beaulieu observed in early January 1624, "although His Majesty giveth waye to the Prince and to the Duke of Buckingham in these things wherein they are very fervent and earnest, yett his former affections doe still sticke to him and it will be no small matter when matters come to the push to bring him to a contrarie resolution."[30] The next fourteen

---

[29] Beaulieu to Trumbull, 18 November 1623, Trumbull MSS, VII/136. On Rota's mission, see Valaresso to the Doge and Senate, 31 November 1623 and 16 January 1624, *CSPV*, XVIII, pp. 160–2 and 200–3; and Tillières and Puysieux, 11 and 19 December 1623, PRO 31/3/57, fos. 271 and 281.

[30] Beaulieu to Trumbull, 9 January 1623, Trumbull MSS, VII/142.

months were to provide almost innumerable examples of James's stubborn independence.

In the circumstances, the best response to secret diplomacy was a little of the same. Goring's embassy has rightly been dubbed "a setback" for the war coalition, but it is important to insert the adjective "temporary" into this judgment.[31] On 9 January, Buckingham and Conway wrote a series of letters to Elizabeth, Maurice and Carleton which all stressed the necessity of Dutch assistance in the "blessed revolution." The rhetoric is worth closer attention for it clearly reveals the awkward position of Charles and Buckingham with a new Parliament a month away. Conway began his letter to Maurice by emphasizing the certain results of Dutch caution. The Anglo-Spanish discussions earlier in the year, Conway revealed, had often strayed from the topic of Charles's bride; the Spaniards were in fact eager to connect "la Restitution du Palatinat avec le recouvrement de la Souveraineté de vos Estats." Having captured Maurice's attention, Conway assured the prince that this danger would soon pass – provided the Dutch acted in time. Currently James followed the lead of his son and favorite, but he warned "les Roys sages and experimentez sont froids aux changemens violens principalement en ceux qui sonts hauts et hazardeux." Given the king's unpredictability, "les instrumens qui conseillent a tels desseings, courent grands risques aux moindres accidens et evenemens de disgrace ou mauvaise conionction." The success of this risky operation therefore "en grand partie depend de prudence et resolution de Votre Excellence et de votre Estat." Hence, "si le Roy n'est confirme par vos ouvertures conceils et offres," James would be unable "parler rondement et franchement a son peuple" in the impending Parliament; the result would inevitably be "une disgracieuse rupture entre luy et son Parlement," the collapse of the "Patriots" and the revival of the Spanish match. No official sanction, the Secretary of State confessed, could be attached to this plea; he was only speaking in his own name and that of the duke, "qui est Favori de Roy, [et] intime et cordiall amy de notre Prince."[32]

With Carleton, Conway was more explicit; the Dutch response to Goring "could bee raysed to noe more than generalities upon which nothing of certaine can be concluded. And with generalities wee have been soe punished and in them mispent soe much time as now wee can rellish nothinge but that which is Catagoricall." Since James had resolved that "if he may bee seconded, to seeke by all means the establishment of the peace in Germanie recoveringe of the Palatinate and the boundinge of every man with in his owne," Conway was baffled that there was "no eager poursuit" of an English alliance. At this point all he could do was beg;

---

[31] Adams, "Foreign Policy and the Parliaments," pp. 155–6.
[32] Conway to Maurice, 9 January 1624, SP 84/116/11.

it is certain nowe the time, the high time and the precious time for States to make use of the opportunities and of the advantage of the humor of the King more than at a stand and bendinge to the waie of them [the Dutch] the gallant and stronge affections of the Prince seconded by the brave and powerfull favorite and the rest of the good and stronge part of our world, to offer counsel, persistance and assurance.

On the other hand if the Dutch succumbed to "negligence, pride or artifice to pretend advantage, they will hazard their owne ruine and our harme," which he prayed God would prevent "for his Church sake." Finally, while he confessed to have "noe commission to imbarque you into this business," he assured Carleton, "you cannot doe aniething to stirr up that State to seeke ayde and protection here that will not bee well understood." As Mr. Secretary noted to his son on the following day, "it is in their power . . . to bringe his mayiesty [*sic*] to an open declaration."[33]

Conway's letters are particularly revealing. The most significant point was that at the beginning of 1624 James could contemplate a war "to bound every man with in his owne" provided "he may bee seconded." Thus the hysterical pleas for Dutch envoys becomes comprehensible. The letters also illustrated the nearly crippling effect of nonexistent credentials. Since the king would not alienate the Spaniards by publicly soliciting alternative allies, any anti-Habsburg proposals would formally have to be made to him, not vice versa. Unfortunately, no prince was anxious to commit his prestige to a major English embassy when James's mind remained unsettled; Charles and Buckingham could promise assistance but they could not guarantee the king's decision. The state most likely to overlook the peculiarity of the situation was the Dutch Republic. The United Provinces had the most to gain, and the lines of communication between the two states were broad and well-travelled; it was not an unknown foreign politician but rather Edward Conway, an old friend of the Republic, who begged for Dutch help.

These calculations ultimately proved correct; at the eleventh hour, the Dutch sent over envoys – but only after the English Secretary of State confessed his master's embarrassing difficulties with, and dependence on, Parliament. To be sure, Conway exaggerated in order to dramatize the situation, and it is heartening to see that James's minister was not above employing this lamentable constitutional problem to good effect in a diplomatic crisis. But there was more than a grain of truth in the Secretary's statements about Parliament; his master's bad luck with previous sessions was simply too notorious for him to deny. In fact since this was common knowledge, contemporaries must have read the "Patriots'" willingness to present their case to Parliament as an impressive illustration of their determination

---

[33] Conway to Carleton, and same to Conway, 9 January 1624, SP 84/116/15 and 25. See also Buckingham's note to Carleton, 9 January 1624, SP 84/116/20.

and desperation. Conway certainly argued as much to Maurice; his prediction of "une disgracieuse rupture" in Parliament was linked to his mention of the "grand risques" that "les instrumens" of an Anglo-Dutch entente ran. Parliament, far from being a powerless institution, was rapidly becoming the only means of breaking Spain's hold on the king. The force of these arguments cannot be underestimated, for two ambassadors extraordinary from the United Provinces arrived in London just as Parliament was about to begin. They represented the only foreign success of Charles and Buckingham, and as will be seen, this single diplomatic triumph was to save the "Patriots" from disaster later in the session.[34]

THE FOUNDATION OF A FRENCH MATCH

An Anglo-Dutch entente was to have been simply the foundation of a more ambitious foreign coalition. And well before the crisis over the Dutch envoys, the prince and Buckingham were already busy retailing their proposals elsewhere. After the Dutch republic, the most essential foreign confederate would be France; when James spoke of his willingness to consider a war "if he may bee seconded," the person whose assistance James had in mind was Louis XIII. Logic dictated a military league be successfully negotiated before it was publicly discussed in Parliament "rondement et franchement." Otherwise Parliamentary suspicions and the possibility of "une disgracieuse rupture" would dramatically increase. In the end, the "Patriots" had to accept these risks; the lack of official warrant, which severely hampered their overtures to the Dutch, completely paralyzed those to Louis's ministers. Consequently before Parliament, the supporters of a Spanish war had to appear in a weaker and more vulnerable position. Even more damaging in the long run, they were unable to probe the French position before the session; consequently Charles and the duke were unable to discover the fallacy on which they had constructed their French policy and the entire common cause.

In 1623 Louis XIII had valid, but not compelling reasons to support a military struggle on Frederick's behalf; as his ministers repeatedly noted, the Elector was Louis's ally, not his kinsman. The most promising means of overcoming this dynastic defect was to marry Frederick's brother-in-law to Louis's sister, Henriette Marie. Once Charles lost interest in a Spanish match, various Dutch and German ladies were discreetly proposed to him, and all politely declined.[35] Admittedly none of them were royal princesses, but it should not be forgotten that Charles was more interested in the family's military strength and religion than in its lineage. Henriette Marie had high

---

[34] See below, pp. 234–8, 255–9.
[35] Carleton the younger to Carleton, 1 November 1623, SP 14/154/2.

marks in both vital categories; her brother's army was second only to that of the Habsburgs, and his title of Eldest Son of the Church would ensure a war for the Palatinate would not degenerate into James's *bête noire*, a war of religion.

What made sense to James did not necessarily make sense to a domestic audience, and some contemporaries had a sense of *déjà vu* as one Catholic princess replaced another. Later in the 1624 session Charles dispelled these fears with his public promise not to marry a Catholic on terms prejudicial to English law, but in light of later events, it is possible to argue that "the Prince and Buckingham hoped to use this promise as a bargaining point in the marriage negotiations with the French." Yet this analysis ignores the fact that Charles and Buckingham anticipated minimal bargaining. Indeed until June 1624 they assumed that the French would not demand as much as the Spaniards had. Conway told Carleton in April 1624, the same month as Charles's oath, that if Louis should seek to strive with Philip for the title of "Most Catholic," "I conceive that . . . will break the business." The bridegroom's own words on this subject deserve close attention: in late August 1624, Charles informed Carlisle, "if you fynd they persis in this new way that they have begunn in making an article for our Roman Catholiq Subjects, dallie noe more with them but breake of the treatie of Marriage . . . and believe it ye will have as greate honnor with breaking upon these tearmes as with making the alliance."[36] Rather than cynical duplicity, pious naiveté may best characterize Charles's parliamentary oath.

Popular myth as much as any fact was responsible for this assumption. When the English spoke of the French king, they often seem to have meant Henry IV, not his son, Louis XIII. The previous thirteen years of French history, which provided ample evidence of Louis's anti-Huguenot and pro-Habsburg sympathies, were ascribed to "bons catholiques" and Jesuits about the young king. Louis reportedly required only a little encouragement to assume his father's role as the steadfast anti-Habsburg warrior. Similarly the English tended to exaggerate the independence of the Gallican church: the French church which had defied Clement VIII in the coronation of Henri IV would surely resist papal punctiliousness in an Anglo-French marriage. It is unnerving to witness Henry of Navarre, a stock character in the Elizabethan cycle of popular history, enter into sober diplomatic deliberations over a decade after his assassination. Yet as Russell has observed, "for a generation brought up during the Armada war, the myth mattered as much as the reality."[37]

---

[36] Conway to Carleton, 16 April 1624, SP 84/116/58; Charles to Carlisle, 13 August 1624, SP 78/73/40; and Ruigh, p. 240.

[37] Conrad Russell, "Parliament and the King's Finances," *The Origins of the Civil War*, ed. Conrad Russell (New York, 1973), p. 101.

More substantial reasons also encouraged a belief in French pliancy. Earlier in 1623, as Spanish demands rose, Englishmen recalled with longing the Anglo-French marriage treaty which granted religious toleration exclusively to the household of Princess Christine, Henriette Marie's elder sister. This 1613 arrangement, which James eventually rejected in favor of a Spanish match, comforted those Englishmen who later again looked to France. "Bons français" noblemen like the Duc de Bellegarde and the Duc de Chevreuse also insisted that the 1613 treaty could be revived without significant alterations.[38] But the most important source for this assumption was the French government itself. Although the French were aware as early as October 1623 of belated English interest in Christine's marriage treaty, they went to great pains to avoid disabusing hopes of its revival.

The first contact between the two sides occurred rather improbably in Spain. There, Father Grey, a Scottish cleric resident in France, met the prince and duke through his fumbling attempts at conversion, and before the favorite left Madrid, Grey volunteered his services if the Spanish match ever foundered. Since he had "beaucoup de connaissance" of the Queen Mother, Marie de Médicis, Grey "seroit un instrument fort propre pour mettre sur la tapis celuy of France." There the affair ended until an astonished duke saw Grey in England late in October. The Queen Mother, the friar reported, welcomed the prospect of an English son-in-law; consequently Grey spent the rest of the year carrying friendly messages between the duke and Marie.[39] As this unexpected secret contact developed, Buckingham began to visit the Comte de Tillières, the French resident ambassador, to feel the official French pulse.

Most English courtiers found the comte difficult to understand, but perhaps that was because he was more interested in the recusants than in them. For example, this "devot," or in the English translation "bigot," was characteristically scandalized to learn that Inijosa philandered widely among Catholic ladies. The morality of the situation which was common enough in Madrid and Paris did not trouble him. Yet he grieved for the good name of the Catholics once the news reached the Protestants. His fascination with the local Catholics sprang from a blend of piety and politics; any concessions that he could secure would redound to the temporal as well as spiritual glory of Louis. James had responded to recent French attempts to reduce, if not to eliminate, the political autonomy of the Huguenots by championing Huguenot liberties, a subject which the French regarded as an exclusively

---

[38] Bellegarde to Buckingham, 9 and 31 December 1623, Bodleian Library, Add. MSS D.111, nos. 433 and 434; and Pesaro to the Doge and Senate, 2 October 1623, *CSPV*, XVIII, p. 124.
[39] Tillières to Marie de Medicis, and same to Puysieux, 31 December 1623, SP 31/3/58, fos. 1 and 2.

internal matter. Therefore the English Catholic community, whose numbers and militancy were often exaggerated, appeared as an ideal counter-weight to the Huguenots. Unfortunately, much to Tillières's chagrin, the recusants themselves undercut this policy with their clear preference for the Spaniards.[40]

His brooding over the English Catholics ended with the rapid disintegration of the Spanish match late in 1623 and the discovery that some English courtiers were extremely curious about Louis's youngest sister. Earlier in 1623 he had grumbled that no one except Carlisle ever came to visit him or his staff "comme s'ils eussent esté attaqués de la contagion."[41] Yet with the return of the prince, Tillières's popularity rose dramatically. A casual day trip to Royston quickly led to a dinner party given by the Marquis of Hamilton and a bed in the Earl of Montgomery's apartment where the favorite dropped in for a midnight tête-à-tête. His visit, Sir Philip Mainwaring observed, "was wonderfully well interpreted and to expres the same they feasted him, and filled him with wine and treated him in that free and familiar manner that some spectators would ever since looke noe way, but french." By way of contrast the Spanish envoys a few days later were not invited to dinner and had to spend the night in an inn with Lord Keeper Williams. The ambassador soon took the hint and came "croire qu'ils reviendront bientot à nous."[42] By 16 November he requested immediate instructions on his response to queries about an Anglo-French dynastic alliance, and by 11 December, events had developed so fast that he begged for his own recall and the dispatch of an ambassador extraordinary to handle the question.[43]

Buckingham whole-heartedly approved of the comte's request, for Tillières had regularly remained cool to the duke's glittering prospects for both nations. Unfortunately, the French extraordinary, Marquis d'Effiat, arrived only in July 1624; thus until March, when Kensington was in place in Paris, Buckingham had no other choice but to deal with Tillières. What the duke failed to appreciate was that Tillières was following orders as well as his own prejudices. The English interest placed Tillières and his superiors in a quandary. While apprehensive of arousing the Habsburgs' wrath by cutting in too eagerly on the frustrated bridegroom, they also shared Maurice's reluc-

[40] Tillières to Ville-aux-clercs, 7 February 1624, PRO 31/3/58, fo. 27. See also A. D. Lublinskaya, *French Absolutism: The Crucial Phase, 1620–1629* (Cambridge, 1968), pp. 146–212; and V.-L. Tapie, *France in the Age of Louis XIII and Richelieu* (New York, 1975), pp. 89–126.

[41] Tillières to Puysieux, [summer 1623], and the same to Ville-aux-clercs, 7 February 1624, PRO 31/3/57, fo. 286, and 31/3/58, fo. 27.

[42] Tillières to Puysieux, 4 November 1623, PRO 31/3/57, fo. 261; Mainwaring to Trumbull, 12 October 1623, Trumbull Add. MSS, XV/113; and Williams to Conway, 16 October 1623, SP 14/153/58.

[43] Tillières to Puysieux, 16 November and 11 December 1623, PRO 31/3/57, fos. 264 and 271.

tance about acting before James formally ended the Spanish talks. Yet even a devot like Tillières could appreciate that the Anglo-Spanish marriage would have been a major calamity. Louis's ministers had not forgotten Charles V's adage, "peace with England and war with everyone else"; and they readily grasped that a large proportion of "everyone else" spoke French fluently. Thus, the French moved cautiously at first and more openly later to disrupt the match with Spain. M. de Ville-aux-clercs, the Secretary of State for England, repeatedly urged the ambassador "traverser le mariage d'Espagne par touttes voies", "fortifier la volonté du Prince" to break with Spain, and to point out to the duke that "sa propre seureté qui ne se peut trouver qu'en la ruine de la faction Espagnolle."[44] A match with England, however, was another matter, one that filled Tillières with grave reservations. The preliminaries of the Spanish match had convinced him that a marriage treaty would be impossible to enforce and that a marriage across religious lines would lead only to recurrent quarrels and perhaps even war. Moreover, he strenuously argued that Louis should not get involved with losers. The Stuarts were "en misèrable estate... sans argent, sans amis et sans reputation, neantmoins leur gloire et leur vanite leur reste." Parliament alone could rectify the situation, and the envoy doubted if the MPs would follow Charles's lead as easily "comme l'on pense." Indeed, the institutional impoverishment of English monarchs made him warn that they may well have "non seulement appuyer une vieille maison mais en soustenir une tombante" as well.[45]

Tillières's superiors in Paris ignored these objections for the time being; as a result, the major stumbling block was the ambassador's old friends, the recusants. In spite of the common English assumption, which Tillières found insulting, that a French marriage would prove "meilleur marche que avec l'Espagne," the French ministers had already resolved to insist on at least the same terms as the Infanta. The blunt declaration of this resolution, however, might very well backfire and revive the Spanish match. The answer to this problem was simple: tell the English only as much as they needed to know. As Tillières explained to Louis, the French requirements should be concealed until after James had formally broken with Spain; then "peu a peu, vous le [James] menez beaucoup plus loing qu'il n'a desseing d'aller." The policy of "peu a peu" required the French envoy to encourage English hopes of "les avantages qu'il peut esperer de la france" while declining to discuss an Anglo-French entente until after the rupture of the Spanish treaty.[46] Tillières under-

[44] Ville-aux-clercs to Tillières, 5 and 6 February and 19 March 1624, BL Add. 30,646, fos. 1, 31 and 109v.
[45] Tillières to Puysieux, 30 December 1623, PRO 31/3/58, fos. 2, 9 and 21.
[46] Ville-aux-clercs to Tillières, 7 February 1624, BL Add. 30,646, fos. 38v–40; and Tillières to Puysieux, 11 and 30 December 1623, PRO 31/3/57, fo. 271 and 31/3/58, fo. 2.

standably sought to avoid this role. To his mind, the *rapprochement* of the duke and the godly was the prelude to an anti-Catholic backlash. Yet the policy of "peu a peu" tied his hands and closed his mouth; the English Catholics could not become a major issue until James steered towards Paris. Ville-aux-clercs soothed him; although "il sera bon de proteger les catholiques," it was essential "de traverser le mariage d'Espagne et d'advancer celuy de France." Such equanamity in the face of a mounting anti-Catholic hysteria disturbed Tillières, and the Secretary repeatedly preached the benefits of self-control. The Catholics would be taken care of, but the French had to await "la conioncture de temps qu'elle fast composée de telle sort que cela ne refroidist point le Prince et le Duc de la recherche de Madame"; Ville-aux-clercs was confident that in a little while after Charles and the Duke had insulted the Spaniards, James's "timidité naturelle" would force them to accept "les conditions desquelles ils ne voudroient pas ouir parler."[47]

The "Patriots" made the London post even more uncomfortable by repeatedly testing Tillières's discipline. In late January, for example, an unnamed Privy Councillor, whom the ambassador described as normally sensible, inquired if a French match could be negotiated in two months and without a papal dispensation. Privately Tillières ridiculed the question and questioner: "j'estonne comme les personnes icy si peu connaissans le trictrac du monde." Publicly, however, he replied vaguely that Louis was a Catholic prince.[48] His severest trial came from Buckingham and the two leading francophiles, Hamilton and Carlisle. In late December, the favorite and Carlisle pressed for much closer ties between Louis and James who alone could check the Habsburgs' "desseing d'engloutir tout le monde." French cooperation was essential "parceque se sentant fortifié de ce costé là, il [James] pourroit prendre courage." To this impassioned oratory, the ambassador could only reply that he had no commission to treat and did not expect one as long as the Anglo-Spanish negotiations continued. Carlisle returned alone the following day to try to draw out Tillières; he fared no better. The tight-lipped ambassador drove the frustrated Englishmen to replace blandishments with threats. One casually mentioned that thanks to Tillières's coolness, Charles "estoit resolu de se marier ailleurs;" another warned him that Louis was upset with "ma trop grande retenue;" and a third maintained "je serois cause que le mariage d'Espagne se renouveroit." The

---

[47] Ville-aux-clercs to Tillières, 26 February and 26 April 1624, BL Add. 30,646, fos. 52–54v and 165.

[48] Tillières to Puysieux, 1 February 1624, PRO 31/3/58, fo. 21.

ambassador, however, continued to offer general statements of support while declining to discuss a match.[49]

The favorite found Tillières's reticence incomprehensible; and he insisted that Kensington proceed to Paris even though he too would have to travel without a royal commission. Perhaps he might be able to feel the official French pulse more firmly, and the reading was of crucial importance before James formally broke with Spain.

THE REVOLT OF THE GRANDEES

During the Dutch crisis, Buckingham had closed a note to Carleton with the hope that things "goe as well on your side as it doth here." His comment reveals the perfectly logical view that barring a few mishaps such as Rota all was proceeding reasonably well in England. Closer examination, however, reveals that the coalition's formidable domestic position was due to the invaluable assistance of Inijosa and Coloma; they seemed intent on reversing the reputation for craft and guile that Gondomar had earlier earned for Spanish diplomats. They had blundered into a verbal sparring match with the favorite, forgetting that he might enjoy trading insults tit for tat. The energy devoted to denying any linkage between the Palatinate and the marriage treaty was not used to conjure up a new formula for restitution. Consequently desperation more than conviction drove James closer to his son and favorite. So badly had the envoys' position eroded that they lived in almost complete isolation at Exeter House; Tillières noted with satisfaction, "le peu de monde . . . va en leur maison maintenant et qu'il semble estre crime de les visiter." Thus it was possible to think, as the duke did on 9 January, that all was proceeding apace in England.[50] Six days later Inijosa and Coloma administered a sobering lesson; less than a month before the new session opened, Charles and the duke would learn how much their position owed to Spanish sufferance and how fragile their hold on James and the coalition was.

The new year had begun well enough. Frederick Henry's education eventually wrecked the Palatine–Bavarian marriage just as it had the Imperial–Palatine match, and on 13 November James at last admitted the unwisdom of consigning a potential British heir to near certain Catholicism. Thus a Munich education was something his grandfather "ne pouvait nullement condescendre." Furthermore, the longer Rota stayed at Court, the more suspicion grew about his real mission. As Valaresso remarked, "it is a strange

[49] Tillières to Puysieux, 19 December 1623 and 1 February 1624, PRO 31/3/57, fo. 281, and 31/3/58, fol. 21.
[50] Buckingham to Carleton, 9 January 1624, SP 84/116/20; and Tillières to Puysieux, 17 January 1624, PRO 31/3/58, fo. 15.

thing to send a friar to treat with a heretic about restoring a heretic." In late January, James finally ended the talks by dispatching Rota on a fool's errand; the discussion could continue provided the child's parents approved the match, and their negative was assured.[51] The Anglo-Spanish negotiations appeared just as doomed as Rota's proposal. 13 January found the Junta busy composing James's response to Philip's "punctual answer" and searching for the proper language to express the king's dismay "to see our expectation soe much disappointed." Philip's reply was plainly "a direct negative," and yet "wee have understood that the king would assist us with his Armes to the restitution of the Palatinate." James thus had only one option; since "our patience and confidence on on [*sic*] Treaty and mediation hath given an opportunity to the Emperor and Bavaria with the assistance of the Armes of Spaine to possesse themselves wholly of the Palatinate," the time had come to conclude the discussions. Unfortunately this eloquent letter was not sent; on the following day Inijosa and Coloma appeared with a new answer promising "monts et merveilles."[52]

Their master had had a change of heart and now "would doe whatever His Majestie did desire of him." Philip proposed the Infanta's arrival in March and the restoration of the Lower Palatinate in June. In addition a Viennese accent for Frederick Henry was no longer mandatory, and the Spanish king expressed a willingness to support Frederick with arms as well as diplomats. Further details would arrive with Padre Maestro.[53] With good reason James was "extremement satisfait" with the new proposals; with equal cause, the prince and Buckingham emerged from the audience "very sad," and the duke took to his bed. "I assure you," Chaworth wrote Trumbull, "this from Spaine hath infynitely turned manie of the junto to whom this busynes ys dayly disputed, they sitt dayly are amazed at it, but no man can be in his witts and more trobled then our Great Duke whose house stands next to the fyre."[54] Buckingham had ample reason for alarm. The basic premise of all his arguments had been that the Spaniards would never restore the Palatinate; as Conway's brother observed, "the eloquentest Ambassadore that can be sent will never talke them out of soe good a cuntry as the pallatinat." Yet Inijosa and Coloma had just made the common cause and the "Patriots" redundant with a timetable which placed Frederick and Elizabeth in Heidelberg by June.

---

[51] Rusdorff to Frederick, 22 January 1624, *Mémoires*, I, pp. 188–90; and Valaresso to the Doge and Senate, 21 November 1623, *CSPV*, XVIII, p. 160.

[52] "A letter propounded [from James to Aston]," 13 January 1624, SP 94/30/11–11v.

[53] Valaresso to the Doge and Senate, 16 and 23 January 1624, *CSPV*, XVIII, pp. 200–4 and 207–9.

[54] Chamberlain to Carleton, 17 January 1624, *Letters*, II, p. 539; Rusdorff to Frederick, 22 January 1624, *Mémoires*, I, pp. 188–90; and Chaworth to Trumbull, 16 January 1624, Trumbull Add. MSS, XVII/unfoliated.

In the circumstances, Beaulieu's lament was apropos; "we are anew intangled in the nett of that treatie." The new crisis transformed Exeter House into "a Faire-Markett of the Papists, they now upon the conceite of this newe revolution floode thither again, as freely and as thicke as they [ever] did."[55] The English Catholics plainly knew their monarch well; saber-rattling from James's son and his favorite notwithstanding, the king himself had never concealed his longing for new Spanish offers, which Philip had at last answered.

The new offers were not the chief problem confronting Charles and the duke. St. Albans had earlier warned Buckingham "me thinks you do not draw up your troops," and he reiterated his concern a few days later with the query, "do you draw up your troops well?" His apprehension over discipline no longer was academic after "the newe Catastrophe" of 14 January which "had brought the altered course of the Mariage into its old bias againe." Conway was quick to denounce the new proposal; "tout cela n'estoit que mocquerie."[56] The majority of his colleagues, however, did not share his opinion. Arundel, Middlesex, Williams, Calvert, and Weston, who had been conducting a rear-guard action in defense of the match, readily embraced the new proposals; at last they had something concrete to stop the duke's loud cries against Spain. Even more damaging than the encouragement of the peace faction was the confusion among the "Patriots". The "advantagious conditions," Chamberlain remarked, "do so stagger some of the counsaile that were thought to stand fast, that the sway seems to go on that side, and surely unles God set to his helping hand we are like to be caried away by these sirens songs and suffer shipwrecke in calme and faire weather." Buckingham ran true to form; he "openly doth oppose it and cries warr with Spaine." Yet Pembroke reportedly declared "yf the Spaniard performed the conditions agreed on, he saw not how the King in honor could fall from the conclusion." The Junta not surprisingly decided five to three in favor of the new offer; Buckingham, Carlisle and Conway voted "nay" and Lennox, Hamilton, Pembroke and Belfast abstained. The Committee then dispatched Lennox to carry the resolution to James at Newmarket.[57]

This decision was without question an embarrassing reversal for Charles and Buckingham who had no other choice than to ride after Lennox. The vote forced Charles to play his trump card; he refused under any circumstances to

---

[55] T. Conway to Conway, 18 October 1623, SP 84/114/231; and Beaulieu to Trumbull, 16 and 28 January 1624, Trumbull MSS, VII/144 and 145.

[56] "Notes for a Conference with Buckingham," 17 December 1623 and 2 January 1624, *Letters and Life*, VII, pp. 443 and 445; Rusdorff to Frederick, 22 January 1624, *Mémoires*, I, pp. 188–90; and Beaulieu to Trumbull, 28 January 1624, Trumbull MSS, VII/145.

[57] "Notes for a Conference," *Letters and Life*, VII, pp. 443 and 445; Chamberlain to Carleton, 17 and 31 January 1624, *Mémoires*, I, pp. 539–42; and Sterrell to La Faille, 23 January 1624, HHStA, Belgien PC, fasz. 60/unfoliated.

marry the Infanta. After a game of tennis he told Tillières that "le mariage d'Espagne ne s'accompliroit jamais parcequ'il estoit si alliené des Espagnols qu'il contracter amitié n'y alliance avec eux."[58] After the prince's intervention to save the nascent war effort, the next task was to reclaim the mutinous grandees. Pembroke's statement in support of the Spanish offer cannot be taken at face value. Even a hispanophile like Sir George Chaworth, who delighted in Buckingham's discomfort, could not take the Spanish offer seriously. After posing the question, "will he [Philip] put in a block betwixt himselfe in the Lowe Cuntries and Germanie," he asked Trumbull to "answer me with a greater reason then for the good of a sister whom for a neede he might cheaper bestoe in a Monasterie." Thus he judged the offer was "admiranda sed non credenda." A much more likely reason was that the grandees "ayme to take down his [the duke's] greatnes." Only with great difficulty had Pembroke, Lennox and Hamilton concealed their contempt for the favorite, and Pembroke had quarrelled with Buckingham only a few days earlier over a minor patronage question.[59] The only problem with their reversal was that it was far too ideologically inconsistent. Thus since Pembroke's vote did not really correspond with his well-known opposition to Spain, "yt is much marvayled and spoken of that the Lord Chamberlain should be so backward." Covert support for notorious Spanish councillors completely mystified less sophisticated analysts who had always presumed that "the Earle [Pembroke] favored not the Spanish cause."[60] Indeed, Sterrell, the perennial hispanophile, simply ignored the formality of abstention and added the grandees to the "peace" faction. As Van Male judged, Buckingham "a usurpe tant l'authorite sur tous les grandees du royaume qu'il trouve maintenant une terrible faction bander contre sa personne et procedures".[61]

Fortunately for the "Patriots," this "terrible faction" was so obviously the result of personal animus that the breach between the grandees and the dukes was far from irreparable. The new super-faction Valaresso ascribed to the grandees who "do not give him [Buckingham] credit of leading him [James] to a rupture, which they themselves desired, but which has displeased them when done by him." Thus they could not ruin Buckingham without sacrificing credibility. In a political arena demanding guile, deceit and cynicism in ample measure, a distinguished pedigree and an honorable reputation were

---

58   Van Male to La Faille, 23 January 1624, HHStA, Belgien PC, fasz. 60/unfoliated; and Tillières to Puysieux, 17 January 1624, PRO 31/3/58, fo. 15.
59   Chaworth to Trumbull, 16 January 1624, Trumbull Add. MSS, XVII/unfoliated; and Valaresso to the Doge and Senate, 9 January 1624, *CSPV*, XVII, p. 196.
60   Chamberlain to Carleton, 31 January 1624, *Letters*, II, p. 542; and Pelham to Conway, 12 February 1624, SP 14/159/28.
61   Van Male to La Faille; and Sterrell to same, 23 January 1624, HHStA, Belgien PC, fasz. 60/unfoliated.

distinct liabilities. Contemporaries regularly looked to Lennox, Hamilton and Pembroke for a clear lead, and they were regularly disappointed. Abbot had earlier complained that Pembroke "looketh only to his own ends and whatsoever leagues, promises and confederations are made within one hour they come to nothing." Likewise when Hamilton died in February 1624, Ville-aux-clercs found consolation in the thought that France had lost "non beaucoup en effet estant un Esprit assez foible et peu puissant."[62] These were not the men to stand out after Charles "les exorte de quitter touttes haines privées pour le bien publicq et tous autres interests pour le bien qu'il tenoit grandement engage en cette affaire." Hence on 3 February Goring was able to report "the great distemper amongst our greate lords begins to aswadge."[63]

Having reunited the coalition, Charles and the favorite could focus on the Spanish proposals, which the Junta in a second vote rejected as unsatisfactory. The prince's intervention had even more far-reaching consequences; his declaration also effectively terminated *all* discussion of Anglo-Spanish marriage. In fact, immediately after this crisis, it was confidently reported that Charles "never loved hir further then outwardly and the passion he seemed to carry towards hir was but to serve him as a plancke to convey him well out of Spayne." Certainly the Spaniards adopted this interpretation. One of Infanta Isabella's ministers attempted to look on the bright side; thanks to Charles's bluntness, "nous viendrons a espargner une grande somme d'argent".[64]

One question remained unanswered; should the treaties be formally terminated in the Junta or the Parliament? Eventually the Junta settled on the latter venue. The committee's action is much clearer than its reasoning. It has been argued that "in order to prevent parliamentary discussion of the Spanish negotiations, which offered an opportunity for an attack on himself as well as the risk of alienating the king, Buckingham proposed in the junta for foreign affairs that the treaties with Spain be repudiated by the Council before parliament met." This analysis, although accurate, glosses over some important ambiguities. Only two sources record the duke's position, and both are contradictory. On 22 January Rusdorff noted the favorite supported a decision in the Junta, not to forestall a discussion of the Anglo-Spanish negotiation, but rather "pour complaire et gagner le peuple." Yet on

[62] Abbot to Carleton, 12 December 1617, SP 105/95/15v, quoted in Adams, "Spain or the Netherlands," p. 92; Ville-aux-clercs to Tillières, 26 February 1624, BL Add. 30,646, fos. 52–4; and Valaresso to the Doge and Senate, 6 February 1624, *CSPV*,XVIII, p. 216.

[63] Goring to Carleton, 3 February 1624, SP 14/149/9; and Tillières to Puysieux, 1 February 1624, PRO 31/3/58, fo. 21.

[64] Bonham to Trumbull, 22 January 1624, Trumbull Add. MSS, XV/13; and La Faille to Van Male, 5 February 1624, HHStA, Belgien PC, fasz. 60/unfoliated.

31 January Valaresso noted "Buckingham would like to have it made in Parliament." Pembroke, however, resolutely supported Parliament for the task; when the Venetian envoy urged him to put his private animosity behind him, he coolly replied "they must consider internal foes before external ones, and they must punish those who err seriously."[65]

In the confusion Chamberlain's view that "what passed [in the Junta] is not perfectly knowne" initially seems tempting. On the other hand Rusdorff and Valaresso may well have accurately described events on two separate occasions. Although Charles and Buckingham would have been pleased with either outcome, they clearly preferred the Junta over the Parliament.[66] What they longed for above all else was the fastest possible conclusion, and the Junta would have been at least several weeks swifter than Parliament. Thus Rusdorff may not have mistakenly placed the duke in favor of the Junta on the 22nd. As the grandees' defection illustrated, the Junta was far from Buckingham's rubber-stamp. Five councillors were obviously in no hurry to sever Anglo-Spanish ties and would have plumped for leaving the matter to Parliament; perhaps in the interim Padre Maestro would arrive with better offers. Likewise, if Valaresso reported Pembroke's sentiments correctly, there can be no doubt about the grandees' position, which again left Charles and Buckingham without the votes. In order to make the best of the situation, Buckingham and his two creatures came around to the majority, where Valaresso observed them on 31 January.

CONCLUSION

St. Albans had hoped that before the new session Buckingham would have performed "some remarkable thing." In the event, his most remarkable achievement was simply to maintain an anti-Spanish posture. Far from appearing before the new session in a commanding position, Charles and Buckingham limped into it somewhat battered. The "English match" had done little to overcome foreign uneasiness about dealing with what was at best a powerful Court faction. Consequently, Buckingham has been seen without "a foreign policy to present to parliament."[67] Two gentlemen in London at the parliamentary opening who would have disputed this judgment: two Dutch envoys, Aerssens and Joachimi, were in England exclusively at Buckingham's insistence and would play a critical role in the

---

[65] Rusdorff to Frederick, 22 January 1624, *Mémoires*, I, pp. 188–90; Valaresso to the Doge and Senate, 31 January 1624, *CSPV*, XVIII, p. 211; and Adams, "Foreign Policy and the Parliaments," p. 156.

[66] Ruigh, p. 42; and Chamberlain to Carleton, 31 January 1624, *Letters*, II, p. 541.

[67] "Notes for a Conference," *Letters and Life*, VII, p. 445; and Adams, "Foreign Policy and the Parliaments," p. 156.

new session. Indeed, as will be seen, they later saved the coalition from disaster. Therefore while Charles and Buckingham certainly did not have much of a foreign policy to present for parliamentary approval, they did have the bare minimum to inspire them with enough confidence to face Parliament. They would have to be cautious in their discussion of foreign policy and so to accept the greater potential for parliamentary turbulence. Nevertheless, Parliament and Parliament alone could give life to their plans.

A successful session was also the only means of outflanking the unsympathetic Junta. The recent turmoil in the select Council amply confirmed French and Dutch suspicions about the "Patriots'" ability to control events. Admittedly the prince overruled the Junta and effectively terminated the Anglo-Spanish negotiations. This victory, however, cannot obscure his defeat in the Junta over timing. By deferring the decision to Parliament, the Junta left Charles and Buckingham to twist in the wind for several more months. Given James's track-record with previous Parliaments, this resolution was rather like a challenge to a chivalrous knight; provided he performed a near impossible task, in this case working with Parliament, then his request would be granted. Small wonder that Valaresso noted after the crisis in late January "the prince does not perhaps trust the Council entirely."[68] Thanks to the Junta's decision, the new Parliament had become the court of final appeal for Charles and Buckingham.

The situation on the eve of the opening understandably did not fill the "Patriots" with a great deal of confidence. At the moment when it was imperative that James present his most unambiguous visage to MPs, he was half enchanted with Spanish offers; as the duke complained a month later, the king was more willing to spend time with Spanish agents than he was with his own subjects. Furthermore, the public had learned in recent weeks, not of James's firm desire to recover the Palatinate by main force, but rather of the coalition's fragility. Thus Charles and Buckingham entered the Parliament of 1624 with their attention divided; they had to keep one eye on James who might bolt at any moment and another on their confederates who were whispering among themselves in a disconcerting fashion. And to compound the difficulties of reconciling James and the Commons, the Junta's decision had made sure that the critical opening weeks of the session would take place underneath the shadow of Padre Maestro. It was clearly distressing to learn that after having ushered one Catholic cleric, the Bavarian Rota, out of the royal closet, another, this time a Spaniard, was hurrying to take his place. Maestro, Conway grumbled, "brings the hartie affection of a Spaniard to England and the pietie and sinceritie of a ffryer, as mercifull as Chaucer's ffryer, that would only eate the heads and liver but have nothing killed for

[68] Valaresso to the Doge and Senate, 31 January 1624, *CSPV*, XVIII, p. 21.

him." Yet "Chaucer's ffryer" was the imminent danger under which the session would labor. These facts together with the lack of a firm Anglo-Dutch military league made Mr. Secretary occasionally lose his nerve. He confessed his apprehension to Rusdorff; the MPs "fera animé et incité a braver resolutions" if they could have been presented with such a league, but "voyant cette alliance avoir empechement," then "nous avons sujet de craindre que le Parlement ne prenne autre chemin."[69] Nonetheless, this powerless institution was the only means left to Charles and Buckingham to break the deadlock at Court and to start the clocks moving again in the "Patriots' " favor.

[69] Conway to Carleton, 23 February 1624, SP 84/16/154; and Rusdorff to Frederick, 12 February 1624, *Mémoires*, I, pp. 216–20.

Part II

WESTMINSTER, FEBRUARY–MAY 1624

"A wise ordering of our affayres": Parliament and the "Patriots"

If Charles and Buckingham were to succeed, they would have to work harmoniously with Parliament, and few contemporaries had any illusions about the difficulty of this task. Van Male, the Infanta Isabella's representative in London, confidently reported "l'opinion de plusieurs" that the new session "finera par une dissolution sans resolution." On the other hand Elizabeth of Bohemia remained modestly optimistic about the prospects, but her assurance rested on nothing more substantial than the correspondence between the birthday of her dead brother, Prince Henry, and the parliamentary opening.[1] More dispassionate observers sided with Van Male. Tillières seconded Valaresso's view that "a successful issue of Parliament seems doubtful," and the Earl of Kellie felt that "theis whoe hes bein chiefe instruments for the calling of it maye be the same that will first repent it." For his part, Sir George Chaworth concluded that since "there ys much labor to make it of no use to the King and Cuntrie," he could expect "no myracles of itt, the King ys now impatient and most with his Minion." In fact he wagered that the new session would be "of little good use as the too last were."[2] In any sober assessment on the situation on the eve of the 1624 Parliament, these views, not those of Elizabeth, must be judged more realistic.

In this initially unpromising position, the key to the eventual success of Charles and Buckingham was the extension of the "Patriot" coalition from Whitehall to Westminster. The result was the organization of one of the most effective lobbying groups in the history of early modern Parliaments. Under Charles's aegis several prominent Parliament-men joined hands with leading courtiers in an effort to break the Spanish match and to lead James belatedly into the continental fray. The words with which one fictitious country gentleman concluded his *rapprochement* with an equally stereotypic councillor

---

[1] Elizabeth to Roe, [February 1624], TCD MSS 708, I, fos. 262–3; and Van Male to La Faille, 13 February 1624, HHStA, Belgien PC, fasz. 60/unfoliated.

[2] Chaworth to Trumbull, 16 January and [late February] 1624, Trumbull Add. MSS, XVII/unfoliated; Valaresso to the Doge and Senate, 12 January 1624, *CSPV*, xviii, p. 192; and Kellie to Mar, 5 February 1624, *Mar and Kellie*, p. 191.

could easily have done service in similar understandings reached before the 1624 session: "though we be constrained to play an after-game," he noted, "yet by the assistance of God and by the wise ordering of our affayres, we shall quickly make him [James] see as well our injury as his owne errour."[3] The confusion before the Parliamentary opening generally obscured the important steps taken for "the wise ordering of our affayres," but before beginning a close analysis of the session, an assessment is in order of the general mood before the parliamentary opening and of those who agreed on the necessity of "a wise ordering."

PARLIAMENTARY EXPECTATIONS

"A greate expectation there is," Beaulieu reported, "of the actions and successe of this assemblie," and the most popular expectation was the demise of the Anglo-Spanish entente. While some Englishmen argued passionately against the Habsburg marriage for geopolitical reasons, many others could not be distracted from the grim meditation on the match's implications for England and the foreign brethren. Sir Robert Phelips's assessment of James's extended dalliance with Spain succinctly illustrates this anxiety: "we have lost our friends abroad by this treaty, ourselves at home, and almost God which is the greatest loss of all."[4] An overly-excited concern about "the greatest loss of all" was characteristic of Jacobean Englishmen, but by 1624, many thought there were solid grounds for grave concern. Even before the suspension of the anti-Catholic legislation in 1622, the recusants, confident that the Spaniards would protect them, had become more daring; at Easter 1621, Archbishop Abbot could scarcely express his amazement over "what height of pride our Papists did carry themselves." Convinced that "all things had bene loose to their advantage," they held an impromptu convention in Westminster Hall, a few hundred feet from the House of Commons, where they "braved it . . . walking confidently 5 or 6 in front." In subsequent months, the Catholics became even more audacious, and given the recusants' long history of involvement in seditious plots, many found James's tolerance dangerously foolhardy. Before the 1624 session, Sir Ferdinando Gorges reminded Buckingham that "within these fewe yeares" the Catholics "are growne to that hedd in every quarter that they are not onely become insolent and unsufferable to particulars, but most dangerous to the publique peace of this Realme."[5]

[3] "A Discourse . . . betweene a Counsellor of State and a Country Gentleman," Somerset RO, DD/Ph 227/16.
[4] Beaulieu to Trumbull, 13 February 1624, Trumbull MSS, VII/148; and 1 March 1624, Nicholas Diary, SP 14/166/33.
[5] Abbot to Trumbull, 22 July 1622, Trumbull MSS, I/42; and Gorges to Buckingham, 8 February 1624, SP 14/159/22.

Reports from around the realm suggested that Gorges was not exaggerating. In London, a recusant attorney vowed that Henry VIII "did pisse the Protestant relligion out of his cod-piece"; in Lincolnshire, a Catholic predicted that the breach of the Spanish match "would cause a tumult"; in Northamptonshire, another concluded a contemptuous appraisal of Frederick, Elizabeth and Maurice of Orange with the hope that the Infanta Isabella would come over "to see fire and faggott amongst us"; and in Yorkshire, a recusant boasted of a planned Catholic uprising in May to be led by men with ribbons in their hats.[6] This last rumor ominously dove-tailed with a report widespread in London of the "Order of the Orange Tawnie Ribband," a secret Catholic society which moved through London taverns "30 or 40 in a company." And since the ribbon-men allegedly originated in Lord Vaux's regiment of English Catholics in the Spanish army, such reports were particularly disturbing.[7]

These rumors generated a fearful apprehension which could be seen in the Gentlemen Pensioners guarding James: in December the watch was doubled, and the men armed with "a paire of French Pistols."[8] Yet the clearest illustration of this anxiety came when the Catholic chapel at the French embassy collapsed on 26 October. So nervous was Tillières about a Protestant riot that he did not summon immediate assistance, and as a result the fatalities numbered almost a hundred. His caution did not prevent a commotion; the crowd, which quickly gathered to taunt the survivors and to exult over the dead, ultimately attacked a half-dead girl in order to finish the job. Such uncharitable behavior prompted the preachers of the metropolis to rebuke their congregations: "our ministers," Beaulieu reported, "will not have us to insult or rejoyce" over the tragedy.[9] Nonetheless, for Tillières discretion was the better part of valor; rather than attempt to remove the corpses, he ordered most of them to be buried on the embassy grounds. As one popular poem reveals, much more than ritual anti-Catholicism was involved in this incident. The poetic attack on "the sons of Antichrist" began predictably enough, but quickly broadened to employ terms which reflected the tensions of 1622–3. The "sons of Antichrist" for example were also "rebellious multitudes" that "Praye for Queene Maryes dayes that sword and fire / May make professors

---

6 Whiteway Diary, BL Egerton 784, fo. 74; Chamberlain to Carleton, 21 February 1624, *Letters*, II, p. 545; various examinations in SP 14/159/12, 38 and 39; and Pelham to Conway, 24 February [1624], SP 14/159/80.

7 Beaulieu to Trumbull, 18 November and 19 December 1623, Trumbull MSS, VII/136 and 140; Chamberlain to Carleton, 6 December 1623, *Letters*, II, p. 530; and anonymous newsletter, [December 1624], Trumbull Add. MSS, XV/149a.

8 Anonymous newsletter, [December 1623], Trumbull Add. MSS, XV/149a.

9 Beaulieu to Trumbull and Castle to same, 31 October 1623, Trumbull MSS, VII/134 and XVIII/105; Valaresso to the Doge and Senate, 31 October 1623, *CSPV*, XVIII, p. 147. See also *The Fatal Vespers* (London, 1623) and *A Dolefull Evensong* (London, 1623).

feele of your ire." Nor was the poet shy about pointing out the real culprit as "proud Spaine, great Brittaines enemy" whose punishment "doth wait, though yet delayde."[10]

Many Englishmen looked to Parliament to administer the long-awaited retribution, not the Crown which had become too involved with Spain to assess matters rationally. Earlier in 1621, the time for the counter-blow to Rome and Spain had apparently arrived. Thus, although

> This faire Island abound in all Crimes
> The Parliament say wee shall have better times
> . . . yea wee shall be saffe.

Parliamentary correction in fact appeared so imminent that one poet called for "a halter for traitors, a figg for the Pope." Such hopes did not survive the second session, after which the situation at home and abroad steadily deteriorated in the two following years. The hopes deferred in 1621 were naturally revived with the election writs for the 1624 session. Consequently "as all the voices of the land," Thomas Taylor observed, "have made you [the MPs] the eyes of the land, so are all the eyes of the land upon you."[11] Parliament alone could restore the body politic to good health, or as a contemporary reminded Secretary Conway, "blessed shall that bone setter be that shall put those partes in their proper places." Thomas Scott for his part reviewed the recent Catholic triumphs and then exhorted the new MPs to do their duty: "we pray the God of everlasting happiness so to direct and prosper all your projects and consultations, that they might extend to the glory of God . . . and the confusion of Antichrist with all his adherents."[12] Parliament in short was widely seen as the only institution capable of breaking the Spanish hold on James and England.

Vehement opposition to Catholics and hispanophiles logically dominated the popular mood. In the elections, "the Countries," Beaulieu observed, "have been very daintie . . . and the Courtiers have much adoe to gett into those places." Electoral fastidiousness moreover was directly related to the recent Catholic revival. In both Kent and Norfolk, candidates were cried down as papists, and in Canterbury another denounced for having a Pope "in his belly."[13] A prospective MP for Ludlow had to fight clear of rumors that he was "inclinable to Popery"; a friend even wrote assuring the Corporation that the candidate "is as sincere and devoted to the Church of England and

---

[10] Tillières to Puysieux, 28 October 1623, PRO 31/3/57, fos. 260–260v; and "On Those who were Killed at their Idolatrous Serivice," Folger Library, V.a.345, pp. 117–18.

[11] "God Marry a Good Scott," Folger Library, X.d.232, fos. 1–1v; Thomas Taylor, *Two Sermons* (London, 1624), p. 2.

[12] Trussell to Conway, 3 January 1624, SP 14/158/6; and [Thomas Scott], *Boarneges*, p. 33.

[13] Beaulieu to Trumbull, 6 February 1624, Trumbull MSS, VII/147; and Derek Hirst, *The Representative of the People?* (Cambridge, 1975), pp. 145–7.

the common weal hereof as any man I know." In Cheshire the Sheriff boldly linked the Catholic menace with the Spanish match in his address to the electors. Sir Richard Grosvenor announced that James's concerted efforts "to procure peace in forraine parts" through accommodation with Spain had only squandered England's military reputation and religious unity. To illustrate the danger of this royal policy he recalled

that an Angell, a Prophett came and told the Israelites . . . that because god had commanded them to make noe Covenant with the Canaanites those wicked Idolators, but to destroy them, and they had not obeyed; Therefore sayth god I will not cast them out before you, but they shall bee as thornes in your sides; and their gods shall bee a snare and destruction unto you.

The transparent application of this text Grosvenor politely left to his audience.[14] So prevalent was this concern that the government sought to relieve it by banishing the Catholic clergy from Ireland. But far from blunting the drive for stronger anti-Catholic measures, James's action only encouraged it and was widely regarded as earnest money towards a more comprehensive solution of the Catholic question. Before any other business in the new session, General Vere assured Elizabeth, "we will first begine with the setting religione into his Joynts that hath beyne put oute of Joynte by this Spanishe treaty."[15]

In the meantime, the shadow of the new Parliament permitted Londoners to express their true feelings for Spain and Catholicism. The guards protecting the Spanish embassy could do little against public mockery; Inijosa, for example, complained that "an apparent Gentleman in a grey suite did with Actions of his hand and Jackanape tricks with his face seem to scorne him much." In the circumstances the envoys could only prepare for rough weather. Once Parliament opened, they forbade that without express order "le moindre serveteur sorte de la porte"; with good reason they feared "quelque tumulte . . . du Common peuples qui est plein de rage and de furie."[16] Other likely targets of parliamentary scrutiny and possibly popular attack also laid low. When "the puritans . . . triumph much," William Sterrell, a recusant, prayed "all chatholicks to be verie scilent and moderate," and so they wisely were. Likewise Giles Mompesson found the thought of a late winter vacation in Brussels irresistible; since the 1621 session had stripped

[14] G. Holland to the Ludlow Corporation, 27 January 1624, quoted in *Transactions of the Shropshire Archaeological and Natural History Society*, 2nd series, VII (1895), p. 22; and Grosvenor's address to the electors in 1624, Eaton Hall, Grosvenor MSS, item 25. See also R. P. Cust and P. G. Lake, "Sir Richard Grosvenor and the Rhetoric of Magistracy," *BIHR*, LIV (1981), pp. 40–53.
[15] Cecil to [Carleton], 21 February [1624], SP 84/116/147; and Beaulieu to Trumbull, 13 February 1624, Trumbull MSS, VII/148.
[16] Conway and Calvert to Kellie, 3 March 1624, SP 14/160/17; and Van Male to La Faille, 5 March 1624, HHStA, Belgien PC, fasz. 60/unfoliated.

him of a knighthood and a controversial patent, both of which he had resumed, he was understandably reluctant to remain in the same country with a new Parliament.[17]

As popular excitement mounted, the government became increasingly paralyzed. It became very difficult, and, in the first two months of the session, impossible for either the Council or the Secretariat to conduct non-parliamentary business. During the first quarter of the new year, the Privy Council handled only routine matters, and as the councillors made clear in a belated letter to the Lord Deputy in Dublin, the reason for this metamorphosis was Parliament; they informed Falkland that "the sitting of Parliament and therein the great affaires now on foote . . . hath soe taken upp most of our tyme as that little or none hath beene left us to assemble in councell and to give answere to your letters soe often as otherwise we would have done." The pressure on leading Councillors was especially acute. Conway ended the session with "more business in his hands than knowledge which waye to turne himself," and he half-jokingly offered to sell his vexatious office to Carleton in April for a knock-down price. Buckingham with characteristic melodrama did more than complain of the toils of office: "the heate of all the business" brought on a nervous breakdown which incapacitated him in the session's final month.[18]

Governmental paralysis before and during a Parliament was a common phenomenon in the 1620s; it is also one historians have largely overlooked. Given the magnitude of the issues before Parliament, any prior decision by either the Council or the Secretariat might well be imprudent. Dudley Carleton learned this lesson after waiting several weeks for a decision: "I do finde to my griefe that whosoever come hither to follow any business at Courte in time of a Parlement had better save his labour and stay at home, for every body is so full of Parlement matters, that there cannot so much as an audience be gotten for anything else." Consequently a major patronage plum like the Provostship of Eton College remained vacant "untill the Parlement businesses (which now take up king and Duke and all time little enough for the publique) be a little better settled and a season of leasure come in to dispatch matters of a more private nature." Unfortunately it was to be years before "a season of leasure" ever arrived. Parliament eventually produced a host of matters to which the government had to attend; Middlesex's impeachment left his Court offices available for redistribution, and a single bill

---

[17] Sterrell to La Faille, 8 January and 12 February 1624, HHStA, Belgien PC, fasz. 60/ unfoliated; Chamberlain, 12 July 1623, *Letters*, II, p. 506; and Woolley to Trumbull, 15 February 1624, Trumbull MSS, XLVIII/110.

[18] Council to Falkland, 12 May 1624, APC, XXIX, p. 213; Carleton the younger to [Carleton], 21 May 1624, SP 14/165/12; and Sterrell to La Faille, 3 June 1624, HHStA, Belgien PC, fasz. 60/unfoliated.

created fifty-two new positions for officers to command the 6,000-man expeditionary force. With good reason "many hang allready upon my Lord of Buckingham like burres." In the circumstances, Archbishop Abbott's advice to Trumbull was inspired: all suits should be delayed in light of "this present conjunction and crisis of things, namely of the Marriage, where of this Assemblie of the Parlement is like to cleere the issue."[19]

The government's riveted attention on Parliament was not singular; a large continental audience also watched intently. "Tout demeure en suspens," the English agent in Mainz maintained, "et ha le ieux fiches sur le Parlement de la grande Bretagne," of which God himself would be "par son sainct esprit le president et Directeur." With the collapse of Frederick's last army in 1623, German patriots could only pray that in the eleventh hour James would begin "a prendre aultre chemin."[20] German attention to an English Parliament paled before the Dutch excitement. "All our discourses [in the Hague] being of what passeth in Parlement," Carleton wrote to Chamberlain, "and the speeches there are scarce owt of men mowthes when they are here in Duch." As the session came to fulfill the wildest Dutch expectations, their exultations were unbounded. One Englishman in a Dutch regiment wrote to Lord Zouche that

to dilate unto youre Lordeshipe, the unspeakable ioy that these inhabitants doe conceive; as well the Gentry as the communalltie; in that itt semeth by letters from those parts that his Maiestie is somwhat inclined to favour their Cause and hath founde out the iniurious and infidelious dealinge of the Kinge of Spaine, it is in my pen not to express.

Dutch interest in parliamentary news eventually led the Estates General to initiate a weekly packet between Brill and Gravesend, and to the English amazement, to assume the cost themselves. As Carleton explained, the Dutch were normally "Flagmaticke enough," but when decisions crucial to their welfare were being taken on the other side of the North Sea, even their composure could not stand the inherent delays in merchants' schedules. In the United Provinces and Germany, "all the expectatione that is left is turned towards England."[21]

Equally interested were Louis XIII and his ministers. The major addresses and even some of the debates were forwarded to Paris, and Louis's own comments reveal that he followed the "great business" with considerable attention. On learning of one parliamentary offer of supply, the French king

[19] Carleton the younger to Carleton, 10 and 28 March and 14 April 1624, SP 14/160/58, 14/161/49, and 14/162/60; and Beaulieu to Trumbull, 13 February 1624, Trumbull MSS, VII/148.
[20] [Bachoffen] to Carleton, 10 March 1624, SP 81/30/73.
[21] Carleton to Chamberlain, 8 March 1624, SP 84/116/204; Fowkes to Zouche, 30 March 1624, SP 84/117/270; and Carleton to Conway, 7 April 1624, SP 84/117/12.

announced that "il a este bien aise d'avoir apris la continuation des resolutions fortes du Parlement."[22] James's evasive reply to this offer, however, threw Louis into a panic. He rebuked Tillières for lax intelligence-gathering and even dispatched a secret agent to London with instructions to submit a full report on "qui est puissant dans le Parlement," and on "ce qu'il faudroit faire pour gagner les plus puissans." He awaited the news of the successful conclusion of the subsidy debates "avec impatience," and the results made him "tres content." His formal congratulations were promptly sent to James who "a d'estre honnoré de ses subiects" with "preuves signalees de leur affection."[23]

The most avid parliament-watchers, however, were the great mercenary captains: Duke Christian of Brunswick, the Thurn *père et fils*, Duke Bernard and Duke Ernest of Saxe-Weimar and Count Ernest von Mansfelt. When a frustrated Louis XIII suspended all payments to his German captains late in 1623, the market for mercenaries entered a sharp depression. Mansfelt subsequently disbanded his army in Emden and withdrew to The Hague where Brunswick and he squabbled over their arrears with the French ambassador. Brunswick's embarrassment increased when his mother publicly begged him to abandon knight errantry and return home.[24] This ignominious existence in Holland drove Mansfelt to plan a final appeal to Louis before retiring to Venice. The news of the English Parliament, however, quickly altered these arrangements: Carleton alerted Conway to the fact that Mansfelt and Brunswick "will long to crosse the seas into England." Letters from these *condottieri* offering James their services left no doubt that business rather than pleasure lured them to London. Since neither James nor his son had any wish to complicate the delicate parliamentary negotiations with the presence of several mercenaries, Carleton spent much of his time dissuading prospective tourists.[25] The ambassador, as will be seen, was only temporarily successful.

These illustrations suggest something of the obsessive attention that some foreigners devoted to the 1624 session. The most remarkable example, however, came two years later in a camp near Hamburg where Christian IV anxiously waited for Parliament to vote a subsidy for his army. Hitherto the

---

[22] Mémoire de ce qui s'est passe; and Ville-aux-clercs to Tillières, 19 March 1624, BL Add. 30,646, fos. 66v–70v and 109v.

[23] Ville-aux-clercs to Tillières, 1 and 6 April 1624; and Autre mémoire baille . . . Seton [late March 1624], BL Add. 30,646, fos. 115, 124–7 and 129.

[24] Carleton to Calvert, 14 January 1624, SP 84/116/56; Conway the younger to Conway, 14 February 1624, SP 84/116/123; and Dowager Duchess of Brunswick to Christian of Brunswick, 12 March 1624, SP 81/30/75.

[25] Carleton to Calvert, 14 January 1624, SP 84/116/56; Valaresso to the Doge and Senate, 26 February 1624, *CSPV*, XVIII, p. 233; and Christian of Brunswick to James, 6 January 1624, SP 81/30/5.

Danish king had confined the advice he offered his young nephew to general strategy, but as it became increasingly apparent that the session was heading for dissolution, Christian plunged into parliamentary tactics. To an astonished English ambassador, he announced he "doeth offt call to mynde when the Parlament of England did most earnestlie maike suite to our laite kinge and maister . . . to enter in to warre against spaine." Yet whilst he "doeth much wounder to see the parlement chainge ther former propositions," he also rebuked his nephew's stiffness. Alternatively he cited the example of his brother-in-law, Charles's father:

This kinge doeth much approve his maiesties speech to the Parlament, I meane our laite kinge of happie memorie, comparinge the callinge of a parlament to the meetinge betwixt man and wyffe, booth in honnour and profit and to prevent all inconveniences that might happen unto them, for preventinge of anie mistaiking and to understand treulie one the other . . .

The speech Christian quoted to his nephew was James's opening address to the 1624 Parliament.[26]

It has been suggested recently that early Stuart Parliaments were in fact comparatively powerless.[27] To be sure, Parliament's erratic existence made its influence equally intermittent. But when a Scandinavian monarch quoted a parliamentary address two years after the fact, much less when a French king impatiently awaited parliamentary news, it seems obvious that parliamentary influence could mushroom quite spectacularly once MPs began to fill the Chapel of St. Stephen.

A COALITION ANATOMIZED

Under interrogation in 1621, the Earl of Southampton did not deny that MPs "ordinarilye and familiarilye" met with him to "receive directions from him, what to doe in theyr house." In his defense, Southampton argued that he had done no more than "every one else did."[28] In 1624, when Buckingham did as "every one else did," he met a remarkable group of MPs "ordinarilye and familiarlye." In the excitement before the opening, a second series of *rapprochements* united Charles and the duke with prominent contemporaries. In these weeks, that loose network of persons which hispanophobia and the reversionary interest bound together expanded to include MPs.

---

[26] Anstruther to Conway, 22 July 1626, SP 75/8/176v; and Carleton to Christian V, 1 March and 1 April 1624, abstracted in *46th Report of the Deputy Keeper of the Public Record Office*, Appendix II, p. 48.

[27] Russell, "Parliamentary History," pp. 1–3.

[28] "The Earle of Southampton's Examination," Inner Temple Library, Petyt MSS, 538, vol. 19, fos. 1–1v.

Consequently the "Patriots" were able to field a formidable phalanx in the Commons.

Prior tactical coordination was not novel to early modern Parliament-men. This fact plainly emerges in the embarrassed responses to the accusation that the attack on the favorite in 1628 had been planned. Although several members denied knowledge of a "confederacy," they defended the idea in principle; as Sir Edward Coke insisted, "I have had no conferences, yet we may do it." William Strode opposed introducing a "new oath . . . amongst us to forbid us to confer," and added "I know private conference is not only fit but necessary to the service of the House and has advanced much the business of it." Equally emphatic was Sir Thomas Wentworth: "God forbid but we may speak with one another out of this House concerning those things which concern this House." After all, "a man may light his candle at another man's fire." Edward Alford characteristically had no time for coyness. His question, "may we not confer one with another beforehand?", prefaced the confession that he had done as much. In self-defence he noted "it is not my fashion to speak suddenly to anything. I am old." Besides "in ancient times 14 of us or more usually went privately and had conferences what was fit to be moved." Indeed, so important was this practice that Alford maintained "if you will now single us, you will take away Parliaments."[29] These frank comments illustrate that the mere existence of prior coordination was not unique in 1624. Since there was in 1624 a good deal of candle-lighting "at other men's fire," the "ancient times" to which Alford referred were not too distant. But what was unique in 1624 was the size of the "confederacy" and the range of its members.

It has been argued recently that Charles's eagerness to work with Parliament in the 1620s was due to his inherent fondness for the institution, not simply for its financial grants. Unquestionably Charles preferred the traditional way. Yet it was not his inherent fondness for Coke, Sandys, Phelips and Digges that led him to work in 1624 with men he had earlier dubbed "such seditious fellows."[30] It seems instead that he reversed his opinion later because he had to; without them, he could scarcely hope to persuade the House to accept a decidedly peculiar agenda. Substantial "inside" assistance was imperative, because Charles and the duke faced a complex tactical problem akin to squaring the circle. Their fundamental goal was for James and Parliament to agree on a war. But before any parliamentary final agreement, James insisted on the organization of a broad foreign

---

[29] 3 June, *Commons Debates 1628*, IV, pp. 65–6, 70, 73 and 75.
[30] Charles to Buckingham, 3 [30] November 1621, Bodleian Library, Tanner 73/68. I am grateful to Christopher Thompson and Richard Cust for many discussions of this valuable document.

coalition to support the war. Parliament on the other hand was not likely to share his taste for certain alliances, particularly with Catholic states. To complete the conundrum, the allies James had in mind declined to discuss an English alliance until Parliament broke off the Spanish match and voted an ample supply. Finally, any solution to the puzzle was certain to meet with the vigorous, if less than subtle, opposition of Inijosa and Coloma. This near impossible task makes quite clear why, when Buckingham collapsed in April, contemporaries were prepared to believe that he had gone mad.

Charles and Buckingham had sought to avoid this mediatory nightmare. They had petitioned James to be more reasonable – without success; and they had hastily attempted to organize an agreement, however tentative and informal, with potential allies. The Dutch had responded very reluctantly, while the French refused even to discuss an alliance until after the Parliament. Tillières repeatedly coached his superiors in Paris on the importance of the English Parliament. James, when in financial straits, "ne peut se recouvrer que par cette voye," and the current session could easily end "en mauvaise intelligence entre le Roy et ses subiects." Therefore, for the "patriots" as well as Louis XIII, "il est necessaire de voire ce que produira ce parlement."[31] Charles and Buckingham therefore had an exceedingly awkward brief which constrained them to request an unprecedented sum of money for something they did not wish to discuss in public. James was to accord the Commons broad freedom of speech in foreign affairs, but whenever MPs descended to particulars, supporters of the prince's war policy quickly rose to cut off debates: as Secretary Conway maintained, "it is not for us to dispute where the King would make the war."[32] The steadfast defense of a limited royal prerogative was essential because any discussion of strategy would have opened a veritable Pandora's box. The debate in the royal closet over the war was complicated enough with the legalism of the king, the chivalry of the prince and the requirements of potential allies. Additional advice from the Commons only muddied the water further and made James even more anxious to read the new terms Padre Maestro was carrying to London. Similarly, James's refusal to enter a war without foreign Catholic allies would not have sat well with many MPs' notion of England's power. Clearly the war was a topic that would be best avoided altogether.

In the circumstances the subsidy bill and the campaign for a Spanish war would almost certainly have failed if the "Patriots" had not plunged into parliamentary politics. The resulting war coalition may well have been ephemeral; as Russell has suggested the union of Buckingham and Edward

---

[31] Tillières to Puysieux, 9 and 18 January 1624, PRO 31/3/58, fos. 2 and 9. See also above, pp. 114–27.
[32] 19 March 1624, Holles Diary, fo. 105.

Coke was like the brief encounter of ships passing in the night.[33] Nevertheless, the 1624 session makes little sense without an analysis of the surprisingly rich information on the parliamentary coalition. In an appropriate martial metaphor, the coalition consisted of three detachments each covering the other, and the most important of these was the prince himself. His mere presence in the ranks of the coalition protected it from his father. Without his support, the maneuvering room of Buckingham, not to mention the MPs, would have been sharply restricted. But under his aegis, they could publicly dare to press for a policy which did not have royal favor. Charles was an invaluable asset inside as well as outside the Parliament House. The regular physical presence of a peer who was not above drawing attention to his future eminence and to his memory certainly aided the MPs' concentration wonderfully. Only a desperate man could have ignored Charles's statement to both Houses on 11 March: "when time shall serve hereafter, you shall not think your labors ill bestowed." His assiduous attendance constantly put Parliament in mind of his interests. "His Highness," Woolley reported, "assisteth dayly in person, taketh infinitt paines and by reporte, speaketh as well and as bravely as ever man did, continuing most constant and desirous to have the resolution thought on by the said Parlement."[34] Charles also earned affection as much as he commanded it. In a session when at least four MPs voiced fears of Parliament's continued existence, the prince's devotion to representative institution was reassuring. Moreover, his mediation between Parliament and his irritable father defused several crises and earned additional popular praise. It was Charles who offered more favorable constructions on James's messages and who delayed the prorogation for a week. The prince thus occupied a commanding position which allowed other elements of the coalition to function.

Charles's cloak was worthless unless he had people to protect, and in this respect Charles and Buckingham had their greatest success. An uninformed observer might easily have presumed that the pressure for war came, not from the government, but rather from those who had been, in Castle's memorable phrase, "our Tribuni plebis in the last Parliament." The "Tribuni plebis" formed the crucial second element of the coalition. "Monye of theis parlament men that did disturbe the last Parlament," Kellie noted early in the session, "are now als mutche for my Lord of Bukkinghame as theye warr then against him."[35] The recruitment of Sir Dudley Digges, Sir Edwin Sandys, Sir

---

[33] Russell, *Parliaments*, p. 202. For the background on early seventeenth-century "undertakings," see Clayton Roberts, *Schemes and Undertakings* (Columbus, Ohio, 1985), pp. 3–30.

[34] Ruigh, p. 208; and Woolley to Trumbull, 6 March 1624, Trumbull MSS, XLVIII/115.

[35] Castle to Trumbull, 25 October 1622, Trumbull MSS, XVIII/86; and Kellie to Mar, 4 March 1624, *Mar and Kellie*, p. 193.

Robert Phelips and especially Sir Edward Coke was a public relations coup of incalculable importance. Buckingham and his known agents, such as Conway, Goring and Harley, could remain in the procedural background and allow prominent "undertakers," as yet untarred with the brush of "dukism," to handle sensitive financial issues. Buckingham's few public speeches therefore became extraordinary occasions, the equivalent of a media event in which the duke would be wheeled out to deliver a carefully prepared address. Unexpected difficulties exposed the value of the scheme. On 5 March, a controversial message from the Lords about the subsidy bill led to heated exchanges in the Commons and ultimately to the rejection of the message.[36] The peer who moved the message and the MP who delivered it had each suffered for their opposition to the king in the 1621 Parliament. It is hard to imagine that the "Patriots" could have escaped as lightly if the personnel involved had been less acceptable to Parliament, if, for example, Buckingham and Goring had replaced Southampton and Sandys.

These "undertakers" of the coalition do much to explain the success of Charles and Buckingham. But the importance of Sandys, Digges, Phelips and Coke extends beyond anything they said in support of the war. Sir Richard Weston, the Chancellor of the Exchequer, remarked in the middle of the session that "there is no such fencing as there hath been in former parliaments." In this respect 1624 was indeed singular, and the credit should not be attributed solely to the House's unanimity on the war; Ruigh and especially Russell have noted that the mood of the Commons was often non-fractious.[37] Rather, the relative quiet of 1624 was due directly to the fact that the old swordsmen of 1614 and 1621 were now drawn up in defense of Charles, Buckingham and the war. It is worth considering how the Commons conducted business. In the early seventeenth century, as in later periods, there seem to have been no more than forty to fifty MPs ready to "speechify," to hold forth at any length, and of this number, only a dozen could be regarded as orators of the first rank. Those MPs hesitant about public speaking can only have been encouraged to hold their peace after witnessing the often brutal displays of the House's intolerance. In 1624 Sir George More, a veteran MP and the head of a prominent Surrey family, was cried down, and Sir George Chaworth ejected from his seat; both had merely dared to voice their opinions. Both discovered that the consensual model of proceeding placed less emphasis on independence of thought and more on speaking after the current "sense of the House." This fact only serves to underscore the importance of the first rank orators who could direct as well as develop the

[36] For a detailed discussion of this incident, see below pp. 184–7.
[37] 12 March 1624, Nicholas Diary, fo. 73; Ruigh, p. 205; and Russell, *Parliaments*, pp. 158–66 and 145–203.

"sense of the House." Indeed one contemporary likened the parliamentary talents of Coke and Phelips to those of "a good director."[38]

The conversion of Phelips, Digges, Sandys and Coke therefore represented a major blow to back-bench "country" sentiment, which in their absence was only fitfully articulated. The Commons were railroaded through the initial debates without serious objections. Finally, on 19 March when the question had become whether three or four or six subsidies would be adequate, Sir John Savile posed the question that the war coalition had sedulously avoided; he wanted "to know first *what* we should do." Sir Francis Seymour rephrased Savile's query: "Howsoever it [supply] be said to be necessary, yet to consider to what end we give it and it is fit that should be known . . . War is spoken of and an army but where and against whome is fit to be known." A body of Crown officials, courtiers, and pro-war MPs, all fair speakers, echoed Thomas Wentworth's response: "the particular of what is to be done is not here to be handled."[39] But the most persuasive responses to Savile's question came from Phelips and Coke. The "old duces gregis" of the back-benchers had abandoned their traditional charge for the war coalition. The defection of these men was critical to the course of the 1624 session; in fact the Earl of Clare in the following year was even willing to forego a second session of the same Parliament since "their orators beeing becum servers of turns and the instruments of great men."[40]

The third division of the coalition was the mass of major and minor Crown officials, those in the duke's inner circle and those who aspired to be there. While their rhetorical ability ranged from passable to respectable, the best among them could not hope to best an "oracle" of the House, such as Sir Edward Coke, because their Court connection undercut the force of their oratory. Sir Henry Mildmay, the Master of the Jewel House, met this problem head-on when he assured the House that "this he speaks not as a courtier or in regard of his dependency but as a lover of his country."[41] Most of his colleagues at Court adopted a less forthright approach and simply avoided drawing attention to the matter. Yet even with this limitation, the officials remained useful especially if deployed *en masse*: they could second and in general swell the progress toward a resolution.

With the "duces gregis," the courtiers and officials formed a tactical relationship which can best be described as symbiotic. Phelips, Sandys and

---

[38] Owen Wynn to Sir Thomas Wynn, 17 February 1624, NLW, Wynn of Gwydir MSS, 9061E/1391; and Russell, *Parliaments*, pp. 5–26. I am grateful to Richard Cust for the loan of a microfilm of the Wynn Papers.

[39] 19 March 1624, Gurney Diary, fos. 128 and 133; Holles Diary, fo. 104.

[40] Chamberlain to Carleton, 20 March 1624, *Letters*, II, p. 549; and Clare to Somerset, 2 March 1624, *Holles Letters*, II, p. 298.

[41] Valaresso to the Doge and Senate, 12 January 1624, *CSPV*, XVIII, p. 192; and 20 March 1624, Spring Diary, fo. 143.

Coke walked a fine line between the "political" Court and Country; excessively close identification with one naturally raised the suspicion and distrust of the other. Thus the corps of officials and courtiers was useful in relieving some of the pressure on the "Tribuni plebis." Conversely the officials and courtiers would have been emboldened to speak on sensitive issues by the knowledge that they were roughly of like mind with the "duces." Heath, Eliot, Edmondes, Harley and May undoubtedly must have risen to speak with a more cheerful heart knowing that at worst they would only have to face Savile, Seymour and Alford, and that at a pinch they could look to Coke for support. The aura of a box-office star often dwarfs supporting actors. But the officials and courtiers in 1624 proved the value of a well-trained troupe of supporting actors on a very crowded stage.

It should be noted that willful ignorance is not responsible for the treatment of the royal officials and courtiers as a collective unit. Recent scholars have emphasized that the Court, far from being a political monolith, was invariably divided within itself. These divisions in turn make nonsense of any attempt to see contemporary politics in terms of Court versus Country; more often than not the two were interdependent rather than antithetical. Needless to say, notions of "the government" and "the opposition" are hopelessly anachronistic when applied to early modern Parliaments.[42] Invaluable though these historiographical corrections have been, particularly with controversial figures such as Eliot and Phelips, the fact remains that the absence of an organized Country opposition does not necessarily negate the possible existence of a Court grouping. In 1624, although the Court was sharply divided into antagonistic factions, these divisions appear to have made little real difference to the parliamentary positions of leading officials and courtiers. To select two extreme examples, Calvert shared with Arundel a pronounced sympathy towards Spain and, for a time in 1622, a house; but in the Chapel of St. Stephen he provided timely assistance in the drive against Spain. Similarly, the Chancellor of the Exchequer, Sir Richard Weston, was a protégé of another hispanophile, Lord Treasurer Middlesex, and yet he too supported the "Patriots" in the Commons. The only courtier to break ranks was Sir George Chaworth, and his defection cost him so dearly that he later confessed "it was madness in me" to have done so.[43] Other officials and courtiers were either "hotter" Protestants with pronounced continental sympathies or ambitious men eager for advancement, and they toed the "Patriot" line with few of the reservations which doubtless troubled

[42] Russell, *Parliaments*, Pp. 5–26.
[43] Castle to Trumbull, 16 August 1622, Trumbull MSS, XVIII/80; Chaworth to same, 8 April 1624, Trumbull Add. MSS, XVII/unfoliated; and M. V. Alexander, *Charles I's Lord Treasurer* (London, 1975), pp. 5–7, 17 and 33. For the parliamentary speeches of these three, see below pp. 203, 209 and 213.

Weston and Calvert. The result was a remarkable parliamentary unanimity among the leading royal servants.

Given their importance the members of the Court phalanx deserve a brief introduction. Of the six Privy Councillors, Sir John Suckling, the Comptroller of the Household, was even less conspicuous than Weston and Calvert in the major debates. His silence may have been linked to his concerns about war's economic repercussions, which appear in internal government memoranda. In Parliament, however, he kept these reservations to himself.[44] More enthusiastic support came from Secretary Conway, his predecessor, Sir Robert Naunton, and the Treasurer of the Household, Sir Thomas Edmondes. Legal officials such as the Solicitor General, Sir Robert Heath, and the prince's solicitor, Sir John Walter, lent their vocal support as did two other aspiring Councillors, Sir Henry Mildmay, the Master of the Jewel House, and Sir Humphrey May, the Chancellor of the Duchy of Lancaster. Rounding out the Court group were lesser officers notable for their devotion to the duke and their own careers; Sir Miles Fleetwood, Sir John Coke, Sir John Eliot and Sir William Beecher. Lastly several courtiers, Sir Robert Harley, Sir Robert Killigrew, Sir Thomas Jermyn, John Maynard and Sir George Goring, were to prove quite helpful in the subsidy debates.[45] This is not to say that all royal officials moved in lock step; as will be seen, considerable opposition to the "Patriots" came from some lesser officials. But the men who were prominent in the government and close to the favorite clearly worked together, and constituted a distinct group that Christopher Thompson has dubbed the "political" Court.[46] The irony of the charge about prior coordination in 1628 was that it came from Beecher; in 1624 Beecher and his colleagues gave ample evidence of their own talent for prior coordination.

These brief descriptions beg questions about motivation. Open support for the war plunged officials directly into the intense Court struggle and might well incur their employer's anger. For the "undertakers," Court ties were a liability as much as an asset and could easily damage their standing in the country and in the Commons. Why did they become involved? The most obvious answer, self-aggrandizement, has some validity: active parliamentary service was an excellent way to score points with influential people.

---

[44] Suckling to Buckingham, 12 February 1625, SP 14/183/49.

[45] For further details on these men, see Schreiber, *Naunton* (Philadelphia, 1981); Michael Young, *Servility and Service: The Life and Works of Sir John Coke* (London, 1986); Jacqueline Levy, "Perceptions and Beliefs: The Harleys of Brampton Bryan" (Ph.D thesis, University of London, 1983); J. N. Ball, "The Parliamentary Career of Sir John Eliot" (Ph.D thesis, University of Cambridge, 1953); and *DNB* under Edmondes, Heath, Walter, Mildmay, May, Fleetwood, Beecher, Killigrew, Jermyn, Maynard and Goring.

[46] Christopher Thompson, "The Divided Leadership of the House of Commons in 1629," *Faction and Parliament*, p. 277.

Almost non-existent, however, is direct evidence of later political pay-offs; the most illuminating piece is the persistent rumor in 1624–5 that Phelips would become a Master of Requests, if not Carleton's replacement in The Hague.[47] Whether Buckingham dangled these posts before him is unclear, but Phelips was doubtless aware that a successful stint in Parliament could lead to an exhilarating leap to the head of the duke's patronage queue. Harley who hailed Phelips for "your further power in England" clearly recognized this phenomenon. So too did Sir Peter Manwood who commented at the end of the session that "it is sayd of the Parliament men of accompt that they have done there indeavours to be of the courte. Lord Coke hath gon his old way" with rather than against the Crown.[48] Certainly Eliot and Coke operated on similar assumptions, for they were later disgruntled that Charles and Buckingham did not fully appreciate the value of their 1624 performance. Devoted parliamentary service could also stabilize a deteriorating career. Sir Richard Weston, for example, managed to scramble out from under the collapse of his patron, Middlesex, in part through his parliamentary labors.

To assign the main explanatory burden to cynical careerism, however, would be to miss the reason for the extraordinary appeal of the coalition. People who worked with Charles and Buckingham did not feel that they were being "bought"; they were not laboring to foist by chicanery and guile something like the Union or the Great Contract on an apprehensive populace. Rather they assisted in achieving a popular goal – avenging Elizabeth and Frederick through a Spanish war. The problem this time was foisting the goal on the king, not the people. In this delicate task, Parliament played a major role, but given James's sensibilities and Spanish practice, it had to perform it discreetly. Thus the coalition's main task was the restraint of the MPs' best impulses. Events would rapidly lead to an open breach with Spain, if the Commons played their part and if they did not, as they had in late 1621, become overly enthusiastic. Publicly, the direction of foreign policy and the planned war had to remain veiled from Parliament, but privately the talk within the coalition was of a diversionary war, a "blue water" policy. Indeed, this strategy was probably one of the coalition's main cohesive bonds. The other was the Protestant credentials of the "Patriots." Tillières repeatedly petitioned anyone who would listen to resist the popular pressure to crackdown on Catholics; his least receptive audience was Charles and Buckingham who, he grumbled, "semblent se jetter a corps perdu entre les bras des puritans." The contemporary biographer of Dr. Preston, the Puritan divine,

---

[47] Carleton the younger to Carleton, 26 June 1624, SP 14/168/47; Woolley to Trumbull, 23 April 1625, Trumbull MSS, XLVIII/169; and Phelips to [Buckingham], [1624–5], Somerset RO, DD/Ph 216/18.

[48] Harley to Phelips, 23 March 1624, Somerset RO, DD/Ph 216/33; and Manwood to Trumbull, 6 June 1624, Trumbull Add. MSS, XVII/unfoliated.

confirmed the ambassador's assessment; Charles and the duke were "cryed up by all the Godly party in the kingdome . . . All things now are fairely carried for Religion, as represented by the Duke of Buckingham, the Prince's and the people's favorite."[49] Finally the coalition bore Elizabeth's banner. Early in the session, Sir Thomas Crewe, the Speaker of the House of Commons, privately told Sir Francis Nethersole, Elizabeth's secretary, of his desire to assist Elizabeth. In reply she thanked him for his "respect and affection" and told him to follow the lead of her brother.[50] The coalition therefore implicitly subsumed the Palatine interests as well as seconded the Protestant cause.

To a cynic, the most noble goal might seem inevitably tarnished by association with Buckingham. But the company that the duke kept in the first half of 1624 dispelled any lingering sense of sordidness that the scrupulous might have felt over intimate liaison with the favorite. The prince and the Archbishop Abbot flanked him on either side, "popular" lords like Southampton and Warwick pressed close about him, with Essex, Oxford, Saye and Sele, Hamilton and Pembroke near at hand, and over all the group hovered the presence of Elizabeth and Frederick. Working with Charles and Buckingham therefore was an ideal political arrangement; the advancement of the public good and one's own career went hand in hand.

PEMBROKE AND THE TRIBUNES

Two fundamental questions arise about the validity of this sketch, the first of which is simply the inclusion of the Earl of Pembroke and his client, Sir Benjamin Rudyerd. Rudyerd was to figure prominently in the grand debates of 1624, and indeed his suggestion eventually formed the basis of the subsidy bill. Rudyerd was closely bound to Pembroke; in 1621, for example, the earl referred a correspondent to an accompanying letter from Rudyerd for the particulars of recent political developments.[51] And yet Pembroke early in 1624 had been involved in the Junta's attack on Buckingham. These details have led Simon Adams to speculate that "in 1624 the Duke of Buckingham did not make an alliance with a parliamentary war party, but rather that the inspiration for the proposals actually carried in parliament probably emanated from the Earl of Pembroke." Unfortunately this tantalizing theory must ultimately be counted as unpersuasive. Adams disputes Russell's

---

[49] Tillières to Ville-aux-clercs, 30 April 1624, PRO 31/3/58, fo. 83; and Thomas Ball, *The Life of Renowned Doctor Preston* (Oxford, 1885), p. 105.

[50] Nethersole to Carleton, 20 March 1624, SP 81/30/88; and Carleton to [Nethersole], 3 April 1624, SP 84/117/22.

[51] Pembroke to Aston, 10[?] October 1621, BL Add. 36,452, fo. 1. See also above, pp. 103–5 and below, 175, 189–90 and 200.

analysis that Rudyerd was a "government spokesman" when he proposed the Four Propositions on 1 March; rather, Adams asserted, he was acting at Pembroke's behest, not Buckingham's. Sir Robert Phelips, however, warmly seconded the Four Propositions: "He that shall go out of the way Sir Benjamin Rudyerd set down, shall go walk in a maze."[52] It is interesting to note that Phelips was so closely identified with Buckingham that he had difficulty getting re-elected in 1625. A scene in which Buckingham's client supports Pembroke's client would suggest prior coordination rather than an attempt by Pembroke to steal a march on the duke.

Coordination was unlikely in Adams's analysis because Rudyerd's Four Propositions were antithetical to "government policy" and Buckingham's desires: therefore, "it is probable that these proposals came from Pembroke's circle." Given the confusion in the closet throughout 1624, James and Charles would probably have been surprised to learn of "government policy" on the war. As for Buckingham's own views, Conway's early strategic treatises indicate not surprisingly that the Lord Admiral inclined to a naval war. The Four Propositions therefore could have easily subsumed the duke's desires as well as those of Pembroke. Yet, Adams concluded, Buckingham could not have approved of Rudyerd's motion because on 4–5 March in the Lords, Southampton moved for an "open offer" of supply. Unfortunately the documents do not reveal a sharp polarity between the motions of Rudyerd and Southampton. The fact that Pembroke himself drew up Southampton's motion and seconded a motion to present it to the Commons only further undercuts his case.[53]

The most crippling difficulty with Pembroke's alleged control of Parliament is the complete lack of any contemporary reference to the coup. Negative evidence generally reveals more about contemporary record-keeping than it does about contemporary events. Nonetheless, such a move by Pembroke would have been sensational news. Many Englishmen regarded Pembroke as the aristocratic ideal, and many dreamed that the earl would do what Adams suggested he did in 1624 and wrestle control of the government out of the hands of the godless parvenu. His attempts to do so in January 1624 and in the winter of 1625–6 attracted widespread attention. It is hard to believe that any success that Pembroke had against Buckingham in 1624 would have gone unmentioned. Gardiner concluded an analysis of the earl with the observation that Pembroke was the early seventeenth-century prince of Denmark. Scholars who sought to link Pembroke to Shakespeare's

[52] Adams, "Foreign Policy and Parliaments," pp. 139 and 165; and 1 March 1624, Nicholas Diary, fo. 33.

[53] Adams, "Foreign Policy and Parliaments," pp. 165–6. Set against this, *Notes on the Debates in the House of Lords 1624 and 1626* (London, 1879), p. 20; Ruigh, pp. 192–3; and above, pp. 69–76.

Sonnets ignored a more obvious connection; "if anybody had spoken of him as the original begetter of *Hamlet*, it would have been difficult to prove the negative." Against Adams's Pembroke as the new Leicester, Gardiner's casting seems more appropriate.[54]

Adams, however, has focused scholarly attention on Pembroke, the most prominent courtier after Buckingham, and his role in the 1624 session requires clear definition. With Hamilton and Lennox, he had clashed with Buckingham immediately before the opening. But Charles had reconciled the factions, and circumstantial evidence, such as the coordination of Rudyerd and Phelips, suggests that their reconciliation lasted through the session. Rudyerd's address on 1 March, Ruigh observed "signified to all present that an alliance had been concluded between the parliamentary forces of the Earl of Pembroke, Rudyerd's patron, and those of the Duke of Buckingham." Yet in spite of the outward show of amity, the two patrons moved together in the Lords rather stiffly. In January, Pembroke and the grandees had called off their attack because of the realization that their action would only doom hopes of any English assistance to Elizabeth and allow the Spaniards to repair their faltering position at Court. An assault would also anger Charles, and later in the session, the earl declined to join in Middlesex's desperate plot against Buckingham because "he perceived the Prince to be so much for his Grace." Consequently Pembroke, as Russell observed, "allowed his hostility to Spain to beat his hostility to Buckingham by a short lead."[55] Their uneasy *rapprochement*, however, survived the prorogation; Pembroke sat on the select committee for French affairs where no one outside Buckingham's inner circle ever penetrated. Tension between the two surfaced again in the spring of 1625. Yet until that time, Pembroke and Rudyerd worked with Buckingham for a war to restore Elizabeth and Frederick.

The second question about the coalition concerns the four undertakers so important in the eventual success of the "Patriots." What led them to cooperate with Charles and Buckingham? The best documented of these four is Sir Robert Phelips whose mass of surviving letters provides an extraordinary insight into the actions of a "Parliament man of accompt." At first glance the reason for Phelips's cooperation appears all too obvious; the most striking theme in all his correspondence was Sir Robert's desire for advancement, a desire which at once tormented and emboldened him. When he thought there was a chance that, as he wrote to Buckingham in 1624, "by your means I may be brought into his Maiesties service," he could be as

---

[54] S. R. Gardiner, "The Political Element in Massinger," *New Shakespeare Society Proceedings*, 1st series, I, p. 317; and same, *A History of England* (London, 1884), VIII, p. 133.
[55] Brett to the Countess of Middlesex, Kent Archive Office, Sackville MSS, ON 245, quoted in Ruigh, pp. 314–15, n. 32; Russell, *Parliaments*, p. 148; and Ruigh, p. 178.

uxorious as any courtier and declare himself "your Graces most humbly and truly devoted creature."[56] Yet when the lines to the Court were less open, he could react quite differently; when Tomkins suggested that one of Phelips's two possible responses to the forced loan was to refuse "handsomly" and to set himself up as "a leader of those who shall refuse," he was not proposing a novel mode of political behavior for Phelips. On another occasion he explained that given "the impossibility of my ever getting into the favors and service of the court," pliancy to royal, or ducal, demands was "not to be purchased with the least abatement of a good fame." In such circumstances, he would "glorye to suffer martyrdome for the commonwealth."[57] Therefore 1624 was an occasion when such theatrics were not in order; then he could at last enter "his Maiesties service."

This portrait of an MP endlessly vacillating between servility and opposition, however, does not explain all; and a tract Phelips probably composed late in 1623 underscores this point. "A Discourse by way of a dialogue betweene a Counsellor of State and a Country gentleman who served in the last assembly of the estates in the yeare 1623" is one of the more remarkable documents to come to light in recent years, and any question about the author of this anonymous tract is answered in a note in Phelips's characteristically tortured handwriting. Conrad Russell has made the phrase out to be "El Hombre de Marq[uis] male dicto" and suggested that "El Hombre" was Nathaniel Tomkins.[58] To be sure Tomkins and Phelips were close political associates. Yet it was Phelips, not Tomkins, who prided himself on his Spanish and counted himself as a client of Buckingham both as Marquis and Duke; Phelips insisted in 1621 that the favorite was the man "upon whom . . . I principally relyed." Tomkins on the other hand served first Lord Kensington and then Charles himself.[59] The author becomes more clearly Phelips if the phrase is read to attribute the tract to "El Hombre de bien malo dicto." Confusion about Phelips's handwriting of course is far from a modern phenomenon; one Somersetshire gentleman complained to Sir Robert that "you write so hierogliphically that I know nott how to decypher itt." If this second gloss of Phelips's hierogliphics is correct, then it fits the conventions of the Tomkins–Phelips correspondence which cast Tomkins as "el hombre

[56] Phelips to [Buckingham], [1624–5], Somerset RO, DD/Ph 221/18.

[57] "El hombre fiel" [Tomkins] to Phelips, 27 November 1626, Somerset RO, DD/Ph 219/33; and [Phelips] to anon., [early 1622], DD/Ph 224/88.

[58] "A Discourse," Somerset RO, DD/Ph 227/16; and Russell, *Parliaments*, p. 149. I am grateful to Derek Hirst for the loan of his typescript of "A Discourse."

[59] Phelips to [Goring?], [early 1622], Somerset RO, DD/Ph 224/82. On Tomkins, see H. F. Brown, "El hombre fiel," *Somerset and Dorset Notes and Queries*, XXX (1970), pp. 238–41; and I I. Berry, "The Globe Bewitched and 'el hombre fiel'," *Medieval and Renaissance Drama in England*, I (1984), pp. 211–30.

de fiel" and Phelips as "el hombre de bien."[60] The attribution to Phelips is further reinforced by the existence of another hitherto unnoticed copy of the "Discourse" among some Phelips papers now in the Beinecke Library.[61]

Given that "A Discourse" was probably written by as well as about Phelips, it becomes a compelling piece of evidence about Phelips's motivation. In response to Phelips's Councillor who argued in favor of non-parliamentary taxation, the Country Gentleman clung to the traditional ideal of sovereign and estates united in Parliament "for the apparent advantage of them both, to witt to releeve and supplie the sovereigne, to protect and secure the subiect." He had no objection to Parliament's use in diplomatic negotiations, provided that "in the meane time" James allowed the Commons "to shake off those vexations and oppression, under which . . . they now sensibly groane." The gentleman had several "vexations" in mind. "First that the honour of the kingdome, now restinge upon a sick and doubtfull bedd, may timely be recovered and preserved." He did not insist on an immediate breach with Spain: rather military and naval preparations would quickly recover English honor and the Palatinate either by diplomacy or by force of arms. In addition, English trade, which "is now languishing and even givinge up the ghost," had to be encouraged, and "the increase and growth of a most pestilent and dangerous party" of Catholics checked. Finally his glowing reference to the Elizabethan practice by which she preserved "her people . . . from beinge oppressed by corrupt and haughty ministers" illustrated his enthusiasm for its revival.

Phelips's belief in a reciprocal exchange between king and Parliament reveals the problems inherent in using the term "undertaker" to describe him. The gentleman contemptuously termed the notorious undertakers of 1614 as "practized and corrupt men" whose "hopes of advancement were . . . placed and fixed upon this Parlement." Phelips in 1624 obviously did not see himself as following "their degenerate wayes . . . to governe that Councell [Parliament] and to cause to pass whatsoever fitt or unfitt according to the force of their disordered appetites should be propounded."[62] Instead, he accepted the noble, and daunting, task of leading both Parliament and sovereign back to the ideal of a balanced polity. The dream of wedding Court and Country together clearly dazzled Phelips, and given the actions of Sandys, Digges and Coke, his may not have been a private fantasy. Being a popular man, as any

---

[60] Barkeley to Phelips, [1610s?], Somerset RO, DD/Ph 219/58. For an example of the Spanish pen-names, see "Hombre de fiel" [Tomkins] to "Hombre de bien" [Phelips], SRO, DD/Ph 219/42.

[61] "Short Collection out of a Dialogue," Beinecke Library, Osborn 652, pp. 61–72. This volume also contains Phelips's letters from Spain and eulogies on the death of Sir Robert and his daughter Bridget; see pp. 90–124 and 160–1.

[62] "A Discourse by Way of Dialogue," Somerset RO, DD/Ph 227/16.

of these men could have testified, was pleasant enough, but if one had risen to that fame at the expense of Court connections, then the applause of neighbors and tenants celebrated a Pyrrhic victory.

A clearer understanding of Phelips's motivation makes his *rapprochement* with Buckingham more comprehensible. Their relationship had begun in the 1621 session when Phelips insisted that he had acted as Buckingham's agent and had supported Goring's motion because he thought it had Buckingham's support. His parliamentary service eventually landed him in the Tower with several other MPs. His punishment admittedly was less dangerous than that of Sir Peter Heyman whom James sent to Heidelberg. Nonetheless Sir Robert's punishment was equally humbling. Having returned to Somerset-shire he was almost immediately summoned back before the Privy Council which placed him in close confinement for over seven months.[63] While isolated there, denied access to his wife and children and, for a time, even pen and paper, he learned a painful object lesson in the importance of deference and compromise. No formal charges were made, but he soon learned that "my liberty is not to be purchased att a lower rate then . . . utter blemishing of my fair reputation." Weston, the Chancellor of the Exchequer, although sympathetic, stressed "the necessity of a wysman to comply with the tyme." Phelips in response insisted that "I would doe any thing to recover his Majesties grace," provided of course "I might doe it without wounding my conscience." His reservation proved excessive. Weston "tould me playnely the king must have the victory", exhorted "good Sir Robert consider the difference between a prince and a subject" and reiterated the maxim, "the wysest men doe governe theyr action by due according to tyme."[64]

Several months of confinement eventually brought Phelips around to Weston's point of view. A renewed plea for forgiveness of his "unpardonable presumption" in attempting "to putt his hand to the arke of Government which is the proper work of kings" included no saving clauses for his delicate conscience. Instead he pleaded his offence had been entirely unintentional, and if the session had continued, James would have seen "my utmost endeavours to have procured a graunt of such a proportion of supply as I thought the house would possibly be drawn to." His most important state-ment, however, concerned his future conduct; henceforth he would "with a loyal and faythfull hart always apply himself to his Majesties service and wil carefully avoyd and shun the ways and occasions which may hear after iustly give offense." After Phelips at last governed himself "by due according to

---

[63] Phelips to [Goring?], [early 1622], Somerset RO, DD/Ph 224/82; and Council to Friend, 28 December 1621, and same to Vere, 2 May 1622, *APC*, XXVII, pp. 107 and 206.
[64] "Hombre de bien" [Phelips] to [Tomkins], [early 1622], Somerset RO, DD/Ph 224/85.

tyme" and yielded unconditionally, the Council shifted his confinement to more pleasant quarters at his house at Montacute.[65]

Sober meditation on the folly of "unpardonable presumption" doubtless contributed to Phelips's later cooperation with Buckingham. Yet the desire to repair his bridges to the Court cannot on its own account for his later compliance. On his return to Somerset he had to report the failure of the extraparliamentary benevolence for the Palatinate. His report, however, employed a phrase which perhaps best accounts for his later conduct; the extraparliamentary levy was "not fitt for any man" to be seen as "a voluntary advisor or a confident undertaker of this business." The implication is quite clear that for Phelips there *were* occasions in which a similar project would be worthy of "a confident undertaker." The local gentlemen, far from being indifferent to the Palatine cause, "did extraordinarily affect the service and restitution of the princes [Elizabeth's children]." Nor should we assume that this was simply a polite excuse to avoid taxation, for Phelips's personal papers and parliamentary addresses testify to a strong interest in the continental crisis. The problem with the 1622 benevolence therefore was not its goal; rather it was that Phelips and many of his neighbors were not prepared to "forgett what the word parlament meanes" in order to help the Palatines. On the other hand, an occasion when a Parliament could at once support "the princes" and correct "the great disorder and distemper" in the commonwealth would be "fitt" for "a voluntary advisor." For Phelips, that opportunity came early in 1624.[66]

Actual sightings of Phelips outside the Palace of Westminster in 1624 are infrequent, but they all reveal his intimacy with the duke's inner circle. In late March, he was in contact with Harley, a courtier and MP whom Russell has pointed to as an intermediary for his busy father-in-law, Secretary Conway. Later in the session Phelips wrote Buckingham a lengthy letter about the delicate Bristol case, and his detailed advice indicates Phelips had long passed the initial sycophantic stage with the favorite.[67] But the most revealing glimpse of Phelips occurs in relation to a West Country trade dispute with Breton rivals. Certain St. Malo merchants claimed the loss of a ship and cargo worth £1,000 in one of Sir Henry Mainwaring's privateering ventures and eventually secured French letters of reprisal for £15,000 of English goods. Taunton merchants, fearful for their goods in Brittany, had vainly petitioned the Council and the king to head off the crisis. On 9 March, Phelips discussed

[65] Phelips to James, [early 1622], Somerset RO, DD/Ph 224/83; and *APC*, XXVII, p. 308.

[66] Phelips to "my lord" [summer 1622], Somerset RO, DD/Ph 211/61; "Hombre fiel" [Tomkins] to Phelips, 27 November 1626, DD/Ph 221/18. On Phelips's attention to continental events, see DD/Ph 215; 211/62–67v; 99–106v; and 160–163v.

[67] Phelips to Buckingham, 21 August 1624, Somerset RO, DD/Ph 211, fos. 199–200v (also printed in *Cabala*, I, pp. 264–6); Russell, *Parliaments*, pp. 46–7; and note 38 above.

the matter with Conway, who immediately reacted. He wrote to Annandale to relay the details to James and to press the king to write to Tillières. Conway then hurried to see the French ambassador and persuaded him to write to Paris to revoke the letters of reprisal. The secretary then organized an express to carry Tillières's letter and his own instructions to Herbert to press for a revocation. On the 10th, Conway wrote to tell Phelips that the danger had been averted. "When you shall have occasion," he concluded, "you shall find me assuredly Yours."[68] While Conway was addicted to the ceremonious, he was not often so energetic. Phelips doubtless realized that the secretary's alacrity was more the result of the government's current parliamentary anxiety than of an inherent concern for Taunton. Nonetheless, the thought that a "popular man" during a parliamentary session could make the central government jump over a decidedly "country" issue may have encouraged him to see the Parliament of 1624 as the beginning of a return to "that mutuall and needfull exchange of benefitts and service which they [the king and his people] have in those assemblyes."

A similar line of reasoning may well have led Sir Edward Coke, Sir Dudley Digges and Sir Edwin Sandys to work with the "Patriots," but the evidence about their motivation unfortunately is not as full. We do, however, know enough about them to make an educated guess. Like "Roarin' Robin" Phelips, these three were prominent MPs to whom their colleagues in the House regularly looked for guidance. Thus Chamberlain's tag for them, "duces gregis," the leaders of the flock, was entirely appropriate.[69] Digges could be recommended to prospective electors as "an ancient and well respected parliament man," while Sandys had achieved such fame for his opposition to royal policies that James had earlier begged the Virginia Company to elect anyone other than Sir Edwin, even the Devil himself. Likewise when Bishop Williams wished to poke fun at parliamentary pretensions, he announced that he had no desire to be ruled by Sandys.[70] Yet great though Sandys's prestige unquestionably was, Coke's was greater. He was something of a rogue royalist, a man whom Bacon judged to be "by habit popular," fearful of no one and scarcely the king himself. His independence accounts for the Earl of Kellie's unkind observation; in 1624 an incident nearly drove Coke "madd, whitche is noe difficill matter to doe, he being alreddye almost

---

[68] [Conway] to Phelips, 10 March 1624, SP 14/160/55; Hill to Brereton, 1 March 1624, SP 14/160/2; Conway to Annandale, 9 March 1624, SP 14/160/54; Tillières to Ville-aux-clercs, 12 March 1624, PRO 31/3/58, fo. 53; and Herbert to Conway, 22 March 1624, SP 78/72/71.

[69] Chamberlain to Carleton, 20 March 1624, *Letters*, II, p. 549; and "Libel on Parliament," *Commons Debates 1628*, VI, p. 246.

[70] Lister to Mayor of Hull, 25 January 1621, Kingston Upon Hull RO, Corporation Letters L169; Williams to Buckingham, 12 October 1622, BL Add. 34,727, fo. 45v; and *DNB* under Sandys.

madd."[71] James had already come to this conclusion; after the 1621 Parliament he feigned ignorance of Edward Coke, insisting he knew only "Captain Coke" of the Commons. James's amnesia was in fact warranted; in 1624 one newsletter-writer, plainly not a citizen of Coventry, referred to Coke as "our champion."[72] For Charles and Buckingham, these men were obviously worth a gamble. Indeed given the persistent and ultimately fatal problems the "tribunes" had caused for a comparatively straightforward royal request in 1621, it would have been almost suicidal for Charles and Buckingham to have approached a new House of Commons without some variety of prior understanding with them.

The task of wooing these men was made much less complicated by their evident, and at times almost indecent, eagerness for office. The former Lord Chief Justice was so eager for his rehabilitation that he baited a match between his daughter and Buckingham's idiot brother, Viscount Purbeck, with a lavish £10,000 dowry, and when the reluctant bride-to-be barricaded herself in a house, Coke forcibly broke in to drag her to the altar. As Sir John Holles noted, the entire affair left Coke with "a sent fitter for his house in Norfolk, then for the Court, or any honest cumpany," a scent from which "he may strinke in it all the dayes of his life." The aroma certainly lingered as late as 1621, for a satire on the Villiers family placed Coke beside his demented son-in-law.[73] Digges for his part was spotted late in 1622 "following the Court hard both at Roiston and Newmarket and was in hope somwhat wold fall to his lot." He had learned full well, as he later explained to Charles, that the "dauncing" of "busie men" in the Commons "without your Musicque would appeare poore folly."[74] Not surprisingly Digges's willingness to foot to the tune from Whitehall allowed his opponent in the Kent election of 1624 to denounce Digges as a "royalist." The opponent ironically was his cousin Sir Edwin Sandys, and while Sandys's desire for advancement was not readily apparent before 1624, it certainly was afterwards. Consequently in the next election, Sandys's cousin was able to turn the table, and dub Sandys as the royalist.[75] Hence, none of these men would have rejected out of hand any overtures about their reconciliation with the government.

[71] Kellie to Mar, 30 May 1624, *Mar and Kellie*, p. 204; and "Remembrances . . . touching the Lord Coke," [1616], *Letters and Life*, p. 95.
[72] Anon. to [Trumbull], [April 1624], Trumbull Add. MSS, XXXVIII/unfoliated; and Mead to Stuteville, 2 February 1622, *Court and Times*, Ii, p. 289.
[73] Holles to Lady Burley, 29 August 1617, *Holles Letters*, II, p. 196; and "The[y] saye Sejanus doth bestowe," Chester RO, 63/2/19, fo. 29v. For the entire affair, see C. D. Bowen, *The Lion and the Throne* (New York, 1956), pp. 393–411.
[74] Digges to Charles, [April–May 1625], SP 16/19/107; and Chamberlain to Carleton, 21 December 1622, *Letters*, II, p. 468.
[75] Chamberlain to Carleton, 17 January 1624, *Letters*, II, p. 540; and Hirst, *The Representative of the People?*, pp. 144–6 and 174.

Not only was their interest in a reconciliation well-known, but thanks to their difficulties after the 1621 session, the avenues of communication between them and leading officials were open and well-travelled. Sandys had got into hot water in the first session which had scarcely been dissolved before he began a five-month stint in the Tower. When the opening of the second session eventually forced his release, Sandys was apparently advised to consider the advantages of domestic obscurity. Thus the polite excuse of an illness covered his absence from the entire second session.[76] Digges nearly shared Sandys's fate, but he was reportedly let off with a timely warning. Consequently his sudden moderation after his earlier passion "hath utterly lost the house." His subsequent self-restraint in 1621, however, was not regarded an adequate penance; hence James sent Digges and his fellow "tribunes," Thomas Crewe and Sir Nathaniel Rich, to investigate Irish problems. Digges seized the opportunity to prove his administrative skills and produced a detailed report on the Irish army. He also concluded his tour of duty in a position to call Buckingham "my especiall good Lord" and himself the marquis's "most affectionate and trew servant." Such good behavior had its reward. On his return, he became an Irish Privy Councillor. More import antly, James permitted him to return ahead of schedule; thus Digges avoided the stormy autumnal crossing and shipwreck that awaited the rest of the commission.[77] Coke, like Phelips, was arrested in late December 1621, but Coke alone suffered the added indignity of having his house searched and his papers seized and of being confined so closely that his daughter could visit him only in the presence of the Lieutenant of the Tower. After eight months in an old kitchen which the guards quipped "needed a cook," he was confined to his house in Buckinghamshire where he quietly remained until summoned before the Privy Council in late December 1623. James, having abruptly discovered in mid-winter "an extra ordinarie care for . . . his realm of Ireland," dispatched Coke and Sandys to follow up on Digges's report. Given the generous pay – £2 per diem, £120 for transport, and a £100 advance – the Irish commission had obvious advantages over confinement. But the Council's eagerness for the commission's departure suggested that the real reason for the mission was, as Chaworth insisted, "to prevent the lower house of so usefull members."[78] Two points emerge from the histories of these men.

---

[76] *Commons Debates 1621*, II, pp. 436–8; and Zaller, *The Parliament of 1621*, pp. 139–41 and 158.

[77] Digges to Buckingham, 19 April and 26 July 1622, Bodleian Library, Carte MSS, 30/117–117v and 125–125v; "The True State of the Army in Ireland," July 1622, 30/119–23; *Cal. of SP Ireland*, XVI, p. 389; and Chamberlain to Carleton, 22 December 1622, *Letters*, II, p. 416.

[78] Chaworth to Trumbull, 16 January 1624, Trumbull Add. MSS, XVII/unfoliated; and *APC*, XXXVIII, pp. 106, 107, 140, 307, and XXXIX, pp. 157 and 159. See also Bowen, *The Lion and the Throne*, p. 454.

First they had all suffered for the commonwealth and so become heroes like Coke, "our champion." Second their popular martyrdom had expanded their acquaintance with the leading royal officials.

Motive and opportunity led to reconciliation. Digges's Irish letters to Buckingham suggest that he had made his peace well before the decision to summon a new Parliament. Phelips was briefly rumored to have joined Coke and Sandys in Ireland, but his name never appeared in any of the official documents. He too seems to have reached an understanding with the duke well before the opening. More problematic are the cases of Coke and Sandys whose departure out of the country James had reportedly made the *sine qua non* for issuing the election writs. Sandys at first sought safety in his old refuge – ill-health. Since the summons found him so sick that he expected to die rather than recover, a wintertime jaunt through Ireland, he argued, would be a certain death warrant; he had not been on top of a horse in over a decade, and the primitive Irish roads and inns would not permit him to travel as he did in England, by coach and easy stages. The government, however, remained unconcerned about either the Commissioners' comfort or Sandys's health. Less than a month before the parliamentary opening, James made Coke and Sandys members of the Irish Privy Council, while their new brethren on the English council continued to press them to be on their way. Eventually the electors of Coventry saved Coke from his first voyage abroad just as those of Kent reprieved Sandys. The Council went so far as to seek legal advice which confirmed that the commission took precedence over the election. But in the end the Council allowed them to take their seats because their exclusion would "trouble and distemper the very first entrances of our session" and because of strong pressure from the prince.[79]

While the precise time of their *rapprochement* remains uncertain, it is nonetheless clear that arrangements were reached. Digges recalled that before his Irish jaunt Charles assured him "I should bee accompted one of your men," and by the 1624 Parliament Digges numbered himself among the duke's "honest servants."[80] Coke's dramatic interventions in the 1624 session on behalf of the "Patriots" also reveal that he had come to some arrangement. Russell suggested that Coke may have dealt exclusively with the prince. To be sure, in the midst of several hyperbolic testimonials to Buckingham in 1624, Coke reportedly said the favorite "had not deserted the loss of his head" since

[79] *Cal. of SP Ireland*, XVI, pp. 454–6; Van Male to the Infanta, 1 January 1624, HHStA, Belgien PC, fasz. 60/unfoliated; Beaulieu to Trumbull, 28 January 1624, Trumbull MSS, VII/145; Bonham to same, 22 January 1624, Trumbull Add. MSS, XV/13; and APC, XXXIX, p. 165.

[80] Digges to Hippesley, 8 January 1626, Bodleian Library, Rawlinson MSS, A 346, fos. 226–7; and Digges to Charles, [April–May] 1625, SP 16/19/107. I am grateful to Conrad Russell for the first reference.

his return from Madrid. His reservation is indeed ominous. However, since Charles and Buckingham were political Siamese twins during the 1624 Parliament, it would have been a remarkable piece of work if Coke had formed an alliance with Charles alone. Furthermore, since only one account recorded Coke's judgment about the duke and that unique account was composed after the fact, it is safe to say that Coke's views of his daughter's brother-in-law were at least benign in 1624.[81] As for Sandys, he ended the session on such good terms with Charles that one of the new monarch's first acts in 1625 was to call Sandys to his side. The basis of this relationship was a promise early in 1624, "of all manner of conformity" in lieu of obligatory participation in the Irish commission. As in so many other matters, John Beaulieu made the nature of Sandys's promise a little clearer. He reported that Coke and Sandys had been confronted with a choice: either they could go to Ireland or they could explain "how they made good the proffer [*sic*] in the Protestation of the last Parliament" which offered James the "lyves and fortunes" of his subjects for the recovery of the Palatinate.[82] Rather obviously they had taken the latter option.

Thanks to these preliminary arrangements before the session convened, Charles and the duke stood more of a fighting chance than many foreign and domestic observers thought. Smart money might have been placed on James who, as Van Male noted, "a quelque desseing en teste assez contraire aux intentions de ceux qui pensent gouverner ce monde a leur mode." On the other hand those who thought to govern James had made some unprecedented arrangements. Although the "Patriot" game plan would call for an impressive display of close order drill on the floor of the House, "the great men" who sympathized with Charles and Buckingham had agreed, as Digges later suggested, to work closely with "their friends and followers" among the MPs. More importantly, in 1624 the prince and Buckingham would not have to become as wildly apprehensive as they had been in 1621 about conferences between Sandys and Phelips "by the fyre syde at ten of clocke at night the sarvants being put out and none but you ther"; the two were doubtless discussing how they might, as Phelips had promised in 1622, "procure a graunt of such proportion of supply as . . . the house would possibly be drawn to."[83] Affairs could scarcely have been ordered more wisely.

---

81 Russell, *Parliaments*, p. 162; and 27 February 1624, Pym Diary, fo. 10. I am indebted to Christopher Thompson for emphasizing the importance of the late composition of the Pym Diary.

82 "Hombre fiel" [Tomkins] to [Phelips], [late] March 1625, Somerset RO, DD/Ph 219/33; Chamberlain to Carleton, 31 January 1624, *Letters*, II, p. 543; and Beaulieu to Trumbull, 26 December 1623, Trumbull MSS, VII/141.

83 Van Male to the Infanta, 13 February 1624, HHStA, Belgien PC, fasz. 60/unfoliated; Digges to Carleton, [April–May 1625], SP 16/19/107; and Phelips's examination, 25 January 1622, SRO, DD/Ph 216/11.

5

"That mutual and unhappie jealousie": exultation and despair in the opening weeks of the session

Simon Digby insisted that the new Parliament, not the Council or the king, "will soone tell us what is to be done in the great affaire" of Spain and the Palatinate. He was ultimately proven to be correct – after the issue had swung uneasily in the balance for almost four months. In the long process of parliamentary resolution, the first step was for the Commons to thrash out a basic position on Spain and "the war likely to ensue." Thus in the opening weeks parliamentary business revolved around a series of extended discussions about strategy and war finance. Unfortunately, although the Patriots assumed an unambiguously Protestant stance, the peculiarity of their brief and the waywardness of James soon led to the resurgence of what Beaulieu termed "that mutual and unhappie jealousie . . . betweene the Head and the members."[1] The emergence of this sentiment had customarily signalled disaster in earlier Parliaments, and in 1624 it promised to destroy the early hopes of harmony "betweene the Head and the Member" and all plans of breaking the Spaniards' grip on England.

STRIKING THE KEYNOTE

Charles's allies in the Commons had an awkward assignment. They had to persuade their colleagues to recommend terminating the Spanish treaties, to vote a generous supply, and at the same time, avoid any general discussion of the proposed war itself. The first hurdle, the breach of the Anglo-Spanish treaties, was not as easy as it might initially appear. While there was broad unanimity on the Spanish match, some MPs had reservations about abandoning the pursuit of a peaceful diplomatic solution to the Palatine problem. The war coalition therefore had to prevent any moves to separate one set of negotiations from the other. On 1 March, Dr. Gooch illustrated the need for this arrangement: "howsoever it is apparent that the Spanish arms and forces

---

[1] S. Digby to Aston, 17 January 1624, SP 94/30/21; and Beaulieu to Trumbull, 8 March 1624, Trumbull MSS, VII/115.

have been the means of dispossessing the Palatinate of the right owner ... but what cause have we to war with him . . . Our friends cause is not just cause for us."[2] To minimize the appeal of such arguments, the "Patriots" sought to create a mood of crisis: the distance between Court and Country, it was hoped, would markedly diminish and the proper response to the Palatine crisis appear obvious if a Catholic fifth column seemed to threaten England and if the Habsburgs appeared ready to overrun the "outworks" of Holland and Ireland.

On the first day of the session, James delivered his extraordinary request for parliamentary advice on the future of the Anglo-Spanish negotiations and pleaded for an expeditious response. Two weeks later the MPs debated this supremely important question. This delay is indeed quite striking. Yet it cannot justly be interpreted as an indication of the House's general unwillingness to shoulder the burdens of war. Rather it is clear that the Commons delayed the debate at the government's request. Contemporaries anxious to fathom royal intentions always scrutinized the opening addresses of king, Lord Keeper and Speaker, which set the official tone for the session. In 1624 the result of such a close inspection justifiably could have supported the interpretation that a major assault on the recusants at last had royal sanction.

James's request for advice also advanced an extended apologia for the preceding two years. The Anglo-Spanish discussions had no other goal than "to settle a peace in all Christendome and here at home." More importantly he confessed that such a goal was unattainable, "it being come to this that our welfare, or our ill-faring, must grow out of war." But his role in disrupting "peace ... here at home" concerned him the most; indeed he spent more time justifying the suspension of the penal laws in 1622–3 than he did discussing Spain and the Palatinate. He vowed that he was "a Protestant King " with no desire "to tolerate another and adverse religion in my kingdom." After attempting to reassure his audience, he gave Parliament *carte blanche* to discuss the domestic religious situation as well as the diplomatic one abroad. "I pray God," he ended, "your counsels may advance religion."[3] As the first drum-beat for a return to the Elizabethan consensus of war against Spain and religious unity, James's address deserves much more attention than it has received. Contemporaries certainly had no trouble deciphering his message, which refuted rumors of a royal command that Parliament "shold neyther treate nor touch on Spaine or the Catholicks." Simonds D'Ewes delighted in the "most admirable" speech "shewing his dislike of the Spaniard," and Sir Dudley Carleton hailed the speech as a fundamental shift in royal policy; after

---

[2] 1 March 1624, Spring Diary, fo. 56.
[3] Bodleian Library, Rawlinson MSS, B151, fos. 58–9.

James revealed his "good inclination to the change of affaires," Philip IV "will undoubtedly have nothing to doe with us heretiques."[4]

Lord Keeper Williams and the new Speaker of the House, Thomas Crewe, continued the emphasis on religion. The selection of Crewe as Speaker was itself a vivid illustration of the ascendancy of "us heretiques"; one of the 1621 "martyrs" who had served with Digges on the 1622 Irish Commission, he was also notable for his godliness. "He was warm," Hacket recalled, "in the Care of Religion, and a Chief among them that were popular in the defence of it." His favorite concern emerged quite plainly in his list of pressing grievances which gave pride of place to a plea that "good Laws for establishing of Religion may be confirmed." In particular, he petitioned "that the Generation of Locusts, the Jesuits, and Seminary Priests, which were wont to creep in Holes and Corners, and do now come abroad, may . . . be blown away into the Seas" and that the Irish Church be buttressed against a resurgent Catholicism. Given the obvious value in wartime of the "Wall of Brass, the Bond and Unity of Religion," he urged James to follow Elizabeth's example and "find Safety in the Ark of True Religion." With good reason a French reporter noted Crewe spoke "furieusement contre les Jesuites."[5] James's response, which Bishop Williams delivered, readily accepted Crewe's suggestions: "Your House was anciently a Chapel, and still it may be said *non Domus, sed Templum*; so many Men as ye are, so many Churchmen . . . His Royal Majesty hath given Leave of us that are His Chaplains to put him in Mind of this. God is ever careful of Kings, and Kings cannot be too careful of him." This public exchange apparently signalled James's approval of a campaign against the recusants. While D'Ewes predictably applauded the new Speaker "whoe spake exceeding boldlie . . . against the papists," he was particularly impressed with the Lord Keeper; the cleric who had hitherto been "of the popish faction" now "turned the note of his tune another way." Little wonder then that Conway described James's reply as "manna which pleased all tastes."[6] The parliamentary Israelites proved to be a ravenous audience; before the MPs begun scrutinizing the disputed elections, they quickly gave a first reading to a bill against "divers Abuses on the Lord's Day" and pressed for a national fast in addition to the customary communion and sermon. On 24 February the Sabbath Bill passed a second reading and a bill for "repressing of popish Recusants" had its first. On the 26th, fears of a popish *coup de main* prompted Sir John Jephson and others to propose a guard for

---

[4] Carleton to Roe, 1 March 1624, TCD MSS 708, I, fo. 265; D'Ewes, *Diary*, p. 179; and Chaworth to Trumbull, 16 January 1624, Trumbull Add. MSS, XVII/unfoliated.

[5] *LJ*, III, pp. 211–12; Hacket, *Scrinia Reserata*, I, p. 176; and "Mémoire de ce qui s'est passe," BL Add. MSS 30, 646, fo. 67v.

[6] *LJ*, III, pp. 212–13; D'Ewes, *Diary*, p. 179; and Conway to Carleton, 23 February 1624, SP 84/116/154.

the House. Although the House eventually rejected Jephson's plan, Sir John Packington again revived fears of another Gunpowder Plot on 8 March.[7]

However wildly extravagant these apprehensions may now seem, two prominent ministers vigorously supported them. Joseph Hall gave the opening sermon to the ecclesiastical Convocation which began at St. Paul's almost simultaneously with the Westminster Parliament. Hall's selection for this task symbolized the fundamental alteration which seemed imminent early in 1624. Taking full advantage of his opportunity, Hall delivered an impassioned call to theological arms. He rebuked his colleagues for sitting "still with our hands folded," eager "to take our ease, to say nothing, to doe worse," when all could see "how proudly the Tridentine faith hath advanced her crest, and hath dared to flie fiercely in the very face of the Gospell: the Romish forces putt themselves openly into array, and have dared to sound not an alarum onely, but . . . a victory." The only solution was to exchange the 1622 Directions concerning Preaching for a more aggressive evangelical style before it was too late. "If ever ye have wrought heretofore," Hall asked his colleagues, "if ever ye will worke hereafter, Now worke . . . Preach the Word . . . Rouse up your selves, o ye holy Fathers . . . destroy this Tyberine Monster (Popery, I meane) with the breath of your mouthes." The impending struggle also required the rejection of a notion, so common earlier in the decade, equating Puritans with Papists; since "we are by Gods grace reformed, let us take heed lest we be deformed againe by mutual dissentions." Consequently "let us forget there were ever such . . . as Luther, Melancton, Calvin, Zwinglius, Arminius."[8] Such a bold design, Hall recognized, was not in the Convocation's power to approve; hence he begged fellow clerics to use "what ever grace and authority yee have with our Gratious King, with the Peeres, and commons of this Realme" to join in the "utter extermination of Idolatry."

Lest there was any trouble in relaying his message, Isaac Bargraves repeated it directly to both Houses in a fast sermon a week later. In contrast to Hall, Bargraves was known for his acute sensitivity to the temperature at Court, and he left no doubt about his reading of the contemporary political climate. The first priority of the new Parliament, he maintained, should be a concerted assault not only on recusants, but also on the church Papists, those "Hermaphrodite Christians," and on the Catholic agents "of Forraine States" who had infiltrated "our Court, our Parliament." Spain and Rome employed either dangerous fanatics who "professe they drinke the blood of Christ" but actually make themselves "drunke with the blood of Christians

[7] *CJ*, I, pp. 671 and 673–4.
[8] Joseph Hall, *Noahs Dove*, printed in *The Works of Joseph Hall* (London, 1634), pp. 515–16 and 519.

and Christian Princes," or "such World-wormes, as sell their consciences." The only secure defense was Protestant solidarity; "beleeve it," Bargraves insisted, " . . . the very Axell whereon they winde about the whole body of their Machiavilisme in England, is our division and dissension." Consequently the Parliament-men should banish "those distracting names of Lutherans, Calvinist, Puritan" and instead remember "Wee are all the children of the same father."[9] For those reluctant to heed broad hints from the Court, Bargraves's message must have been very hard to ignore, and the fact that the same sermon a few months earlier would have earned Bargraves a stint in the Tower only underscored the magnitude of the recent shift in policy.

The Commons reluctantly deferred further anti-Catholic measures on 26 February when Goring proposed closer attention to the "more effectual businesses" of the match and the Palatinate. No one seconded Goring, and although the House agreed to his motion, no debate ensued on the "great business." "The impression," Russell observed, "is not of a House of Commons eager to seize the initiative in foreign affairs but rather of one deferring the involvement which was asked of it until the last possible moment."[10] Yet in fact there is no mystery about the lack of a debate on the 26th; Secretary Calvert asked the MPs to defer the discussion until the next day to allow for a thorough debate. On the 27th the Commons formally heard Buckingham's history of the Spanish entanglement and received their charge: should James continue the treaties "or else stand upon himself." Afterwards Heath, the Solicitor General, proposed, and the House accepted, that the MPs spend the weekend pondering over Buckingham's revelations and that the debate should begin on Monday 1 March, the day after Bargraves had preached to Parliament.[11]

It is hard to detect any widespread desire to avoid debate when the MPs dutifully followed the lead of royal officials. Suspicion, as will be seen, certainly ran high in the Commons about royal intentions, and some MPs, as Russell suggested, were apprehensive about involvement in the war. Nevertheless, very few MPs could resist the allure of more information and an opportunity to voice their fears about the Spanish match. This may have been precisely what Charles and Buckingham were gambling on. In any case, the members, after venting their Catholic fears in the first week of the session, agreed to interrupt their investigations: they had initially wished to pursue the Catholic question, but Beaulieu noted that "upon riper consideration it

---

[9] Isaac Bargraves, *A Sermon Preached before . . . the Lower House* (London, 1624), pp. 22, 26–7, 32–3, 39; and Hall, *Noahs Dove*, p. 516.

[10] 26 February 1624, Nicholas Diary, fo. 24; and Russell, *Parliaments*, p. 161.

[11] 26 February 1624, Nicholas Diary, fo. 25; 27 February 1624, Pym Diary, fo. 8; and *CJ*, I, p. 271.

was thought fitt to forebeare and put [off] till the great Point of the Marriage and the Palatinate were resolved on and concluded." The MPs could, however, take comfort in their preliminary labors: the English Catholics, Woolley reported, "begin to feare, and not without reason, that they shalbe all banished; their heads like to the snaile they begin to pull in already and by reporte many of late goeth to Church which before declared themselves otherwise."[12]

The "Patriots" now attempted to expand this domestic concern to international politics, and for this task, the coalition had to establish its bona fides as the English representatives of the Calvinist International. A flood of information helped accomplish this goal. Buckingham's relation on 24 February, which Weston reported to the Commons on the 27th, was one of the significant events of the 1624 session and indeed in early-seventeenth-century history. S. R. Gardiner, for example, interpreted the address as an announcement of Buckingham's usurpation: "If Buckingham had said, 'I am the King,' he could not have expressed himself more plainly." This long and well-documented account of Anglo-Spanish negotiations in 1622–3 is notable for its amnesia on points which might have compromised Charles and the duke. Yet in spite of its sins of omission, Buckingham's narrative remained a powerful story of a prince constant to the true religion in the face of repeated popish threats and blandishments: in the discourse Charles repeated several variations of the line, "he was come settled in his religion which was dearer unto him than all other things whatsoever."[13] Those contemporaries whose suspicions might have been aroused by such a disingenuous story in which Buckingham played a major part were not free to probe the question. The negotiations, the duke emphasized, had merely become stalled, and Padre Maestro was hurrying with new terms which might easily break the deadlock. And if the Spaniards succeeded, England would have to abandon its ancient allies, the Dutch, as well as its old prejudices against Catholics, while Prince Frederick Henry, a potential English monarch, would have to be consigned to Vienna and Catholicism. The address was in short a finely wrought piece of theater appealing to the audience's altruism – and its *amour propre*.

Parliament scarcely had time to comprehend the new information before learning of fresh revelations. On the 28th, they received further archival gleanings from Bristol's dispatches. On 3 March, Bishop Williams in the Lords and Sir Edward Coke in the Commons delivered reports on Spanish machinations to disrupt an Anglo-French match and to forestall English

---

[12] Beaulieu to Trumbull, 5 March 1624, and Woolley to same, 28 February 1624, Trumbull MSS, VII/151 and XLVIII/114.
[13] Gardiner, *England Under Buckingham*, I, p. 15; and Buckingham's Relation, 24 February 1624, Lansdowne MSS 498, fo. 38.

intervention on behalf of Frederick. They also retailed "the heroical Act and Resolution of the Prince" who urged James to forget him if he should be detained in Spain and instead "to reflect his royal Thoughts on his Sister and her Children." On 4 March, Digges produced new information in which Pembroke supported Buckingham's earlier claim that the Spaniards really aimed at the reduction of the United Provinces. This last report prompted Sir Isaac Wake, Sir Thomas Edmondes, Sir Robert Cotton and Coke himself to offer recollections of various nefarious Spanish dealings.[14] Many MPs doubtless had trouble analyzing this mass of information, and many may have been certain only that, as Russell suggested, "Spain was a Bad Thing, and negoations ought to be broken off." But since a copy of the Relation was almost de rigeur for a gentleman's separate collection, we would do well to uncover the reasons for the remarkable popularity of this document.[15]

The widespread interest underscores an important point; while modern scholars might carp at the selection of materials, contemporaries were transfixed by an extended presentation of the hitherto closely guarded Mysteries of State. Compared with their neighbors in Amsterdam, Brussels and Paris, Englishmen in the early seventeenth century knew precious little about their government, aside from rumors and the odd proclamation. Indeed a few months earlier they were constrained from discussing affairs of state altogether. Yet in late February 1624, they were offered an apparently authoritative account of involved diplomatic negotiations which had deeply troubled the English polity in preceding years. In addition they were freely offered documents. The sheer volume of information should not be underestimated. Several collectors quite rightly ordered a precis of the Relation as well as the text itself, which took Buckingham and Charles several hours to deliver. Hence the Relation was the early-seventeenth-century equivalent of Khrushchev's celebrated address to the Twentieth Party Congress in 1956. Not until the publication of Rushworth's *Historical Collections* and the *Cabala* thirty years later could Englishmen find a more impressive piece of contemporary history. Finally MPs were also enjoined to discuss this information among themselves and their constituents; as Coke explained, the information was such that the king "thought fit to communicate to us, and we to the whole Kingdom."[16] Such boldness a few months earlier would have earned all of them a jail sentence. In the circumstances therefore it is scarcely surprising that the duke's auditors made little immediate response to his

---

[14] *CJ*, I, pp. 725–7; and 3 and 4 March 1624, Pym Diary, fos. 15–18. On Cotton's address, see Kevin Sharpe, *Sir Robert Cotton* (Oxford, 1979), pp. 172–5.

[15] Russell, *Parliaments*, pp. 158–9; and Thomas Cogswell, "Thomas Middleton and the Court, 1624, *A Game at Chess* in Context," *Huntington Library Quarterly* XLVII (1984), p. 288, n. 46.

[16] *CJ*, I, p. 725; and Alnwick Castle MSS, vol. 12, fos. 136–51 (Relation) and 152–3 (precis).

address; they were too busy writing out all the details, much less analyzing them.

Once they had a little time to digest the data, they were not quite as baffled as Russell would have them. Archbishop Spottiswoode of St. Andrews reported that the Relation "hath wonderfully affectit the hearts of all the good subjects of this kingdom." For this service, "your graces honor shalbe Immortal," for Buckingham had "savit al our lives, liberties and religione." Lord Falkland in Dublin concurred; the Relation would redound to "your eternall honnor." Falkland's letter also makes the reasons for the duke's "immortal" and "eternal" fame much clearer; "yt hath begott in us heare a stronge expectation that the Advise of the two howses will conclude uppon warr." It certainly bred in Falkland an overwhelming need to justify his ability to rule Ireland in wartime.[17] Falkland's reaction was what the duke seems to have expected. In the polarized international situation, Anglo-Spanish negotiations alone prevented open war, and as Gerbier recalled, the point of the Relation was "that all the world might see that with the Spaniards theire was nothing to be effectued by a Treaty." This interpretation did not elude an English Catholic. In spite of the favorite's address, "I hope our kinge will not enter into a warre." But after late February he could rely on nothing more solid than hopes and prayers.[18] As a statement about future domestic policy, the Relation was equally evocative. Even the crudest analyst could not help noting it as a major departure from the standard operating procedure of the Stuart regime. "In handling these Matters," Beaulieu observed, "there have been such things discovered and delivered that passed in Spaine which never came hitherto to any mens knowledge out of that sanctuarie." In the words of another newsletter-writer the Relation was a remarkable "expression of his Maiesties singular trust."[19] And this example of James's "singular trust" after so many months of mistrust heralded a major move to close the perilous gap which had developed between Court and Country over the Palatine crisis.

Just before the crucial debates on the subsidy, the coalition's dire warning that Protestant liberty stood in imminent peril received timely confirmation; in January 1624 a large detachment of the Army of Flanders crossed the frozen Ijssel into the unprotected heartland of the United Provinces. The Spaniards soon withdrew, but not before the Dutch alarm spread to England.

---

[17] Spottiswoode to Buckingham, 19 March 1624, Bodleian Library, Add. MSS D111, no. 440; and Falkland to Buckingham, [March 1624], Bodleian Library, Carte MSS, vol. 30, fos. 183–4.

[18] Gerbier's Relation, BL Add. MSS 4181, fos. 19v–20; and Sterrell to La Faille, 11 March 1624, HHStA, Belgien PC, fasz. 60/unfoliated.

[19] Beaulieu to Trumbull, 5 March 1624, Trumbull MSS, VII/151; and "A Succinct Relation," [late February 1624], Trumbull Misc. MSS, XXXIV/91.

James "much inquires," Conway reported, of the Ijssel crisis, and "wee are yet in a fearefull expectation what is become of the troopes that passed the River." Charles, on Mr. Carleton's arrival from The Hague in late February, was "very particular" about details of the raid, and "shewed no small contentement that things had gon no worse with the States." The English anxiety was not confined to Whitehall: "I finde," Sir Edward Cecil wrote "that this whole kingdome dothe take a great alarome at this accedente and espetically our Parlements and I hope that this ill accedente will turne to our good (by Gods favore) in the same kind as the Princess goinge into Spaine which was so terrible to us at the beginning."[20] The Spanish raid therefore inclined even the reluctant to listen more attentively to the calls for immediate military intervention. Pleas for an offensive war might have left some MPs unmoved, but a Spanish army before Utrecht was a striking illustration of the need at the very least to buttress England's "outworks."

RELIGION AND SPAIN: THE FIRST DEBATE, 1–2 MARCH

Having prepared the House by emphasizing the dangers of parliamentary diffidence, the war coalition now introduced the question of the Spanish treaties. The chief goal of the session, James had insisted on 19 February, was for the Parliament to "give me your honest advice and to shew what you shall think fittest" in the "match of my son to a sister of Spain." For additional details, he referred MPs to the duke, who ended his Relation by asking the Parliament if James "with anie safetie" could "relie upon" Spanish promises about "the reliefe of his onlie daughter [Elizabeth]."[21] It was these questions that the Commons debated on 1 March in the first of three extended discussions.

The tactical problem confronting Charles's parliamentary allies should be clearly understood. Almost all Englishmen in 1624 assumed that the breach of the treaties would inevitably lead to an Anglo-Spanish war; as Phelips's Country Gentleman succinctly put it, "no Maryage, no peace." Therefore given the logical result of the Commons' resolution, it made sense that before reaching any decision the House should consider what it was getting into. Logic in this case, however, would have sorely tempted fate. As will be seen, one of the few constants in the many tactical maneuvers of the "Patriots" was their eagerness to throttle any discussion of the "war likely to ensue" after the

---

[20] Conway to Carleton, 20–3 February 1624, SP 84/116/141 and 151; Carleton the younger to Carleton, 1 March 1624, SP 84/116/186; and Cecil to [Carleton], 21 February [1624], SP 84/116/147. On the raid itself, see Jonathan Israel, *The Dutch Republic and the Hispanic World, 1606–1661* (Oxford, 1982), pp. 104–6.

[21] February 1624, Bodleian Library, Rawlinson B 151, fo. 58; and Ruigh, p. 166.

breach of the Spanish treaties.[22] On 1 March this apparently contradictory goal of a war coalition took the form of holding the discussion to the fate of the treaties and nothing but the treaties.

Rudyerd began the debate with a sobering assessment of the Spanish negotiations: "we have lost the Palatinate altogether and almost all our party of the religion abroad, besides a great bulk of papistry grown and knotted within our own bowels at home." Moreover the projected match had "exceedingly threatened" the United Provinces: "the whole power of the Emperor and King of Spain coming down upon it, nothing to divert, nothing to give it breath, Bethlen Gabor retired, Count Mansfelt's army dissolved, besides a rotten faction of Arminians among themselves which is likely to hasten their ruin by revolt." The Dutch themselves, Rudyerd conceded, might have objectionable characteristics, but they had provided refuge to Elizabeth, "the inestimable jewel of this crown," and they formed "our outwork, which, if it be taken, we shall be more than in danger." The deteriorating Dutch situation alone required the prompt breach of the treaties: "Believe it, Mr. Speaker, the day of the loss of the Low Country will be no eve of a holiday to us." He then delivered his strategic proposals, the famous Four Propositions. Rudyerd proposed that the navy and the militia be set on a war footing, that Ireland be reinforced, and that England "really and roundly assist the Low Countries." The war for the Palatinate, he suggested, should be waged by diversion and nearer to home where the Dutch could render effective assistance. But the purpose of these measures was to allow James to "enter into a consideration with his friends abroad and endeavour to recollect and revive that scattered and broken party of the religion in Germany." Thus these proposals were, when initially delivered, more ambiguous than Dr. Adams has allowed.[23] For Rudyerd and others in 1624, a diversionary war and the revival of the German princes were not mutually exclusive.

In the ensuing debate, few MPs explicitly endorsed all four of Rudyerd's Propositions. Sir John Strangways alone voiced concern about the English coastal defenses and the preparation of the militia; Sir John Eliot was singular in his call to prepare the fleet; and Rudyerd's proposal to buttress the Irish defenses received no vocal support.[24] The call to assist the Dutch fared slightly better. Christopher Brooke argued that with "the loss of the Hollanders which are our surest friends and strongest bulwark against Spain for our state . . . we should not only lose their assistance and friendship but be subject to the mischiefs of their power and shipping to annoy us." Sir Robert Harley dwelt on the dangers of a Franco-Dutch *rapprochement* which

---

[22] "A discourse by way of dialogue," SRO, DD/Ph 227/16; and see below, pp. 179–80, 189 and 222.

[23] 1 March, Pym Diary, fos. 10–11; and Adams, "Foreign Policy and Parliament," p. 165.

[24] 1 March, Spring Diary, pp. 46 and 50.

continued Anglo-Spanish negotiations made almost inevitable: "it is high time to make sure with the Hollander who wants not offers and will assuredly join with support and friends elsewhere, if they should be still made jealous of us by continuing the treaties, either of them."[25] Given the lack of enthusiasm for the Four Propositions, Rudyerd's speech can be seen only in retrospect to have been, as Pym recalled, "the mould of the resolution of the whole Parliament." It certainly did not dominate the debate on 1 March.[26]

What did captivate the House on that day was religion and Spain, topics which Phelips first developed. Ruigh rightly observed that it was Phelips much more than Rudyerd who excited the House. The Spanish treaties were "the most advantageous weapon for Spain" and had "debased us in reputation in all christendome." When Phelips thought "of the loss of religion, the cruelty and oppression of the Papists and Spaniards to the [continental] protestants and . . . of the distress of that royal lady [Elizabeth]," he could not mention the Palatinate "but with sighs and sobs." More dramatically, he had the boldness to insist that "if we speak of revenge yet, whether should we look but towards him that hath wounded us . . . Spain must be the enemy."[27]

Given the earlier discussions about the recusant revival, most MPs found the opportunity of linking their fears for religion publicly and directly with Spain more appealing than a discussion of what Russell termed "practical belligerence": coastal gun emplacements, militia powder stocks, and Irish garrisons. Sir Miles Fleetwood moved quickly from "all our mischiefs we suffer is from Spain" to the praise of "Religion" which is "like the ark that carries a blessing with it."[28] Sir Francis Seymour spoke at length of "the increase and insolencies of the papists how they are of late enlarged both in numbers and boldness." His philippic against Catholicism and Spain concluded with a plea to enforce the penal laws as well as an immediate end to the Spanish treaties. Sir John Eliot next proposed, and Sir John Strangways supported, a special tax on the recusants to finance the outfitting of the fleet.[29] Others simply wanted the negotiations broken off. Sir George Chudleigh maintained that "all they [the Spaniards] had aimed at was to move rebellion here in England." Sir Robert Harley exhorted the House to consider that while "our foreign enemies be great . . . those at home are much more, who lie in our bosoms and are not distinguished nor known of us but are familiar and conversant in all companies and all councils." Indeed as long as the negotiations continued, Richard Hutton insisted "we nourish the wolf in our bosom."[30]

25   *Ibid.*, pp. 58 and 60.
26   1 March, Pym Diary, fo. 10; and Adams, "Foreign Policy and Parliament," p. 166.
27   1 March, Spring Diary, pp. 43–4; Holles Diary, fo. 29v; and Ruigh, pp. 180–1.
28   Russell, *Parliaments*, p. 164; and 1 March, Spring Diary, p. 45.
29   1 March, Rich Diary, fo. 28v; and Spring Diary, pp. 45–6 and 50.
30   1 March, Spring Diary, pp. 59–61; and Rich Diary, fo. 23v.

Religion, and the Spaniards' manipulation of it, was clearly behind the Commons' resolution later in the day to advise terminating the treaties. The willingness to talk about Catholics and Spain, however, should not be ascribed to what Russell has termed their unwillingness to talk about "practical readiness to prepare for war." Rather it seems that most MPs felt a "nuts and bolts" discussion of the war could wait while they publicly vented frustrations and fears which had tormented them in preceding months. More importantly, as Sandys pleaded with his colleagues, they were not asked for advice about a Spanish war; "he moved to keep ourselves within the limits of the King's proposition, whether fit the treaty of the match should continue or no, and not to go on with war."[31] And to have moved faster than the king on such a delicate subject would have been to invite a repeat of the second session of the 1621 "assembly".

This logic ensured that the House's mind on strategy was never clearly developed. War would almost certainly follow the breach of the treaties, but what kind of war remained vague. Since the Palatinate was "a lost place not recoverable," Rudyerd called for English defensive preparations and especially an Anglo-Dutch league which "will take away all jealousies and distastes of foreign princes," and the foreign princes he had in mind were German and French.[32] Rudyerd's "diversion of a war" was quite simple; the English acting as Frederick's proxies would make themselves so troublesome to the Habsburgs in the Low Countries and on the Atlantic that the Spaniards would eventually restore the Palatinate just to be rid of the English. Phelips, on the other hand, thought "we must war for it [the Palatinate] or something better than it." The notion of securing "something better" as a means of Frederick's restoration was an ambitious extension of the diversionary strategy. The English would seize and hold a Habsburg or Catholic possession to be exchanged for the Palatinate. Such a strategy had been discussed before, both in and out of Whitehall, and it explains the attractiveness of Mansfelt's later proposal to secure the Rhenish bishoprics and more improbably Bavaria, and Wimbledon's instructions in 1625 to capture Cadiz and Seville.[33] Of these two options, Seymour alone seconded Phelips and hoped "that [the Palatinate] or a better portion may be gained in spite of the King of Spain's teeth." Others were less emphatic about their view of a war. Digges asked the House to consider how they might correct the danger that the Anglo-Spanish negotiations had done to "the professors of the religion with us both in Germany and elsewhere."[34] Dr. Gooch agreed with Rudyerd

---

[31] Russell, *Parliaments*, p. 164; and 1 March, Holles, fo. 87v.
[32] Russell, *Parliaments*, pp. 175–6; and 1 March, Spring, p. 42.
[33] [Mansfelt's Proposal], [April–August 1624], SP 81/31/80; and Instructions to Wimbledon, 26 August 1625, SP 16/5/87.
[34] 1 March, Spring Diary, pp. 46 and 55.

"that the recovery of the Palatinate is impossible" but denied the necessity of the defensive preparations, much less a war. Aside from these few comments and those on the Four Propositions, MPs seem to have had only the dimmest view of what they were getting into.

This state of ignorance seems to have been precisely what the "Patriots" desired: a pause might bring on the one topic that the war supporters had to avoid at all costs – the war itself. But any further reflection would have been difficult on 1 March amid the coalition's echoing pleas for haste and expedition. Rudyerd first sounded the note of urgency: "now we must make as quick an entrance and dispatch of this business as the Prince did of his journey into Spain." Sir George More requested "that in so weighty a cause we should move slowly" only to have his plea for due consideration "interrupted with the noise of some that misliked his tediousness." Phelips scorned such timid ways: "since we have lost so much by the talking way already it is now like Englishmen to do."[35] Eliot repeated Phelips's refrain: "it is now time rather to do than speak." Sergeant Hitcham adopted a less aggressive tack: the evils of the treaties were "so clear and manifest . . . that every man cannot but be of the opinion that all treaties must cease." Against the benefits of mature deliberation, Hitcham set the public relations coup "that it may be reported abroad that the parliament House at the very first propounding of it did determine all treaties with Spain to be concluded and broke off."[36]

There were, however, limitations to how fast the members would let themselves be pushed. Towards the end of the morning, a request from the Lords for a conference on the following afternoon agitated members about the precipitous proceedings. Since "the business is not yet so well deliberated as it should," Digges suggested that the Commons rather than the Lords should set the time of the conference. Sir Edward Cecil, however, maintained that an afternoon's debate on the subject was more than enough: the issue, though admittedly "weighty," was "no strange or new matter to any man but that it hath been long known and often disputed of." In conclusion, "it is now time," he warned, "to begin to deal with Spain or else he will soon deal with us." Phelips then proposed that the joint committee meet the next day, "if conveniently we can." Although Edward Alford seconded Digges, Phelips's motion eventually passed.[37]

The resolution of the question about the joint committee led to another on the afternoon's agenda. The House ultimately decided on a Committee of the Whole House to debate the treaties, but not before the question of deliberation or expedition again immediately arose. Earlier in the day when More had unsuccessfully attempted to slow the pace, the Patriots had answered him

---

[35] 1 March, Spring Diary, pp. 41 and 43; and Rich Diary, fo. 30.
[36] *Ibid.*, pp. 46–7; and *ibid.*, fo. 28v.   [37] 1 March, Spring Diary, pp. 48–9.

with catcalls. Yet Digges soon revived More's suggestion and proposed that the attorneys and the country gentlemen who would have to pay for the war led a detailed analysis of a war. Digges's proposal was clearly aimed at the question his fellow "Patriots" had to avoid, and it immediately brought Sandys to his feet with another plea for expedition: "when thou enterest into the presence of God, let thy words be few." The Commons, he warned, should not play too long at "the Spaniards' own games . . . ambassadors and treaties." Whatever resolution the House might take, it should do so quickly, if, he added ominously, "it be not too late."[38]

Once in committee, Digges again proposed a thorough discussion of "how we are able to maintain a war." His motion, however, never survived the warm endorsement of Dr. Gooch, Vice-Chancellor of Cambridge. Given that England did not have enough munitions "for one day's good service," Gooch chided the House for its juvenile enthusiasm for war, "a pleasing word to men without experience." Not surprisingly, "the noise did interrupt" his school-masterly speech, and "he was taken off." Digges's proposal went with Gooch. Sir Robert Killigrew called Digges to order: "the proper point to be now treated of is whether the treaties should hold or not and to leave other things to their due time." Sir William Strode endorsed Killigrew's strict delineation of the debate and ridiculed Gooch's military analysis. Eventually Coke resolved the question. On 1 March as on later occasions he employed his prestige and reputation to head off a debate that would have endangered the coalition. The Parliament writ, he argued, held the answer: "the advice is *ex arduis*, the speed of it implied in *urgentibus*."[39] To conclude the debate on the right note, Jermyn proposed "to thrust the word treaty out of the House, for every man is weary to hear of it." The breach of the treaties, which "we have desired and prayed for long," should not be delayed: "other things will fall in their own time and place to be considered on."[40]

The outcry against Gooch thus quickly slid into a unanimous resolution that James should promptly terminate the Spanish negotiations. Attempts to inject more objectivity into the debate had been thwarted, and instead religious zeal and jingoism carried the day. Yet it is vital to remember that this curious procedure had been adopted, not because a majority was fearful of the burden of war, but rather because of the necessity to avoid a full discussion of the war. Admittedly there certainly were those in the House, as young Carleton reported, "that by the consideration of the whole charge of war like to rest upon their shoulders, were waivering and ready to advise the continuance of the treaty of restitution [of the Palatinate]." And just as

[38] *Ibid.*, pp. 50–1.
[39] 1 March, Pym Diary, fo. 13; and Spring Diary, pp. 54–8.
[40] 1 March, Spring Diary, p. 61.

certainly to have soothed their apprehensions through a thorough examination of the question would have been to tempt fate by wandering into an exceedingly dangerous topic. Therefore the "Patriots" countered Digges's call for "reason, not will" with emotion; only a prompt and unambiguous decision, they insisted, could begin to repair the damage the Spanish treaties had done England and the continental brethren.[41] Anyone bold enough to repeat James's old adage, *dulce bellum inexpertis* was ridiculed for their timidity. These tactics would later bear bitter fruit; logically the supporters of a war should have seconded More and Digges, but thanks to the peculiar shape James forced the war to assume, chauvinism would have to replace reason on 1 March.

In this confused debate, Russell has perceived a general lack of interest in a war: "If it is to be maintained that the Commons demanded a war with Spain, the evidence used for this case must be taken from some other place than the debates of 1 March." His plea of "not proven" is undoubtedly the wisest option, although not for the reason he advances. First of all it must be remembered that the question before the House was not war with Spain; it was simply the fate of the Spanish treaties. As one anonymous MP noted, some of his colleagues urged a resolution on a Spanish war, but "this opinion was resolved against, because the King asked our advice, not for war, but for proceeding or disisting from the treaties." Granted "a highly organized team of the Duke's supporters" desperately sought to hold the Commons to the treaties alone, but this fact does not lessen the force of their argument.[42] That the MPs eventually resolved to do only as much as James asked of them can scarcely be held against them; after all the king who had given them this charge was the same one who had abruptly dissolved Parliament and laid the "duces" by the heels for putting the cart before the horse in 1621.

Personal preference also went hand in hand with caution. MPs brought to Westminster profound anxieties about the Catholic problem, which the coalition had raised to the point of near hysteria. When given their lead on 1 March, many MPs quite understandably wanted to talk about recusants. It is clearly a little too much to expect the MPs to have jumped immediately into planning a Spanish war when they were deeply apprehensive about a domestic fifth column. Their ordering of priorities did not necessarily imply that they were uninterested in war: they merely had a more immediate problem on their minds. Finally those who were more interested in Spain rather than the recusants would have been bold to press for a Spanish war. All the information which the MPs had received emphasized the serious and immi-

---

[41] 1 March, Holles Diary, fo. 87v, and Carleton the younger to Carleton, 5 March 1624, SP 14/160/33.
[42] Bodleian Library, Rawlinson MSS, B 151, fo. 61; and Russell, *Parliaments*, pp. 175–6.

nent danger that Spain *directly* posed to England. Therefore, the fact that some Parliament-men talked about defensive preparations does not necessarily imply that they were uninterested in an offensive war: reason and apparently the government itself dictated their selection of topics. Indeed, it could be argued that until Buckingham's speech about the West Indies on 3 March, the war coalition itself was apparently not interested in an offensive war. Thus Russell's observation is eminently judicious; the Commons on 1 March were not yet ripe for the question about "a war with Spain."

THE EMERGENCE OF THE OLD KING

The early success of Charles and the duke was in part due to the belief that the Crown for once was moving in tandem with the Commons. In the coming week, however, the illusion vanished. James, it became apparent, was not as quiescent as Charles and Buckingham confidently gave out. Excited rumors had run through London in the first week of the session that James would follow the wishes of Parliament and his son. "A man of credit," told John Woolley "that his Majestie . . . would consent to anything the Parliament should thinck convenient, and if upon a warr, rather than they should want a generall he would goe himself." Another story portrayed a more superannuated monarch and lends contemporary credence to the Spanish ambassadors' later accusation against Buckingham: after opening the session, James retired to Hampton Court "with an intention (as I am tould) not to truble himself with anything but leave it all to his Highnes, the Duke and Parlement being resolved to take all in good parte, that they shall agree upon."[43] James himself would reveal on 5 March the vanity of these hopes. Until that time, however, the illusion that James was securely in tow behind Charles and Buckingham did much to allay the Commons' suspicions about royal intentions. But once it became apparent that a distinct third party, that of James himself, had entered the field with the Commons and Charles, parliamentary apprehensions of a double-cross revived and were not easily dispelled.

Just before James's emergence, Buckingham made a significant pronouncement on strategy. On 3 March Buckingham delivered a short address on the Habsburg design for a "western monarchy," much of which had already been achieved. Many MPs, as the debates on 1 March had revealed, accepted such Spanish designs as axiomatic. But the logic of the duke's closing remarks certainly left his auditors riveted: "what remained [in their design] must be gotten with arms, arms maintained by money, money with the Indies, the profit of the Indies must come by sea, and if the King and the Low Countries

[43] Woolley to Trumbull, 28 February and 6 March 1624, Trumbull MSS, XLVIII/114 and 115.

joined they shall be masters of the sea and Spain's monarchy will have a stop." Ruigh observed that "in a few sentences the Duke had synthesized the prejudices and purposes of the majority of the Commons."[44] It should also be added that the duke synthesized his own ambition and that of the war coalition.

To the younger generation of the 1620s raised on tales of Elizabethan naval triumphs, the West Indies had a potent and almost irresistible allure. Many of the older generation, who should have known better since they had seen the Elizabethan reality, played up to a wide-eyed audience by minimizing the inherent dangers and by maximizing the potential profit of an Indies voyage. "Many thinck," William Monson, an old Elizabethan veteran, observed in 1625, "that the name of Indies and the spoiles we shall commit there, will affoard wealth and riches sufficient to the king and kingdom to maintayn a warr and to themselves preferrment and gaine." But in the late sixteenth century, Monson's contemporaries had learned the bitter truth, as Drake had done at Nombre de Dios: "in stead of riches, he found a most miserable infection and sickness, but wealth it affoarded none."[45] Yet by the 1620s, Drake's legend had come to obscure his fate. It was no coincidence that his nephew issued in the mid-twenties the seadog's authorized biography, *Drake Revived, Calling upon this dull or Effeminate Age to folowe his Noble Steps for Golde and Silver.* And as we have seen, one of the most enthusiastic Drake devotees was the Lord Admiral himself; he was to recruit officers for action in the Atlantic in 1625 by calling for men "covetusnes [*sic*] to measure gold by theire hatts and other spoyles by shippes lading."[46] The West Indies Company, a Dutch joint stock company for colonization and privateering, revived the cult of Drake in 1623. Its early growth excited Sir Dudley Carleton, who pleaded for English involvement in the venture. The profits seemed assured, and if the English could get in on the ground floor, Anglo-Dutch rivalry, which poisoned the East Indies, could be avoided.[47] The scheme and the area so enchanted the ambassador that he commissioned Hondius, the celebrated cartographer, to prepare a map of the West Indies. Conway certainly required little convincing: a proposal for an Anglo-Dutch West Indies Company exists in the secretary's distinctive hand, and in his

---

[44] Pym Diary, fos. 16 and 16v; and Ruigh, p. 192.

[45] [William Monson], "The Copy of a Letter . . . Concerning the Sea Iorney to Cales 1625," *The Naval Tracts of Sir William Monson* (London, 1908), III, pp. 135 and 139. For a contemporary copy, see Nottingham University Library, Newcastle Correspondence, NeC 15,406, pp. 41–77.

[46] P. Nichols [F. Drake], *Drake Revived* (London, 1626); Buckingham to Cecil, 5 May 1625, SP 84/127/22v; see also above p. 97.

[47] Carleton to Conway, 23 September 1623, SP 84/114/137; and same to Buckingham, 23 January 1624, SP 84/116/62.

"Three-Year Plan" he argued forcefully for an English expedition to the Caribbean.[48]

Buckingham's speech on 3 March reveals that these arguments were not lost on him and that he realized full well that he was not alone in his interest in the West Indies. If for reasons of state and security, the precise details of the war strategy could not be discussed in Parliament, it was vitally important that some inkling of the Crown's intentions should be given to quiet suspicions. And so much the better if the government's heart appeared to be in the right place. It is significant that one of the few things that Sir Edward Coke and the Duke of Buckingham shared aside from kinship was a common delusion about the West Indies. A "blue water" policy with a decided Caribbean flavor may well have bound the coalition together as much as the prince's reversionary interest.

The exhibition of the duke's favorite enthusiasm came as the Commons were waiting for James's response to the resolution of 1 March, which his reported "fierce rheum and cough" delayed. But after Buckingham chided James for preferring stags and Spaniards to his own subjects, he agreed to an audience on the 5th, provided Parliament removed religion as one of the reasons for the breach of the treaties. After the MPs regretfully complied, he received the delegation.[49] His response to the amended petition quickly dashed any hope that he and his son moved in step. He agreed "seriously [to] think upon" the advice, but given his own financial straits and those of "the beggarly Dutch," and given the recent Spanish offers which he mentioned, he offered little hope of immediately following Parliament's advice. Instead, he challenged them to "shew me the Means how I may do what you would have me [do]." If the Commons offered him a firm financial support, then James *might* consider a breach of the treaties. To sweeten his new request, James offered two concessions, which had not been heard in Parliament in over a century. Parliamentary deputies could administer the subsidy: "I will not take your money unless I take your Counsel." Moreover, "I will not treat nor accept of a Peace without first acquainting you with it, and hearing your Advice." Finally he left no doubt about his independence. While his son and favorite spoke of a war, James continued to speak of a negotiated settlement: after the Commons voted a war subsidy, "haply conditions of Peace will be the better when we are prepared for War, according to the old Proverb, That Weapons boad Peace."[50] After James artfully rephrased the question the

---

[48] Hondius to Carleton, 21 May 1624, SP 84/117/213; and Proposal [in Conway's hand, late 1623], SP 14/157/64.

[49] Buckingham to James, [2 March 1624], *Hardwicke State Papers*, I, p. 460; and Ruigh, pp. 190–5.

[50] *LJ*, III, pp. 250–1; and Castle's report, Trumbull MSS, VII/90.

"Patriots" had sedulously avoided on 1 March, there were no further reports of James as a silent partner of Charles and Buckingham.

Many Englishmen did not share Kellie's assessment that James's speech "did mutche satisfye a great number of the houses." After all, as a Scots Catholic and a Spanish sympathizer, Kellie was no judge of parliamentary opinion. More sensitive observers came to a much different conclusion. The speech caused Castle to abandon his earlier optimism: since the king's speech, "the hope of the publick stands not so well." Lamentations for "the faire beginnings . . . [of Parliament] to cast off the witchcrafte of Spayne and to prop up the cause of the religion" ended with a fervent prayer that God who can turn the hearts of kings "as the water-courses, will never suffer us againe to be charmed with the former sorceries."[51] John Woolley shared Castle's gloss, if not his emotional response: James's public announcement of "his desire . . . to have peace almoste at what rate soever . . . gave no great satisfaction." John Beaulieu interpreted the speech to mean that James was "doubtful and undetermined." Hence "no small crosses and perplexities" awaited the rest of the session. "That mutual and unhappie jealousie," Beaulieu noted,

seemeth still to worke betweene the Head and the Member, he suspecting that they have no mynde to relieve him but to engage him into a Warre and they on the other side that his onely end is to drawe contributions from them; which they are very cautious in this Assemblie not to give the lesse hope of, before the Maine Businesse be resolved and agreed on.

After James's speech, Beaulieu thought another round of fasting and prayers "most seasonable."[52] Notwithstanding repeated admonitions to banish the memory of previous parliamentary "abortions," recollections of the 1621 Parliament were now clearly foremost in the minds of many contemporaries. Behind the admirable visage of the constant prince and the worthy duke, they could now perceive the old king they knew all too well.

While James delivered his reply at Theobalds, the Commons revived other unpleasant memories of 1621. Sandys reported on 5 March Southampton's motion from the Lords that Parliament should anticipate James's acceptance of its advice and agree to "assist his Majesty with our persons and fortunes according to our abilities." His seemingly innocent motion set the MPs by the ears. Before Sandys's motion could find a seconder, Edward Alford denounced it as a violation of "the liberties of the House." Behind his defense of parliamentary privilege clearly lay painful memories: "our former engage-

---

[51] Kellie to Mar, 11 March 1624, *Mar and Kellie*, p. 195; and Castle to Trumbull, 8 March 1624, Trumbull MSS, XVIII/90.

[52] Woolley to Trumbull, 6 March 1624; and Beaulieu to same, 8 March 1624, Trumbull MSS, XLVIII/115, and VII/152. Set these against Ruigh's judgment, p. 200.

ments in this kind have got us nothing; and that it is fit something should first be done for the country and grievances reformed, and then this motion may have his proper time."[53]

The clash between Sandys and Alford reverberated through the House. Phelips and Sir William Strode both attempted to defend Sandys and Southampton, while Sir John Savile supported Alford, warning that by this motion "we shall stand engaged to generalities, even to all our estates for who shall be the judge of our abilities." He was not "against assisting the King according to his fortunes, but desires us to be advised how we engage ourselves." Christopher Wandesford reiterated Savile's plea for caution and suggested "a parliamentary way not generally." Sir Heneage Finch then argued that the entire debate was "unfit . . . for the manner and time." The House did not know "whether the King will have wars or not, nor what assistance his Majesty will demand."[54] William Mallory then moved that the Commons ignore the Lords' motion and expel the MPs on the joint committee who had even proposed it. The committee, he remarked, had driven the House with "much diligence," but "double diligence is not good." Mallory's accusation brought two committee members, Weston and Digges, to their own defense. Weston attempted to shame the sticklers of privileges: he "shall be glad to go out of the House," since "Spain and Rome would rejoice to hear that we have given advice to the King to break the treaties with Spain and that we will not assist his Majesty therein." Sir Francis Seymour, unmoved by Weston's threat, was anxious only that the written proposal itself be "suppressed lest it be thought that the King did accept of our advice upon promise and contract." In Sandys's defense Sir William Beecher and Sir Edward Giles argued that the motion was "no more than they did the last parliament." Sandys himself assumed the same line of defense: his motion "was propounded . . . to rest upon the protestation of the last parliament."[55] Coke as usual resolved the debate when he joined the attack on Sandys's motion, although not on the committee itself. Glanville then identified the central issue: "to provide for war before it be propounded to us is to christen a child before it was born." Meanwhile, Sandys, Phelips, Digges and Coke had fallen back and proposed, instead of Southampton's "generalities," to offer to support a war "in a parliamentary manner." Alford and Seymour on the other hand proposed that the House simply ignore the message completely. The Commons eventually sided with Alford and Seymour and ordered that Southampton's motion "be not so much as spoken of."[56]

[53] 5 March, Spring Diary, fo. 84.
[54] 5 March, Nicholas Diary, fo. 50; and Spring Diary, p. 85.
[55] 5 March, Nicholas Diary, fo. 51; and Spring Diary, pp. 86–7.
[56] 5 March, Spring Diary, p. 88.

The horror at Southampton's motion, Russell has argued, "can be taken to show the comparative importance they attached to their privileges and to their constituents on the one hand and to war on the other." Yet the issues involved were in fact less clear-cut. To be sure, a concern for privilege could veil less honorable motives. Ruigh remarked that royal officials were apt to view "pleas for the liberties of the subject and the due process of Parliament" as "an excuse for obstruction and greed rather than a guarantee of the citizen's security." Yet to conclude, as Russell does, that "at the crucial moment, members' local loyalties had proved stronger than their national ones" is questionable.[57] Doubts first arise about equating the failure of Southampton's motion with the passing of "the chance that King and Commons would be united in a successful war effort." It is perfectly true that "it seemed like military suicide to enter on a war, which would necessarily depend largely on Parliamentary supply, without some assurance, however vague, that supply for the war would be available and would continue beyond the first flush of enthusiasm." Nonetheless, it seems a little hasty to assume that only Sandys's motion would have met this requirement. In fact, another motion which did pass the House on 12 March sounded very similar to the alteration of Sandys's motion which Coke, Digges and Phelips urged a week earlier: "uppon your Majesty's declaration we have with one voice agreed in a parliamentary way to assist your Majesty with our persons and abilities."[58] Hence mourning for the war effort on the afternoon of 5 March seems a little premature.

The misunderstanding arose because most of the Commons made a distinction between Sandys's motion and the war; Russell unfortunately did not. The demise of the motion certainly did not augur well for the war's success, but they both did not pass away together. Some of Sandys's opponents seem to have been mere "wreckers" who would have looked on with dry eyes as Sir Richard Weston left the House and took the "great business" with him. But others seemed sincere when they objected, as Finch did, that the motion was "unfit, not for the matter, but for the manner and time." Finch, in short, inverted Russell's dictum: it would have been just as suicidal to promise subsidies for a war when "we know not whether the King will have wars or not" as it would have been to begin a war without adequate parliamentary support. Russell acknowledged that to most MPs, the Parliament of 1621 had been a "traumatic experience"; at least one MP of that session was still trying to explain away in 1624 his parliamentary actions

---

[57] Russell, *Parliaments*, pp. 180 and 182; and Ruigh, p. 195.
[58] 12 March, Spring Diary, p. 112; and Russell, *Parliaments*, pp. 180 and 182.

three years earlier.[59] Southampton's motion, as Alford had immediately pointed out, was 1621 writ large. Against this background Russell's analysis can easily be accepted as valid with the addition of a dependent clause: the Commons' reaction to Southampton's motion does indeed illustrate that MPs' local loyalties were stronger than their national ones – when the national ones called for their political self-destruction at the hustings. The 5 March debates were not really about the war: they were about the elementary rules of political survival.

The Commons from 5 to 11 March occupied itself largely with legislation until Weston delivered on the 11th the account of royal finances that James had promised on the 5th. It is important to appreciate, however, that MPs were dutifully awaiting events and that when topics relating to foreign policy arose, they dealt with them immediately. They were not avoiding involvement; rather they were proceeding with all deliberate speed. The members officially heard the king's response only on the 8th. Sir John Eliot then proposed that given the "many strange Reports" of James's speech, "all members may take Copies" of James's reply in order to prepare "for debating and treating of the Things herein propounded by his Majesty." Weston then announced that he would deliver on 10 March the Lord Treasurer's financial address. In the event, however, the report was a day late; it "had been made sooner," Weston explained, "if Computation could have been made, what would be lost in the Customs, if a War" and if the Customers had not been tardy in their reports.[60] Immediately after Weston's financial assessment, the Commons then engaged in prolonged debate on supply.

It is possible to see in the interval between 5 and 11 March a relative difference in the martial enthusiasm of the peers and the Parliament-men. "When they [the MPs] could," Russell noted, "most of them were happy to leave high matters of state to the court and the House of Lords." But it would be unwise to press the distinction too far. The Commons then dutifully marked time in the "great business," not because they were too skittish to assume the financial burden of war, but because they were waiting on two successive reports. One diary, for example, recorded the king's speech of 5 March but added "meanwhile, that this answer was in coming, we went on with other matters in our House."[61] Once the speech was officially reported and Weston's study delivered, the Commons began a detailed two-day discussion of war finances. It is worth remembering that on 8 March, Sir John Davies complained that the Commons had spent too much time, not too little, on

[59] R. Cust and P. Lake, "Sir Richard Grosvenor and the Rhetoric of Magistracy," *BIHR* (1981), pp. 40–53.

[60] *CJ*, pp. 679, 682 and 731.

[61] Bodleian Library, Rawlinson MSS B 151, fo. 62; and Russell, *Parliaments*, p. 189.

"this great matter of advice." By then, only five public bills and one private had passed the House, and the other measures "will have but a slow proceeding until the main businesses" were resolved. Likewise "the grand transcendent business" meant that the complaints made to the Committee of Grievances were "little dispatcht."[62] As Davies made clear, foreign affairs were blocking domestic business, not vice versa.

In addition, the difference between the Commons' patience and the Lords' bellicosity is hardly surprising. After all, the Commons, not the Lords, had aroused James's wrath in 1621. Given the regularity with which pro-war MPs reminded their colleagues that this could be the last Parliament, it should be no wonder that the Commons in 1624 studiously minded their procedural Ps and Qs. Finally, a "localist" MP may well have grumbled that saber-rattling was cheap among their lordships who did not have to face constituents either in tax collection or at the poll. Money matters, Glanville reminded the Commons, should "proceed originally from us who sat there for shires and boroughs whereas the Lords were only for themselves."[63] In any event, the question of parliamentary interest in the war in these six days is really beside the point because on 11–12 March, the Commons gave ample testimony of its views on the war.

MAKING GOOD THEIR ADVICE: THE SECOND DEBATE, 11–12 MARCH

The second of the three major debates on the "great business" was in Ruigh's analysis "diffuse and disorganized." The House on 11–12 March had to "make good" the advice it had unanimously given James on the 1st, and although the coalition remained tactically efficient, it gave indications of being less well drilled: Sandys and Coke crossed one another, as did Conway and Phelips. Nonetheless, even in the confusion, it was hard to perceive, as Russell has argued, that the various conflicts between James, Charles and Buckingham over the war spilled over into the Commons' debate.[64] Only Rudyerd and Coke on the 11th and Conway on the 12th proposed "particulars" about the Commons' general offer of assistance, and they all did so in a backhanded fashion. On these two days when James's desire was put forward so faintly and half-heartedly, a description of parliamentary events in terms of conflict between sovereign and favorite is inappropriate.

More than any dispute, fundamental unanimity was most noticeable in the debate. No one was delighted with James's response on the 5th, but all were prepared to "make good their advice." "If the Commons were not prepared

[62] Davies to Huntington, 8 March 1624, *Cal. of SP Ireland*, XVI, pp. 470–1.
[63] 11 March, Holles Diary, fo. 97.
[64] Ruigh, p. 205; and Russell, *Parliaments*, pp. 177–8.

to accept something on the lines of Southampton's motion [of the 5th]," Russell remarked, "they could not with any consistency advise the King to undertake a war." By the 12th, the House cleared up this inconsistency when it agreed that, if James terminated negotiations with Spain, it would "in a parliamentary way . . . assist your Majesty with our persons and abilities." Admittedly both Charles and Buckingham expressed concern over the precise definition of the phrase, "in a parliamentary way"; Charles for instance wanted to know "what Parliamentary way they meane." But the phrase was first proposed by Sir Robert Harley, one of their most loyal servants in the Commons, and Southampton quickly persuaded them to overlook any ambiguity in the phrase. In the earlier furore over Southampton's motion on the 5th, Sir Heneage Finch suggested that once the "manner and time" became fit, such a motion would easily pass; on 11–12 March the manner and time were propitious for something very much on the lines of the earl's earlier motion.[65]

Such conflict as there was on 11–12 March came from those who wanted to talk about the war in more detail and those who did not. The coalition, with the notable exception of Sandys, fell into the latter category. Their common response to the confusion of the 11th was to hold the debate to the question. Indeed, the confusion arose partly from persistent motions to return to the question, almost all of which came from pro-war MPs. Whenever Sir Robert Mansell and John Glanville in their enthusiasm or curiosity wandered beyond the narrow topic of "making good" their advice, Sir William Herbert and Sir Robert Heath quickly rose to shepherd them away from potentially vexatious topics. This sequence of events was characteristic of these debates when the Commons began to perceive that the boundaries of the *arcana imperii* had not vanished; they had merely been adjusted.

Rudyerd opened the debate by dwelling at length on the intimidating refrain which was fast becoming the leitmotiv of the "Patriot" coalition in 1624. "As long as we can maintain parliaments," he maintained, "we can never want liberty." Since the preservation of the institution itself was ultimately the most important issue before any session, he begged the House "not be over-curious and ingenious" and "not distaste" either the young prince or the old king. Otherwise, "I am afraid if this parliament fail it will be the last of the parliaments." Having sufficiently sobered his audience, Rudyerd then returned to his pet project, the Four Propositions: he proposed a joint committee to assess the cost of implementing these as well as a "present" for James's debts.[66] Discussion of Rudyerd's proposals immediately stalled when

---

[65] *Notes of the Debates in the House of Lords, 1624 and 1626*, ed. S. R. Gardiner (London, 1879), p. 30; Russell, *Parliaments*, pp. 179–80; and above, p. 85.
[66] 11 March 1624, Pym Diary, fo. 25.

Sir James Perrot offered his own suggestion of a second committee to consider the estate of the kingdom as well. More provocatively, he proposed to tie redress of grievances with assistance towards the war: "that the King might be acquainted with the grievances in traffic, and that if he please to redress that and to pass laws prepared, then to think to give him what we may." Sir Henry Mildmay, the Master of the Jewel House, moved promptly to head off Perrot's motion by echoing concerns about Parliament's imminent peril; unless "our fears and jealousies" were abandoned, "we shall be but spectacles of ruin and desolation." Instead of backing either prior motion, he simply proposed that "we make good our advice by contributions and that our contributions may follow the King's declaration."[67] Mildmay, not Rudyerd or Perrot, ultimately defined the bounds of the day's debate. Thomas Wentworth of Oxford seconded Mildmay and tacked on a characteristic reminder of dangers confronting the Dutch Republic; as Pym reported, he "did more honestly than necessarily labour with many reasons to excite us to the assistance of the Low Countries." Secretary Conway and William Coryton then steered the discussion back to Mildmay's motion. After the king's declaration of the breach, Conway assured the MPs that they could discuss the war, but now "till we have resolved what we will do for the enabling of the King for a war, we shall not know his Majesty's resolution." Coryton added the important clause, "if he follow our Advice," which Conway omitted from Mildmay's formula.[68] In spite of these admonitions, Sir George More again proposed a broader debate which would include "what we must now do" and "how to be maintained." More may well have been one of those whom Pym referred to as "entangled in the considerations of the general poverty and want in the kingdom."[69] In any event his motion would have steered the debate directly into danger. Sir Edward Cecil attempted to answer More's objections; "no king makes war of his own purse, the people must bear it." But his own labors to limit the debate gave way to martial fantasies, which he doubtless regretted two years later at Cadiz: "with 10,000 men he durst undertake to run through Spain." Since Cecil had set "2 hares . . . on foot," Edward Alford requested the Speaker "to hold everyone to the question."[70]

The chaotic cycle repeated itself when Sandys assumed Digges's position on the 1st and held forth on the dangers of "precipitation," which Perrot and More had earlier raised. A discussion of the war was inappropriate without a valid *causa belli*; James had yet to issue an ultimatum for the return of the

---

[67] 11 March 1624, Spring Diary, p. 102; and Nicholas Diary, fo. 68.
[68] *CJ*, p. 682; 11 March, Pym Diary, fo. 25; and Nicholas Diary, fos. 68–9.
[69] 11 March 1624, Pym Diary, fo. 25; and *CJ*, p. 682.
[70] 11 March 1624; Nicholas Diary, fo. 69; and Holles Diary, fo. 96.

Palatinate and Philip to defy it. Moreover, since the charge of a war "will be great," the estate of the kingdom must be examined in order to redress grievances and to restore the flagging cloth trade. He proposed a fourth response to James's address, which directly linked redress and supply: "we should promise that as we shall be enabled we will extend our aid."[71] Sandys's sudden volte-face was almost total: the sober advocate on the 11th of mature deliberation had been a week earlier one of the most precipitous men in the House. His public humiliation on the 5th may have taught him the merits of circumspection and the need to recover some of his old standing among back-bench "country" MPs. In any event, Charles and Buckingham may have begun to wonder if a promise from Sandys of "all manner of conformitie" was worth the bother.

From Sandys's very cautious motion, Christopher Brooke, his ally in Virginia Company disputes, veered back to Rudyerd's motion. Since "general terms and conditionally" were not likely to serve the turn, he pressed for a particular grant to cover the implementation of Rudyerd's Four Propositions. By this point the bewildering array of proposals alarmed Sir Henry Anderson, who moved that "we will make good our advice and no more."[72] As the resolution of the House faltered, Coke stepped into the breach. First, he dispatched Sandys's fears. Apprehensions about the country's ability to maintain a war were groundless; from his experience as a commissioner of the Treasury, he proclaimed "under the rose" that in order to increase trade, "divers understanding citizens said no better way but by war with Spain." Moreover, Sandys's search for a *causa belli* Coke dismissed as excessively nice. Instead of Sandys's polite international law, Coke urged the merits of "cannon law": "Some say they have not denied it. Did not the King demand it and said he would take delay for denial. We see it is delayed, and so denied, and then just." After such marvelous logic-chopping, Coke delivered a brisk pep-talk to the faint-hearted. Once Ireland and the Dutch were reinforced and the Navy strengthened, England itself would be impervious; "and come Spain, pope or devil . . . we fear them not." Indeed the mere mention of a Spanish war made him feel seven years younger. Yet while he embraced these proposals, he also placed them in proper perspective: "but first it will be necessary to have the King declare himself . . . to draw on the King to an absolute declaration."[73] Coke's speech was a *tour de force*. With cajolery and bluff patriotism, Coke at once overturned Sandys, co-opted Cecil and steered the debate firmly back to the simple question of "making good" the Commons' advice.

Even Coke, however, could not discipline his colleagues. Sir Robert

---

[71] 11 March 1624, Spring Diary, p. 104.
[72] *Ibid.*, pp. 104–5.   [73] *Ibid.*, p. 105; and Holles Diary, fo. 97.

Mansell initially supported Coke only to wander off at the end. A war was already justified "for the honor of the royal blood and for the honor of Christ's blood too." Moreover, he scoffed at the "bugbear" of Spanish power; Philip "holds his greatness by our charity." Yet having disposed of Sandys, Mansell then moved that the Commons consider the cost "for the preparation of the war" and then "the means how to raise it." Sir William Herbert immediately objected to Mansell's motion, and, to forestall any other attempts to put the cart before the horse, he asked that "if any shall wander from the question . . . that the Speaker should hold him to the question." Sir William Strode and Sir Robert Harley both seconded Herbert and backed Mildmay's motion, although one diarist has Harley add "in a parliamentary way."[74] Such a simple motion, however, displeased John Glanville who had doubts about "the honor and justice of the war" and about the declaration of assistance, which should be "carefully couched that it may not prejudice us." Heath, the Solicitor General, rose to refute such fears. Coke had earlier argued that a debate on the justice of the war was merely inappropriate, but Heath stated it was unwarranted: "it is not proper to us to determine whether there shall be war or not." The cost of the war could not yet be debated "because we understand not the particular necessaries of the war," and these particulars were best discussed in a Council of War rather than Parliament "since this place can better give counsel than keep it." Therefore, "to draw on the King," a simple declaration of their assistance was the most acceptable course.[75]

The issue at last seemed resolved, and Phelips, Digges, Sir Nathaniel Rich and Sir Heneage Finch supported Mildmay's motion for a general declaration. Only Phelips and Finch specifically objected to broader discussions. Phelips argued plausibly that the House's convenience rather than the royal prerogative prevented any discussion: "it will make much dispute among us." Finch on the other hand warned "that we now should not deal in an unnecessary and improper question of war or of the justice of war." After such chastening, all that remained was to settle the form of the declaration. Finch proposed that if James followed the Commons' advice about the treaties, Parliament should "assist him and make it good with our bodies and goods to the uttermost." Alford then objected to "uttermost" and Coke to the "bodies and goods." Sir Thomas Jermyn mildly chided them for falling out just when they were about to find the political "philosopher's stone," and he proposed an alternative formula, which was in the end adopted – "persons and abilities in a parliamentary way."[76]

---

[74] 11 March 1624, Spring Diary, pp. 105–6; and Nicholas Diary, fo. 70.
[75] 11 March 1624, Spring Diary, p. 106; and Nicholas Diary, fo. 70.
[76] 11 March 1624, Spring Diary, p. 107; Holles Diary, fo. 97; and Nicholas Diary, fos. 70–70v.

Even in a debate which, Pym remarked, was "not altogether without variety of propositions," a fairly clear pattern emerges.[77] A large group of MPs wanted to talk about the war. Wentworth, More, Cecil, Brooke, Mansell, Glanville and the newly regenerate Sandys shared an interest in discussing either war aims and strategy or the possible effects of war on the nation, all eminently reasonable questions for a nation on the brink of a foreign conflict. But any detailed discussion of these points was cut off; another large body of MPs, all of whom, except Alford, had close connections to the "Patriots," successfully held the House to generalities. Rudyerd's Four Propositions seem to have been an acceptable fall-back position, but they appeared at the time too confining when the king might still agree to an open war. Consequently the coalition did not then solidly line up behind the Four Propositions.

The debates on 11 March were the first signs of a phenomenon which would become more pronounced on 19–20 March: the enthusiasts resolutely sought to prevent others from discussing their cherished policy. Against this background, it becomes more understandable why there was so little discussion of the war in the lengthy subsidy debates of mid-March. Notwithstanding Russell's comments on "very little . . . practical readiness to prepare for war" in the Commons, the debates on 11 March testify that there was interest in "practical belligerence," but compelling extraparliamentary reasons forced those who should have had the most interest in fostering its growth instead to muffle it at every turn.[78] It is scarcely surprising that parliamentary views of the war emerged from the session in a stunted form.

A brief debate on the following morning formed a coda to the second discussion of "the great business." As the Commons on the 11th had moved to a resolution, the Lords grappled with the fear that "some Doubts might arise" among the MPs about James's reply of the 5th. Charles eventually delivered a message to a joint committee "to clear such Doubts as have risen amongst them and may, peradventure, arise amongst you," a message which Secretary Calvert reported to the Commons on the morning of the 12th. The prince assured them that James actually did not insist on parliamentary help with his debts and that the resolution of "the great business" would decrease rather than increase the intervals between parliamentary sessions. He then exhorted the House to proceed swiftly, and, as Beaulieu reported, "not to shew themselves as those dogges that would only snarle and brake and not bite; but to use their teeth as well as to shewe them." Anxious for a successful resolution, Charles even wagered his personal prestige. "If ye go on with Courage and

---

[77] 11 March 1624, Pym Diary, fo. 25.   [78] Russell, *Parliaments*, p. 164.

shew Alacrity and Readiness in this busines," he promised, "ye shall so oblige
me unto you now, that I will never forget it hereafter."[79]

His "most heroical" speech, though reported too late to influence the
Commons' debate on 11 March, did prompt a round of backslapping among
MPs and an extraordinary message of compliment to the prince. Almost as an
afterthought, it also led to a motion to enumerate the particulars of their
assistance to the king. Sir Thomas Edmondes, the Treasurer of the Household, waxed eloquent over the prince's virtues; Phelips exulted over "our
good genius" that "led us to resolve of assistance to the king before the Lordes
had done it"; Sir Humphrey May, the Chancellor of the Duchy of Lancaster,
praised the current session for their "clear and plain dealing"; and they all
supported a message of "due thanks" to Charles. Some of their colleagues,
however, grew restive during this contest between the two Court officials and
a prominent "undertaker" in the composition of anthems to Parliament and
Charles. Both Alford and Digges approved of the sentiments behind a complimentary message to the prince, but questioned the propriety "to compliment with others than the king." Sir John Savile, who had been asked to help
frame the compliment, was even more emphatic: since "he understands not
compliment nor never saw it used in parliament before," he asked to be
excused. Conway at this point returned to the question of supply. What
would "best content the Prince," the Secretary announced, would be to "set
down in that declaration particulars what we will do if the King shall
declare." Conway's attempt to tack on "particulars" about supply was somewhat lame, and Sir John Eliot quickly dispatched the proposal. "Particular
subsidies," he pointed out, "cannot so fully answer the charge of a war, as an
engagement to assist to the whole war." Finally Coke returned to the question
of a complimentary message wrapping the proposal in ancient precedent, the
fairest possible parliamentary clothing: "the Black Prince and Henry the 5th
did both sit princes in parliament and had thanks often given them by the
House."[80]

By the conclusion of the debate, everyone seemed pleased with one another.
James had, his son reported, dropped the matter of his debts and announced
willingness to summon frequent Parliaments if the Commons made good
their advice. By the time the Commons learned of these concessions, they had
already approved a general offer of assistance. Moreover, the prospect of
regular sessions obviously pleased them, but the fact that they had acted more
expeditiously than the Lords put them in an especially contented mood. In the
past, they had been accused of dragging their feet in important financial

---

[79] *LH*, III, pp. 256–8; and Beaulieu to Trumbull, 12 March 1624, Trumbull, VII/153.
[80] 12 March, Spring Diary, pp. 109–11; Nicholas Diary, fos. 72–3; Pym Diary, fos. 26–7; and
CJ, pp. 683–4 and 734.

matters, and now they had for once turned the tables. No wonder then that the Commons decided on 12 March to revive the custom of complimenting the Prince of Wales.

The euphoria proved short-lived. On the 14th, after delivering Parliament's resolution and receiving James's reply, Archbishop Abbot immediately took to his bed. Notwithstanding Charles's report to the contrary, James himself still insisted on parliamentary assistance with his debts: his creditors apparently mattered as much to him as his grandchildren did. Moreover, he had not resolved on a war as Charles and Buckingham had earlier intimated. Indeed, at the beginning of this speech, James pointedly emphasized the distinction between Buckingham and himself. These contradictions, however, paled before James's response to Parliament's offer of assistance. Personally, he was delighted by the general offer: "I confess it is without Example, that any King hath had so large an offer, and with God's favour, I need fear nothing in this World." Unfortunately, James explained, "I must not only deal with my own people, but with my Neighbours and Allies . . . General words will not carry it: therefore I must resort to particular means." The particular means he had in mind were five subsidies and ten fifteenths for "this great business" and one subsidy and two fifteenths annually for his debts. To balance his extraordinary requests, he offered three concessions as testimony of his willingness to meet Parliament half-way. He reiterated his earlier offer that a parliamentary commitee, not the royal Treasury, could disburse the subsidies, and he repeated his promise not to conclude a peace "without your Advice." Finally, he announced his intention "to make this a session" and to summon another at Michaelmas and a third in the following spring. He encouraged Parliament to report "the Grievances of My people," and he spoke of his desire "to make good Laws and to reform Abuses."[81]

James's concessions could in no way overshadow the size of his new demands nor his contradictions of the prince and favorite. One account related how James's response "much discomforted" Abbot and the joint committee; a second how it "much dishartened" them; a third how it "peeved" them; and a fourth how the committee was so surprised that they omitted the customary "God save the king."[82] They had good reason for chagrin. Initially the passionate desire to repair the damage done in 1621–3 had bound both king and parliament together, and this common interest in turn had promised an early end to the Spanish treaties. Yet on 5 and

[81] *LJ*, III, pp. 265–6.
[82] Carleton the younger to Carleton, 17 March 1624, SP 14/160/89; D'Ewes, *Diary*, p. 186; Nicholas to Nicholas, 18 March [1624], SP 14/160/91; and Beaulieu to Trumbull, 19 March 1624, Trumbull MSS, VII, no. 154.

14 March, James delivered repeated checks to any hopes of a harmonious conclusion. After James's speech, the Earl of Huntington commented that "I desyre and pray for" and "wish the Parliament may succeed." Nevertheless he could not ignore that "the kings last speech hath many waighty and considerable things to be consulted." In particular, "soe many difficultys wille arise" from James's request for "a great masse of mony."[83] The "Patriots," to be sure, pressed on, rallying the Parliament-men to strive again for James's approval, but after the second royal response, no amount of optimism could dispell the fact that the old sentiment of "mutual and unhappie jealousie" had again arisen between James and his latest Parliament. Notwithstanding the auspicious opening in mid-February, the followers of the prince and favorite had no other option a month later than to attempt to reconcile sovereign and estates for a third time. And this time, thanks to James's demands, they could no longer avoid the discussion of the potentially dangerous topic of the war itself.

[83] Huntington to Davies, 17 March 1624, Huntington Library, Hastings Correspondence, Box 10, HA 5482.

"The high crisis of this most important business": Parliament and the war, 12–24 March

The committee members whom James had stunned on 14 March would doubtless have been even more amazed if they had known that in less than ten days their dejection would become delight. On 23 March royal rebuffs gave way to a gracious acceptance of the Parliament-men's third offer, and James's volte-face laid the foundation for both English military intervention and parliamentary turbulence later in the decade. Given the later contemporary confusion over precisely what had been discussed and resolved in these nine days and given the current historiographical debate over contemporary interest in military intervention, this final grand debate merits careful attention. Anything less can scarcely permit us to understand the importance of the decision reached in what Beaulieu dubbed "the high Crisis of this most important business."[1]

PRELUDE TO CONFRONTATION

Credit for bringing king and Parliament together for a third time belongs to Charles and the duke. After a brief period of shock over James's address on 14 March, they informed James "how tenderly that answeare of his would be apprehended by the House" and pressed him for more pleasing modifications. Conway confessed on the 17th that James's response "was construed by many to admit iealous interpretations." But in the intervening days, his address "by the endeavours of the prince and the mediation of the Duke of Buckingham betweene the king and his people is now settled with good Comments and interpretations."[2] Endeavors and mediation, however, are excessively polite descriptions of their frantic lobbying from 15 to 18 March.

Charles and Buckingham not only had to persuade James to relent, but also to convince the Commons to accept the new royal concessions. Abbot's

---

[1] Beaulieu to Trumbull, 5 March 1624, Trumbull MSS, VII/151.
[2] Conway to Carleton, 24 March 1624, SP 84/116/264; and Beaulieu to Trumbull, 19 March 1624, Trumbull MSS, VII/154.

psychosomatic illness delayed the formal report of the royal audience and so allowed Charles and the duke a few days' respite. On the 15th, at a meeting of the joint committee, Buckingham and Charles offered verbal corrections of certain "misinterpretations" of the royal speech. The king in fact had not disavowed Buckingham's relation and had no doubts about the justice of a war. But since Charles's verbal corrections to the royal speech of 5 March had partially prompted James's displeasure in the second speech of 14 March, Buckingham and Charles wisely resolved to secure written authorization for the new emendations. After a visit to James at Woking on 16 March, Buckingham returned with a signet letter containing "some Amendments but no Alteration at all," which was eventually presented to both Houses. There were two significant modifications: James was now content to add the one subsidy and two fifteenths, initially requested for his debts, to the other five subsidies and ten fifteenths earmarked for the "great business," and he was resolved "in Honour and in Conscience" on a war. When Heath reported the news to the Commons, he followed a practice that was rapidly becoming normal procedure: he distributed copies of the address, allowed two days for "ripe deliberation," and set a debate for two days later.[3]

The ensuing discussion on 19–20 March was indeed, as Ruigh has remarked, "the climax of the session." Not only was it essential to arrive at a basic framework of agreement, it was also imperative to act quickly. Buckingham had earlier referred to the imminent arrival of Padre Maestro with new Spanish proposals. By the time the debate opened on the 19th, the Spanish envoy was at Calais awaiting the arrival of a Mr. Bond, an English "special agent," to escort him through any possible Dutch naval interference. A few days earlier near Abbeville, he had been robbed of his instructions, although it is unclear if the news of this event reached London before 19 March. In any event, there was considerable anxiety over his arrival before James had broken the treaties. In late February, Conway had confidently assumed Padre Maestro would arrive too late: "before hee arrive I doubt not, but the Parliament will have interpreted the end of the preparations in Spaine, and cutt out an answeare for the ffryar."[4] But events did not proceed as Conway had expected. On 6 March Woolley expressed concern that the mere rumor of his arrival "being once blowen into his Majesty's eares may hinder our proceedinge." Four days later, Mr. Carleton reported that Rota had finally left London only to have "a worse beast," Padre Maestro, hurrying to take his place: "I hope matters are gon too farre for any enchanting ouvertures to take place any more." By 17 March even Conway's optimism

[3] *LJ*, III, pp. 165–6; *CJ*, p. 738; and Ruigh, pp. 210–16.
[4] Conway to Carleton, 23 February 1624, SP 84/116/154; Introduction to John Bond, 12 March 1624, SP 78/72/60; and Ruigh, p. 270, n. 16.

began to falter. "You may preadventure here wavering coniectures," he warned Carleton, "and noe marvel if you doe, for wee admitt them here."[5] The close conjunction between Parliament's resolution and the Spanish envoy's arrival in London had become more than a little uncomfortable. "Chaucer's ffryer" pacing at Calais left Charles and Buckingham a narrow margin of error.

The delay of the parliamentary resolution was also becoming an awkward bottleneck to the coalition's plans. In late February, the Dutch envoys, Aerssens and Joachimi, whom the English had so insistently requested a month earlier, arrived in London and were received "with more ceremony then they expected." Whatever the course of their future negotiations, "sure I am," Woolley remarked, "the common people did much reioice to see them as they passed alonge." Yet nearly a month later, the envoys still waiting to begin negotiations, and Joachimi and especially Aerssens, never the most patient of men, were becoming restive. Conway attempted to explain the delay by pointing out that the English "would by noe meanes enter into treaty with the States Ambassadors, until his Majestie had declared."[6] The lack of this vital declaration, which hung on Parliament's resolution, likewise stalled the preliminary French negotiations. Kensington reached Paris in late February to find a very attentive French audience, but "I directlye finde," he mournfully reported on 2 March, that the negotiations could not begin until "our Parliament shall have delivered our yonge maister clearlye from that unhappy and tedious treatye of Spaine." He beseeched Buckingham to "let me with speede hear from you for I languish until I understand your resolutions."[7]

Amid the rising tension outside Westminster, the coalition had to concentrate on its most difficult task. The discussion of the exact number of subsidies and fifteenths was always a very delicate operation, and the royal request for six and twelve respectively meant that in 1624 the coalition had to proceed with the steadiest possible hand. Two problems complicated their task. The one clear result of the debate on 11 March was the majority's unwillingness to vote any public money until presented at least with some outline of the projected military plans. Having been duped in 1621, many MPs were determined to avoid a repeat performance in 1624. Chamberlain

[5] Woolley to Trumbull, 6 March 1624, Trumbull MSS, XLVIII, no. 119; Carleton the younger to Carleton, 10 March 1624, SP 14/160/58; and Conway to Carleton, 17 March 1624, SP 84/116/235.

[6] Woolley to Trumbull, 28 February 1624, Trumbull MSS, XLVIII, no. 114; Carleton the younger to Carlerton, 1 March 1624, SP 84/116/186; and Conway to Carleton, 24 March 1624, SP 84/116/264.

[7] Kensington to [Buckingham], 26 February 1624, SP 78/72/46; and same to Conway, 4 March 1624, SP 78/72/48.

observed that the Commons on the eve of 19 March "are so warie and cautious on all sides as yf they were to treate with ennemies and in daunger to be over-reacht." Yet James refused to discuss any war, much less an Anglo-Spanish one, until the Commons voted supply. Just as 1621 haunted his subjects, so too the fear that "I should be bound and they leap free and leave me naked and without help" consistently troubled James during the 1624 session.[8] In this unpromising situation, the Four Propositions at last proved their merit. Obviously a massive grant for a conflict which had the full parliamentary approval would have been ideal, but if the war itself could not bear close scrutiny and discussion, then Rudyerd's Four Propositions were an acceptable second choice. They would provide funds for necessary defensive measures, which would allow negotiations to begin with potential allies. In a later session, it was hoped, a more detailed discussion of the war would lead to further parliamentary grants. For the "Patriot" coalition, therefore, a sizeable allocation for the Four Propositions represented an acceptable alternative.

The lengthy debate over the subsidy on 19–20 March, in which over fifty MPs spoke, was the most sustained of the entire Parliament. Yet what is most surprising about this babel of voices is as much who did not speak as who did. Digges made two comparatively minor interventions, and Phelips three. Rudyerd, as usual, broke the ice on the 19th, but his later silence in the rambling discussion underscored the difference between a set-piece orator, who always relied on a prepared text, and a skillful debater.[9] The most frequent speakers were Savile and Alford who in four speeches each led the only significant opposition to the subsidy bill. Of the two, Savile developed his ideas more fully while Alford confined himself to terse objections. But the frequency of their speeches probably reflects more on their supporters than it does on themselves. It appears that they took the floor as many times as they did more out of frustration than conviction: few others fundamentally questioned the subsidy bill as searchingly as they did, and few MPs expressed support for their ideas. Their criticisms and those of Seymour and Mallory were trenchant enough, but in a long debate, the sheer depth of the coalition bench ultimately proved more telling. Edmondes, Heath and Mildmay could certainly equal the eloquence of Alford, Savile and Mallory, but perhaps most decisively the former trio had no lack of support as Fleetwood, Weston, Conway, Harley, Walter, J. Coke, Wardour and Jermyn testified.

The debate not only brought an exceptional number of speakers to their

---

[8] Chamberlain to Carleton, 20 March 1624, *Letters*, II, p. 548; and James to Conway, [22 April 1624], quoted in Ruigh, p. 242.

[9] On the size of the House, see Nethersole to Carleton, 20 March 1624, SP 81/30/88; and on Rudyerd's art, see Sir John Eliot, *Negotium Posterorum*, pp. 66 and 68–9.

feet; it also sharply divided them. The tension arose from the coalition's efforts to press for the "particulars" of a subsidy for a war which could not bear public discussion. MPs must have found the lines of conflict on 19–20 March all too familiar. On the 1st, at the insistence of the "Patriots," Parliament-men could discuss only the Spanish treaties, but not the Spanish war; on the 11th, they had to confine their remarks to the basic question of making good their advice and eschew any particular ones. After the latest tactical deployment of the war coalition, MPs found that they would be carefully shepherded away from any general questions about the war and held simply to *the* particular one of funding the Four Propositions. This debate not surprisingly became so intense that a chorus of MPs began to chant a sober counterpoint to the coalition's anthem about "the crisis of Parliaments." Rudyerd and Mildmay argued that the future existence of Parliament and English liberties depended on acquiescence to royal demands. But Savile, Alford and Seymour countered that if the Commons acquiesced to such a vaguely worded subsidy bill, MPs would not be able to live with themselves, or with their constituents for that matter. The debate must have been truly unpleasant for the "silent majority" of MPs, who doubtless echoed Sir Henry Anderson's lament: "Dangerous, to return into the Country, and tell them of Subsidies: dangerous again, not to give."[10]

The circumstances of the debate understandably aggravated tempers. Sir Dudley Digges and Sir Peter Heyman, for example, had an unusually brisk exchange on the 20th. Heyman sat for one of the Cinque Ports, customarily exempt from a parliamentary subsidy, and when he voiced a common concern about the burden of taxation, Digges could not resist pointing out the incongruity of the situation: "whereas Sir Peter Heyman said before that we that serve for the countries must look for their satisfaction, he wondered those that served only for the ports would say so." To relieve Heyman's embarrassment, he proposed to "have the ports, that never yet gave, to be brought in" the provisions of the subsidy bill. The member for Hythe did not appreciate any comic relief either at his own or his constituents' possible expense, and he retorted by commenting that the noted martial advocate was in fact a mere tyro: "he [Heyman] had been an apprentice to the wars and should understand them better than he that never had been in them [meaning Digges]."[11] The tone of the Digges–Heyman exchange was playful compared with several comments on the mercenary aspects of the legal profession. The enthusiasm of Sir John Walter, the prince's solicitor, and John Glanville, a prominent London attorney, for four subsidies drove a normally silent MP, Sir Thomas Bellasyse, to remind them that "Subsidies come not in so easily as

[10] *CJ*, p. 742. For these references to a potentially restive electorate, see below, pp. 205–6, 211 and 214.
[11] 20 March 1624, Holles Diary, fo. 109v.

Fees." Similarly, at the end of the debate, Sir John Savile in a passable imitation of Cassandra warned that the 1624 subsidy bill would haunt the MPs at the next election, and he singled out the lawyers for leading the Commons down the primrose path: "his masters of the gown ran very high in giving but they counted without their hosts, and so he thinks we have done, and that we must both reckon again." Little wonder that Baptist Hicks attempted to relieve the tension with a pun that appealed to a common Foxean heritage: "God be thanked, though all we have bee at the Stake, yet not that Stake our Enemies would have us."[12]

The tension, according to Russell, did not result from the coalition's attempt to railroad the subsidy bill through the House; rather it was simply the extension of a factional struggle at Court that set Charles's war party against James's "peace" party. Unfortunately, the "clash of wills" between James and his son and favorite cannot properly account for the alignment of MPs and the intensity of the debates. The coalition lodged James's demand for six subsidies and twelve fifteenths so feebly that it seems to have been mentioned more as an inflated figure useful in bargaining than as a serious proposal. The first half of 1624 unquestionably presented the spectacle of "the Crown . . . divided against itself," and this generational conflict strongly affected parliamentary debate, as the lack of discussion of a war amply illustrates. But to argue that the parliamentary dispute over the subsidy was actually about "a clash of generations in the royal family" seems less justified, unless of course Edward Alford and Francis Seymour can be seen as the king's men on 19–20 March.[13]

The alternative description of what happened on these two days must revive a somewhat discredited historiographical concept. Given the fact that of the original undertakers, only one, Coke, vigorously intervened in these debates, Crown officials and courtiers were left to handle these critical discussions about the subsidy bill largely on their own. Although the coalition pressed a popular idea, a Spanish war, which attracted some "non-aligned" support, it appeared to be almost exclusively a Court coalition on 19–20 March. Historians in recent years have generally sought to minimize the use of a polarized model of centralists against localists to describe parliamentary struggles. Rather, they have preferred to see these conflicts as those of rival Court factions. Unfortunately, the task of "cherchez le patron" produces unsatisfying results when applied to those who opposed the coalition. Since the Court itself was sharply divided between war and peace factions, the logical alignment of those MPs who opposed the former would be with the latter. Sir Francis Seymour's support of Middlesex initially indicates the crucial Court link in 1624, but Seymour's associate in the opposition to the

[12] 20 March 1624, Holles Diary, fo. 110; and *CJ*, p. 742.   [13] Russell, *Parliaments*, p. 145.

coalition's subsidy bill, Sir John Savile, joined in the assault on Cranfield. Even more confusing was Savile's attempt to outstrip his local rival, Sir Thomas Wentworth, for Buckingham's favor. A more promising way of identifying the opposition to the Court coalition presents itself with the cases of Edward Alford and William Mallory. The latter, in Russell's analysis, was an MP "whose natural habitat is where angels fear to treat" and whose Court connections, if any, are unknown; and the former "fits the archetypal image of the 'country member'."[14] Both men clearly depended on some Court favor for their local offices, but this did not apparently circumscribe their independence in Parliament. Therefore, pending further research on Court connections, there seems no other verdict: the conflict on 19–20 March was a dispute between a pro-war coalition dominated by courtiers and an *ad hoc* group of MPs who were deeply suspicious of the arrangements being pressed upon them and who appealed during this struggle to "Country" sentiments.

THE PARTICULARS OF THE WAR: THE THIRD DEBATE, 19–20 MARCH

Sir Benjamin Rudyerd assumed his customary position at the head of the debate. The Spanish treaties would soon end if the Commons offered "a particular sum" as well as a general offer of assistance. The figure James had in mind admittedly was breathtaking, but Rudyerd was quick to point out mitigating factors: indeed most of his speech dwelt on how James's demand could be juggled into a relatively painless form. First of all, James's sacrifice of his debtors to national service could only encourage magnanimity and generosity in the Lower House. More importantly, Rudyerd emphasized that the timing of the payment, in another royal concession, could be spread out so that the subsidy "shall be no greater burthen to the subject than if it were not granted till our next session after Michaelmas." Such easy payment terms, which Edmondes would develop more fully, were not without precedent. The proponents of the idea had the 1601 subsidy in mind, which granted four subsidies over four years. Likewise Rudyerd and Edmondes seemed to have proposed that the collection of the 1624 subsidy bill be spread over at least two years. The money, Rudyerd continued, would be deposited not in the Treasury, but rather "into the hand of committees of both Houses and that it should be still in our power to dispose of." He also reiterated his Four Propositions, although he now envisaged a large expeditionary force of 10–12,000 men to second the Dutch. Finally he concluded with a theme that was rapidly becoming hackneyed. This vital issue, Rudyerd argued, had to be

---

[14] *Ibid.*, pp. 34 and 109; Ruigh, pp. 316, 329 and 332. For the emphasis on faction, see, for example, Derek Hirst, "Court, County and Politics before 1629," *Faction and Parliament*, pp. 105–37.

resolved quickly or else it would grow cold, and "coldness is a degree of deadness so that if we be not very careful we may leave all our hopes dead and buried in this place."[15]

A trio of war supporters, Sir John Eliot, Sir Thomas Edmondes and Sir Miles Fleetwood, then expounded on these themes. Eliot in a rousing address exhorted the House to pay up cheerfully: "he cannot but think a sudden pain better than a continued grief." Those apprehensive about the poverty of the country were urged to reflect "that the war with Spain is our Indies, that there we shall fetch wealth." Edmondes adopted a more sober approach; "the interests of religion and state," not a desire for maritime larceny, compelled England to break with Spain. The only remaining question was the discovery of "a fitting measure and an easy proportion," and he proposed "for the present" a subsidy of £300,000 to fund the Four Propositions, together with a promise "to afford more aid hereafter if occasion serve." Fleetwood echoed Eliot's plea for " a chearful and plentiful Resolution this Day."[16]

Unfortunately for a coalition, saber-rattling and pious hopes could not dissuade some MPs from lodging searching questions – as Sir George More again did. Although it was "time to do, not speak," More referred the House to "the ancient course." "So great a sum," as either James requested or Edmondes proposed, demanded that "it will be fit to know the present occasion." And to justify the propriety of his request for further information, he cited a telling precedent: "In queen Elizabeth's time there was an account given to the parliament what enemies the Queen then had, the Pope, Spain, etc." The striking contrast with 1624 he discreetly left in silence, as he went on to propose two subsidies and four fifteenths. Sir John Savile then embodied More's request for information in a motion that the day's debate proceed in three stages: "to know first what we should do, then how we should do it, and how to levy it."[17] After one short speech and a seemingly innocent procedural motion, the debate seemed about to drift onto that dangerous topic, "to know first what we should do."

The war supporters, as on earlier occasions, quickly deployed themselves to head off such a debate. Before they could get into position, however, two speakers plumped for Savile's motion. Sir Robert Mansell pointedly "dissents" from Rudyerd and opened the discussion of Savile's first point, "what we should do," with his own strategic proposals. Ever the naval officer, he dismissed Rudyerd's call for a large English military force; "to assist the Low Countries by sending thither will be to no purpose." Instead he

---

[15] 19 March, Pym Diary, fos. 32–3. On the 1601 subsidy bill, see J. E. Neale, *Elizabeth I and her Parliaments, 1584–1601* (New York, 1958), pp. 411–22.

[16] 19 March, Spring Diary, pp. 124–5; and *CJ*, p. 740.

[17] 19 March, Holles Diary, fo. 104; and Spring Diary, fo. 125.

called for £3–400,000 to fund an amphibious force comprised of forty-five vessels and 20,000 soldiers which could at once defend Ireland and the Dutch Republic and assault Spain itself. Edward Alford abandoned strategy to press home some truths about "this the greatest matter in parliament." Each of Savile's points, he advised, should be well debated, and the precedents for parliamentary treasurers explored. Otherwise "whatsoever we do the King is free and the people will say that we (if we exceed their abilities) oppress them."[18]

In less than four speeches, Fleetwood's cheerful optimism had given way to Alford's somber vision of a sullen electorate, a vision which dominated the rest of the debate. Weston interrupted the flow of pro-Savile speakers in an attempt to dispel their suspicions: James "hath not sought to bind us and keep himself free." Such thoughts were unworthy of men who were about to reclaim "the honor of the old English nation." Since "the sound of 6 subsidies and 12 fifteenths" was "very fearful," Weston dared "not say for so much but for what will be necessary." Like Rudyerd, he dwelt on the royal concessions; the parliamentary treasurers and "the reasonable limitations of an easy and unburthensome levying." He may also have introduced an additional concession when he urged the House to "consider the charge shall continue no longer than the occasion last."[19] Weston's best efforts, however, could not diminish the appeal of Savile's motion. Sir John Perrot assumed that Savile's first question swung wide the door into the *arcana imperii* and that Mansell had already rushed in. Not to be outdone, he proposed that James terminate "all other Treaties with foreign Princes . . . which may be prejudicial to our Religion" as well as the Spanish negotiations. Perrot's reflection on the nascent French match could at least claim Buckingham's speech of 15 March as justification. But Sir Francis Seymour's foray into continental strategy had no other warrant than Savile's motion; "generals can give satisfaction neither to the King nor us." The recent royal descent to particulars led to Seymour's pointed question: "he would be glad to know where and with whom the war shall be." In the meantime, he announced his aversion to a war in the Palatinate; "the charge is too great and it hath been, far from our thoughts." Then, in a touching display of deference, after his own strategic pronouncements, Seymour conceded that "we must leave that to the King." If James passed "good laws" and if the Catholics paid double, Seymour was willing to give one subsidy and two fifteenths.[20]

John Pym broke the pro-Savile flow to support Weston. Six subsidies and twelve fifteenths would be an acceptable exchange for a Spanish war, and

[18]   19 March, Pym Diary, fo. 33; and Nicholas Diary, fo. 91.
[19]   19 March, Holles Diary, fo. 104v; Spring Diary, p. 127; and Nicholas Diary, fo. 91.
[20]   19 March, Nicholas Diary, fo. 91; Spring Diary, p. 128; and *CJ*, p. 741.

especially so "with the King's limitations for the time of levying, for the ceasing with the occasion, and of having our own disposers." But Sir Edward Giles, who next spoke, immediately returned to Savile. Obviously both sovereign and subject, he argued, were willing to work together, "but we must consider what we do before we do it and to what end." This demand should not be casually dismissed, for he reminded the House that "we conclude not for ourselves but our countries, and we must account for it; when we know for what we do it, we may give freely."[21]

Secretary Conway then attempted to stop the flood. The growing insistence for more information was then inappropriate: "where the war shall be who can declare until the King declare himself." Implicitly a discussion of "where the war shall be" would follow James's declaration. But Conway took pains to assure MPs that this procedure was a mere formality since James "is resolved in Conscience, he may break." In sharp contrast to 1621, James now "makes no doubt of Spain's ambition to the western world's monarchy . . . Now the whole pack [of lies?] is discovered the King will not stick to think and speak of Spain's ambition." Moreover, Conway argued that James's willingness to reveal the details of the Spanish negotiations indicated the tenor of his designs: "we may guess by that, what he intends." In 1621, Charles, Buckingham and the Council inclined to a Spanish treaty, but now they too "have manifested another opinion." Given these changes, the Spanish treaties "can never be knit again," and Conway pleaded with the House to believe that "this fear then arises from nothing." He seconded Weston's proposal for "the whole" which would be divided "under the reservations that the King allows." In conclusion, the Secretary issued further unofficial assurances about a Spanish war. The subsidy, he pointed out, would be spent not merely on martial preparations, but "to go farther to provide for the inheritance of the heirs of our state . . . which in time shall be done by weakening of Spain."[22] Following Buckingham's discussion of a West Indies enterprise, the Secretary of State's oration on the inevitability of an Anglo-Spanish war may have moved some MPs to find the Four Propositions more acceptable when draped in fairly open hispanophobia. As Conway confidently assured them, a generous subsidy bill was simply the downpayment for a Spanish war.

Notwithstanding Conway's impassioned plea for good will, one MP at least remained skeptical. William Mallory "wonders to see so much Importunity put on us at this time." Since "we are but stewards and accountable for what we do," governmental softsoap should not lead the House to abandon its sober consideration of the question: he seconded Savile and moved, in defiance of Conway's arguments, "first to consider what we have

---

[21] 19 March, Spring Diary, p. 128.   [22] 19 March, *Ibid.*, pp. 129–30.

to do." If the administration really wanted to encourage "the world and our allies abroad," then it merely had to order that "the parliament may be kept together."[23]

For all the cogency of Savile's argument, Mallory proved to be its last effective spokesman. Three speakers later, Sir Arthur Ingram tersely announced, "he concurred with Savile, he would know what is to be done," but it was a feeble barrier against the rising tide of pro-war speakers.[24] If Ingram's intervention and Sir Thomas Bellasyse's later attack on the generosity of attorneys are discounted, Edward Alford ranks as the next speaker to express dismay about what was happening in the House that day, and by the time he either struggled to his feet or caught the Speaker's eye, a host of pro-war MPs had already spoken: Sir George Chudleigh, Sir Robert Harley, Thomas Wentworth, Sir Henry Mildmay, Sir John Walter, John Glanville, Sir Henry Vane and Sir Baptist Hicks. By the time Alford spoke, the first proposition of Savile's motion, "what is to be done," had already been swept under the carpet, and the question then before the House was the second proposition, "the Charge."

Savile's pressure for more information prompted these war supporters to produce an array of blue-chip reasons against such information. Conway claimed a discussion of war aims could not precede the royal declaration, but the speakers who followed him seemed to vie with one another in formulating novel arguments. Instead of Conway's temporary prohibition, Chudleigh posited a permanent stay: "it is not fit for us to enter into the particulars of what war is necessary." Consequently the MPs should be grateful for the "needful particulars" that James had deigned to reveal. Harley, although equally anxious to avoid a full discussion, seemed a little confused about the exact reason. His uncertainty about the merits of Conway's or Chudleigh's argument was relieved only by his certainty that one of the two had to be right; thus Savile's first question was "not proper for this place nor time." Thomas Wentworth put forward a third argument, that of security: "what is to be done is not here to be handled lest our enemies, being forewarned, should be forearmed." Nonetheless, he hoped that the Commons would receive "assurances of some noble enterprise." Finally Sir John Walter, not content to be merely repetitive, advanced a fourth reason to forestall any debate. The nature of warfare itself rendered any public discussion futile: "to dispute what war shall be undertaken is in vain, for that war is changeable of occasion." Walter concurred with Wentworth that "it is more proper for a private council than for one so public."[25]

Their most effective response to Savile, however, was not this catalogue of

---

[23] 19 March, *ibid.*, p. 130; and *CJ*, p. 741.   [24] 19 March, Holles Diary, fo. 105.
[25] 19 March, Spring Diary, pp. 130–9; and *CJ*, p. 742.

prohibitions. Indeed, rather than dwell on Savile's motion directly, they spent most of their time dangling the breach of the treaties and its results before the House. The distinct impression that a bargain was being pressed on MPs pervades these debates of mid-morning. Harley frankly outlined the situation: the House wanted details of the war and the king wanted parliamentary supply before he would declare. He begged the House to "consider which demand is greater, ours or the King's." And for those who plumped for the former, Harley drew attention to the "danger of this summer... It is not only our wealth we must respect, but our friends and confederates, and how with advantage to endamage our enemies. Where lies this? In the King's declaration."[26] Mr. Wentworth also urged the House to be neither willful nor petty: "to fail now from fighting with Spaine to fight with fees, is to save a drop of our purse to lose the drops of our hearts. The peace with Spain hath and doth ruin the state, religion and honor." Similarly, Mildmay repeated his earlier admonition to the House that "if we fear not too much, we are safe."[27] For Walter, the breach of the treaties overrode all other considerations, even those of Savile. The recent economic difficulties were obviously divine retribution for abandoning "the professors of the gospel." A breach of the Spanish treaties and a war were therefore necessary as an economic cure and as an occasion to recover England's lost honor and reputation; "we have been famous heretofore, now our honour is in the dust. Yet this free gift for so good cause shall declare us to be the offspring of the ancient English." In order to "resist the increasing pride of Spain and to regain the Palatinate and defend religion," Walter proposed tightening the national belt; "let our pride of clothes be abated, our great portions to our children, our back and belly lose rather than suffer so just occasions to want assistance." Glanville returned to the dilemma of choosing between James and Savile: "we have a hard choice, but with David let us rather fall into the hands of God than of men, let us rather fall upon God's providence and our own estates than into the hands of Spain."[28] Vane for his part revived the old theme of the war coalition: "there is no kingdom that hath better conditions for the subjects than this hath and he would not that our carriage this day should draw us to as bad conditions as others have beyond the seas."[29] Although the details varied among the speakers, a common sentiment prevailed: to probe Savile's first position would be to endanger the breach of the treaties, the Anglo-Spanish war, and even Parliament's future existence.

This troop of speakers also advanced the discussion of the subsidy bill. Edmondes's earlier suggestion of £300,000, together with some formula for further assistance if needed, received the blessings of these MPs, and they

---

[26] 19 March, Spring Diary, p. 131.
[28] *Ibid.*, pp. 134–5.

[27] *Ibid.*, pp. 132–3.
[29] 19 March, Nicholas Diary, fo. 94.

developed the idea of "nominative subsidies"; six subsidies and twelve fifteenths would be approved in principle but tied to future parliamentary approval. At the same time, the pro-war speakers were careful to propitiate "country" sensibilities. To protect "the poor subjects," Chudleigh proposed an exemption for all men with "under 5 li lands." Mildmay meanwhile first espoused a key argument: "we must conceive that this is not given to the King, but for the safety of the King, religion and state; and this well understood, the name of subsidies cannot affright the poor country."[30] The usefulness of Mildmay's argument lay in the fact that it did more than mitigate the sound of the subsidies; it also effectively countered any attempt to link redress of grievances directly with supply.

The individual speeches of Chudleigh, Harley, Wentworth, Mildmay, Glanville, Walter and Vane were far from remarkable. But collectively the effect of one speaker after another seconding and developing the same arguments had a crucial steadying effect. They halted a run among backbenchers for Savile's motion, while beginning the discussion of the subsidy bill. When Mallory sat down, the war coalition faced a serious challenge, and when Alford finally rose, the sense of the House was well developed towards the subsidy itself.

The troop of pro-war speakers cannot, however, claim full credit for this transformation. As on the 11th, nascent opposition to the coalition received its shrewdest blows from its supporters. Between Harley and Wentworth, Sir George Chaworth delivered a controversial speech. The MPs, he argued, were being bamboozled with cries of "the King's honor, the commonwealth, religion and all at the stake" into granting money for the breach of two treaties which were already broken: "the marriage is certainly [ended] and that of the Palatinate cannot stand without it." Likewise the Dutch actually "are not in so desperate case" as to require English help; "one small town less than the borough of Westminster [Ostend] held Spain 3 years nor such great danger abroad as is thought." His speech convulsed the House and soon led to his expulsion.[31] It also revealed the ease with which one speaker, "not of the mind of any before him," could single-handedly tar the opposition to the coalition with the brush of "averseness" and hispanophilia.

After Chaworth and the pro-war troop, Edward Alford wisely abandoned Savile's three questions in a last-ditch attempt to halt a precipitous resolution on the subsidy bill that morning; Alford strove at the very least to prolong the debate into the afternoon. "This is a dear year," he objected, and in those

---

[30] *CJ*, p. 742; and 19 March, Spring Diary, p. 133.
[31] Spring Diary, p. 132. Thanks to the discovery of a series of Chaworth letters in the Trumbull Add. MSS, the background to his outburst on 19 March becomes much clearer. I hope to compose an article on the subject in the near future.

circumstances the notion of voting twelve fifteenths, however collected, seemed preposterous: "last Parliament would give no Fifteens because fell upon Poor Men. When they then would not give two, shall they now give twelve?" He urged "that more deliberation be had of these points," and that the debate be deferred until the afternoon.[32] Unfortunately, Alford was followed by Sir Edward Coke who neatly resolved his reservations about an early decision. First, Coke delivered a decisive blow to Savile's first proposition, ironically by concurring whole-heartedly with Savile's desire for information about the war: "there can be no estimation of the charge of a building till the model be seen and resolved on and the materials appointed forth. To give the King satisfaction it will be needful to know what is our work to be done." Then, doubtless having caused considerable apprehension among his fellow war advocates, Coke dexterously resolved the question that had perplexed the House in the first half of the morning. He cited the Four Propositions, proclaiming: "this is our work and for this we must give." Nominative subsidies he disdained as "never heard before." Instead, Coke simply proposed to vote £300,000, or a third of James's demands, leaving the remainder for the "other sessions at Michaelmas and the spring."[33]

On the 19th, as before, Coke's intervention was decisive. Sir Robert Heath, the Solicitor General, delivered the official stamp of approval to Coke's subsidy proposal. He formally moved three subsidies and three fifteenths together with an assurance of more in the future sessions, and propounded the full array of mitigating factors. The money would be given "not to the King but to the business." Parliamentary compliance with the royal demand would assure James's affection not "only to the business, but to the House also." The subsidy, while admittedly large, would not leave the country: "it doth only change the hand." Heath sought to deny the recusants "so great an honor" as paying double in taxation, although he promised the House that "better blood shall be wrung out of them." Finally, since parliamentary treasurers would disburse the money, if the need for subsidies vanished, the money "is not lost."[34] With Heath's embodiment of Coke's proposals, the coalition hurried to an agreement.

After Coke and Heath, the cautious approach of Savile appeared vanquished. Unfortunately, a formidable and possibly noisy opposition now arose, not so much from several MPs' throats as from their stomachs. Heath had begun his speech with a quick voice vote "whether to sit in the afternoon or go on now," and the House voted to proceed. But either the vote was sprung on an unsuspecting House or several MPs quickly reconsidered the question. Earlier in the morning, the charge of "precipitation" meant a hasty resolution of vital public business, and it attracted some support in the

---

[32] *Ibid.*, p. 136; and *CJ*, p. 743.   [33] *Ibid.*, pp. 136–7.   [34] *Ibid.*, pp. 137–8.

House. As it came near to 2 o'clock, however, precipitation also came to mean no lunch, and this dawning realization led to a back-bench revolt. Almost immediately after Heath sat down, Sir Thomas Lucy rose to argue the merits of dinner: "the House hath ever done well when they have not run into Precipitation." Sir Thomas Jermyn responded by proposing a "civil fast" to complement the Commons' earlier spiritual fast: "he would . . . sit out this business." Jermyn's equation of abstinence with patriotism, however, was not persuasive. Mr. Ravenscroft averred that he "never knew any Subsidy granted but a Committee [of the Whole House] before, to debate."[35] Six MPs then seconded Ravenscroft's motion for a committee in the afternoon. Where Savile and Alford had failed to block the passage of the subsidy bill, lunch time succeeded.

In the sudden devotion to due deliberation, several speakers tacked on comments which indicated that some opposition to the coalition's proposal still remained, if only fitfully articulated. Sir Charles Morrison's famous phrase, "the country thought [of] the last parliament that we and our money were soon parted," preceded his revival of Savile's motion: "let us know what to give and for what and then no man shall give more cheerfully than myself." Sir Henry Poole thought that the House was not ready for the question, and Sir John Savile added that even to propose the question at that time was "one of the [most] dangerous and unseasonable Motions he ever heard." Since the House was still divided, "if the King should fail [in a division], it would be a great discredit." But John Selden the antiquary delivered the sharpest rebuke to the "Patriot" attempt to hurry the subsidy bill: "[he] will not speak to the great matter in hand nor to the orders of the House, being so young a parliament man, but he hath been no stranger to the journals of either House and found that the pettiest business hath not been so precipitated."[36] In the face of such unexpected opposition, the coalition drew back. Digges in the end supported adjournment while lamenting the passing of the "nominative subsidy," an idea he thought "a good one, but now is changed." Finally, Phelips concurred with the motion for a committee which was set for the following morning.[37]

The "Patriots" may have consoled themselves with the thought that they had, if nothing else, scotched Savile's motion. If they did, they quickly learned the extent of their error on the next day. Difficulties began as soon as Sandys took the chair at the head of the committee. His humiliation on 5 March apparently still stung him. On 11 March he had supported Savile's motion for

[35] 19 March, Holles Diary, fo. 107; *CJ*, p. 743; and Nethersole to Carleton, 20 March 1624, SP 81/30/88.
[36] 19 March, Holles Diary, fo. 108.
[37] 19 March, Spring Diary, p. 139; and *CJ*, p. 743.

due consideration and so compelled Sir Edward Coke to intervene to extricate the coalition. Sandys was equally troublesome on the 20th when the admirable desire to structure the debate led him to reformulate Savile's motion; it was necessary for the Commons to balance the demands of "honor," what must be done, with those of "necessity," what could be done. And to facilitate a consensus, he proposed five heads for debate:

the first is what the work of this year is in the great action for the defence of this kingdom against the great monarch . . . 2, what charge will defray it . . . 3, the means how this is to be raised, 4, when this money is levied a caution to know how it shall be disposed. 5, . . . what answer we shall give to his Majesty's demand, wherein we must have care to give such an answer as may satisfy his Majesty and not engage the subject for more than this year.[38]

If he sought to conciliate "country" back-benchers for his past as an undertaker, Sandys's structure for debate on 20 March should have succeeded: neither Savile nor Mallory could not have phrased it any better.

Christopher Brooke immediately objected to this structure: "the war is not properly to be handled in this place, it is fitter for the King's cabinet and Council. That it is no policy to tell here what shall be done this year." Brooke's view of Parliament was surprisingly limited: "it will be fit only in this place to treat of the matter of supply," and it was "not fit here to dispute the work among 460 persons." Since the members should not "put our sickle too far into the King's corn," he proposed that the committee limit its debate simply to Sandys's last point, the answer to James's demand. Sir Thomas Hoby was "of the same mind." But instead of three subsidies and three fifteenths, he proposed another general offer of supply dependent on the royal declaration.[39]

The notion of a general offer at this point was as alarming to the "Patriots" as Savile's motion. Their success in screening the war from public debate would verge on the pyrrhic if the Commons, as a result, only voted another general offer of assistance. Consequently, Hoby's apparently innocent motion and Sandys's motion for a discussion of "the work of this year" led to assurances about the royal war aims in general and an Anglo-Spanish war in particular. Sir John Coke, a Navy Commissioner, followed Hoby, and ostensibly he defended the prerogative: "where the war shall be or what it shall be, this must proceed from the King." Informally, however, he insisted that "the king in his speech looks farther" than the Palatinate. Of the Four Propositions, "the 3 first have no dependency with the war of the Palatinate and the last but a little." Indeed, instead of a Palatine war, Coke bluntly stated his opinion that "the general aim and the necessity is apparent to be a war

---

[38] 20 March, Nicholas Diary, fo. 96.
[39] 20 March, Holles Diary, fo. 108; and Spring Diary, p. 141.

with Spain."[40] Coke's performance was the first of several on the 20th which formally protected the royal prerogative while informally assuring the House of an imminent Spanish war.

Mildmay's explanations stabilized the situation, and in the next group of speakers all but one concurred with Mildmay. Characteristically the lone dissenter was Mallory who proposed a lesser sum so that MPs might "cut our coats to our cloth and consider well the present state of the countries." Sandys conversely announced his satisfaction with Mildmay's proposal since "this is not particularly to determine a war but to be prepared for it." Similarly Sir Edward Coke was confident that James "doth certainly intend a war but will not be prescribed to the particulars of it" and when war came, "he must be advised." He concluded on a note of optimistic belligerence: "by these good beginnings he yet hopes to live till he see the King of Spain lose his Indies." Sir Robert Phelips, although he did not address the question of the future war, approved Mildmay's proposal before he eagerly sketched out the next task before the Commons: "after we have provided for the dissolution of these [treaties], we shall find a torn commonwealth, which must necessarily be carefully regarded." Secretary Calvert then rose to voice his support of Mildmay's resolution, and he added further unofficial assurances: "De modo [of the war] is not here to be handled, though the wisdom of the House is capable enough of it." However, he told the House: "we have passed the river Rubicon, there is no going back. A war must follow, both offensive and defensive."[41]

The last three speeches reveal some of the reasons which may have persuaded waivering MPs to back Mildmay's proposal. A certain degree of faith in royal intentions was necessary in order to accept the peculiarities of the proposed subsidy bill, and on 20 March, Coke publicly announced that, on the basis of a few implied understandings, he was prepared to trust James. Phelips attempted to distract attention from the proposal itself by dangling one of the results of parliamentary compliance to royal demands – free rein in the investigation of the "torn commonwealth." Finally, of all the unofficial assurances of an imminent Anglo-Spanish war, Calvert's may have been the most impressive. The others all had the character of special pleading since they came from coalition members or fellow-travellers. But Calvert's view of the subject was more interesting and possibly satisfying. Calvert's intervention in the 1624 debates was minimal, but his certainty about an Anglo-Spanish war must have been especially soothing to some anxious MPs when it issued from one of the House's most notorious closet Catholics. Finally, after a little comic relief in the Digges–Heyman tussle over the Cinque Ports,

---

[40]   20 March, Spring Diary, p. 141.
[41]   20 March, Holles Diary, fo. 109v; and Spring Diary, pp. 144–6.

Sir Thomas Edmondes could not resist a public sigh that the Commons had at last declined Savile's lure: "He is glad that the particulars of the war are declined."[42]

Congratulations among the war supporters at this point, however, would have been premature. Having finally halted the press for more information about the war, another potentially disastrous drive rapidly gained momentum in the house. Earlier in the day and in the session, several MPs, when faced with an irregular subsidy bill, had consoled themselves with visions of the Commons presenting the king a subsidy bill festooned with grievances. As the House moved towards agreement on the subsidy bill, so too the drive rose to tack on redress of grievances. Nathaniel Tomkins began the discussion of possible "riders" with his own shopping list of grievances: "for the satisfaction of the country" in order to sweeten the pill of the subsidy, he requested that James pass "bills of grace," grant "a free and general pardon and a large one," and redress various grievances, "especially that of concealed titles." Mr. Coryton approved the idea in principle and proposed that "the laws may first pass and the act of subsidies last." Seymour repeated his previous demand that the recusants pay double. Sir George More at this point attempted to head off the discussion of riders before it got out of hand: "there needs no further labor or doubt upon this point, whether it will content the people or not: all the well affected people will undoubtedly rejoice." Heath then moved to put the sum to a question and the bill into committee.

Savile rose in response and apologized in advance for running "a contrary course to others," but he could not help regretting that "we have declined the first part that should have been considered first, for that we were to give, and are leaped over this, what to give." In a pointed comment to the coalition, he recalled his early hope "that they might make the King a good sword. Now it is said the King only best knows how to use his sword." Then in an attempt to make the best of a bad situation, he proposed that the subsidy be divided among "the particular ends" of the Four Propositions. This arrangement might placate the people, but he was certain that the royal concession of parliamentary treasurers "is no security nor satisfaction to them."[43]

Sir Edward Coke quickly dismissed Savile's latest motion as impractical: "to say what shall serve to this or that is not possible." Savile's comments on popular irritation with the subsidy bill, however, may have disquieted Coke for he proceeded to announce his own list of crying abuses: along with "bills of grace" and a pardon, he expressed his wish to see bills against informers, supersedeas, and certiorari, although he was careful to request these by petition, "not by way of condition, merchant-like." Savile then requested that pretermitted customs be added to Coke's petition. Sir William Herbert, how-

---

[42] 20 March, Spring Diary, p. 147.   [43] 30 March, Spring Diary, pp. 147–8.

ever, deployed Mildmay's argument of the previous day to forestall any further discussion of riders: "we give this sum not to the King but to the kingdom and when we give towards the King's necessities then to petition for those things that the gentlemen spake last [Savile] desired." Jermyn and Glanville repeated this reasoning, and the subsidy bill proceeded towards a vote. Alford made another attempt to delay the question; he requested time to consult with his constituents, but his motion was swept aside as the House agreed "without a gain-saying voice" to vote three subsidies and three fifteenths "towards the Support of the War, which is likely to ensue" after James had declared "the utter Dissolution and Discharge of the Two Treaties."[44]

Once the Commons approved a supply of three subsidies and three fifteenths on 20 March, Charles and Buckingham hurried to present the formal offer to James, which they did on the 23rd. The "acceptation of this offer . . . or rejection," Nethersole noted on the 20th, "will be the Crisis of this Parliament and therefore all men long to be at that day." In the event, Abbot for once returned from the audience without immediately having to take to his bed; James, to everyone's delight, accepted. In recent years, historians have seen James on this occasion as less than excited with the Commons. Ruigh viewed the royal acceptance as the work of "a dejected and dispirited man"; Adams asserted James accepted the parliamentary offer " with little enthusiasm"; and Russell implied James was disappointed with the offer.[45] But these sentiments, while certainly present, should not overshadow the dominant theme of the address: James simply felt pleased and expansive.

James began with thanks for the Commons' offer, and he seems to have been quite sincere when he remarked "it is without Example, that ever any Parliament, for a Beginning, Gave to a King so great a supply, to be levied in so short a time." His emphasis upon the subsidy "for a beginning" was not facetious or pointed: rather it was a construction which the MPs themselves put on the bill. He repeated his earlier pledge that he would not accept their money and reject their advice: he begged them "think Me not that man."

James then again sought to justify his actions in the previous years: "I pray you have a charitable Opinion of Me." He had never forgotten the plight of his daughter and his grandchildren; he had merely attempted to secure their restoration without the effusion of Christian blood. Indeed, he insisted very heatedly that the Palatine question had obsessed him in recent years: "God is My Judge and Saviour, I never had any other End . . . for my part except by such Means as God may put into My Hands I may recover the Palatinate, I

---

[44] 20 March, Spring Diary, pp. 149–50; Holles Diary, fo. 110; and Nicholas Diary, fo. 102.
[45] Nethersole to Carleton, 20 March 1624, SP 81/30/88; Ruigh, p. 230; Adams, "Foreign Policy and the Parliaments," p. 169; and Russell, *Parliaments*, p. 189.

could wish never to have been born." James pledged himself and his family to this task. He even offered to go in person "if it might do good to the business." Even though James, given his advanced age, might not be equal to the task, he reminded his audience, "My only Son is young." He promised to begin preparations for a war using the money that Parliament was to provide. His debts he left to their later consideration, and he spoke of a certain fall in Customs revenues as a consequence of a war. But in spite of these problems, "undertaking the War, I must go through with it one way or another, though I should sell Jewels and all." And to underscore his commitment, he made an oath which Parliament would recall sixteen years later: "If I should spare any Means possible for the Recovery of it, then let Me not be thought worthy to reign over you." In the next session he promised to submit the accounts of the subsidy expenditure, and "it will spur you the more to enable Me for the rest." Although his previous parliamentary record was admittedly lamentable, James expressed the hope that the 1624 Parliament "shall be a happy Parliament and make Me greater and happier than any King of England ever was." He repeated his promise to consult Parliament over any peace terms and to respect the independence of the parliamentary subsidy treasurers. But he did insist on his absolute control of the war: "whether I shall sent twenty thousand or ten thousand, whether by Sea or by Land, East or West, by Diversion or otherwise by Invasion upon the Bavarian or the Emperor, you must leave that to the King." Such a statement should have been hardly surprising to MPs since they had ultimately agreed not to force their way into the *arcana imperii*. Finally, James returned to his opening justificatory theme. "Assure yourselves, My delay hitherto was upon Hope to have gotten it without a War." But that hope had proved vain. Now God and Parliament advised "that I shall clear My Reputation from Obloquy and in Despight of the Devil and all his Instruments, shew that I never had but an honest Heart."[46]

James's acceptance of the subsidy, and "the war likely to ensue," was scarcely a "Blood and Iron" address. It was more that of the reluctant warrior, that of the honest, peaceable man provoked beyond the limits of Christian forbearance to take arms in defense of his daughter and his honor. In retrospect, the speech was potentially unsettling for its vagueness in critical points: the breach with Spain, for example, was never made explicit. On mature reflection some contemporaries would spot these ambiguities, and consequently their doubts and suspicions would return. But when James delivered the address, it seemed to please all parties involved. James at long last had publicly announced that he was prepared to adopt a non-diplomatic solution to the Palatine question. He donned his armor rather wearily, but at the time everyone was overjoyed that *Rex Pacificus* had been able to speak of becoming a warrior, however reluctant.

If there was an overtone of pessimism and lack of enthusiasm in James's address, contemporaries chose to ignore it. After the speech, James consulted with Lord Mandeville, who had been delegated to take notes: after looking over Mandeville's copy, the king remarked that "he thought never any speeche of his had beene so well taken, which my Lord President . . . sayd he thought was true too in another sense." Mandeville's sentiments seem to have been common. Sir Richard Harrison, an MP, told Carleton that when James was offered the subsidy, "the king dothe take this exceeding well," and for the Parliament's part, James's acceptance "hathe so pleased the Parliament that I think the king may have anything that hee will desir." Parliament, in short, was "over joied that the king hath given way to us." Indeed, Valaresso noted after recording James's speech, "one cannot say with how much consolation, feeling and almost tears, such a reply has been received."[47]

The government itself was equally delighted with the speech. Charles dispatched an express courier to announce the news to his sister who was excited to learn of "the good conclusion betwixt his Majesty and Parlement." Earlier reports about the Parliament, Carleton reported, "had filled us full of dispaire of any good from that meeting," but "it seems the God will shew his power and wisedom . . . and I now beginn to hope we shall see the effects of Gods further blessings in reparation of those crosses and losses which he hath hitherto suffered his Church to suffer for our sinnes." Conway wrote to inform the diplomatic corps of the event, and he could not restrain himself from gloating over the fact that the Spanish ambassadors had had "an unsuccessful Parlement." James's speech, he reported, was "soe much to the contentiment and ioyes of both houses, who are the representative body of his kingdome, as I cannot compare it with anything but their ioy for the return of the Prince."[48]

The people for their part rose to the occasion. Captain Hamilton reported that James's speech was greeted with "the unexpressable content of all well affected." Many Londoners, however, did find means of self-expression. "I am sure," Beaulieu wrote Trumbull, "your earies doe glow to hear what passeth in our Parlement." James's speech was greeted "with so generall an applause and demonstration of joye as that at night our streets were all full of bonefires for it . . . there was a mightie one kindled by the Boys and Common

[47] Nethersole to Carleton, 25 March 1624, SP 14/161/36; Harrison to Carleton, 24 and 27 March 1624, SP 14/161/35 and 47; and Valasesso to the Doge and Senate, 24 April 1624, *CSPV*, XVIII, p. 261.

[48] Carleton to Trumbull, [late March 1624], Trumbull MSS XVII/96; and Carleton to [Nethersole], 7 April 1624, SP 84/117/22. See also Conway to Herbert, 24 March 1624, SP 78/72/82; and same to Kensington, 30 March 1624, SP 78/72/83.

people of the Strande before the Spanish Ambassadore Dore, which were kept very close." And amid the scenes of celebration in London streets, Padre Maestro made his way to the ambassadors' House. He had come, Nethersole remarked, a day "after the fayre."[49]

ANALYSIS

The character of the debate over the 1624 subsidy bill changed abruptly on 23 March. The grand set-piece parliamentary conflicts, and the records of these conflicts, largely ended on 20 March as the subsidy bill disappeared into committee. Glimpses of it appear periodically in the later part of the session, but these are generally in relation to extraparliamentary events. Therefore before plunging into the murkier later period, an assessment of the early and more strictly parliamentary phase of the subsidy debate is appropriate.

The reasons for the ultimate success of the "Patriot" coalition emerge clearly from the month-long debate about treaties and supply. Initially, the role of "undertakers" in Parliament seems to supersede all other explanations. Their position in the coalition's corner would have been highly significant even if Phelips, Digges, Sandys and Coke had remained completely silent. Without them, any opposition to the "Patriots" had considerable difficulty finding formidable champions whose oratory could stir emotions and command the House. They did of course play a prominent and vocal part in the coalition, yet curiously they did not consistently dominate it on the floor of the Commons. Although all four had a leading role in the 1–2 March debates, Phelips no longer appeared in the limelight in the two later debates; Sandys seems, at times, to have reversed his position after Southampton's motion backfired on 5 March; and Digges often proved an awkward ally. Pressing for the breach of the treaties of course was one thing and pressing for a large subsidy quite another: these three may have been reluctant to assume a prominent role on a sensitive financial issue. They may also have noted with alarm the rapid rate at which their own popularity dwindled once they were publicly associated with a government policy, even a comparatively popular one. By 20 March, Chamberlain reported that Sandys, Digges and Phelips had "so little credit" among the MPs, "though they speake well and to the purpose sometimes, yet yt is not so well taken at their hands for still they suspect them to prevaricate and hold them for undertakers." By the end of the session, the Earl of Clare dismissed these reputed popular champions

[49] J. Hamilton to Trumbull, 25 March 1624; and Beaulieu to same, 26 March 1624, Trumbull MSS, XXVI/114; and VII/155; and Nethersole to Carleton, 25 March 1624, SP 14/161/36.

as "servers of turns and the instruments of great men."[50] They may have fallen back on 11 and 19 March in hopes of preserving some modicum of credibility.

Coke, on the other hand, never waivered. His prestige and popularity may have been so much higher than that of the other three that he could afford to draw down his account with less anxiety. In spite of his constant and vigorous support of the coalition, he does not appear to have shared the public relations problems of the other three. His characteristic position in the major debates may account for the phenomenon. Unlike the other three, he never led a debate, and he never appeared to run with a pack of courtiers and officials. Rather he always spoke near the end of the debate, and his remarks, which always provided timely support for the coalition, were invariably original. Indeed, by preserving the illusion of standing at a slight distance from the coalition, Coke could intervene on its behalf regularly without appearing to be currying favor at Court. Phelips may have provided critical guidance behind the scenes, but in the actual debates, Coke, of all the "duces gregis," unquestionably lent the most valuable assistance to the coalition. In 1621 after a presentation from Coke, Charles announced he "was never weary with hearing him, he mingled mirth with business to so good purpose."[51] In 1624 he should have been even more delighted with the old attorney who had done so much to advance the prince's own business. Had Charles ever distributed kudos and rewards for meritous parliamentary service in the 1624 campaign, Coke should have been at the head of the queue.

Since the other undertakers hung back in the final mêlée, a major exception, if not a revision, is in order for one of the sturdier historiographic generalizations about early Stuart Parliaments. D. H. Willson accounted for the Crown's unique success in 1624 by pointing out that Charles and Buckingham "found themselves in sympathy with the people and were able to form a temporary alliance with the popular party in parliament." Yet, as we have seen, there was considerable, albeit ill-organized, "popular" opposition to the coalition's plans, and in the crucial final debates, the leaders of Willson's "popular party" (excepting always Sir Edward Coke) were secondary. Willson's analysis would make the agreement on 20 March one of the great mysteries of the century. Ruigh, however, provided a resolution for this difficulty: of the forty-odd speakers on the 19th, "a significantly large proportion were privy councillors or royal officials closely dependent upon the Court." In a debate when less than fifty MPs actually participated and

---

[50] Chamberlain to Carleton, 20 March 1624, *Letters*, II, p. 549; and Clare to Somerset, 2 March 1625, *Holles Letters*, II, p. 299.
[51] 15 March, *CD 1621*, V, p. 43.

when roughly half of the speakers confined themselves to brief comments, it was possible for thirteen to fifteen courtiers and officials to dominate the debate. In 1624, the frequent and often verbose efforts of Mildmay, Rudyerd, Eliot, Edmondes, Fleetwood, Weston, Conway, Harley, Walter, Vane, Heath, J. Coke, Jermyn, Tomkins and Calvert enabled the government largely under its own steam to maneuver its way through a major debate. This fact might lead us to question if, in 1624, the Crown's "parliamentary tactics ceased to be efficacious" and if the royal officials and courtiers "were reduced to impotent spokesmen of the crown in an assembly that had slipped from their control."[52] In that year at least, the officials and courtiers equalled the performance of Willson's fabled Elizabethan councillors.

Unfortunately, the shrewd co-option of potentially troublesome parliamentary leaders and a high degree of organization and dedication among the corps of royal servants in the House cannot fully explain the Crown's success. Conciliation also played a key role. One striking example illustrates this point. On the morning of 9 March, Sir Thomas Edmondes, Privy Councillor and the Treasurer of the Household, exchanged words with John Glanville. Edmondes, though not a committee member, attended the meeting of the Committee for Privileges, which Glanville chaired, and as the room was crowded, he proposed that the committee rise to a larger room. Glanville in response had the list of committee members read and then "stoutly told the treasurer that he had no voyce nor was of the Committee." Edmondes "in grande passion" retorted that "the chaire hathe made you forgete your selfe and autres parolls in grande scorne et disgrace." The Treasurer then left, and the committee considered reporting the scene to the whole House. An hour later, however, after cooling down and having received mature advice, Edmondes returned and asked Glanville as his old friend to accept his apology. "Being slighted by Mr. Glanville," he explained "he was very tender of it, having been long employed in public by his Majesty and that made him the more tender of a disrespect because he would not his place should lose any of its dignity whiles [*sic*] he holdeth it." Nonetheless, since "he is unwilling the House should be troubled in the great affairs now there in hand," Edmondes swallowed his pride and asked that "those words of his may die." Mr. Glanville magnanimously received the Treasurer's apologies.[53]

Edmondes's public humiliation is of course an indication of the social reversal that often took place during a Parliament. Nevertheless, it is an extraordinary indication; Willson gave it pride of place in his chapter on the councillors' "Loss of Influence in the House." If a similar exchange had taken

[52] Wilson, *Privy Councillors*, pp. 4 and 160; and Ruigh, p. 218.
[53] 9 March, Nicholas Diary, fo. 61; and Hawarde Diary, pp. 189–90. I am particularly grateful to Mark Kennedy for this last reference.

place when Parliament was not in session, Glanville for all his friendship with Edmondes would probably have felt himself fortunate only to suffer Edmondes's fate. Councillors were often taunted and ridiculed in Parliament, but they rarely, if ever, publicly submitted to a barrister. Edmondes himself indicated that his submission was an extraordinary gesture: he sacrificed the dignity of his office and his personal pride for the "great business now there in hand." Secretary Calvert with good reason singled out Edmondes for praise at the end of the session for his role in the Parliament. The success of the Parliament of 1624 cannot be ascribed simply, as Russell argued, to the fact that the coalition presented Parliament with a "programme" and a pocket watch; the "Patriots" were also anxious to avoid the slightest ruffling of parliamentary feathers.[54]

Concessions were as important as conciliation in the success of Charles and Buckingham, and it is necessary to examine the former more closely. In the first half of the session there were two constitutionally significant innovations, or more properly revivals of medieval practice. James in his address on 5 March proposed that if Parliament agreed to financial assistance, he would allow the subsidy to be allocated for specific purposes and disbursed by parliamentary treasurers. James's proposals which the Commons accepted have recently prompted a historiographic debate. Russell has concluded that since Buckingham had earlier proposed the idea to James and since the Commons had not discussed such ideas until after James's address, "another supposed constitutional advance was the result, not of the initiative of the Commons, but of conflicts at court." It is patently obvious that the Commons did not push for these concessions. But it is dubious to argue that "it was not a concession by the King to the Commons, but by the Commons to the King."[55] When Rudyerd, Weston, Edmondes and Conway pressed these proposals on the Commons, they were not acting out "conflicts at court." Rather they were dangling royal concessions in front of the MPs in hopes that they would reciprocate and agree to a massive supply without asking too many questions. Factional conflict at Court over the war certainly explains many of the peculiarities around the coalition's proposal for supply in 1624. This fact, however, should not obscure another and more important one – James's offer to allow the 1624 subsidy to be appropriated for particular ends and administered by Parliament was clearly a concession to soothe anxieties in the Commons. The proposals did not Minerva-like arise discretely from the duke's brow. As Russell noted, they had been discussed in earlier Parliaments; in fact the government in the 1621 Parliament was

---

[54] Willson, pp. 241–2; Russell, *Parliaments*, p. 202; and Calvert to Conway, 21 May 1624, SP 14/165/11.
[55] Russell, *Parliaments*, pp. 177–8; and "Parliamentary History," pp. 7–8.

tormented by the fear that Southampton would propose such conditions to the subsidy bill, and a few days before Buckingham proposed the idea to the king in 1624, Mr. Carleton reported that the MPs were willing to vote supply, but they "will have officers of their owne (as some say in private) to receave and manage their moneys."[56] If we appreciate the important caveat that the Commons did not wrestle the concession from a reluctant Crown, then the hallowed constitutional assessment of these innovations still remains valid. "When the Parliament of 1624 met," J. R. Tanner observed, "the Commons were ready to vote large supplies if they could be sure that the money would really be devoted to providing for the impending war with Spain."[57] The royal concessions over appropriation were simply a means of relieving this parliamentary anxiety.

If the preceding analysis of the importance of tribunes and councillors, conciliation and concession in the opening debates on supply is roughly correct, then it calls several earlier assessments of 1624 into question. Harold Hulme viewed the Parliament of 1624 as one of the great milestones in the "winning of Freedom of speech by the House of Commons": "[James] permitted them, nay urged them, to speak freely on all those vital subjects, foreign affairs, religion and the prince's marriage, which he had declared in the last parliament to be under his prerogative and not even to be mentioned by the Commons. They were now free to speak on any subject."[58] Hulme's assurance on this subject is nothing short of remarkable. Savile undoubtedly would not have known what Hulme was talking about. He and several others tried repeatedly to speak freely on foreign affairs, but they were always politely but firmly ushered away from this topic. The only foreign policy that James allowed the Commons to discuss and advise him on was the breach of the Spanish treaties, and since there was no one in the Commons who dared support these treaties publicly, it can scarcely be considered a profound concession. On the other topics that mattered in 1624, particularly the question of war aims and strategy, they were left out in the cold as completely in 1624 as they had been in 1621. Indeed, in terms of public resolutions, the Parliament in 1621 developed its views on foreign policy more clearly in the 3 December Petition on Religion than in anything it produced in 1624.

An analysis of the parliamentary debates on supply also bears on a common criticism of Buckingham, which finds a clear formulation in Adams's article. Buckingham, he argued, had a "cavalier attitude towards the Subsidy

---

[56] Southampton's Examination, [July 1621], Inner Temple Library, Petyt MSS, 538, v. XIX, fo. 1v; and Carleton the younger to Carleton, 1 March 1624, SP 84/116/186.

[57] J. R. Tanner, *Constitutional Documents of the Reign of James I, 1603–1625* (Cambridge, 1952), p. 374.

[58] Harold Hulme, "The Winning of Freedom of Speech by the House of Commons," *American History Review* (1956), p. 851.

Act . . . he never had any real interest in its terms." The incident which provoked such a severe verdict was the payment of Count Mansfelt out of the
1624 subsidy "in direct violation of the terms of the Subsidy Act." Similarly,
Adams rebuked Buckingham for failing "to accept parliament's suggestions
regarding a new foreign policy." Before we examine the passage of the
Subsidy Act in more detail, it is sufficient to note here that, while the
Commons were quick to remove a clause in the text which spoke of the
recovery of the Palatinate, they left in among the Four Propositions, the
phrase "the assistance of your neighbours, the States of the United Provinces
and other your Majesty's friends and allies."[59] Mansfelt was notoriously
eager to lay claim to any stray title or bit of property, but one of the few titles
he could quite legitimately claim in 1624 was that of James's "friend and
ally." If the MPs were as strategically exact in their goals as Adams would
have them, then it is odd that such precise men allowed so large a loophole as
the phrase, "other your Majesty's friends and allies," a loophole through
which Mansfelt would literally march an army. Early in 1624, there had been
discussions within the government of James's possible friends and allies, and
the results ranged far afield: the King of France, the Duke of Savoy, the
Venetian Republic, the King of Sweden, the King of Denmark, the Duke of
Brandenburg, the Duke of Saxony, the Swiss and Grison cantons, the Prince
of Transylvania, various Berber pirate communities and, last but far from
least, the Duke of Bavaria himself. Since any of these potentates easily could
have come under the Commons' rubric, and so qualified for parliamentary
assistance, it seems a little ungenerous to exclude Count Mansfelt.

It could be argued that Mansfelt's subsidy violated the spirit, if not the
letter, of the subsidy bill. Buckingham, as Adams has maintained, refused to
abide by "parliament's suggestions regarding a new foreign policy." Here, as
with Hulme's assertion of parliamentary freedom of speech, Sir John Savile
undoubtedly would have been startled: the Commons never formally
debated, much less resolved on, "a new foreign policy." Surely it must have
been difficult to violate something so amorphous as the views of the MPs on
foreign policy in 1624.

Finally it could be objected that the Commons understood the phrase,
"other his Majesty's friends and allies," to mean a naval diversionary war
against Spain. This argument has more validity. Buckingham and other
members of the government went to great lengths to assure the House
unofficially that the government regarded the Palatinate as "a lost piece" and
a "blue water policy" as the most efficient way of punishing Spain. Yet in
spite of this near-consensus on a naval war, the precise form of the other

---

[59] Adams, "Foreign Policy and Parliament," pp. 159 and 170; and the 1624 Subsidy Bill,
printed in *The Stuart Constitution* (Cambridge, 1966), edited by J. P. Kenyon, p. 76.

aspect of the diversionary strategy, the holding action on the other side of the North Sea, was decidedly vague. All the MPs, except Chaworth, wanted to assist the Dutch Republic, but a number of MPs took a very broad definition of that assistance. As Alford noted on 11 March, "the Low Countries are a large field to speak of." For Adams, Rudyerd was crucial in the attempt to develop the "new foreign policy." Yet when Rudyerd first outlined the Four Propositions on 1 March, he named as its goal "to recollect and revive that scattered and broken part of the religion in Germany."[60] On the 20th, Mildmay developed this notion when he broke down the "Dutch" propositions into three sections: "First, the aid of the states of the Low Countries; 2, the uniting the disbanded princes of Germany; 3, the aiding and assisting them to encounter their and our adversaries." Digges was more concise: "the princes of Germany and the King of Denmark must be drawn into assistance."[61] These sentiments easily could have subsumed Mansfelt's expedition. Indeed, if there were apprehensions about Mansfelt, the Commons should have said so, or if nothing else, removed the loophole in the subsidy bill. He was in London as the Commons were refining the subsidy bill, and although initially some observers reported the count had come to retire in England, the Paul's walkers quickly learned what he was really about when he was closeted with James, Charles and Buckingham.

The one thing that does seem clear is that the prospect of a major English expeditionary force operating deep inside the Empire, and the cost of such a venture, filled the Commons with horror. But there are indications that the Commons' abhorence did not extend to "stirring up the German princes" with a few loans in order to get the German diversion rolling. A naval diversionary war would be of little use unless the Habsburgs were occupied in several places at once. Moreover, the policy of bankrolling confederates could boast quite respectable Elizabethan precedents. In short, the members seem to have made a distinction that would be quite understandable today: they were willing to assist a distant ally with money and advice, but they drew the line at direct military involvement. MPs certainly did not envisage monthly subsidies of £20,000 to Mansfelt and £30,000 to Christian IV of Denmark, but they may not have found the principle of foreign subsidy abhorent.

Finally, Adams implied that Buckingham manipulated parliamentary sentiments about the war only to discard them cavalierly once he had secured his goal, the subsidy bill. For the early period of the Parliament, however, it is interesting to note that Buckingham and his fellow advocates of war give every indication of sincerity when they spoke fondly of a "blue water" policy.

---

[60] 11 March, Holles Diary, fo. 96; and 1 March, Pym Diary, fo. 11.
[61] 20 March, Spring Diary, pp. 143 and 149.

In short, their public statements at Westminster corresponded with private discussions at Whitehall: thus duplicity is not readily apparent in the first half of 1624. Buckingham was obviously not above deceit, but our understanding of history will not be advanced if we accord that characteristic to all his actions.

In more recent years, Professor Russell has lodged an equally controversial assertion. Against the common view that in 1624 the MPs clamored for war, Russell argued that parliamentary enthusiasm for a war consistently proved "lukewarm": the resolutions on the war reveal that "the House of Commons, with a few exceptions, were almost as reluctant partners in the enterprise as King James himself." In the debates of 19–20 March, for instance, "almost all members," Russell maintained, "showed that their commitment to their own countries was much stronger than any commitment they might have to war." There is a good deal of evidence to support this view. Solicitor Heath's frustration after weeks of pleading is palpable when on 19 March he exclaimed, "wee desire to be embuckled from the false and feigned amity of the King of Spain, yet will not prepare so much as to defend ourseloves."[62] The prospect of a war apparently did not seize the Commons with excitement.

Unfortunately, an application on behalf of the 1624 House of Commons for a posthumous peace prize would be premature. We still have to consider what variety of a war failed to excite them. The Four Propositions quite simply were not anything to take to the streets and cheer about. In fact, as James told them, they were not voting on a declaration of war; they were voting instead on a bill to increase the defense budget. Given this fact and given the coalition's insistence on preventing any debate on a war, Russell's judgment is surely too harsh. Men cannot justly be termed "lukewarm" when they were never allowed to air their views. The only solid evidence of their views on this subject is also mute, the subsidy bill itself, and that speaks volumes.

The House's grant in these circumstances of "the greatest aid which was ever granted in Parliament" in fact reverses Russell's interpretation: the subsidy bill of 1624 stands as silent testimony that their belief in the Crown, and in a war, outweighed the fear of their constituents – if only slightly. They voted in 1624 for the proverbial pig in a poke. Several MPs pleaded with their colleagues that they would require details of the planned war in order to justify the heavy taxes in the country. But these "localist" MPs were ultimately ignored. Given that the Crown asked the Commons to pay for something they could not even talk about, it is remarkable, not that the Commons declined six subsidies and twelve fifteenths, but that the Crown got anything at all. In the final analysis, in return for a breach of the Spanish treaties and

---

[62] Russell, *Parliaments*, pp. 189–90; and 19 March, Holles Diary, fo. 107.

for the *possibility* of a Spanish war, the MPs were willing to overcome their great apprehensions and to trust James and Charles, even though it meant that they might experience difficulties at the next election. Localism cannot fully explain what happened in the Parliament of 1624. It does, however, render the MPs' sacrifice even more striking. It also explains their later rage when they felt they had been duped for a second time.

7

"Other circles": redress of grievances and supply, April–May

After the celebrations on 23 March, the government's obsessive efforts to reach an agreement with the Commons over the subsidy might appear largely completed. There were no more extended debates on supply, and in the last half of the Parliament, Middlesex's impeachment and the Spanish attack on Buckingham overshadowed the subsidy bill itself, which eventually emerged in substantially the same form as outlined on 19–20 March. This shift in the session's agenda may explain Russell's decision to conclude his effective analysis of the 1624 subsidy bill on 23 March. Yet if this had been the case, the members of the administration would have been spared much anxiety and Buckingham might have avoided his physical and mental collapse in May. The subsidy campaign in fact did not end in late March: a month later, Secretary Conway privately lamented that in the Commons "all things seeme to move in other circles than they were wont." More importantly, "the maine business" of the subsidy bill, he confessed, "goes on slowly."[1] What had happened was that the grand set-piece parliamentary battles of March had ended only to give way to a more irregular pattern of conflict. To be sure, the Crown eventually won the subsidy campaign, but in the last partisan phase of the struggle it paid dearly for its triumph.

The unilateral prorogation of the 1624 session on 23 March therefore is a particularly unfortunate decision in a study of the Parliaments of the decade. The documents for this period, while admittedly sparse and ambiguous, bear directly on some of Russell's general axioms about early Stuart Parliaments and politics. Parliament in this period, he has argued, "was not powerful," and because it could not tie redress of grievances to supply, the institution "was heading for extinction."[2] It is true that in 1624 the Commons did not link one with the other. It is also true that in 1624 the Crown granted with

---

[1] Conway to Kensington, 14 April 1624, SP 78/72/136. Compare Russell's analysis of events before 23 March (*Parliaments*, pp. 145–90) and that afterwards (*Parliaments*, pp. 190–203).
[2] Russell, "Parliamentary History," p. 3.

reluctance and considerable bad grace a public declaration of the breach of the treaties, a Proclamation against Jesuits, several bills on economic and legal regulation, a generous pardon, and an extra week to the session's existence. In the same period it concluded a treaty with the United Provinces on less than favorable terms.

The Commons never made any of these measures a *sine qua non* for the subsidy bill. Rather the MPs quickly discovered that they did not have to press for anything as provocative as direct linkage. They merely had to allow the subsidy bill to languish in some committee chamber, and the Crown of its own volition would find a burning interest in the grievances of the commonwealth. In fact, by 1624 the policy of royal concessions to a Parliament was well established: at the beginning of the session, the Earl of Carlisle advised James, "cast but away some crums of your Crown amongst them, and your Majestie will see those crums will make a miracle, they will satisfie many thousands." By the end of the session, the "crums" had become largish. Bishop Laud by 1627 was scarcely sympathetic to Parliament, but his assessment of the situation in 1624 is interesting: in "the last Parliament of King James, they gave three subsidies, and had that from the King that was worth eight, if not ten, to be bought and sold."[3] And all this took place without the House of Commons ever having, as Coke put it, "to bargain merchant-like."

Russell has observed that "the timing with which . . . the Parliament moved on from the breach of the treaties to the trial of Cranfield has the smoothness of clockwork." The only question, however, is whose watch was the House following in the last half of the 1624 session? Russell was confident that it was Buckingham's timepiece, but the question needs to be examined carefully, if only because the answer is vital to a sound understanding of the 1624 Parliament and the pattern of early Stuart politics.[4]

MANSFELT AND RELIGION

James's speech on 23 March initially seemed to resolve the major problems separating James and Parliament on how to avenge, if not to restore, Elizabeth and Frederick. Unfortunately the "Patriots" were to discover that waging war was bureaucratically onerous and physically dangerous. Conway's memoranda began to include long lists of preliminaries for military action; one from late March called for James to reinforce Ireland, to ready the militia, to dispatch Wake, Anstruther and Carlisle, to conclude a naval league with the Dutch and above all to ensure sufficient reserves of powder. Not surprisingly, comments about "the stresse of business which depends on this

---

[3] Carlisle to James, 14 February 1624, *Cabala*, I, pp. 269–70; and Russell, *Parliaments*, p. 53.
[4] Russell, *Parliaments*, p. 202.

Court" began to figure prominently in Conway's correspondence as did his longing for summer and leisure. The Secretary was perhaps the first "Patriot" to appreciate that the vindication of English honor and the salvation of Europe from the Habsburg Antichrist was tedious work. It was in fact hard to be glamorous from behind a desk full of unanswered dispatches. Nevertheless, those as yet ignorant of the crushing administrative burden planned a jousting match to display their élan. The result was prophetic; the Earl of Oxford broke an arm during practice, and the event was first postponed and eventually forgotten.[5]

The full appreciation of these problems of course lay in the future. In the meantime the result of James's speech of 23 March was a flurry of bellicose statements; "les choses," Tillières remarked on 31 March, "s'acheminent au grand galop à la guerre." Buckingham spent the Easter recess at Chatham where he inspected the fleet and placed on his own credit a large order for beer and salt beef. He also spoke openly of his desire "to go Admirall" with an Anglo-Dutch fleet of ninety sail in which the London watermen would man the English contingent. The fleet's goal was mysterious: sometimes he said it would wrest control of the Channel from pirates, freebooters – and Dunkirkers – and at other times he boldly outlined naval raids against Spain under the Palatine flag.[6] "Les preparatifs de guerre resiouissent fort tout ce peuple," who, Tillières added, were "si animé contre l'Espagne" that they did not consider "les malheurs qui leur en peuvent arriver."[7] Jingoistic fervor found additional support in two widely reported exchanges at Court. Cecil's boast about marching 10,000 men through Spain understandably outraged the Spanish ambassadors who told Conway that "an army of their women" would "beate them backe." The Secretary reminded them that "one woman [the Infanta] would have served the turne to have kept all English from going thither otherwise then in friendship," but he agreed on the formidable nature of women as he was sure the Spaniards had "heard of the like at home in '88." This exchange concluded with both sides promising in the approaching conflict to take care of any captured kinsmen. In another report, Inijosa "merrily" proposed a *rapprochement* to the duke: "Come Buckingham let's be friendes agayne, or if we cannot let's have warre and not stand thus betweene." The duke reportedly was in no mood for playful fencing: the English had "made one good step towards a warre on our parts make you another on yours and see what we will say to you." Both Conway's appeal to

---

[5] Remembrances to the Duke [in Conway's hand], [late March to early April 1624], SP 14/162/53; and Tillières to Ville-aux-clercs, 30 March 1624, PRO 31/3/58, fo. 64.

[6] Carleton the younger to Carleton, 11 April 1624, SP 84/117/31; Valaresso to the Doge and Senate, 2 April 1624, *CSPV*, XVIII, pp. 263–9; and Beaulieu to Trumbull, 26 March 1624, Trumbull MSS, VII/155.

[7] Tillières to Ville-aux-clercs, 30 March 1624, PRO 31/3/58, fo. 64.

Elizabethan imagery and the duke's dare found an attentive domestic audience eager for confirmation of the Court's bellicosity. Little wonder then that Buckingham's widespread popularity in late March led Sterrell, an English Catholic, to predict "a popular tumult" in support of the favorite who "swayeth all."[8]

The wild euphoria proved short-lived. When someone asked Buckingham if the king had approved his naval plan, "he confessed not yet but he assured it would be easily obtained." Buckingham's confession, rather than his aspirations, seemed to reflect reality in early April. Contemporaries could easily judge if the duke was talking through his hat by examining the government's compliance with the parliamentary offer. James had to name a Council of War to disburse the subsidy, negotiate an Anglo-Dutch league, dispatch the English diplomatic corps to organize the continental confederates, and formally terminate the Spanish treaties. By mid-April, the government had taken none of these steps. Faith in James's sincerity consequently dwindled as the Dutch envoys grew increasingly restive over the constant delays in opening negotiations, and it evaporated as their Spanish counterparts had frequent and lengthy private audiences with the king. Beaulieu on 9 April retracted his earlier high hopes and remarked that nothing appeared certain "but sure we will go very discretely to worke and not lightly engage our selves into anie great inconvenience."[9]

The dawning realization that the government was not moving in step with Parliament soon affected the passage of the subsidy bill. But when the Commons re-assembled after Easter, it was apparent that the subsidy bill and the war were secondary in the minds of many members. Buckingham on 1 April greeted the returning peers and MPs with the alarming news that the Spaniards were preparing at Dunkirk "a far greater and stronger Navy than that of '88," replete with "at least an Hundred Flat Bottoms" to ferry over Spinola's army. In light of the present danger, the Lord Admiral requested, and the Lords quickly approved, an advance against the forthcoming subsidy. He also informed the Lords that the letter to Philip terminating the treaties had been drafted and that the Spanish ambassadors had been informed of James's resolution. But in the Commons, although Eliot confirmed having seen the letter, the duke's impassioned plea fell on deaf ears. The House instead followed the lead of Phelips and Heath; it formally deferred the discussion until 5 April and informally ignored the motion altogether. On 3 April, Buckingham moved the Lords to remind the Commons of the need

---

[8] Nethersole to Carleton, 29 March and 3 April 1624, SP 14/161/50 and 14/162/12; and Sterrell to LaFaille, 8 April 1624, HHStA, Belgien PC, facz. 60/unfoliated.
[9] Beaulieu to Trumbull, 9 April 1624, Trumbull MSS, VII/157; and Carleton the younger to Carleton, 11 April 1624, SP 84/117/31.

for "some speedy Provision of Money to be made for this great business," but his colleagues dissuaded him from forcing the issue. On 5 April Lord Keeper Williams again returned to the issue, but Charles asked the House to have patience: "they [the MPs] have it in agitation."[10] The Commons in fact did not have it in agitation, but at least by the 5th, several peers appreciated that the forgetfulness was a polite excuse concealing a more serious problem. On 11–12 March, the Commons had been beforehand with the Lords, and by early April they were beforehand with James. They had taken the first step, and a large one, towards an agreement, and they justifiably felt that it was now James's turn to make a corresponding move. The House, Conway's son reported, "is firmly fixte" that James publicly had to break off the Spanish treaties.[11] Unfortunately, James was very reluctant to do so, and as the Commons waited, they scrutinized his speech of 23 March.

On more sober reflection many found the address to be uncomfortably vague on crucial points, and doubts naturally arose about whether more had not been read into James's speech than was actually there. John Castle by early April was certain that this was the case: the Commons then regarded James's Easter speech as "an individuum vagum, which hath given small satisfaction." In this situation, recollections of the previous session overwhelmed many MPs. Mr. Carleton observed that the MPs in 1624 "feare nothing more than that when they had disbursed money towards the warres, an idle and rotten peace may quickly denonce the same according to former experience."[12] Quite clearly their "former experience" made MPs willing to risk hampering naval operations that summer rather than repeat the debacle of 1621. Consequently, the Commons' demands insensibly expanded in the remaining weeks of the session. "We have bin heretofore," Carleton remarked, "so deceaved in our expectations when we tooke our selves to be in so faire way as might in all likelyhood have carried us forward to very good resolutions, that many will not yet go from their doubtes, because here is no preparation made for warre." Signs of some preparation for war came to merge with the demand for a public declaration, and Secretary Conway wearily wrote that the administration now had to secure "some executions on the kings part of the Resolution promised to the House to bee taken by the King."[13]

At the end of the debate on 20 March, Phelips had made a linkage which many MPs found appealing: after a resolution on the subsidy, "we shall find

---

[10] *LJ*, III, pp. 284 and 288; *CJ*, pp. 751–2; and *Lords Debates*, p. 32.
[11] Conway the younger to [Carleton], 18 April 1624, SP 14/163/1.
[12] Castle to Trumbull, 16 April 1624, Trumbull MSS, VIII/115; and Carleton the younger to Carleton, 19 April 1624, SP 14/163/16.
[13] Carleton the younger to Carleton, 28 March 1624, SP 14/161/49; and Conway to Carleton, 16 April 1624, SP 84/117/58.

a torn commonwealth, which must necessarily be carefully regarded." On 1 April, they doubtless agreed with Phelips that Buckingham's proposal came "unexpectedly"; it interrupted the House's enjoyment of its reward for earlier good behavior, the unimpeded pursuit of legislation and of the "crying grievances" of the kingdom. This sentiment emerges clearly from the relative treatment of Buckingham's proposal and the recusant question. Mr. Delbridge, just before Buckingham's suggestion, voiced a *cri de coeur* about "nothing done about Recusants yet." The daily resort of Catholics to the Spanish ambassadors' chapel would, unless checked, "breed Suspicion still in men's Hearts." Buckingham's proposal was then delivered, and Phelips smoothly shifted the House from the subsidy to Delbridge's query with his remark that "Spain can do us no harm, unless he have a Party here in England." This led naturally to a motion for a Committee on Religion which Solicitor General Heath seconded.[14] Having testified to their devotion to "the great business" by breaking off their discussion of the Catholic question before the 1 March debate, and since James had yet to make reciprocal testimonials, the MPs' sense of priorities on 1 April was not misplaced: they had earned a little self-indulgence.

The involvement of Heath and Phelips suggests that the coalition decided to humor the Commons a little before attempting to lead it over the next hurdle. If that was the plan, then the Petition on Religion which emerged on 3 April, revealed the danger of giving the Commons their head. The petition, largely a revival of a similar one in 1621, was prefaced with a lengthy denunciation of Spain based on Buckingham's earlier report of the threat of a Spanish invasion. The proposed text, Sir Dudley Carleton noted, contained "many aromatical points in it which I believe must be qualified before it hath his Majesties placet."[15] His prediction was accurate. On news of the "stinging Petition," James stayed the courier carrying the letter to Philip. "You know," he told Conway, "my firm Resolution not to make this a War of Religion, and ... I would be loth to be Conny-catch by my People." Hence, Charles and the Lords spent 5–7 April in the awkward task of persuading the Commons to water down the petition. Eventually the Parliament-men yielded to heavy pressure and removed the offensive preface, but they insisted on retaining the request for a Proclamation banishing the Jesuits. "Now we were to expect a forrayne warre," Nethersole explained on 3 April, "the contentment which the country would receyve by the newes of some good course taken herein, and the triall this would be of the truth of the good hopes conceyved which one man was so wise to say and I thinke more had in their thoughts by the full

---

[14] *CJ*, pp. 251–2; and Holland Diary, fos. 74–74v.
[15] Carleton to [Nethersole], 19 April 1624, SP 84/117/78; *LJ*, III, p. 289; and Ruigh, pp. 239–45.

cry went uppon this sent."[16] The list of trials that the Commons set for James was rapidly becoming impressive.

A day after the House intemperately went after the recusants' scent, it started another hare, Lionel Cranfield, Earl of Middlesex and Lord Treasurer. Apart from the breach of the Spanish treaties, "hewinge downe . . . the glorious tree of the Middlesex Earle" was probably the most popular act of the 1624 session. "Never was theire any man less pittyed," Castle gloated, "he was neither good in ramo or radice, and every man now hath a hatchett to cutt at both." Likewise Lord Falkland "mightely" rejoiced on receipt of the news "that Lucifer is fallen."[17] The "Patriots" certainly had an interest in ruining the "plus fort arboutans" of James's Spanish inclinations and an alleged conspirator with Arundel "to oust Buckingham." But the timing of the attack was not in the coalition's favor. "The action of enquiring and proceeding against him is good," Valaresso remarked, "but the time is perhaps unfortunate and the delay certainly harmful . . . Thus the energies and abilities of the parliament are involved in what one may call a private affair while the more important public resolutions are delayed and suspended."[18] Secretary Conway fully shared Valaresso's misgivings. To Sir Edward Herbert, he complained that the Commons "have turned a little aside from the great business" to pursue Middlesex; to Carleton, he confessed that the impeachment was "the maine impediment in all the publique proceedings" and would delay passage of the subsidy bill; and to Kensington, his close friend, Conway lamented that "all things seeme to move in other circles then they were wont . . . the maine business goes on slowly, the houses diverting themselves to examine the error of the tyme."[19] As befitted a man rumored to be Cranfield's replacement as Master of the Court of Wards, Conway was pleased to see him ruined; nonetheless, as a public official he was distressed that the Commons had gone off in full cry after the Lord Treasurer and abandoned the subsidy bill.

The obvious solution was a compromise, but neither James nor the Commons was eager to make the first move. The Commons, after a generous opening, now looked to James, who for his part was very shy of bargaining. In early April, he questioned Conway about a possible linkage between the subsidy and the Petition on Religion: "I mean whether they will go on with

---

16 Nethersole to Carleton, 3 April 1624, SP 14/162/12; and James to Conway, quoted in Ruigh, p. 241.

17 Falkland to Buckingham, 22 May 1624, Bodleian Library, Carte MSS 30, fos. 161–161v; and Castle to Trumbull, 16 April 1624, Trumbull MSS, XVIII/115.

18 Tillières to Ville-aux-clercs, 14 April 1624, PRO 31/3/58, fo. 79; and Valaresso to the Doge and Senate, 2 and 16 April 1624, CSPV, XVII, pp. 268 and 278–9.

19 Conway to Herbert, 14 April 1624, SP 78/72/42; same to Carleton, 16 April 1624, SP 84/117/58; and same to Kensington, 14 April 1624, SP 78/72/136.

the subsidies according to their promise and trust to my wisdom and discretion in answering their petition, or if they will make it in effect, a condition, *sine qua non*, though not say it plainly." Charles and Buckingham attempted to negotiate a settlement. On 9 April Heath told the Commons that since the letter to Philip, which Buckingham and Eliot had earlier reported, had now been sent to Spain, this act "did actually dissolve the Treaties, according to the advice of his Lords and Commons." Sir Francis Seymour, however, adopted a more cautious assessment. The Parliament's offer of aid was predicated on the public dissolution of the Spanish treaties; thus he asked "whether the House conceives this public Declaration to be already made." The House decided in the negative.[20]

Having failed to lure the Commons into further displays of faith in the king's sincerity, Charles and Buckingham could only ignore James's fear of a *sine qua non* and establish some link between the Petition and the subsidy bill. The Lords resolved on 10 April that Charles, speaking on his own and not for the Upper House, should most delicately posit the linkage before the Commons. Charles announced that he would personally carry the petition to the king, but added that his task would be easier if "we will take a course to begin with the bill of subsidies that his Highness may say that we are in the way with the subsidies." Sir Thomas Jermyn then brandished the threat of Tyrone's return to Ireland while Sir John Savile in an apparent volte-face addressed the problem directly; some had told James that "we have said we will give subsidies but that we will then have all we desire. He saith it can do no hurt to begin with the bill." The Commons, however, stood its ground. Although the House agreed to enter in its book of record Buckingham's sighting of James's letter to Philip, it also resolved to follow Coke's dictum, "till Signification made to the other king, no dissolution of the treaties."[21]

This intransigence understandably made Conway eager to provide "some executions on the kings part of the Resolution promised to the House," and the likeliest place to start was the Dutch treaty. By early April, after cooling their heels in London for six weeks, Francis Aerssens and Albert Joachimi, were "not a little discontented." Earlier in the year, Charles, Buckingham, Conway and Elizabeth had implored the Dutch to send over ambassadors extraordinary. Yet on the envoys' arrival, the English employed one excuse after another to postpone the negotiations. The situation was particularly galling for the Dutch who were deeply apprehensive about becoming "shoing-horns" to slip James into a Spanish entente.[22] The delays, moreover, made Aerssens, never a model of discretion, seem "as impatient of stay . . . as

---

[20] James to Conway [4 April 1624], quoted in Ruigh, p. 242; and *CJ*, pp. 760–1.
[21] 10 April, Nicholas Diary, fo. 138; and *CJ*, p. 761.
[22] Beaulieu to Trumbull, 23 April 1624, Trumbull MSS, VII/160; and Carleton to Conway, 4 February 1624, SP 84/116/95.

a little childe is for a thinge he sees and desires and cannot be speedily given." The fact that both ambassadors knew England and English politics fairly well only complicated the situation: they spoke, Mr. Carleton reported, "to everybody," and the stories of their neglect only added fuel to popular suspicions of James's intention. "Many will not yet go from their doubtes, because here is no preparation made for warre, and Monsieur Aerssens is the forwardest of twentie to cast in his doubtes."[23] Domestic politics as much as foreign policy demanded that the English quickly attend to the Dutch.

English enthusiasts of an aggressive foreign policy constantly advocated a course "as Queen Elizabeth did" in Anglo-Dutch relations. It is perhaps appropriate, given the high English expectations of the Dutch, that they should have been the first to point out that the times had changed in a generation. Devotees of the Elizabethan era simply could not imagine that the Dutch Republic might now be embarrassed with its earlier subservient role. Equally, even Carleton's coaching from The Hague had not prepared his superiors to absorb the fundamental fact that a revival of the Elizabethan foreign policy towards the Dutch would immediately precipitate a bidding war with France and that the Dutch might actually enjoy playing one suitor off against another. The Dutch negotiations of April to May 1624 served as many Englishmen's first plunge into the icy waters of early seventeenth-century *realpolitik*.[24]

A *coup de théâtre*, Charles and Buckingham planned, would open the Dutch negotiations; immediately after James accepted the parliamentary assistance on 23 March, Buckingham would usher Aerssens and Joachimi into James's presence. Unfortunately, although the ambassadors arrived on time, Buckingham did not, and the audience was postponed until 1 April. Aerssens glumly told Mr. Carleton that in his conferences with Conway and Buckingham, "he had not heard that day one worde . . . that sounded resolutely for a warre . . . nothing had bin sayd to them of their business that day or at any time else." When on 1 April the envoys finally met the king, James did not relieve their suspicions. He agreed to appoint a commission to consider their offer of an offensive and defensive alliance. But he added that since he "is not resolved as yet to enter into war," an offensive alliance was unnecessary, and if he should decide on an enemy, "he did not thincke [it] would be the king of Spaine." In that case, both James and Aerssens agreed that an alliance was pointless.[25]

[23] Conway the younger to Carleton, 18 April 1624, SP 14/163/1; and Carleton the younger to Carleton, 28 March 1624, SP 14/161/49.
[24] Carleton the younger to Carleton, 11 April 1624, SP 84/117/31; and Grayson, "From Protectorate to Partnership," pp. 290–4.
[25] Carleton to Trumbull, 16 April 1624, Trumbull MSS, XVIII/115; and Nethersole to Carleton, 3 April 1624, SP 14/162/12.

The English commissioners were not appointed for another two weeks. In the meantime, Conway warned the duke that, given James's preliminary comments, the greatest possible care must be taken with the "difficult poynt," the selection of "well affected Commissioners." And "this Parliament tyme" further delayed the selection, not to mention the actual meeting, of the commissioners. Thus to soothe the restive ambassadors, Conway on 3 April opened unofficial discussions "to the end wee might describe a foundation and circle of a Treaty."[26] The Dutch simply asked "wheather the chaunge of his [James's] Councells and affaires would stretch to the declaring of a warre or noe? and that against the king of Spaine." Conway chided the ambassadors for pressing James too fast: "it became not a wise king to make violent chaunges . . . and kings love to have Reason on their sydes and found of a good cause." The paramount difficulty was to arrange a mutually advantageous alliance: how could they agree on an offensive alliance, and "not an Enemy declared," or on a defensive alliance which "would advantage them but . . . moves nothing towards the recovery of the Palatinate." Although some hope remained for a joint fleet operating under the Palatine flat, the discussions came to center on a strictly defensive treaty. Such a limited agreement distressed Aerssens and Joachimi, but not as much as Conway's proposal that the English "lend succours as Queen Elizabeth did." The most singular aspect of the Anglo-Dutch Elizabethan tradition had been the deposit of Dutch towns under English control as a caution for the Dutch debt, and in 1624, Aerssens and Joachimi were "utterly against" any revival of this earlier practice. The unofficial conference ended very coolly: since the envoys "observed a coldness and unripenes in our affaires," they asked for permission to withdraw, and "when his Majesties resolution should bee better prepared they knew the States would ever bee ready to attend him."[27] Indeed the mere mention of cautionary towns reportedly made the negotiations "very colde and heavy on both sides"; and the Dutch ambassadors "are much startled . . . and take it for an argument that we will doe nothing." Aerssens emerged from the discussion to tell Mr. Carleton not to bother including his greetings to Carleton's uncle in The Hague; the envoy would soon perform that office in person.[28] By 10 April, when Charles made his personal plea for expedition with the subsidy bill, the Paul's walkers had already picked up the

---

[26] Conway to Carleton, 16 April 1624, SP 84/117/58; and "The States Ambassadors Propositions," 22 April 1624, found in two parts in SP 103/41 and 42, unfoliated.

[27] Conway to Herbert, 14 April 1624, SP 78/72/42; same to Carleton, 16 April 1624, SP 84/117/58; same to Kensington, SP 78/72/16; and Castle to Trumbull, 16 April 1624, Trumbull MSS, XVIII/115.

[28] Beaulieu to Trumbull, 16 April 1624, and Castle to Trumbull, 16 April 1624, Trumbull MSS, VII/159 and XVIII/115.

news that the MPs might well waste their labor if they allocated one of the Four Propositions of the subsidy bill to the defense of the Dutch Republic.

At this point, the prince intervened, and the envoys agreed to wait until formal negotiations could begin. On 15 April, James finally named five commissioners – Buckingham, Hamilton, Pembroke, Weston and Conway – who first met with the ambassadors two days later. The close popular attention to the troubled Dutch negotiations allowed opponents of the "good Patriotts" to use the Dutch talks to turn the tables on their tormentors without tarring themselves as crypto-Papist hispanophiles. Consequently, the Elizabethan Anglo-Dutch tradition, Conway mourned, was "taken up and earnestly followed by those who hoping of an averseness in that State to give satisfaction to theise poynts [the cautionary towns], may cast a breach betweene this Crowne and that State." The Secretary probably had in mind Arundel and Middlesex whom the Dutch ambassadors had earlier reported as eager to be included on the commission. Mr. Carleton also feared that the Dutch refusal of cautionary towns might well play into the hands of the anti-war faction: the Dutch stiffness

is knowne to be their act to marchand a cheap bargain but it will prove an ill craft if by the occasion they make none at all, and their good friendes feare that may happen if they bid no fayrer for the friendship of the kingdome, the King continuing still more inclinable to deale with Spayne.[29]

Almost two months after the Dutch envoys had arrived in London, the official negotiations began. Yet even though Conway expressed relief over "the choyce of a good Committee" who "desire a perpetuall Amity and Alliance between these Kingdomes and those States for the conversion of Religion and mutuall surety of both," the first official conference was as unsatisfactory as the unofficial one. All talk quickly centered on a defensive league and its attendant problem, cautionary towns as security for James's loan. Aerssens and Joachimi in response played their trump; Dutch envoys currently were in Paris completing a three-year loan package in which Louis XIII did not receive any cautionary towns. Aerssens and Joachimi therefore reportedly protested that "France doth more for them gratuito then is possible for us to do for the present, though we do our best." Moreover, they pronounced cautionary towns "a very strange demande from us, when we have neede of them for recovering of our own and have made them come over upon our own invitation."[30] Appeals to Elizabethan glories led only to

---

[29] Carleton the younger to [Carleton], 19 April 1624, SP 14/163/15; Conway to Carleton, 16 April 1624, SP 84/117/58; and Carleton to Conway, 4 February 1624, SP 84/116/95.

[30] Beaulieu to Trumbull, 23 April 1624, Trumbull MSS, VII/160; Carleton the younger to [Carleton], 4 April 1624, SP 14/162/13; and Grayson, "From Protectorate to Partnership," p. 291.

the reply that the Republic was "not at so low an ebbe as they were at when not onely the protection of these provinces was desired but the souveragnitie of them tendred to Queen Elizabeth." In short, if James openly joined the Spanish war, cautionary towns were a possibility; otherwise they were out of the question.

The opening negotiations thus simply confirmed a number of fears. To Rusdorff, Aerssens confessed his suspicion that the English "n'ait autre intention si non de faire menaces aux Espagnols par le beau semblant de leur negotiation."[31] As the Dutch negotiations foundered, parliamentary tempers rose in mid-April to the point where "the Iron of our great and public matters is hott." Castle reported rumors of James's refusal to publish the declaration ending the Spanish treaties until the Commons passed the subsidy bill; "but they meane to be at even hand with him, having so penned the Acts, that the ceasing the treaties is made the preface and Inducement to the Subsidies."[32] Furthermore, James's response to the Petition on Religion, Sir Henry Goodere observed, had become "a touchstone to discerne cleerely his Majesty's reality," and as he delayed his response, Conway's son reported, "the house doth violently fall upon the worst consequences." Castle blended these points into a pious hope:

Wee pray God his Majestie may returne such answere as may be to their encouragement to go on cheerfully in matters of the subsidie, which it is thought they will not yeeld unto, unless his Majestie vouchesafe his favor to this request, as also shall declare himself more absolutely and Categorically in the annullinge of the Treaties.

A survey of the same problem also led Edward Conway to pray for divine intervention: "I hope well for I hope since we desire to worke in Gods vineyard, he will not hire other labourers."[33]

Human intervention may also have had a role in the resolution of this crisis, although historians have been reluctant to consider the possibility. While strolling on the night of 14 April, Mr. Carleton was surprised to meet a large number of the "Cavaliers and followers" of Count Mansfelt. "Yf he is not come," Carleton immediately wrote his uncle, "I believe he will not long be absent." The count had in fact arrived in London that day. Ruigh perceptively commented that "London, for a brief moment, had become the diplomatic capital of Europe, yet Parliament seemed almost isolated from this maelstrom

[31] Rusdorff to Frederick V, 12 April 1624, *Mémoires*, II, pp. 278–80; and Carleton to Conway, 19 April 1624, SP 84/117/62.

[32] Castle to Trumbull, 23 April 1624, and Beaulieu to same, 16 April 1624, Trumbull MSS, XVIII/116 and VII/159.

[33] Conway the younger to Carleton, 18 April 1624, SP 14/163/1; Goodere to Carleton, 18 April 1624, SP 14/163/2; and Castle to Trumbull, 16 April 1624, Trumbull MSS, XVIII/115.

of Machiavellian intrigue."[34] One might only wish to underscore the word "almost."

Certainly since Gardiner's day, assessments of Ernest von Mansfelt have been so universally hostile that the count now requires a word in his defense in order to make the contemporary English response to him comprehensible. "If there was a man in Europe who was unfit to stand at the head of any serious movement in Germany," Gardiner judged "that man was Mansfelt." Admittedly Mansfelt was a public relations man's nightmare, but it should be remembered that, given the contemporary reliance on the contribution system to finance a war, all the generals of the Thirty Years War, even Gustavus Adolphus, had very similar "image" problems. Rhetoric could not adequately dispel the overtones of extortion that attended the extraction of "contributions" from the local inhabitants, whether neutral or hostile. Moreover, to pronounce Mansfelt as "unfit" for service because "he had not even the merit of success" was a verdict few contemporaries would have accepted.[35] Indeed his singular quality was his generalship. Until the arrival of the Swedish king, he was the most successful anti-Habsburg commander. He was defeated in 1622 at Wimpfen and Fleurus, but he also won in the same year at Wieslock, and to the wonder of the Dutch, he succeeded in relieving Bergen-op-zoom, a task which had defied Prince Maurice. In 1623, he held East Friesland against Tilly and for the Dutch and Louis XIII. The main blot on his career, and one which Gardiner oddly ignored, was the slight pull that loyalty exercised on him. His "variableness" and "juggling" caused Carleton to name him aptly "the Duke of Savoy's scholar," and at times, the general "doth exceede his master," Charles Emanuel. No one had forgotten the time in 1621 when he had very nearly sold his services and that of Frederick's last field army to the Emperor. Nonetheless, as Carleton observed, the count had "the luck thereof to come opportunely in the nick of two occasions . . . and may doe the like againe." To many opponents of the Habsburgs' "Western monarchie," Mansfelt was on sober reflection a "malum necessarium."[36]

Mansfelt had restlessly spent the first three months of 1624 in The Hague in the company of his fellow *condottieri*, John Ernest and Bernard of Weimar and his premier rival, Christian of Brunswick, the Administrator of the

---

[34] Carleton the younger to Carleton, 14 April 1624, SP 14/162/60; and Ruigh, p. 196.
[35] Gardiner, *England Under Buckingham*, I, p. 55. On the practice of contributions, see F. Redlich, "Contributions in the Thirty Years War," *Economic History Review* (1959–60), pp. 274–54. For a general discussion of the effects of early modern warfare, see Myron Gutman, *War and Rural Life in the Early Modern Low Countries* (Princeton, 1980), pp. 41–53, and for a specific illustration – the 1632 Swedish campaign in Bavaria – see Michael Roberts, *Gustavus Adolphus* (London, 1958), II, pp. 694–714.
[36] Carleton to Conway, 28 May 1624, SP 84/117/229; same to Chamberlain, 11 July 1623, SP 84/113/28; and same to Calvert, 5 February 1623, SP 84/111/67. See also Anton Gindeley, *History of the Thirty Years' War* (New York, 1898), I, pp. 320–42.

Bishopric of Halberstadt. Christian was noble, valiant and wholly devoted to Elizabeth in whose service he lost an arm. Yet even his admirers had to confess that as a general, he was "careless." In 1623, Tilly massacred his army at Stadtlohn because Christian neglected to send out sentinels. With England's possible shift in foreign alignment, tension between the two generals rose dramatically: Christian and Mansfelt eyed each other nervously as they jostled for the English contract.[37] Only Sir Dudley Carleton's strenuous efforts persuaded the two men to submit their applications in writing rather than in person. Frederick, Elizabeth and Carleton supported Christian's candidacy by a slender margin, and James responded graciously to his application; "whensoever there shall bee occasion to imploy a Person of his ranke and worth, his Majestie will have him the first man in his memory for that purpose." In the meantime, he instructed Carleton "by all meanes to dissuade his coming over hither at this tyme." The first round apparently went to Christian.[38] Unemployment and suspicion quickly led to a series of public quarrels and one near duel between the two rivals. In early March before retiring to Venice, Mansfelt resolved on a final personal appeal to his former patron, Louis XIII. But as the count prepared to board ship in Rotterdam, Christian became fearful that the French trip was a ruse to cover an impromptu visit to London. Given the "dayly goode newes of our parlement proceedings which are blowne over to the place he [Mansfelt] still waytes for a winde," Christian argued that in these circumstances Mansfelt would certainly head for England, and he requested permission to precede him. Carleton and Maurice again had to persuade Christian of the merits of patience and of having Mansfelt out of the way.[39]

The count did sail to France where his presence provoked a furore. His request for a royal audience met with the vociferous opposition of the Spanish and Flemish ambassadors, the Papal Nuncio and the dévot party. In early April, Louis politely declined his offer; as one French minister remarked, "wee did not want Generals." Nevertheless the Connestable Lesdiguières, a prominent *bons français*, softened the blow by suggesting "la route d'Angleterre." He did not need much encouragement. Before a reply could be made to his modest and transparent request "to come to London and live privately and unknowne in some citizens house," he arrived on 14 April and

[37] Carleton to Calvert, 30 July 1623, SP 84/113/109. See also Mansfelt to James, 18 November 1623, SP 81/29/271; Christian to James, 6 January 1624, SP 81/30/5; and Christian to Essex, 18 November 1623, BL Add. MSS, 46,188, fo. 20.

[38] Conway to Carleton, 20 February 1624, SP 84/116/141; Elizabeth to James, and Frederick to same, 19 January 1624, SP 81/30/5 and 16; and Carleton to Conway, [19] January 1624, SP 84/116/46.

[39] Carleton to Conway, 15 March 1624, SP 84/116/224; and same to Calvert, 26 February 1624, SP 84/116/156.

quietly settled into lodgings at Millbank.[40] The fact that he chose West-minster rather than London for his retirement home very clearly reveals the reason for his visit. After the collapse of Mansfelt's army in Frisia, his departure from The Hague under a cloud, his rebuff at the French Court, and his arrival in London with only a letter from the Connestable, contemporaries concluded that only desperation led such a notorious opponent of the Habsburgs to seek James's aid. "His friends here have cause to doubt," Castle observed on 16 April, "that his Comfort here will not be much better than those he receaved in France"; Sir Edward Conway remarked that "I am sure it [Mansfelt's visit] will be to noe purpose"; and Valaresso noted that "there is no doubt that his coming has displeased everyone, especially the king."[41]

His luck unexpectedly improved. On the 15th, Abraham Williams, a wealthy merchant devoted to Elizabeth and Frederick, offered the count the hospitality of his house in Palace Yard, next to the Parliament House. There a parade of visitors called on him; first Conway and Carlisle and then Valaresso and Buckingham and finally Charles himself. On the 18th, Charles and Buckingham conducted him in the prince's coach to Theobalds where, Beaulieu stated, "against the common expectation, he received also a very kinde audience." James, it was reported, "used him with extraordinary caresse." Charles again personally escorted Mansfelt back to St. James's Palace where he lodged the count in the rooms next to his own, which had been prepared for the Infanta, and entertained Mansfelt with "a very plentifull table." There Carlisle and Archbishop Abbot constantly attended the general, whom the English accorded "tout d'honneur et courtoisie, comme s'il eut ete un des plus grand Prince, ou un Saint." The canonization of an erstwhile pariah was so sudden, Carleton noted, "that he may thinck himself fallen into a kind of Paradise." Private negotiations and a secret agreement promptly followed, and on 25 April, he left for France carrying letters of exchange reportedly either for £20,000 or £40,000.[42]

The close attention paid to Mansfelt and "his merrie men" illustrates the contemporary interest in his meteoric visit and spectacular success. The habitués of Whitehall anterooms and St. Paul's never uncovered either his precise propositions or the exact terms of his agreement, but they came fairly close. That he had come to solicit financial backing was clear enough, but the

---

[40] Louis to Mansfelt, 2 April 1624, SP 81/30/122; Lesdiguières to Mansfelt, 3 April 1624, SP 81/30/124; Herbert to Calvert, 14 April 1624, SP 78/72/130; and Carleton the younger to Carleton, 11 April 1624, SP 84/117/31.

[41] Castle to Trumbull, 16 April 1624, Trumbull MSS, XXIII/115; Conway the younger to Carleton, 18 April 1624, SP 14/163/1; and Valaresso to the Doge and Senate, 16 April 1624, *CSPV*, XVII, p. 281.

[42] Rusdorff to Frederick V, 26 April 1624, *Mémoires*, I, pp. 289–94; Carleton the younger to [Carleton], 19 April 1624, SP 14/163/16; and Beaulieu to Trumbull, 23 April 1624, Trumbull MSS, VII/160.

pitch he employed to open English pursestrings initially caused some confusion. Sir Francis Nethersole finally pleaded ignorance about what happened in the royal closet "because it is kept so secret."[43] Others experienced only temporary confusion. Castle reported that the count's proposition touched "our matche in France and the meanes by that kingdome to open a war." Similarly Beaulieu quickly learned the rough details of the agreement even before it was formally signed: Mansfelt received the right to levy 10,000 foot, 3,000 horse, and six cannon in England, and James would support the force with £20,000 monthly.[44] Hence Nethersole's plea of ignorance must have erred on the side of caution; MPs in 1624 cannot have been wholly unaware of Mansfelt's business in London.

Nor can they have been ignorant of his popularity. Contemporary English ballads, such as the one lionizing "Illustrious Mansfield, God still guide they Sword," made this champion of Elizabeth no stranger to Londoners; "toute le monde, petits et grands, sont curieux de le voir, criant VIVA, VIVA!." Admittedly this response baffled experienced continental experts like Rusdorff, and Phelips at least knew enough to feel uneasy about the proposed royal subsidy to the adventurer in 1621; "what could be hoped for," his Country Gentleman asked, from "a company of refuge men" who were "undisciplined," driven solely by "spoyle and pillage," and "not unlikely for their better advantage to render themselves at any time to the opposite party"?[45] Yet from a certain distance, his flaws were not readily apparent, particularly to those anxious for a godly Joshua. Simonds D'Ewes, a prim Puritan horrified with immorality around him, nonetheless eagerly recorded the arrival of a warrior who "had done great services to the Protestant party" and would have done more "if moneys for the pay of his army had been supplied in time." Besides, Catholics had witnessed his troops' excesses, and after the brutalization of the Bohemian and Palatine Protestants, some Englishmen felt as though the Catholics deserved equal time. Thus one English corranto strenuously, but selectively objected to a Catholic report that the count's army contained 5,000 campfollowers and the ecclesiastical plunder of over sixty Catholic churches; it was not "only false but scandalous" to report that Mansfelt "should have in his Campe 5,000 women or whores." Nothing, however, was said about the "Chalices and Crosses and Images." "As thou hast done," one ballad intoned, "brave Generall so

43 Carleton to [Nethersole], 19 April 1624, SP 84/117/78; and Nethersole to Carleton, 25 April, SP 16/163/50.
44 Castle to Trumbull, and Beaulieu to same, 23 April 1624, Trumbull MSS, XVIII/116 and VII/160.
45 "The King and Queen of Bohemia," [1622–3], printed in *The Pepys Ballads* (Cambridge, Mass., 1929), I, p. 216; Rusdorff to Frederick V, 16 April 1624, *Mémoires*, I, pp. 283–7; and "A Discourse by Way of Dialogue," SRO DD/Ph 217/16.

proceed / And God with Glory, then will Crowne they meede." Unquestionably by the end of the year many Englishmen, especially in Kent, would feel less charitable, but in the spring, partly for lack of any serious rivals, the count was to many still "Illustrious Mansfield." Thus in honor of his arrival, one "pot-poet" proposed that Londoners

> beate upp the drum,
> for Mansfeild is come
> and receaved in her Ladishipps bed.[46]

The attraction that many both in and out of Parliament felt for the general was rather obviously not what drew a promissory note from James. Rather for the king, Mansfelt was a way out of a labyrinth. Charles and Buckingham had been pressing him to break with Spain and in recent weeks dangling parliamentary subsidies before him. Such crass manipulation was unpleasant enough, but the goal of these maneuverings James regarded as romantic nonsense. Unilateral action against Spain would sharply undermine the English bargaining position with other prospective confederates, and quite possibly eradicate it altogether with France. Mansfelt, as befitted a man whose recent expeditions had been financed by a consortium of foreign states, embodied the rhetoric of the "common cause," but his close English contacts, Sir Isaac Wake, the Earl of Carlisle and Valaresso may well have refined his vocabulary in hopes of gaining James's support. His lack of credentials notwithstanding, Mansfelt purported to represent his last consortium of France, Savoy and Venice, which was interested in linking the Palatine and Valteline questions; Mansfelt's projected army of 20–25,000 men (half of which would be English) would symbolize the union of these two related goals. Initial expenses, while comparatively high, would be shared proportionally and would soon decline "par bon menage et par les contributions." Franche-Comte, or perhaps other hereditary Habsburg lands, such as the Sundgau, could be seized in reprisal for the Imperial occupation of the Palatinate and the Valtelina and would at once serve as an ideal base for operations in either area and remain in easy reach of the Protestant cantons of Switzerland. He also pressed home truths about the proposed Anglo–Dutch naval alliance which James doubtless applauded: it was a nice idea, but "on ne recouvriroit point le Palatinat."[47]

As one of the princes in Mansfelt's new consortium, James found the proposal attractive for the same reason that capitalists prefer corporations –

[46] D'Ewes, *Autobiography*, I, p. 244; *A Relation of Many Memorable Passages*, 14 September (London, 1622); *Count Mansfields Proceedings*, 9 September (London, 1622); and SP 14/163/130. For guidance in the corantos, see the invaluable work of Folke Dahl, *A Bibliography of English Corantos and Periodical Newsbooks, 1620–1642* (London, 1952).

[47] Rusdorff to Frederick V, 14 and 16 April 1624, *Mémoires*, I, pp. 281–7; and Valaresso to the Doge and Senate, 16 and 23 April 1624, *CSPV*, XVII, pp. 280–1.

limited risk. Mansfelt would allow him to do something for his daughter and his grandchildren with the minimum danger and expense and with the maximum éclat. Such an arrangement would unquestionably strain but would not necessarily break Anglo-Spanish relations. Trade dislocations would be minimized, and the consortium would allow James to lay some claim to a major army operating deep within Europe without running through an unconscionable number of Exchequer officials. Finally, the prospect of a league "pour la restitution du Palatinat, Valtoline et Grisons," whose appeal to legal rather than religious ideals cut across confessional lines, simply could not be rejected out of hand.[48] James nevertheless was far from uncritical. Charles and Buckingham could have told the count before-hand of at least one alteration on which James would insist: the consortium would have to be formed before, not as Mansfelt proposed after, the mobilization of his army. Hence Mansfelt's letter of exchange for £40,000 was negotiable only when the representatives of Venice, Savoy and France produced similar documents. As James told Mansfelt, he readily agreed to his plan, "pourvuque je sois auparavant assure, que la France voudra s'y joindre." Buckingham more bluntly informed Tillières on Mansfelt's depar-ture that "everything was referred to France."[49] In short in April 1624 James did not agree to bankroll Mansfelt as much as he allowed the mercenary the opportunity to persuade others of the merits of his plan. Another alteration may owe as much to Charles and Buckingham, and perhaps to Middlesex and Weston, as to James. Although James agreed to begin punctual monthly pay-ments of £20,000 on the formation of the consortium, Mansfelt also agreed in a separate document not to expect any further English installments until after "la seance de premier Parlement qui se tiendra apres celuy d'a present."[50] Plainly Parliament was a convenient vehicle for evading a few payments. Equally the separate agreement could illustrate the sincerity of James's promise of a Michaelmas session and perhaps a desire not to proceed too far in this matter without full parliamentary knowledge and approval. Consequently, in this instance, the Stuarts' well-known shiftiness in financial matters should not overshadow their apparent consideration for Parliament.

Mansfelt's visit coincided with a flurry of activity over the subsidy bill. Because "there is a ielosie rased in the loer hows how that yeet the two treaties are not absolutelie broken off," Charles, Pembroke, Hamilton, Carlisle and the duke all urged James on 16 April that his letter be "shoed to them." He agreed, and on 17 April, Charles proposed to the Lords another joint con-

---

[48] [Draft of the English agreement with Mansfelt], 26 April 1624, SP 81/30/161.

[49] Valaresso to the Doge and Senate, 1 May 1624, *CSPV*, XVII, p. 304; and Rusdorff to Frederick V, 16 April 1624, *Mémoires*, I, pp. 283–7.

[50] Acknowledgements, 24 April 1624, SP 81/30/153. Rusdorff confirmed this arrangement; see *Mémoires*, I, pp. 289–94.

ference to settle "some mistaking" among the Commons. There the duke read the letter in the hope that they "would take all this for a sufficient declaration." He then pulled out all the stops in an effort to put the Commons in a bellicose mood with a *tour d'horizon* highlighting preparations for war in both Spain and England. James had granted commissions "to treat with his ancient Allies," the Dutch and Venetian Republics, France and Denmark, and was in the process of appointing a Council of War. Meanwhile the Spaniards reportedly mocked Parliament and prepared for an invasion of Ireland, which was, Buckingham emphasized, largely undefended. Finally, he dangled before the Commons a generous pardon, which James had ordered his learned counsel to prepare, "in return of the large contributions" which his subjects were about to make.[51]

The government's frustration can be more clearly seen when Secretary Conway appeared on 20 April before the committee preparing the subsidy bill. Then he omitted nothing, not even begging, in an effort to accelerate the passage of the subsidy bill. Any suspicions about royal martial intentions, he insisted, were unfounded; "his Majesty had made a dispatch for Sir Robert Anstruther to goe for denmarck wherein the King desires the King of denmarcks ayde." In addition, "for the regayning of the Palatinate . . . by warr," Mr. Secretary reported "the lyke instructions wilbe for fraunce, the lowe Contryes, the Princes of Germanie, the King of Sweden, the Duke of Savoy, the State of Venice." Nor was activity solely diplomatic; 6,000 troops were to be raised, perhaps to defend Ireland from Spanish invasion. The upshot was quite clear; since "he thought it impossible but that the treatyes were broken," Conway "desired some dispatch of the subsidies or ells these things would be delayed which might be dangerous." His presentation "was much debated." Some, who desired that "the Country might receave satisfaction for the money that was geven," felt a public declaration of the breach of the treaties essential; "though the King hath declared himselfe to the house, yett this not being publiq was not according to the order." The majority, however, sided with Conway; James's letter to Philip, while not a public declaration, was "soe publiq heere in England that the subiects may receave satisfaction." Unfortunately success in this matter immediately raised "another doubt in the house"; before any further action on the subsidy bill, the Committee would like to hear James's reply to the Petition on Religion.[52]

After this point the evidence becomes more fragmentary. We know that on the 22nd, two days after Conway's appeal, the Commons read the subsidy

---

[51] Buckingham to James, [16 April 1624], National Library of Scotland, Denmilne MSS, 33.1.7, vol. IV, no. 67; *HMC Buccleuch* (London, 1926), III, pp. 236–8; and *CJ*, pp. 769–72.

[52] [Anonymous parliamentary newsletter] [April 1624], Trumbull Misc. MSS, XXXVIII/unfoliated.

bill for the first time; and on the following day, James publicly accepted the Petition on Religion and promised a Proclamation banishing the Jesuits. On 24 April, the Commons sent the subsidy bill into committee after reading it a second time. In response, Heath, the Solicitor General, read the details of the pardon and announced the appointment of a Council of War. On the following day, Mansfelt left London.[53] This sequence of events poses a major question: who conceded what to whom? The terse parliamentary accounts in this period make any answer only partial at best. But even with these limitations, an analysis of this period produces some results which bear on the question of Parliament's ability to tie redress and supply together.

First of all, what happened in late April to remove the parliamentary suspicions which had arisen earlier in the month? Buckingham's report of James's letter on the 17th was, as Charles told the Lords, clearly an attempt to remove "some mistaking of the lower house." It was, however, not entirely successful. Mr. Carleton noted on the 19th that "the house is full of jealousies of the King notwithstanding all these remonstrances." Valaresso reported an equally hostile response to Buckingham's address: "when they afterwards came to debate the matter some members grew so heated that they could not refrain from saying that they might as well return home, seeing that they laboured in vain since the king's intention was only too apparent, to obtain the money and then do nothing."[54] Buckingham's *tour d'horizon* admittedly did not depict a nation making major strides towards a war. A handful of diplomatic instructions, a trip to Chatham and optimism about the Dutch negotiations weighed poorly in the balance against an incomplete Council of War and Aerssens telling all who would listen that James was merely using the Dutch to bring on better Spanish offers. It is vital to remember that only after the second conference with the Dutch envoys on the 24th, not the first meeting on the 17th, was it possible to speak hopefully of an Anglo-Dutch league. Buckingham on the 17th had thus nobly attempted to make the best of a bad situation, and he achieved indifferent success.

In such a bleak situation, Charles and Buckingham had one trump in reserve, a favorable reply to the Petition on Religion. James's warm acceptance of it probably had the most to do with easing the subsidy bill over its second, and possibly its first, reading. But it appears that Mansfelt opportunely substantiated the Crown's singularly unsuccessful attempt to present creditable war preparations. As Valaresso exclaimed, "God has sent Mansfelt here." The general certainly proved popular in the streets; "par

---

[53] *CJ*, pp. 769–72 and 774; Chamberlain to Carleton, 30 April 1624, *Letters*, II, p. 556; and 24 April, Holland Diary, fo. 48.

[54] Carleton the younger to Carleton, 19 April 1624, SP 14/163/16; and Valaresso to the Doge and Senate, 23 April 1624, *CSPV*, XVII, p. 291.

toutes les rues ou il passoit," Rusdorff reported, "le peuple en tres grand nombre etoit assemble, les uns s'ecrioitent: Dieu vous benisse, Monseigneur, autres, Viva, Viva! Pleusieurs s'estoimoient heureux de toucher le bord de son manteau." Conversely the Spanish ambassadors, like their colleagues in Paris, reacted sharply to his presence in London and were "very much spighted" with the warm reception accorded him; they "are incensed at such conspicuous honours." And Valaresso added, "many are amazed. All right minded persons rejoice."[55]

There was clearly considerable public relations value in close association with a man who provoked such an extraordinary range of responses. Mr. Carleton rightly assessed the count's value: "we have begunne with him in this high straine," he wrote to his uncle

not out of purpose to keepe him here long or to finde him any such employment as happily he may seeke for, but onely to dispight the Spaniards so much the more, and give contentment to the Parliament; for there is no question of the extreme hatred of the one to him; and the other certainly have so good an opinion of him that they will be better satisfied of his Majesties resolutions by so good a reception given him.

Nethersole made a similar analysis: "the greatest reason" for his warm reception "was the satisfaction . . . thereby given to our house of the sinceritie of his Majesties decleration."[56] D'Ewes in retrospect partially credited Mansfelt with the passage of the subsidy bill. By his entertainment and negotiations "all men now concluded that the King of Great Britain would draw his sword in earnest, and not readily sheath it again till he had restored the prince Elector Palatine." Finally, while Charles and Buckingham were quite pleased with his popularity, they were also relieved at his success with James. After Mansfelt's departure, they both told Rusdorff of "le grand contentement qu'ils ont recu de son arrivee, d'autant qu'ils n'auroient pas si tot ni si aisement porte le Roi a cette resolution, n'eut pas l'occasion presentee par sa presence."[57] Mansfelt had "come opportunely in the nick of two occasions" to rescue Bergen and Frankenthal, and, as far as Charles and Buckingham were concerned, Mansfelt had again arrived in the nick of time in April 1624. He cannot be accorded full credit for this rescue, but unquestionably he assisted the coalition in one of its direst moments during the Parliament of 1624. They probably would have echoed Valaresso's pious ejaculation, "God has sent Mansfelt here."

[55] Rusdorff to Frederick V, 26 April 1624, *Mémoires*, pp. 289–94; Beaulieu to Trumbull, 23 April 1624, Trumbull MSS, VII/160; and Valaresso to the Doge and Senate, 23 April 1624, *CSPV*, XVII, p. 293.

[56] Carleton the younger to [Carleton], 19 April 1624, SP 14/163/16; and Nethersole to Carleton, 25 April 1624, SP 14/163/50.

[57] D'Ewes, *Autobiography*, I, p. 94; and Rusdorff to Frederick V, 26 April 1624, *Mémoires*, pp. 289–94.

If Mansfelt provided the backdrop for the 17–24 April debates, James's reply to the Petition on Religion occupied the foreground. Its utility was apparent in the subsidy debate on 20 April. At that time, Nethersole wrote, "some startled up in one feare and some in another that these three subsidyes might go the same way the two given at the last Convention of Parliament did if the bill of subsidy went thus on winged feete and other bills of grace on leaden ones." Sir Thomas Wentworth, "who thinkes himself wise and sure is bold," pointedly drew attention to the fact that the Petition on Religion was "standing still." Conway countered by observing that "the bill of subsidy [is] not to be passed at the first reading." The Secretary thus suggested the resolution to this awkward impasse; because the technicalities of legislation afforded two further opportunities for bargaining, the Commons could "concede" to the king and garner full royal gratitude without really compromising its position. Later in the day, during a committee debate, Coke again eased the Commons out of a tangle, this time with his famous declaration, "I am no parenthesis man nor no preamble man."[58] The bill was now ready for presentation to the whole House.

On 22 April, the subsidy bill passed its first reading in the face of Sir Francis Seymour's characteristically brisk opposition. He was resigned to the first reading and proposed as consolation "to have the Bill of Subsidy have his first Reading; and then, during our sitting, to go on with publick Bills; that the Honour of the King, and Good of the Subject may go hand in hand." He need not have worried excessively about the "good of the Subject"; scarcely had he sat down, and the bill been passed, before the House learned that James, who "would not be backward with his people," would respond on the next day to the Petition on Religion. Heath, who delivered the message to the Commons, then proposed that the Commons quickly proceed with the second reading, and Phelips suggested a debate on the 24th, to which the House agreed.[59]

The climax of the last half of the session was James's speech on 23 April in which he graciously accepted the entire petition and praised the members for their piety. Not only did the speech signal a major reversal for the English Catholics, who had been maneuvering behind the scenes against a new crackdown, it also represented another public declaration of the end of the Spanish match, for the Petition James approved contained two references to the breach of the treaties. Not surprisingly the response to the address was rapturous. Mr. Prowse reported to the Corporation of Exeter that James's "most noble aunsweare," which comforted "all of his trew hearted subiects,"

[58] Nethersole to Carleton, 25 April 1624, SP 14/163/50; 20 April, Holland Diary, fos. 41–2; and Earle Diary, fo. 152.
[59] CJ, pp. 772–3; and 22 April 1624, Holland Diary, fo. 43v.

was "worthie the keeping in the Citties Chamber."[60] "All I can say of it," Castle wrote, "is that it hath bred an infinite joye in the harts of all well-affected and hath as much dishartened the other parte." Mr. Carleton judged James's response as positive evidence of "good and sounde proceedings" toward "heroicke resolutions." Secretary Conway was so excited with the news that when he found all his secretaries busy, he wrote Elizabeth himself and remarked that, given the news, "she will be very willing to hammer out every word thereof." Carleton sent Elizabeth the text of her father's speech and assured her that James delivered it "in a more ample satisfactory manner and accompanied with more passages of good rellish then are specified in the copie" and that the auditors "upon the very instant [of receiving it] gave demonstrations of their ioy by acclamations and wishings of safety and happines to his Majesty." The speech gave "the greatest contentment to the Parlement that could be hoped for . . . His Majesty sheweth allready that he needes no great spurring to do what they desire and he hath promised."[61] Nethersole simply told his friend Carleton that James's response was "the most joyfull occasion thereof I have yet had" in their correspondence. News of James's speech led Lord Zouche, the staunchly Protestant Warden of the Cinque Ports, to ask Conway if he could now seize a cargo of powder bound for Spain. And it is perhaps no coincidence that in late April after several weeks of discussion by intermediaries, Secretary Calvert offered Carleton the chance to buy his office at a bargain price.[62]

On the day after James's response, the Commons quickly read the subsidy bill a second time, and Heath immediately rose to read the details of a generous royal pardon. Phelips then began exultations that this was "a Beginning and Foundation of much Comfort to us and disheartening to our adversaries." Eliot, not to be outdone, proposed that the House again thank the prince as well as the king. Seymour, however, had not abandoned his role as a spoiler. He stopped Eliot's proposal with a line that the coalition earlier in March had used to good effect: the House should "express Thankfulness rather in Action than Words."[63]

Since the rising parliamentary anxiety in early April and events of 17–24 April form one piece, it is appropriate to tally the scorecard at this point before proceeding into the even more diffuse parliamentary proceedings in May. The Commons in 1624 did not formally attempt to tie supply to redress

---

[60] "Sound Reason," 5 April 1624, Northamptonshire RO, Isham MSS, IL 3556; and Prowse to Mayor, 24 April 1624, Devon Record Office, EC/XI 600/268.

[61] Castle to Trumbull, 31 April 1624, Trumbull MSS, XVIII/117; Carleton the younger to Elizabeth, and same to Carleton, 15 [25]April 1624, SP 14/163/47 and 14/163/48.

[62] Nethersole to Carleton, 25 April 1624, SP 14/163/50; Zouche to Conway, 30 April 1624, SP 14/163/76; Carleton the younger to Carleton, 3 May 1624, SP 14/164/7; and Ruigh, p. 288.

[63] CJ, p. 774.

of grievances. Yet before relegating Parliament to the endangered species list, we should look closely at what happened in April 1624. James himself was alarmed at the prospect of an informal linkage, not a formal one: "I mean . . . if they will make it in effect a condition sine qua non, though not say it plainly." By the middle of April the differences between the Commons and James had been reduced to a simple theological point. Sir Edward Conway, the secretary's son, observed with characteristic whimsy that James argued the merits of faith alone while the Commons insisted as well on the efficacy of good works; therefore "I find no means for their salvation."[64] Conway, while amusing, was too severe in his judgment. Salvation in this instance depended upon a simple act of courtesy: who would go through the door first? It can be argued that the Crown was the first to oblige on 17 March. On the other hand, Buckingham's report of James's letter to Philip and the pardon failed to elicit an excited response from the Commons. Consequently, the Commons' first reading of the subsidy bill could arguably be seen as the first critical concession. Equally it could be maintained that this concession was more apparent than real: after all "the bill of subsidy [is] not to be passed at the first reading." The next candidate for the first real concession then becomes James's reply to the Petition on Religion. It unquestionably was a concession, but since it was so tightly bracketed on either side by the first and second reading, the latter of which in turn led to details about the pardon, the most impartial jury would find itself hopelessly split.

During 17–24 April, the Commons obviously did not have the whiphand; but neither did the Crown. A modern politician would immediately recognize the familiar legislative pattern of logrolling. This observation is so facile as to be hardly worthy of remark, if it did not bear on a modern historiographical controversy. Professor Koenigsberger has proposed a simple rule for parliamentary survival: "a parliament must not agree to grant taxes before the King had met its demands."[65] In light of the events of 1624, his test appears to undercut Russell's assertion about the powerlessness of the English Parliament. An institution which could negotiate the redress of some grievances in exchange for supply appears mature, not moribund.

THE DUTCH TREATY

The session never seemed to progress from suspicion to accord: it wobbled instead unstably between the two extremes. This pattern repeated itself after

---

[64] James to Conway, [4 April 1624], *Letters of King James*, p. 433; and Conway the younger to Carleton, 18 April 1624, SP 14/163/1.

[65] H. G. Koenigsberger, "Dominium Regale and Dominium Politicum et Regale," *Politicians and Virtuosi* (London, 1987), p. 24.

James's acceptance of the Petition on Religion. On 24 April, Inijosa and Coloma launched the last and most desperate of a series of assaults to ruin Buckingham. Anxious to disrupt James's *rapprochement* with Parliament, they hurried to Theobalds to reveal a conspiracy: if James had not conceded to Parliament, Buckingham and some others had resolved on a *coup d'état* in which James would be permanently retired to rural pursuits while Charles ruled in his stead. When other reports gave credence to the Spanish charge, even James's legendary tolerance of his favorite's foibles could not quietly dismiss such an allegation. Later in the day, a tearful monarch told the Spanish accusation to Charles and Buckingham who both vehemently protested their innocence. A few days later, the duke adopted a more effective defense; he collapsed with "many pustules and blaines broken out" over his body. When confronted with the prospect of Buckingham's death in bed rather than on the block, "the King's love for his favorite came flooding back," Lockyer observed, "as strong as it had ever been."[66] James's renewed devotion reportedly climaxed in a scene in the middle of May: "kneeling by his Couch (his hatt off and his hands upp) he [James] said unto him, Steeny I pray God either to recover thee of this sicknesse or els (the teares breaking downe upon his cheekes while speaking) to transfer the same upon me, as one that will stand in the gapp for thee." On his doctor's orders, Buckingham was confined to York House, where James set a close guard "to restraine the continuall resortes of Visitants." The recusants promptly spread the rumor that the duke, like his brother, was insane, while loyal Protestants gave out that Catholic agents had poisoned him. In any case 24 April was the last day he attended Parliament.[67] Against this melodramatic background, the Parliament of 1624 completed the last weeks of the session.

In the short run, the Spanish assault was successful: Buckingham was out of commission for over a month. As any Paul's walker could have testified, the strain in the last few months of keeping the "great business" on track must have been enormous, and when faced with an unusually complex situation, the duke's frail health and highly emotional character made him a likely candidate for a nervous breakdown. Nevertheless the Spaniards' ultimate success depended on the reaction of the coalition and the prince. In this crisis, Charles saved his friend, as he had earlier in January and as he would in later years. He calmly explained to Buckingham on 25 April why the Spanish ploy would inevitably fail: "I cannot think that any man is so mad as to call his

---

[66] Castle to Trumbull, 14 May 1624, Trumbull MSS, XVIII/118; and Lockyer, *Buckingham*, p. 196. Ruigh's chapter, "The Spanish Reaction," presents a comprehensive and persuasive analysis of the Spanish ambassadors' motives and action, pp. 257–302.

[67] Newdegate to Newdegate, 17 May 1624, Warwick County RO, Newdegate of Arbury MSS, CR 136/B345; Castle to Trumbull, 28 May 1624, Trumbull MSS, XVIII/120; and Ruigh, p. 246, n. 163.

own head in question by making a lie against you, when all the world knows me to be your true friend."[68] Under Charles's protection, Conway labored to retain the coalition's momentum.

The development and maintenance of Habsburg power owed as much to diplomats as to soldiers. In April 1624, Inijosa and Coloma signally failed to uphold that tradition. Given James's eagerness to negotiate, it is hard to resist the idea that a tolerably competent ambassador in London would have greatly simplified the Habsburg diplomatic and military problems for the rest of the decade. As it was, however, the ambassadors almost single-handedly destroyed the "peace" party. Later in the year, Sterrell the English Catholic could not help longing for Gondomar who "knoweth howe to negotiate in our courte better than those that succeeded him"; for him, the fact that the recusants were by then riding out a wave of repression painfully illustrated the failure of Inijosa and Coloma. The Spanish counter-attack in late April provided their opponents with two timely martyrs, Charles and Buckingham, and confirmed the popular belief in Spanish deceit. Even worse, they left their allies painfully exposed before a Protestant witch-hunt for Spanish sympathizers. The unsuccessful attack sealed the fate of Middlesex, an alleged co-conspirator in the plot. Consequently what began as a transparent, if popular, attempt to pull down a Court rival ended as righteous retribution for an enemy of the commonwealth. Lord Keeper Williams and the Earl of Arundel had to fight clear of the same net that had caught Middlesex, while Secretary Calvert wisely began to plan his retirement. The Earl of Bristol's long diplomatic service earned him house arrest on his return pending an investigation of his actions in Spain. He stoutly maintained his innocence, but during the last months of the 1624 session, he did so quietly. In late May, John Woolley remarked of Bristol, "there is no more speech than if there were no such man."[69] The earl undoubtedly preferred it that way. Middlesex's treatment at the hands of a frustrated Parliament anxious to flush out closet Spaniards served as a sobering object lesson to all who thought of opposing the prince and the duke.

The Spanish accusations had also, in Conway's words, "slubbered and stayned" Parliament, which understandably rallied to the defense of Buckingham. "The Parliament," Castle observed, "is so nettled at so base a mallice that they are for the present busie to finde out Presidents what course to hold with the Ambassadors and for the Papalls who are judged to be breathers of the information." As for Buckingham, "they generally bewayle him, wishe him all healthe, and publickely utter it that he suffers for the

---

[68] Charles to Buckingham, 26 April 1624, quoted in Ruigh, pp. 286–7.
[69] Sterrell to La Faille, 24 October 1624, HHStA, Belgien PC, fasz. 60/unfoliated; and Woolley to Trumbull, 27 May 1624, Trumbull MSS, XLVIII/122.

publicke good."[70] Their anger over the "Spanish Mallice" unfortunately did not make the Commons more pliant over the subsidy. On 1 May, Conway sought to stir up the Commons. James had ordered Conway and Attorney General Coventry "to provide for some Things in our Petition, by Proclamation" and to consult with the Recorder of London about ending public access to the ambassadorial chapels. Meanwhile the Irish and Dutch projects "standeth at a Stay, only upon the Certainty of Monies." Unfortunately, one *sine qua non* for passage of the subsidy, a favorable response to the petition, had given way to another, the Proclamation against Jesuits. On 6 May, two weeks after James's speech of 23 April the Proclamation finally came out, and if it had not been issued, "the lower house," Mr. Carleton remarked, "would in all likelyhood have fallen into mutiny."[71]

The Proclamation, to be sure, relieved some tension. John Castle's reaction probably was typical, even if a little overwrought; he wrote to Trumbull in Brussels of the Proclamation

banishinge the swarme of your Locusts which thereupon you are like to have come to you in whole Legions. Open the doores of the bottomless pitts againe and take in these Janissaries of his Holynesse and your most Catholique King and lett them have all liberty to serve them and their grand Master the divell so wee bee not pestered any more with their pestilent stinke.

Yet a week later the jubilation had again given way to suspicion. Beaulieu spoke of some MPs who wished to see the Proclamation enforced before passing the subsidy bill. Chamberlain noted that the Proclamation against Jesuits had come out together with another protecting the king's deer; "there is no question," he remarked, "but howsoever the one speed, the other shalbe duly and truly observed."[72]

In order to relieve these doubts, the Commons again searched for signs of some war preparation, and here Buckingham's prolonged absence was crucial. While Charles was helpful in formulating policy and in implementing it in the Lords where he was "full of industrie," the actual administrative burden fell on Conway's already overloaded shoulders. Well before this crisis, Buckingham's success in isolating Calvert meant that Conway effectively had to do the work of both Secretaries; then he half-jokingly observed that he worked for people who called "for the accomptt by a speedier watch then my endeavours worke by." After the duke's collapse, however, the Secretary made no more jokes about overwork; instead he complained about

---

[70] Conway to Aston, 27 May 1624, BL Add. 36,447, fos. 86–7; and Castle to Trumbull, 30 April and 7 May 1624, Trumbull MSS, XLVIII/117 and 120.

[71] *CJ*, p. 606; Carleton the younger to [Carleton], 13 May 1624, SP 14/164/72; and *Stuart Royal Proclamations*, I, pp. 591–3.

[72] Castle to Trumbull, 14 May 1624, and Beaulieu to Trumbull, 14 May 1624, Trumbull MSS, XVIII/118 and VII/163; and Chamberlain to Carleton, 13 May 1624, *Letters*, II, p. 558.

back problems.[73] Sir Dudley Carleton, a perennial candidate for Secretary of State, had a vested interest in Conway's health, and after the duke's collapse the report on the aged soldier was not good; although he continued to "eate his meate well, his looks argue all is not well with him and he is daily more or less in physick." In "the stresse of business," Mr. Secretary delegated the task of shepherding the Subsidy bill through the Commons to his son-in-law, Sir Robert Harley with clear instructions that in the event of any legislative emergency he was to be informed immediately so that "I may labor to dispose humors and make such answears as shal be most requisite."[74] Such radical tactics only underscore the seriousness of the personnel problem which left the "Patriots" unable to exploit fully the popular backlash against the ambassadors. At the same time as the coalition came up lame, the pressure to conclude a successful session mounted. From Paris, Kensington reported with uncharacteristic desperation that thanks to "our delays" and the Spanish ambassadors, "there is not a man in France (myself excepted) that doth not believe but that his Majesty's intentions are changed" about a breach with Spain; and in Dublin, "we attend," Falkland noted, "your Parlement resolution."[75] Hence the necessity to hold the coalition together and to maintain the painfully slow momentum towards war became even more imperative.

At the head of Harley's list for his father-in-law of "most requisite . . . answears" was the urgent need to organize the Council of War to disburse the subsidy. Accordingly the new Council held its first session on 10 May when one of its leading members was already downcast; "for all our indevers and good corispondenc and the expectatione," Sir Edward Cecil lamented, "yet I fear the Great Mountayne will turne but into a Mouse." After a three week delay, the Council finally met, "and accordingly our Bill of Subsidy dothe marche that is after a Parlement manner hand in hand." Yet in spite of Cecil's pessimism, the Council soon approved Sir Robert Mansell's plan to supplement the twelve warships which Buckingham had ordered prepared at Easter, with a rotating force of twenty colliers fitted out as warships. Any satisfaction with Mansell's plan, however, disappeared with the news of the lack of victuals; "it is to be thought," Woolley sighed, "they will scarce stire this summer."[76]

Charles and Conway had better luck setting out the diplomatic corps. For

[73] Conway to Herbert, 31 March 1624, SP 78/72/85; same to Carleton, 26 May 1624, SP 84/117/220; and same to Aston, 9 April 1624, BL Add. MSS. 33,447, fo. 72v.
[74] Conway to Harley, 29 April 1624, BL Loan 29/202v, fo. 122; and Carleton the younger to [Carleton], 13 and 21 May 1624, SP 14/164/72 and 14/165/12.
[75] Kensington to Charles, [mid-May] 1624, Clarendon State Papers, II, Appendix, p. IV; and Falkland to Edmondes, 20 May 1624, BL Stowe MSS, 176, fo. 254.
[76] Cecil to Carleton, 10 May 1624, SP 84/117/199; Woolley to Trumbull, 14 and 27 May 1624, Trumbull MSS, XLVIII/120 and 1220 and BL Loan 29/202, fo. 122v.

months, Sir Isaac Wake, Sir Robert Anstruther and the Earl of Carlisle had assured everyone that they would be leaving for the continent in a few days. As their creativity with excuses dwindled, it became apparent that they awaited neither instructions nor money as much as "to see the kinge passe danger of falling foule with the people." Quite understandably no one wanted to begin a distant embassy only to have a sudden shift at home undermine their labor. But by the middle of May, Wake and Carlisle had departed. Anstruther, ever the by-word for caution, remained in London. "Our house is much troubled with Sir Robert Anstruther his being here still," Mr. Carleton reported on 13 May, "and we have some who feare his Majesty doth still looke backe to Spayne."[77] The attention given to Anstruther was far from idle gossip; he alone was to deal with Protestant princes, those of the Empire and Denmark. His delay therefore was especially unfortunate.

Hope for further signs of war preparations centered on the Anglo-Dutch negotiations, and in May when Conway excused the continued delays by pleading other pressing matters, Aerssens retorted "he can have none of more importance than theirs."[78] Aerssens's comment was perceptive, but unfortunately amidst the spate of loyalty oaths, investigations, and denunciations that followed the Spanish charges, the English commissioners forgot about Aerssens and Joachimi. On 9 May, the disgusted Dutch envoys formally asked for an audience to take their leave. Charles again intervened, and his promise of a swift conclusion to the treaty persuaded them to stay a while longer. In the meantime, the English received Carleton's detailed report on the vexatious question of cautionary towns. Dutch enthusiasm for the "common cause" was matched only by their refusal "to dismember their States." Indeed the Estates General did not have the authority to grant cautionary towns, which would require the approval of each province and town of the Republic. After sampling Dutch opinion, Carleton delivered his sobering conclusion: "wee have more affection to shew towards them and breach with their ennemyes and reputation to recover to ourselves before they will putt the keyes of their Countrey into our hands." Clearly 1624 was not 1584, nor could James be mistaken for Elizabeth. The Dutch also pointed to a tentative Franco-Dutch loan agreement for two million florins annually which had been concluded in April after the French dropped their demand for cautionary towns. Moreover the English regiments served in the Spanish Army of Flanders, "where is not so much as one French Companye." Cautionary towns in the circumstances were out of the question, but Carleton

[77] Nethersole to Carleton, 25 April 1624, SP 14/163/50; and Carleton the younger to Carleton, 13 May 1624, SP 14/164/72.
[78] Carleton the younger to [Carleton], 13 May 1624, SP 14/164/72.

assured Charles and Conway that the Dutch would willingly "give full satis-faction" on any other English request.[79]

Charles, now desperate to succeed in this most public litmus test of war preparation, took Carleton's point, and in two meetings quickly led both sides to an agreement. The defensive treaty stipulated that James would maintain 6,000 English troops to serve in the United Provinces for at least two years and that the Dutch, on the bond of the Estates General alone, would agree to repay the English expenses once a peace or a long-term truce had been concluded. After the agreement, Aerssens and Joachimi dropped their sour visage; instead "they are growne very brag." They had good reason to be pleased. At no immediate expense to their High Mightinesses, four "new" English regiments would join the "old" regiments which had since Elizabeth's day comprised the backbone of the Dutch field army. There was, however, one vital distinction between the "old" and "new" regiments; while the Dutch themselves maintained the "old" regiments, James himself would have to underwrite the latest reinforcements. Admittedly he could look to Parliament to handle this account, but the two year contract would consume almost £200,000, or roughly 80 per cent of the £240,000 the 1624 subsidy would bring in. Thus Sterrell had ample grounds for regarding the Anglo-Dutch agreement as a lucrative free gift to the Dutch Republic rather than a military alliance.[80]

The English could console themselves with the thought that they shared a similarly unfavorable agreement with the French. Unfortunately, in less than a year, concrete examples of the significant differences between the Treaty of London and the Treaty of Compiègne would emerge. The Franco-Dutch agreement, shorn of Louis's request for cautionary towns, simply provided a large "loan" to pay for troops in the service of the United Provinces. But Sir Edward Herbert, the ambassador in Paris, immediately suspected further secret articles. A few days later, Herbert proudly boasted that "I was not deceaved" and reported rumors of several secret clauses. Most limited payment and future peace terms, but there was one "concerning shipping," which Herbert rightly noted would probably trench upon "his Majesties authorities upon the narrow seas."[81] This clause in fact allowed the French at any time to hire up to twenty Dutch vessels; the only restriction was that the vessels could not be employed against the Dutch themselves. Furthermore,

---

[79] Carleton to Charles; and same to Conway, 5 May 1624, SP 84/117/165 and 84/117/171.

[80] Sterrell to La Faille, 17 June and 8 July 1624, HHStA, Belgien PC, fasz. 60/unfoliated; and Carleton the younger to Carleton, 13 May 1624, SP 14/164/72. On the finances of the Anglo-Dutch agreement, see F. G. Dietz, *English Public Finance* (New York, 1932), pp. 216–22.

[81] Herbert to Calvert, 24 April 1624, SP 78/72/163; and same to Conway, 28 April 1624, SP 78/72/172.

the Dutch agreed to deduct the rental charges from the French debt. In return for his "loan," James received the right, if attacked, to call on Dutch assistance.[82] Contemporary analysts regarded this stipulation as unnecessary: an attack on England was unlikely and, if it ever happened, would probably be directed against the Dutch as well. On the other hand, as the Duc de Soubise and Charles himself were surprised to find in the summer of 1625, Louis XIII received a powerful squadron in return for his "loan."

The ineffectual nature of any English diplomatic agreement in this period is scarcely remarkable, but the Stuarts in this instance have good cause to plead extenuating circumstances. The fact that a Parliament, suspicious of royal intentions abroad, was sitting during the negotiations allowed the Dutch ambassadors to secure a hasty agreement highly favorable to the Republic. Although the principle of the *arcana imperii* generally barred the Commons from any direct input on foreign affairs, the Anglo-Dutch negotiations provide a clear illustration of the impact of Parliament on foreign policy; without having formally expressed its view, Parliament could sharply restrict the government's room for diplomatic maneuver.

Having cleared one obligatory parliamentary hurdle with the Dutch treaty, Charles and Conway found another erected before them. If the navy could not be sent out in force in the summer, then the Crown at least could hurry over the four "new" regiments for the summer campaign; everyone, Woolley reported, "expects the drum to beat" for recruits. Yet the government did not get that far until after the prorogation because of what Conway termed "shouldering for Regiments," or more properly for one of the fifty-two positions as officers. "If the King would send an Army of twenty times as many as now he will," Edward Conway was certain that "he should not want men to sue for places."[83] Political patronage further complicated the distribution of military positions since "every nobleman or other of power [is] engaged for some or other of their friends." The sheer number of suitors drove a baffled monarch to inquire with characteristic logic "if men were madd to goe into the low Countreyes seeing they had no enymies to fight against them." Consequently, the delay in the selection of officers led some to wonder if the entire expedition would ever leave England: "itt is generally

---

[82] For the text of the treaties of London and Compeigne, see *Corps universal diplomatique* (Amsterdam, 1728), V, pp. 458–63. On the later role of the Dutch in the internal French war of 1624–6, see V. L. Tapie, *France in the Age of Louis XIII and Richelieu* (New York, 1975), pp. 146–8; and Thomas Cogswell, "Foreign Policy and Parliament: The Case of La Rochelle, 1625–1626," *EHR*, XCIX (1984), pp. 240–67.

[83] Woolley to Trumbull, 22 May 1624, Trumbull MSS, XLVII/121; Conway the younger to Carleton, 26 May 1624, SP 14/165/47; and Conway to Carleton, 26 May 1624, SP 84/117/221.

suspected," Edward Fowkes remarked in late May, "that theire will none goe over."[84]

In these circumstances, the subsidy bill progressed through the Commons slowly. "We are quicke in giving you advertisements of our brave resolutions," Sir William Crofts lamented to Carleton on 7 May, "but slow in the pursuite of them." In May, however, the Commons at least had a valid excuse for the delay: "we have spent extraordinary much time about the Bill of Subsidy," the MPs explained to the Lords on 19 May, "by reason of the new Frame of it."[85] Whatever the appeal of parliamentary control of the subsidy, it certainly was very troublesome to implement. Yet in spite of the trouble, the Commons "are very cautelous to make all sure." On 14 May, the committee presented the bill to the Commons, and Heath, the Solicitor General, offered two significant emendations. One would have added the recovery of the Palatinate to the Four Propositions, and the other labelled the Dutch assistance as "a means to recover the Palatinate." The Commons, however, refused "to alter one sillable of what they have sett downe." This resolution reportedly enraged James. "I feare," Castle noted, "if this distemper be not well sweetened that it may begett an unkind conclusion if not a Rupture."[86] In the end, he was largely correct about an unkind conclusion; the Commons sweetened nothing, and James publicly overlooked the incident – until the bill had passed.

This exchange generally figures prominently in the secondary literature. Adams, for example, remarked that the exchange "was . . . clear proof that, whatever else had been accomplished in the parliament, a new foreign policy had not emerged." He might, however, have missed the point. James's proposed emendations of 14 May appear like his earlier financial demands of six subsidies and twelve fifteenths. Both seem to have been argued lamely and both lacked any support on the floor. In short, the exchange of 14 May was, if anything, proof that two policies had emerged in the Parliament of 1624; that of James, which most of his officials did not even support, and that of his son, which practically everyone else endorsed. The merits of the Four Propositions had initially appeared as a *via media* to reassure suspicious MPs. But, as the events of 19 May revealed, the propositions were equally useful in restraining James himself. The broad diversionary strategy of the "common cause" would become superfluous if James took the subsidy money to blunder off deep into the Empire, or even more disastrously, if he had taken

---

[84] Carleton the younger to [Carleton], 21 May 1624, SP 14/165/12; and Fowkes to Zouche, 25 May 1624, SP 14/165/45.
[85] Crofts to Carleton, 7 May 1624, SP 14/164/14; and *CJ*, p. 706. For a fuller discussion of the difficulties with "new Frame," see Ruigh, pp. 251–5.
[86] Carleton the younger to Carleton, 13 and 17 May 1624, SP 14/164/72 and SP 84/117/91; and Castle to Trumbull, 14 May 1624, Trumbull MSS, XVIII/118.

the subsidy to pay off his debt to Christian IV.[87] It was imperative, therefore, that the coalition hold James as well as Parliament to the Four Propositions. Furthermore, although James had first proposed the idea of appropriations, the scene in the Commons on 14 May reveals that the Parliament-men certainly embraced the idea with enthusiasm and defended it with tenacity. Even if *pace* Russell the concept of appropriations was a concession by the Commons to the king, and it is by no means clear that it was, then paradoxically the grantor was, at least on 14 May, much more distressed with the concession than the grantees were.[88]

The prorogation now drew near, and on 19 May the Commons, Ruigh observed, "practically extorted through the Prince's intercession, a week's extension of the session." Russell, while overlooking the "extortion," maintained the additional week was the result "of the need to complete the second part of Buckingham's agenda, the impeachment of the Lord Treasurer, Lionel Cranfield, Earl of Middlesex." Yet the Lords decided his fate on 13 May, six days before the Commons petitioned for an extension. A better explanation can be found in the petition itself; the difficulties of the "new Frame" of the subsidy bill accounted for the Commons' failure to budget time properly. But in order to interest the Lords in a joint petition to lengthen the session, the MPs offered a concession which more clearly pointed to the cause for the delay: they promised "to entertain no new Matter in any private Cause; but to perfect that, which we have in hand."[89] MPs found solace for the heartburn that James had caused them in an unprecedented volume of public and private legislation. Indeed, given Russell's emphasis on the importance of minor legislation for the average MP and given the fourteen year hiatus in any additions to the statute book, the relatively unrestrained pursuit of country grievances may have inclined many MPs to view the "great business" quite favorably. In any case, the Commons finally passed the subsidy bill on 21 May and sent it up on 24 May to the Lords, who had only enough time to run through three quick readings before the session ended.

James reportedly had not been pleased with the Commons in the last few weeks, and at the prorogation, once assured of the subsidy, he vented his spleen. He repeated his desire to see Frederick and Elizabeth restored and "vowed, that all the Subsidy . . . though it had not been so tied and limited, shall be bestowed that way." James reminded the Commons of his debts, which he expected them to address in the Michaelmas session. And he thanked the Parliament for the subsidy, which "though this be given to the

---

[87] Locke to Carleton, 17 May 1624, SP 14/164/92; and Adams, "Foreign Policy and the Parliaments," p. 170.

[88] See above, pp. 183 and 195.

[89] Russell, *Parliaments*, p. 200; Ruigh, p. 255; *CJ*, p. 706; and Colin Tite, *Impeachment and Parliamentary Judicature* (London, 1974), pp. 167–8.

Palatinate, His Majesty interprets it as given to Himself." Little wonder that, as one MP recorded, "it was made (by evident sign and murmurings) apparent to the King and Lords that we much disliked" the speech. The Lord Keeper in contrast to the other major speeches of the session wisely did not distribute copies.[90] Before James's speech, Mr. Carleton assured his uncle that the one certainty at the session's end was that "our harts faint and are full of doubte of the execution of that which hath been so well meant." James's final speech did nothing to remove these apprehensions. "The parting," Chamberlain observed, "were with no more contentment than needed on neither side." Beaulieu concurred; the session ended with "reciprocal satisfaction" on both sides, "though not fully to the satisfaction of the subjects." He concluded his reportage of the session with a prayer: "God graunt the conclusion and consequence thereof may answeare the wishes of the good people."[91]

PARLIAMENTARY IMPOTENCE RECONSIDERED

Russell has noted that Parliament was "an event and not an institution." But he has also stressed that the sessions did not exist in a void.[92] As we have seen, one parliamentary "event" possessed a very strong collective memory of the preceding "events," and this memory could strongly influence later conduct. MPs operated in 1624 on a vision of the 1621 session as a typically Jacobean drama of faith and betrayal. This vision of the earlier "event" goes a long way towards explaining the caution MPs exhibited in 1624 when handling the sensitive matter of taxation.

The 1624 Parliament not only received a collective memory; it also transmitted one. Many MPs found the subsidy bill and James's position on the war disquieting, but, in contrast to 1621, they at least did not have to return home empty-handed. Russell's argument about parliamentary impotence rests largely on its reputed inability to extract redress of grievances before supply, but at least in 1624, his definition of redress seems to be excessively limited. "In 1624, once again," he maintained "the subsidy was voted before grievances were discussed. The Petition of Grievances of 1624 was presented so late in the Parliament and it received so little attention that the Commons were constrained to present the identical Petition of Grievances again in the next Parliament." This argument, while true enough, ignores the fact that all

---

[90] *LJ*, III, p. 424; Locke to Carleton, 5 June 1624, SP 14/167/17; and Notes on 28 and 29 May 1624, SP 16/165/61.

[91] Carleton the younger to Carleton, 25 May 1624, SP 14/165/43; Chamberlain to same, 5 June 1624, *Letters*, II, p. 561; and Beaulieu, 28 May and 7 June 1624, Trumbull MSS, VII/165 and 166.

[92] Russell, *Parliaments*, pp. 3 and 121.

the grievances that troubled the session were not contained in the Petition. Indeed as James himself remarked, "I find most of them [in the Petition] matters of smal importance."[93] Without question the formal requests to correct Dr. Anian's antics in Corpus Christi, Oxford, or Sir John Meldrum's patent for the Winterton Ness lighthouse were important, but they were nonetheless small legislative potatoes. And the magnitude of these grievances becomes even smaller when compared with the grievances which were not included in the Petition because they had already been redressed. In short, Russell's assessment inexplicably overlooks issues of paramount importance such as the Spanish treaties, Middlesex, Jesuits, monopolies, certiorari, supercedeas and high interest rates, all grievances which the Parliament had successfully redressed in 1624. MPs might have grumbled about James's dismissal of the Petition, but given the extensive list of issues on which James had already given way, they were not likely to be discontent for long.

It could be argued that these royal concessions were relatively minor sops thrown to persuade the Commons to vote three subsidies and three fifteenths. On the other hand, if we accept Heylin's report on financial and legal matters, Justice Dodderidge observed that "his Majesty had brought those Fifteens and Subsidies at ten years purchase." Likewise the Earl of Kellie maintained that he "did never see . . . onye Parlament lyke to it, whitche dois evrye diaye grate upone the Kings prerogative soe mutche as I doe mutche dout hardlye it shalbe recovered."[94] Any definitive judgment of the scale of the concessions, however, must await further research on the extent to which the "generous" 1624 pardon and the Commons' legislation damaged the Crown's financial position. Nevertheless, even if the royal concessions were only of the slightest consequence, the legacy of the 1624 session remained a very powerful one. Against 1621's sober tale of faith deceived, 1624 left a fairly cheerful memory of legislative horse-trading. There should be little surprise that the Commons in 1625, 1626, and 1628 openly attempted to link supply with redress of grievances. The results of these later attempts were of course fearful: they disrupted the session, crippled the war effort and divided the nation. But, if we correct for hindsight, the grim results of these actions recede somewhat and expose instead the reasons for the later attempts to link supply and redress. MPs then were not really being innovative: they were simply perfecting the example of the Parliament of 1624.

---

[93]   Russell, "Parliamentary History," p. 7; and James's address, 29 May 1624, SP 14/165/61.
[94]   Peter Heylin, *Cyrianus Anglicus*, quoted in Ruigh, p. 395, n. 12; and Kellie to Mar, 13 May 1624, *Mar and Kellie*, p. 200.

Part III

THE SUMMER OF 1624

"The revolt of the mice against the cats": reactions to the impending conflict

Gloom certainly can be detected in the air at the closing of the 1624 Parliament. It is important to note, however, that such an ominous atmosphere appears most clearly to those well armed with the knowledge of the parliamentary and military disasters of 1625–8.[1] Contemporaries on the other hand do not seem to have heard in James's concluding remarks the opening chords of a dirge for the war effort. Rather James's speech was an old tune with which they had become all too familiar in the preceding weeks. Several times earlier James had nonplussed his listeners at least as badly as he had done on 29 May. None of these royal addresses had spelled the end of the press for war; they had simply meant that Charles and Buckingham had to intervene with James on behalf of their parliamentary allies. Without question, a pattern of events in which a step backwards followed every two or three forward was frustrating, but as long as forward progress continued, it can scarcely be seen as the cause for abject despair.

And there was considerable forward progress. James might continue to pursue a diplomatic resolution; he had after all vowed to recover his grandchildren's patrimony "by peace or war." Yet if he chose peace, he forfeited the subsidies. A much more likely option was that James after coaching from Charles and the duke would comply with parliamentary wishes and the terms of the subsidy bill. If the king did so, the financial expense of this policy would force him to honor his promise to summon Parliament frequently. Thus landlords in Westminster such as Sir Dudley Carleton faced the happy prospect that rents for "howses in Westminster will hold upp well inough," and at least one MP's wife was eager to take a lease. Rebecca Sherfield in Berkshire had spent the first half of 1624 in increasingly palpable frustration over her husband's extended absence, and on the eve of his return she announced that in the next session, "I dout you would be trobled [with her letters] for sure I should quit turne Londoner for it will not be in my power to have any more

---

[1] See for example, Ruigh, p. 397.

pacience."[2] In addition, the necessity of wartime supply meant that the sovereign would not be able to overlook the "grievances of the commonwealth." Although Wentworth grumbled that James kept back some bills so that "he would draw us to buy our bills and good lawes for money," his complaint could not obscure the fact that Englishmen could expect another round of logrolling and "good lawes," not at some distant date, but later in 1624. Finally the successful conclusion of the 1624 session signalled that James would at last follow a more honorable and martial solution of the German problem. Earlier in 1622 when disaster seemed imminent, John Dod, the Puritan divine, had comforted the wife of Sir Horace Vere with a promising thought: "though for a while some darke clowd doe overshadow them [the godly], yet their innocencie shall againe break forth as the light and their righteousness as the noone day."[3] June 1624 by Dod's timepiece must have seemed like 11 am, if not high noon, for the Protestant cause. Little wonder then that the close of the parliamentary session, far from opening a season of depression and recriminations, inaugurated a period of excitement over the impending conflict. The Spaniards never waivered from their contempt for English military power, but this only increased their amazement of the English enthusiasm for what they dubbed "the revolt of the mice against the cats."[4]

In light of the profound war weariness, that was readily apparent in 1626 and omnipresent in 1628, it is surprising to realize that there was a period, however short, in which the country exhibited signs of excitement over the approaching war. Indeed, either because this period was so transitory or so astonishing, most historians have overlooked it altogether. The popular response to the events of June–August 1624, however, is immensely significant when set against Russell's claim that Englishmen were really uninterested in war, Spanish or otherwise. The wars of the 1620s, he has argued, were "Buckingham's and Charles's wars, and not Parliament's wars."[5] Yet Russell overlooked the coalition's successful campaign to limit the parliamentary discussion of the war; he failed to consider that the agreement between Crown and Parliament over a war might have been implicit rather than explicit; and he effectively prorogued the session two months early. Once we take these factors into full consideration, parliamentary disinterest in the war becomes much less clear cut than he would have it.

The clinching argument in this controversy lies in the period immediately

---

[2] Locke to Carleton, [3?] May 1624, SP 14/164/10; and Rebecca to Henry Sherfield, 2 June 1624, Hampshire RO, Jervoise of Herriard Park MSS, Sherfield Papers, XXXI/31.

[3] Anonymous account of 28–9 May 1624, SP 14/165/51; and Dod to Lady Vere, 30 December [1622], BL Add. MSS 4276, fo. 182v.

[4] Valaresso to the Doge and Senate, 2 April 1624, *CSPV*, XVIII, p. 265.

[5] Russell, *Parliaments*, p. 78.

after the prorogation. The obvious but often ignored problem with parliamentary history is that it presents a necessarily blinkered vision of the past; the very act of vaulting from one session to another inevitably means that the intervening events are given short shrift. Thus just as a tight focus on the Palace of Westminster overlooks the dangerous polarization between the 1621 and 1624 Parliaments, so too it misses the reaction to the parliamentary resolutions in 1624. In less than a year after 29 May, a series of governmental decisions would fundamentally shake public confidence in Charles and Buckingham and revive the tensions so evident in 1622–3. But a vital question remains – before Englishmen absorbed the fact that Henriette Marie came without French assistance against the Spaniards and with English aid against the Huguenots, before they learned of a new Catholic toleration and of Mansfelt's debacle, how did they respond to the impending war? As the Spaniards noted with dismay, many English "mice" did not repudiate the idea of joining the revolt against the Habsburg "cats"; rather they readily embraced it. Van Male, for example, the Infanta Isabella's representative, began to beg for his recall in April so that he could chant a passage from Psalm 114; "in exitu Israel de egypto, Domus Jacop de Populo Barbaro." English clerics had sung this line a few months earlier on Charles's return from Madrid, but Van Male understandably felt he had more ample grounds for rejoicing over his deliverance from "Populo Barbaro."[6] Van Male's judgment can be supported with extensive evidence from sermons, tracts, poetry and one spectacular play as well as from newsletters.

A SEASON OF CONTENTMENT

Although James remained eager for a negotiated settlement in Germany, he would soon have almost no one with whom to discuss a settlement. Parliament not only persuaded him to terminate the Spanish treaties, it also created such a hostile atmosphere that no Spanish diplomat came to replace Inijosa and Coloma after they withdrew. Consequently the Spanish grip on James rapidly withered; meanwhile the nation revelled in the "blessed revolution" and the coming war. One preacher attributed the recent parliamentary success to the fact that "the great Ship of Good Hope" had "such a Master Mate as your Highnesse to perswade" the parliamentary seaman "too obey."[7] And after the session ended, the princely "Master Mate" and his ducal boatswain seemed firmly in control of the helm.

All hope for a Spanish war depended on Buckingham's influence with James. The Spanish ambassadors had left the duke flat on his back at the end

---

[6] Van Male to La Faille, 16 April 1624, HHStA, Belgien PC, fasz. 60/unfoliated.
[7] H. Burton, *A Censure of Simonie* (London, 1624), "To ... Charles."

of the session, and given the magnitude of the Spanish charges, contemporaries were uncertain how James would receive Buckingham on his recovery. "The eyes of this people could not be more fixed on a Meteor," Castle remarked in mid-June, "than they have been upon the motions of the Duke to see whither he dimminshe in his light or holde still the same fulnesse in his Majesties affection and favour." Buckingham's eagerness to return to Court led him to do "too soon too much." His first recovery abruptly ended in his collapse at Greenwich, while Goring's feast to celebrate the duke's second recovery simply brought on another relapse.[8] The duke might almost have proved his own worst enemy had he not had more potent rivals who emerged while he was away from Court. While Mr. Clare, the reputed illegitimate son of Lord Walden, attracted some royal attention, the most serious contender was Arthur Brett, the Earl of Middlesex's brother-in-law. By late May, James was reportedly so fond of Brett that he attempted to marry the young man to the widowed Duchess of Lennox.[9]

Few contemporaries could calmly watch this melodrama. Brett's success would revive the influence of Cranfield who in all his years at Court had evidenced few signs of magnanimity. When Parliament found Middlesex guilty of corruption, fined him £50,000 and barred him from further Court appointments, one poet moralized that "hee loved himselfe alone, / And nowe noe good man doth his fall demoane [*sic*]." Yet the earl, confident of his restoration, accepted his fate cheerfully. When committed to the Tower, "he was so jolie as to carrie his staffe with him." Once the staff was retrieved, Pembroke as Lord Chamberlain called for his set of Court keys, but the prisoner asked him to forbear since "he hoped to make use of them himself ere longe and therefore would not truble his Lordship with them." Three days after James prorogued the session, he released Cranfield who, instead of withdrawing into the country, settled "verie merrie" into his house at Chelsea amid predictions that he would soon be made a Gentleman of the Bedchamber and have "a kinde of superintendencie over the Treasurie." These reports, Chamberlain noted, made those involved in Middlesex's impeachment apprehensive, and they regretted their failure "to crush him low enough when he may live to be a pestilent instrument and to crush some of them hereafter, specially yf Brett his brother-in-law should come in."[10]

Charles, as usual, saved the duke, this time by becoming "a bedchamber man" who "setts the clock to Buckingham's meridian." During the summer

---

[8] Castle to Trumbull, 11 June 1624, Trumbull MSS, XVIII/122; Clare to Somerset, 5 July 1624, *Holles Letters*, II, p. 286; and Lockyer, *Buckingham*, p. 197.

[9] Chamberlain to Carleton, 13 May 1624, *Letters*, II, p. 560; and Castle to Trumbull, 11 June 1624, Trumbull MSS, XVIII/122.

[10] *Ibid.*; Beaulieu to Trumbull, and Woolley to same, 21 May 1624, Trumbull MSS VII/164 and XLVIII/123; and "On Sir Lionel Cranfield," Bodleian Library, Malone MSS 23, p. 27.

progress, the prince insisted that he and the duke attend "more neerely and closely to the King then ever" and that the number of the entourage be strictly limited. Charles also actively undermined Cranfield's position. When Lord Keeper Williams announced the list of subsidy commissioners for Middlesex in early June, Cranfield's name was still on the list; James, at Charles's behest, corrected the oversight. Similarly he quashed Cranfield's proposed entry into the Bedchamber; James could not "offend the gentlemen of the bedchamber to have a Criminall . . . ioyned with them in that highe dignity." Castle judged that "if the Prince had not undertaken his [Buckingham's] defence now in this absence of his, he had been much lower of present than he is."[11]

The prince's vigilance had its reward; when Buckingham finally returned to Court on 16 June, James greeted him warmly. It was Buckingham's singular happiness that he had become so bound up with the war effort, that those who in normal circumstances would have done nothing to assist this Court "mushroom" now eagerly prayed for his preservation. In June, for example, Abbot sedulously attended the ailing favorite.[32] A few months later the archbishop, like many others, were to regret their failure to see in Brett the last chance to humble Buckingham. Nonetheless, at the time they were too involved to consider the matter calmly: on one side, Brett seemed ranged with his brother-in-law, Spain and Rome, while on the other with Buckingham was England. The situation was so polarized that contemporaries could not ignore that "yf buckingham stand he [Middlesex] falles, yf he stand then the other goeth." This somewhat ironic struggle between the duke and his kinsman was probably Buckingham's finest hour. Earlier in the session, "pot-poets" had praised the energetic anti-Spanish campaign of

> . . . the only first of Favorites that ever undertook
> To search and find in every secrett nooke
> Spanish deceivings, yea he hath done more
> Than twenty favorites have done before.[13]

But in June simply by recovering favor with the king, he exceeded even his earlier triumph. "The duke," one commentator reported, "is in great favor with his Majestie and the whole kingdom." Thus, when John Woolley described how James welcomed Buckingham "with one hundred kisses at the lest and continual hanging about his necke, in which manner . . . almoste all

[11] Davies to Huntington, 23 March 1624, Huntington Library, Hastings Correspondence, Box, 10, HA 1929; Castle to Trumbull, 11 and 18 June 1624, Trumbull MSS, XVIII/122 and 123; Chamberlain to Carleton, 19 June 1624, *Letters*, II, p. 564; and Clare to Somerset, 5 July 1624, *Holles Letters*, II, p. 285.

[12] Abbot to Carleton, 18 August 1624, SP 14/171/59. Set against this his letter to Roe, 23 June 1624, TCD MSS 708, II, fos. 311–312v; and Chamberlain to Carleton, 19 June 1624, *Letters*, II, p. 565.

[13] Chaworth to Trumbull, 8 April 1624, Trumbull Add. MSS XVII/unfoliated; and "Of the Duke of Buckingham," Beinecke Library, Osborne b197, p. 225.

that Evening was spent," he seemed more relieved than repelled.[14] Brett made a final attempt to win royal favor in late July when he confronted the king at Wanstead Park. James, ever loyal to Buckingham, ordered the Earl of Warwick to "carry the Foole out of the Forrest." As Lord Haughton had predicted, Brett's only accomplishment would be "to breake his brother-in-laws necke." After the Wanstead incident, "the next Parliament," Woolley reported, "will goe nigh to hange him [Middlesex]." But by late August, the crisis passed, and Buckingham then was reported "in as great favor with the king as ever he was, and I am sure with the prince as much as it is possible for a man to be."[15]

The maintenance of the duke's position effectively signalled the end of the Anglo-Spanish entente. After James lodged a formal protest with Philip in June about his envoys' conduct, Inijosa and Padre Maestro left the country without either kissing James's hand or cleaning up Exeter House which they "made no more esteeme of then a jakes." Since their departure represented the last chance to express "their mortal hatred towards the Spanyard," the citizens bid them farewell by shouting, "all the devills in hell goe with you and for those that staie behind lett Tyburn take them."[16] An equally revealing indication of the deterioration in Anglo-Spanish affairs came in Ben Jonson's portrait of a Spanish scholar in the *Masque of Owls*, performed in August; "had the match gone on," the man stood to make his fortune tutoring aristocratic ladies. "But now," Jonson noted, "since the breach / He has not a scholar to teach." This little portrait of one of six other failed "owls" was nonetheless a significant statement from a playwright who had earlier employed his pen in defense of the match.[17] Thus, the personal tragedy of Jonson's Spanish tutor was a cause for rejoicing among many other Englishmen.

During Middlesex's last desperate attempt to topple Buckingham, most of the Court factions remained loyal to the favorite. The prospect of a military solution of the Palatine question doubtless had much to do with their stance. But it should be remembered that the possibility of self-aggrandizement strongly reinforced any ideological commitment to the war. After Charles's return from Madrid Thomas Adams preaching at Paul's Cross called for a reshuffling as "David used to purge his Court, admitting the righteous into

[14] Woolley to Trumbull, 17 June 1624, Trumbull MSS, XLVIII/128; and Anonymous report, 13 July 1624, Beinecke Library, Osborne fb 57, p. 166.
[15] Woolley to Trumbull, 6 and 20 August 1624, and Castle to Trumbull, 30 July 1624, Trumbull MSS, XLVIII/134 and 136 and XVIII/128; and Clare to Somerset, 5 July 1624, *Holles Letters*, p. 285.
[16] Anonymous report, 19 June 1624, Beinecke Library, Osborne fb 57, p. 165; Carleton the younger to [Carleton], 26 June 1624, SP 14/168/48; and James to Philip, 26 June 1624, SP 94/131/61.
[17] Ben Jonson, *The Masque of Owls*, lines 145–55.

the offices of the unrighteous." In the place of corrupt officials, "here is roome for a good man, which will doe equitie" and "here is roome for one that will love and adhere to the truth."[18] By the summer of 1624, the time for such a purge had finally arrived, and many a "good man" presented himself to replace the "unrighteous."

The eclipse of the Spanish faction produced a spectacular list of Court vacancies. Middlesex's conviction opened the offices of Lord Treasurer and Master of the Court of Wards. Additionally, although the Earl of Bristol, the Vice-Chamberlain, stubbornly maintained his innocence, his post was generally regarded as vacant. "Pride will have a fall," Haughton observed, "for ne Hercules contra duos, much less Digby against the Prince and the favorite." Sir George Calvert seemed resigned to his fate and, in Castle's judgment, "hath made his grave." At his London townhouse on St. Martin's Lane, "scarce a man visiteth his dores," and he eventually retired to Surrey, then Yorkshire and finally Newfoundland in order to make his solitude appear voluntary. Although Lord Keeper Williams had labored throughout the session to "omitt nothing that may doe the Duke honor," he reportedly had also seen the writing on the parliamentary wall. He asked James at the end of the session "to unburthen him of the seales" since his conscience troubled him over having been "so long distracted from the care of his flocke." Castle insisted that Williams was simply "actinge of a part in a Comeadia wherein he hath one eye to the people and an other to the Curtaine." But after Cranfield's fate, a graceful exit with one's ecclesiastical offices intact had much to recommend it.[19]

There was something for every taste in the summer of 1624, and those interested in a comfortable sinecure were not disappointed. Sir Randall Cranfield quickly followed his kinsman into disfavor at Court, leaving his lucrative office as Master of the Mint open. The two pedagogical plums in the Crown's gift, the Provostship of Eton College and the Mastership of Charterhouse, had remained vacant for several months, and when over a hundred suitors had presented themselves for the Eton post, James "much mused what kinde of place it would be for which so many men of so many and different professions should sue for." Those with an eye to the future rather than immediate profit eyed Sir Francis Cottington's weak grasp on his office as the prince's secretary; since he reputedly possessed no talent "save only the spanish tonge, which I thinke he speakes better then English," Castle concluded, "there is noe great opinion of Cottington's constancie in his

---

[18] Thomas Adams, *The Barren Tree* (London, 1623), p. 50.
[19] Clare to Somerset, 5 July 1624, *Holles Letters*, II, pp. 285–6; Castle to Trumbull, 2, 9 and 30 July 1624, Trumbull MSS, XVIII/126, 127 and 128; and Chamberlain to Carleton, 7 August 1624, *Letters*, II, p. 575.

standinge."[20] Thus the ambitious must have found the summer of 1624 a very exciting season.

These posts were not the only ones to be filled; since many of the candidates already held Court positions, a successful suitor would probably open up another post. Applications therefore often included proposals for bureaucratic leap-frogging among clientage networks. The Herberts as usual moved *en masse*. Pembroke was interested in the post of Lord Treasurer, and his endorsement of Salisbury's practice of prompt payment of salaries earned broad support within the bureaucracy itself. He, however, insisted on a package deal: his brother, the Earl of Montgomery, would have to succeed him as Lord Chamberlain.[21] The Exchequer officials also produced their own proposal. Sir Richard Weston and Sir Walter Pye would become Lord Treasurer and Master of the Court of Wards respectively, and Sir Robert Pye would succeed Weston in the Exchequer.

Other candidates requested no special remainders. The shift towards France led Sir Robert Naunton, "the ould French martir," to apply for the Treasurership; Lord Mandeville, who had once before briefly been Treasurer, expressed a willingness for another stint; and Sir James Ley, the Lord Chief Justice, was eager to try his hand at finance.[22] The Court of Wards produced another tangle of applicants. The increasingly overburdened Secretary Conway reportedly angled for the more leisurely and profitable position in the Wards. Sir Benjamin Rudyerd, who assumed Middlesex's duties in the Wards on a caretaker basis, was eager for the official credit and profit of that office. Lord Grandison played on his close Villiers connection in his request to conclude his long royal service in the Court of Wards. Lord Zouche was willing to part with the Cinque Ports, and Sir Edward Leech with £7,000, in order to replace Middlesex as Master. Finally both Ley and Naunton were willing to accept the lesser of Cranfield's offices if they could not secure the greater one. A replacement for Calvert and possibly Conway also stirred imaginations. The Palatine camp produced their own proposal. Sir Dudley Carleton would replace Calvert; Sir Francis Nethersole would succeed Carleton as ambassador in The Hague; and Mr. Carleton would fill Nethersole's post as Elizabeth's Secretary. Others hoped to trump the Palatine influence with that of Buckingham; Sir Albertus Morton maneuvered for Calvert's position, and Sir Edward Barrett for Carleton's in The Hague. Others proposed modifications in the Carleton–Nethersole plan;

---

[20] Castle to Trumbull, 11[?] October 1622 and 30 July 1624, Trumbull MSS, XVIII/85 and 128. Since both Trumbull and Castle were angling for advancement, Castle's letters are particularly interesting in this period.

[21] Nethersole to [Carleton], 14 August 1624, SP 14/171/49; and Castle to Trumbull, 14 June 1624, Trumbull MSS, XVIII/120.

[22] Chamberlain to Carleton, 3 and 24 July, 21 August 1624, *Letters*, II, pp. 568, 572, and 576.

Sir Robert Phelips wanted to succeed Sir Dudley Carleton, as did William Trumbull, the Agent in Brussels. John Castle in turn aspired to Trumbull's post and hurriedly bought some Flemish and Spanish grammar books.[23] Middlesex's fall also promised more than vacant offices; his £50,000 fine only added to the throng of suitors. Although the fine initially was allocated to the war effort, the prospect of a large non-parliamentary windfall for the empty Exchequer brought out royal officials whose wages were far in arrears. In late July, Trumbull was distressed to learn that the queue had already formed for the beneficiaries of the former Lord Treasurer's misfortune; he quickly lodged his own claim for £4,000.[24]

The patronage proposals that circulated over the summer among the Carleton and Trumbull circles are extraordinary. Given the fact that most of the surviving evidence on the Court comes from these two circles, it is likely that other Court factions were in a similar state of excitement. Such vigorous traffic up and down the backstairs helps explain the comparative "era of good feeling" over the summer. Mr. Carleton later remarked that Buckingham "never did anything in his life with post-haste, but when he went into Spain."[25] He was not really referring to the favorite's temperament: he was simply describing his handling of patronage questions. Decisions on appointments, whether governmental or academic, are never a matter of loaves and fishes: a decision on one candidate is bound to create a number of disgruntled suitors. Consequently, as long as there was no immediate need to fill the office, there was no reason for a hasty decision and a good many against one. The applicants obviously found the delay nerve-racking, but they could still entertain some hope of advancement. And as long as there was hope, factionalism at Court was sharply minimized. The patronage log-jam began to break up only in late August, and as Buckingham packed the administration with his "creatures," the resentment of those disappointed, who had often been loyal parliamentary allies, escalated. But until then, Buckingham's languid approach to the problem left the Court reasonably content over the summer.

With the Court temporarily diverted from its favorite pastime of caballing against the current favorite, martial enthusiasts could concentrate on the opening of the long-awaited war. Symptomatic of the new mood was the fate of Thomas Lushington, who in an Easter sermon at St. Mary's, Oxford made a glancing attack on the parliamentary and popular passion for war; when

---

[23] Clare to Somerset, 5 July 1624, *Holles Letters*, II, p. 285; Castle to Trumbull, 28 May 1624, Trumbull MSS, XVIII/120; and Carleton the younger to Carleton, 2 July 1624, SP 14/169/10.

[24] Castle to Trumbull, 9 July 1624, Trumbull, XVIII/127.

[25] Carleton the younger to [Carleton], 18 December 1624, SP 14/176/67.

"the very Name" of peace "growes odious", "nothing," he assured his audience, "now contents the Commonalty but War and Contention." A year earlier, Lushington's sermon would have earned him royal favor; in 1624, however, it led to a humiliating recantation the following Sunday. His short paragraph against the press for war, he explained, had been designed "only to check the inordinate desire for it" which was "somewhat too frequent in most mens mouths." Besides he had found it incongruous "to heare in the Chappell, 'Give us peace in our time, O Lord', and presently in the Chambers, 'God send us warr againe'." On sober reflection he confessed such nicety was "out of season"; he had forgotten Solomon's adage, "there is a time for War and a time for Peace."[26] As Lushington's experience illustrated the time had at last come for war. James with some prodding from his son and favorite was at last preparing to avenge his daughter and grandchildren. A limited war against the Habsburgs opened in the summer of 1624 and inspite of James's reluctance, an open war between the two dynasties was imminent. Realists among the Paul's walkers appreciated that English efforts were unlikely to recover the Palatinate in 1624, but at least they would "breake their [Spanish] pride by beatinge off but some of the feathers of the Aegle." And in the following year, "when wee shall make an ouvert and direct warre, wee hope to break a winge of their birde or at the worst to recover our owne neast or a better."[27]

Several reasons account for the optimism, the most prominent of which was the conclusion of the Anglo-Dutch treaty and the levying of the four "new" regiments. News of the Amboyna massacre in the East Indies, which reached London in early June, delayed the formal signing of the Treaty of London. The news was indeed embarrassing: Sir Thomas Wentworth facetiously remarked that "my Lords the States, to require and appear capable of these Favours [the 'new' regiments] . . . have cut off the Heads of Captain Towerson and ten more of our principal Captains and Factors." James, although initially enraged at the news, was soon mollified as it became apparent that the ambassadors shared his sentiments. On 5 June, after warning the envoys that he expected prompt punishment of all involved, James signed the Treaty of London. The Dutch ambassadors "at last" pronounced themselves pleased with the English, although Mr. Carleton remarked, "they spent a good space before they would entertain any charitable opinion of us."[28] Admittedly James balanced his aide to the United Provinces by permitting Lord Vaux to recruit volunteers for his Spanish regiment. But Vaux's

---

[26] Robert James [Thomas Lushington], *The Resurrection Rescued* (London, 1659), pp. 99–100; and Anthony à Wood, *The History . . . of Oxford* (Oxford, 1796), II, pp. 352–3.

[27] Castle to Trumbull, 2 July 1624, Trumbull MSS, XVIII/126.

[28] Wentworth to Wandesford, 17 June 1624, *The Earl of Strafford's Letters and Dispatches*, ed. W. Knowler, p. 22; Carleton the younger to Carleton, 14 June 1624, SP 14/167/65.

commission was "generally so much distasted" that Mr. Carleton was confident Charles would hinder its execution. One report reveals what Carleton may have had in mind; Vaux would allegedly be given his commission provided "hee nor any other of his company shall ever retorne againe into England nor any issue of theirs."[29] After the domestic crisis of 1622–3, the prospect of exiling a thousand prominent Catholic hispanophiles doubtless struck many Englishmen as an enchanting notion.

The East India Company tried to dramatize the Amboyna incident to excite anti-Dutch sentiments. According to a common calumny, the Dutch "know no God but Gaine, no religion but Reason of State, no heaven but this present World, and no Friend but themselves." Charles and Buckingham eventually would subscribe to this sentiment, which in less than three decades would lead to three violent Anglo-Dutch conflicts. But in 1624 these feelings, while clearly present, did not dominate Englishmen. In the end, the massacre was ascribed to renegades who were "either Atheistical or Arminian," and the incident itself was soon overwhelmed by the prospect of 6,000 troops fighting the Spanish Army of Flanders.[30] There was, Wentworth remarked in early June, "every Day Expectation to hear their drums beat." Meanwhile, London and its suburbs were filled "with great feathers and Buff Jerkins . . . of these gallant Gens d'Armes." In fact so many eager, and needy, recruits were milling around in the City that some inhabitants became apprehensive. John Castle, although a vigorous supporter of the war, was also a householder in Clerkenwell: "if there should be any further delay in recruiting," he remarked nervously, "I do not see but wee should bee in some danger to have our houses broken upp and our throates cutt by the recaille that swarme in this Towne, such as have nothinge more to spend while they attend for the happy voice of the drum." A wave of Scottish recruits only heightened his anxiety.[31]

Extended wrangling over the new officers did much to delay the recruiting. In the middle of June, Conway sighed that "the Sea was never more agitated then the Court hath bin with the nomination of the Colonels and Captaines." Chamberlain expressed surprise "that men of their [noble] rancke and privie counsaillors shold hunt after so mean places." Yet many at Court had younger kinsmen who were at loose ends and who would gladly accept a glamorous, albeit dangerous, job with steady pay. MPs who had been uncertain about the Four Propositions may have found Rudyerd's final argument most persuasive: "every younger brother may take his stock with him

---

[29] Anonymous report, 13 July 1624, Beinecke Library, Osborne, fb 57, p. 166; and Carleton the younger to Carleton, 7 June 1624, SP 14/167/26.

[30] [Thomas Scott], *Symmachia* (Utrecht, 1624), p. 34; and Robert Wilkinson, *The Stripping of Joseph* (London, 1625), p. 51.

[31] Castle to Trumbull, 25 June 1624, Trumbull MSS, XVIII/125; and Wentworth to Wandesford, 17 June 1624, *Letters and Dispatches*, p. 22.

to plant himself in a new fortune."[32] Provided one had the proper Court connections, a vote for the subsidy bill was not only a patriotic act; it was also one which relieved the social tension inherent in primogeniture.

The disputes over a commission in the first military expedition in a generation were understandably sharp. The initial short-list, which Charles and Conway produced, prompted the frustrated candidates to flock *en masse* to Theobalds to present their case to James. But, much to their grief, the king refused to leave his chamber until they had departed. Eventually James named the Earls of Southampton, Oxford, and Essex and Lord Willoughby as the colonels of the new regiments, and the list of junior officers soon followed this announcement. The positions in general went to deserving veteran officers, and one of the few exceptions to this pattern was equally unobjectional. John Knight's celebrated Oxford sermon in 1622 implicitly justifying rebellion against the Spanish match had earned him imprisonment. Southampton, who had met the scholar during his own confinement, secured his release and promptly appointed him chaplain to his regiment. Knight would soon tragically die as a result of illness contracted in prison, but his release and elevation was in itself symbolic of the "blessed revolution" which had taken place in 1624.[33] The qualifications of the new officers did little to soothe the other candidates, and contemporaries received grim evidence of the intensity of the competition when one of the suitors committed suicide on learning of the officers' list: although he had secured a lieutenancy, he felt he deserved a captaincy.[34] While England in the coming four years would mount a series of similar expeditions, the domestic demand for a military command expanded as least as fast as the burgeoning military system. Buckingham's demise in 1628 testified that the competition for these positions never abated.

The selection immediately led to another controversy over precedence among the colonels. Oxford, as Lord High Chamberlain, was reluctant to defer to any of his colleagues, and Southampton argued that his extensive military career, which included a stint as General of the Horse in Ireland, would not allow him to cede precedence to his less experienced friend. This problem between two of the most prominent "Patriots" obviously called for a judicious resolution. Pembroke and Hamilton as Lords Chamberlain and Steward both declined to meddle in the affair and passed it along to the Council of War, which in turn, Nethersole observed, "have a minde to putt it off to the Earle Marshall [the Earl of Arundel]." Finally in mid-July, Southampton issued an ultimatum: if the dispute were not settled

[32] Conway to Carleton, 11 June 1624, SP 84/118/46; Chamberlain to Carleton, 5 June 1624, *Letters*, II, p. 562; and 1 March 1624, Nicholas Diary, fo. 33.
[33] Anthony à Wood, *The History and Antiquities ... of Oxford* (Oxford, 1791), II, pp. 347–8.
[34] Chamberlain to Carleton, 5 June 1624, *Letters*, II, p. 562; and Wentworth to Wanderford, 17 June 1624, *Letters and Dispatches*, p. 22.

immediately, Oxford and he simply "must skrach for it." James at this point intervened to announce a compromise; in all civil ceremonies, Oxford would have precedence, and in all military ones, Southampton.[35] As this decision reveals, James's appropriation of the Solomonic tradition was not entirely without foundation.

Well before this decision, the drums finally summoned volunteers. Castle assured Trumbull in Brussels that if he listened carefully, "you will heare the beating of our drummes" and the jubilation in London. When the day finally arrived, the public response was tumultuous:

At the doeinge whereof the demonstration the people used was as full of ioye as if wee had beaten the house of Austria and were now to enter upon our Triumphe shoutes of voyces and throwing upp of hatts were not sufficient but that they must fall downe uppon their knees to blesse heaven for the hower and crye aloude that this was the Tyme that they had so long expected.

Others at the scene contented themselves with less dramatic displays and merely allowed "their ioye to breake forthe at their eyes by teares."[36] Sterrell, the perennial hispanophile, predicted the government would have to resort to impressment to fill the regiments. Yet the volunteer recruitment proceeded as planned; a week after beginning, Salvetti reported that "we heare thousands of drummes" and more importantly "see hundreth [sic] of feathers."[37] The levying produced one embarrassing moment. The sergeants of Essex's and Oxford's Regiments followed their warrant and called for volunteers to serve the Dutch Republic, but in their enthusiasm they added the phrase "and against the King of Spain and the Infanta." Van Male, the Infanta's agent in London, promptly inquired if the sergeants' recruiting pitch was an oblique announcement of war. The sergeants subsequently spent a few days in prison.[38] Yet notwithstanding James's legalism, contemporaries judged that the sergeants had accurately described the situation; whether James said so openly or not, the regiments were to fight beside the Dutch against the Habsburgs. Hence in Salvetti's metaphor, "the match is very nere the touch-hole."[39] Events seemed to proceeding to the point where James could merely hinder the grand design; he could not block it.

The Privy Council and the Council of War both fostered such an interpretation. Amid a meeting of the Middlesex subsidy commissioners, Sir Robert

[35] Nethersole to [Carlisle], 15 July 1624, SP 14/170/2; and Southampton to Conway, 11[?] July 1624, SP 14/169/36.

[36] Castle to Trumbull, 25 June and 2 July 1624, Trumbull MSS, XVIII/125 and 126; and Nethersole to Carleton, 3 July 1624, SP 14/169/14.

[37] Sterrell to La Faille, 17 June and 8 July 1724, HHStA, Belgien PC, fasz. 60/unfoliated; and Salvetti to Scudamore, 10 July 1624, PRO C115/N1/8487.

[38] Coke to Conway, 1 August 1624, SP 14/171/12; and Woolley to Trumbull, 2 July 1624, Trumbull MSS, XLVIII/140.

[39] Salvetti to Scudamore, 10 July 1624, PRO C115/N1/8487.

Heath warned the merchants to prepare for war. The Privy Council also delivered similar admonitions to the chief Spanish merchants; "they had fair warninge to seek harbour before the storme fell," Archbishop Abbot told one group, "and if they neglected it, they must be held authors themselves of their own ship wracke if they were overtaken." The Council of War meanwhile carefully implemented the Four Propositions of the subsidy bill. Besides dispatching 6,000 men to the United Provinces, the Council also readied 4,000 troops for Irish service and ordered a detailed survey of the coastal fortifications. In so doing, the Council of War quickly proved those wrong who had assumed it would be a pliant tool of the Crown, not Parliament. Sir Richard Weston, Chancellor of the Exchequer, and Sir John Coke, one of the Navy Commissioners, each had an unnerving experience when they conveyed verbal orders from the king and the Lord Admiral for money out of the subsidy account. The Council insisted on proceeding "according to the statute"; Weston and Coke would have to return with James's warrant before they could receive any funds. These incidents apparently confirmed that the war would follow the parliamentary as well as the royal design.[40]

The pace towards a war increased appreciably during the summer. The government distributed a set prayer for "the English companies" who had gone to help "the King and Queen off Bohemia and theire affaires in this warre"; quite clearly the realm was expected to recall its valiant soldiers every Sunday. Earlier in the year a popular poet had begged James to "slacke not thy helpe, relieve the Palatine / Seate him againe hee is a kinne [?] of thyne." The best means to accomplish this end was to give Buckingham "but force, his head for to mayntaine / And like another Scipio hee'le sacke Spaine."[41] While the goal was as yet a little far-fetched, the poem accurately describes what was taking place in the summer; James had given Buckingham the force to "relieve the Palatine." A change in Secretary Conway's clothing perhaps best exemplified the new mood: he began to wear "his sword and feather shewing that he hath as good a stomack to fight for his Majesties children as to write letters at home." "I firmely beleeve," Mr. Carleton assured his uncle, "all will go well in the due time when we shall be more readie for action and fitt opportunity shall offer it self."[42]

Favorable news about the French match only further buoyed the popular optimism. The fact that Parliament had not discussed the French match is scarcely surprising. The "Patriots" had reacted to the topic as they had to

[40] Coke to Conway, 11 July 1624, 14/169/37; Weston to Conway, 31 July 1624, SP 14/170/82; and Castle to Trumbull, 25 June 1624, Trumbull MSS, XVIII/125.
[41] Prayer, SP 14/170/88; and "Of the Duke of Buckingham," Beinecke Library, Osborn b197, p. 225.
[42] Castle to Trumbull, 2 July 1624, Trumbull MSS, XVIII/126; and Carleton the younger to [Carleton], 7 June 1624, SP 14/167/36.

other potentially controversial ones; they forestalled debate. As the session progressed, it became increasingly common knowledge that James and Charles were eager for a match with the Bourbons. But they undercut any parliamentary opposition with public promises that a match would not include terms advantageous to the English Catholics. Heath reminded the House to request such a promise in the Petition on Religion, and James warmly embraced this particular point as "the best Advice in the World." The king added a very reassuring argument, which was to haunt Anglo-French relations in the coming years: "it is against the rule of Wisdom that a King should suffer any of his Subjects to be beholding and depend upon any other Prince than Himself: and what hath any King to do with the Laws and Subjects of another Kingdom?"[43] The public promises of James and Charles were clearly intended to tie their hands in any future negotiations, and if this limitation would not prevent a French match, most Englishmen seemed to have been willing to accept the fact that the strategic value inherent in closer French ties would outweigh the prospect of a Catholic queen. No less a Protestant authority than Sir Walter Raleigh had argued the merits of a French match earlier in James's reign, and in 1621, Sir Robert Naunton had become a martyr of the Protestant Cause as well of France for his advocacy of a Stuart–Bourbon dynastic alliance.[44] Hence a match with France and without prejudice to the domestic religious situation was a very important factor in the explanation of the domestic optimism.

In late May the Earl of Carlisle and Lord Kensington opened formal negotiations in Paris. "Wee talk of nothinge so much," Castle reported, "as of the highe reception of my Lord Carlisle by the French King and in the wishes of the generality of people on both sides, the match cannot but followe." The early euphoria rapidly gave way to despair as the discussions seemed unable to avoid the religious tangles of the Spanish negotiations. On 17 June, John Woodford, Carlisle's chaplain and secretary, arrived in London, where friends such as Nethersole and Woolley pressed him for details. He deigned to report that "some things go as they desire, others quite contrary," and Nethersole added, "these were all the wordes I could get from him."[45] Within a few days, the "contrary" points emerged. Since Louis XIII, Wentworth explained, "was the first Christian King and the Eldest Son of the Church . . . he might not go less in Point of Religion than Spain." With the news of the French intention "to work upon us to the uttermost," Chamber-

[43] *LJ*, III, p. 318.
[44] "Touching the Marriage between . . . England and . . . Savoy" [1612], *The Works of Sir Walter Raleigh* (London, 1829), VII, pp. 237–52; and Schreiber, *Naunton*, pp. 68–84. See also Roy Strong, *Henry Prince of Wales* (London, 1986), pp. 72–85.
[45] Nethersole to [Carleton], 19 June 1624, SP 14/168/7; and Castle to Trumbull, 4 June 1624, Trumbull MSS, XVIII/120.

lain confessed that "I never hoped well of the business since I heard a cardinall [Richelieu] was the prime commissioner."[46]

Yet just as a French match seemed impossible, Kensington unexpectedly arrived in London on 21 June after a break-neck journey from Paris. Although initially as tight-lipped as Woodford had been, Kensington announced that "he would not have come over thus speedily with ill news." As it became apparent that the French would not insist on the stiff terms that Woodford had reported, English suspicions evaporated. Lucy Countess of Bedford jubilantly wrote to a friend with the news that "they are so desirous of that [a match] as I believe itt will presently be both concluded and she heer, eare long, upon less ill conditions then Spayne insisted on for matters of religion." Castle reported that Kensington carried marriage terms "which are so easy and with so little relation to the Pope as there is nothing to impeach the consummation and to have Madame here before Michaelmas." So eager was Louis that he reportedly offered to carry his sister to Calais where he would "cast dyce" to see whether he or Charles would escort her over the Channel.[47] The news prompted one of Lord Haughton's rare moments of excitement in the 1620s. "Thei stand upon no conditions," he wrote "and if the dispensation cum as freely, blessed is the wooing that is not long in doing: but more blessed is the Ariadne that brought us out of the Spanish labirinth into the french Elisian fields." Haughton was so taken with the diplomacy of Carlisle and Kensington that he was willing to vote them a round of "new cloathes [and] perfumed dishes." Woolley recorded "the common report here ... that the Match is in a manner concluded and upon very good terms." With the sudden volte-face in the French negotiations, Chamberlain reversed his earlier opinion: "yt is much otherwise then was given out at first."[48] From Paris an extraordinary ambassador, the Marquis D'Effiat, quickly followed Kensington and confirmed the report of a French match "without sending to Rome for a dispensation or capitulation for favor to the Catholiques here." During July and most of August, observers agreed: "we expect nothing more then a match with france." The sudden fall of the chief French minister, La Vieuville, was to render this pleasing prospect illusory. But until that news reached London in late August, Englishmen enjoyed the agreeable sensation

[46] Wentworth to Wanderford, 17 June 1624, *Letters and Dispatches*, p. 22; and Chamberlain to Carleton, 19 June 1624, *Letters*, II, p. 565.

[47] Bedford to Cornwallis, [late June 1624], *The Private Correspondence of Jane Lady Cornwallis, 1613–1644*, ed. Lord Braybrooke (London, 1842), pp. 122–3; Castle to Trumbull, 23 June 1624, Trumbull MSS, XVIII/125; and Anonymous relation, 30 June 1624, Beinecke Library, Osborne fb 57, p. 165.

[48] Woolley to Trumbull, 17 June 1624, Trumbull MSS, LXVIII/127; Clare to Somerset, 5 July 1624, *Holles Letters*, II, p. 285; and Chamberlain to Carleton, 3 July 1624, *Letters*, II, p. 568.

that events would for once match expectations. James even grumbled to his bedchamber attendants about "the haste" of the French match "as ever he did for the protractions of Spayne." In more leisurely moments, however, James confessed that the easy and reasonable French terms had wholly converted him to francophilia.[49]

To the English observers, an Anglo-French marriage alliance was inseparably linked with a military league. And since James had insisted on such a league as the prerequisite for an open war, the prospect of an Anglo-Spanish war raised English hopes as much as the likelihood of a French princess without a *de facto* Catholic toleration. Thus the amateur strategists of St. Paul's debated a plan to launch Mansfelt's army into Bavaria, something "better" in lieu of the Palatinate, from the French frontier at Sedan.[50] Presented with such a pleasant vista, many Englishmen doubtless found the summer of 1624 the happiest one in years.

OPENING THE TEMPLE OF JANUS

Those close to Court or the Paul's walkers learned of the details of Middlesex's thwarted revival, the steps toward war, and the auspicious opening of the French talks. But, thanks to the unprecedented flood of pamphlets, a broad mass of Englishmen in 1624 were able to share in the optimism of their more well-placed countrymen. "Daily almoste their commeth forth new Pamphletts," Woolley noted in mid-June, and he sent Trumbull a half-dozen of them "not for the worth but to shewe what privilege men take in these days more than heretofore without being once questioned or demanded why they did it." Likewise Van Male was both amazed and amused by "the privilege men take"; he decided to vary the reading diet of his superiors in Brussels with some tracts "de ce puritains enrages que pensent nous faire la guerre avec la plume."[51] The pamphlets that these men found so remarkable merit more than a cursory survey, because they at once influenced and reflected the contemporary satisfaction with the recent Parliament and the "revolution" in political attitudes.

The most remarkable change in 1624 was the flood of anti-Catholic literature openly available for sale. This major genre of theological literature, which had been conspicuous by its absence from booksellers' stalls at the height of the Anglo-Spanish entente, made a dramatic reappearance in 1624

---

49 Carleton the younger to Carleton, 26 June 1624, SP 14/168/48; Woolley to Trumbull, 17 July 1624, and Castle to same, Trumbull MSS, 2 July 1624, Trumbull MSS, XLVIII/131 and XVIII/126.
50 Castle to Carleton, 18 June 1624, Trumbull MSS, XVIII/123.
51 Van Male to La Faille, 16 April 1624, HHStA, Belgien PC, fasz. 60/unfoliated; and Woolley to Trumbull, 17 July 1624, Trumbull MSS, XLVIII/131.

both in sheer numbers and in the virulence of the contents. Although Joseph
Hall and Isaac Bargraves had earlier in the year breached the taboo against
spirited attacks on Rome, a few authors seemed shy about following suit.
John Mayer cited the 1622 Directions on Preaching in order to justify
violating them; since James had suggested that preachers "apply our selves
diligently in this Catecheticall kinde of teaching," Mayer thoughtfully produced a lengthy catechism offering his readers a powerful *Antidote Against
Popery*. An anonymous author also offered the public another work in the
same vein, a catechism guaranteed to be *A Pill to Purge out Popery*.[52] Others,
disdaining such a juvenile audience simply waded in, as Thomas Beard did
with a 400-page tract devoted to proving *Antichrist The Pope of Rome*.
Anthony Wotton likewise offered the public his unequivocal advice in *Runne
from Rome*, and another anonymous author retailed *A Gagge for the Pope
and the Iesuites* which also promised *The Arraignment and Execution of
Antichrist*.[53]

Many of course simply contented themselves with more sober critiques of
Roman practice and theology. William Bedell took advantage of the new freedom to publish pastoral letters illustrating the grave doctrinal errors of the
Catholic church, while George Goodwin analyzed *The Holy Combe of
Romes Religion*.[54] Patrick Symson expanded on this common theme in
another 400-page book conclusively demonstrating the antichristian character of the Pope. Fernando Texada, a former priest, presented an insider's view
of how the Catholics manipulated the Bible to their own advantage, while
Edmund Gurney assailed *The Romish Chaine* binding the Church to antichristian beliefs.[55] Similarly the idolatry of the old faith came under sustained
attack in sermons from John Squire, Thomas Ailesbury and Thomas
Adams.[56] So apparent were the errors of Catholicism and the dangers of
toleration that Alexander Udny urged his congregation to prepare for a major
campaign against "the sonnes of Hell" and "false Apostles" of Rome. The
anti-Catholic bandwagon of 1624 even lured John Wall, who had earlier lent
his eloquence to the cause of peace, to champion a crusade against "those

---

[52] John Mayer, *An Antidote Against Popery* (London, 1625), "To the King"; and *A Pill to
Purge out Poperie, or A Catechisme* (London, 1624). See also above, p. 32.

[53] Thomas Beard, *Antichrist The Pope of Rome* (London, 1625); Anthony Wotton, *Runne
from Rome* (London, 1624); and *A Gagge for the Pope and the Iesuits* (London, 1624).

[54] William Bedell, *The Copies of Certaine Letters* (London, 1624); and George Goodwin,
Babels Balm (London, 1624).

[55] Patrick Symson, *The Historie of the Church* (London, 1625), pp. 300–27; Fernando Texada,
Scrutaimini Scripturas (London, 1624); and Edmund Gurney, *The Romish Chaine* (London,
1624).

[56] John Squire, *A Sermon on the Second Commandment* (London, 1624); Thomas Ailesbury,
Paganism and Papisme Parallel'd (London, 1623); and Thomas Adams, *The Temple*
(London, 1624).

seducers whom the Apostle stigmatizes and brands with the names of Dogges and evill workers," those who "beare him in their names and are termed Iesuites."[57] Finally 1588 and 1605, the two pivotal dates in the Protestant hagiography whose memory the government had attempted to forget in 1621–3, surfaced again in 1624. Bishop Carleton's classic popular history of these events illustrated the simple truth that Catholics were not to be trusted, and Thomas Hering pulled few punches in a sermon which cast the Armada and the Gunpowder Plot as prima facie evidence of Roman perfidy.[58] Quite clearly 1624 was the year when many authors, and readers, made up for the time lost in the ecumenical period of 1622–3 by revelling in unambiguously anti-Catholic rhetoric.

Equally important was the fact that the criticism of the English Puritans almost completely ceased with Charles's return and the opening of the new Parliament. The official line on any objections to James's pro-Spanish policy had regularly featured the charge that the "brainsicke undisciplin'd discipli-narians" within the Church of England posed at least as great a threat as the Catholics without it.[59] In place of the anti-Puritan rhetoric arose another, which Hall and Bargraves first fully articulated in February, emphasizing Protestant unity in the face of the threat from Rome. Hall, for example, cautioned against "mutuall dissentions" which "weakens and lames us and . . . laies us open." John Brinsley echoed this call with his plea for comprehension, "that firme bond of brotherly love" among all Protestants.[60] The real enemies of the godly, Thomas Taylor insisted, were those whose "mouthes run over with Romish Rhetoricke . . . Burne, kill, poyson, blow up," those "cruel Tigers to the life of man," those "unsatiable wolves whom all the blood of the whole fold of Jesus Christ would not satiate." Indeed, even when John Prideaux continued the old argument of a dual threat to the Church, he spent most of his time and energy in 1624 warning against the Roman menace.[61]

Implicit in these anti-Catholic messages, and explicit in some, was a transparent message – it would be highly dangerous, if not fatal, to seek any

---

[57] Alexander Udny, *A Golden Bell and A Pomgranate* (London, 1625), "To Archbishop Abbot"; and John Wall, *The Watering of Apollos* (Oxford, 1625), "To Lord Keeper Williams."

[58] George Carleton, *A Remembrance* (London, 1624); and Thomas Hering, *The Triumph of the Church* (London, 1624).

[59] Richard Gardiner, *A Sermon Preached at St. Maries in Oxford*, p. 23; and see above, pp. 24, 30–1, 38–40.

[60] Hall, *Noahs Dove*, p. 519; and Brinsley, *The Fourth Part of the True Watch*, p. 256.

[61] Thomas Taylor, *A Heavenly Voice*, printed in *Two Sermons* (London, 1624), p. 25; and John Prideaux, *A Sermon Preached on the Fifth Day of October 1624* (Oxford, 1625). See also Prideaux's sermon *Perez-Uzzah* (Oxford, 1625), which continues the same imbalance between Puritans and Catholics.

accommodation with Rome and the most Catholic King of Spain. Hence the collapse of the Anglo-Spanish match in 1624 could be interpreted only as another example of God's providential care of England. Some preachers simply drew attention to the alarming Catholic revival in recent years without assigning responsibility for the increase. Thus Thomas Beard noted, "the Iesuites and Romish Priests multiply Bookes and Pamphlets against us and our Religion"; John Mayer commented on "the daily increase of Popish superstition even within your Maiesties Dominions"; and Robert Barrell pointed to "those croking Frogs of Rome (I meane the Iesuites and Seminary Priests) . . . now more than ever swarme in our Coasts." As John Lawrence asked the crowd at Paul's Cross early in 1624, "doe you not see Masse-priests as ordinary in the streets as Ministers?"[62]

Other preachers were less circumspect. Alexander Leighton attributed the entire problem to James's pursuit of peace and his 1622 Directions; "our bodily leaders are like Oysters in May, and they say to our spirituall Leaders, prophesie not." Thomas Taylor concurred: Catholics had flourished, thanks to the Directions, "by silence and not professing against the Idolatry of Popery." The persistent attempts at general Christian reconciliation also roused Taylor's ire; all "thoughts of reconciling too such contrary religions, which as iron and clay can never be tempered together" only advanced the cause of Rome. Anthony Wotton echoed Taylor's argument in an attack on "Laodiceans" within the Church of England, and Leighton warned of divine wrath against "both Ministers and Magistrates that tolerate false Religion."[63] Thomas Adams pointed out that the blessings accorded to peace-makers did not extend to those who made "matches betwixt him [the Lord] and Belial." In the later case, "maledicti pacifici, cursed are the peace-makers." Likewise Theophilius Higgons asked, "if Rome be Babylon and wee must goe out of it, why doe some men persuade you to goe unto her, or at the least, to meete her?" In the face of "Modificators and temperate men" who insisted the old and new faiths "might bee reconciled together," the worst possible response was "detestable silence," which James had forced on the Church in 1622. Thus the point of all these tracts was to "let Rome understand her sinne; that she is BABYLON."[64]

No one maintained that James had deliberately attempted to undermine the English Church; rather it was clear that a lofty goal, the preservation of continental peace, had led him astray. Nonetheless, some writers boldly

---

[62] Beard, "To Lord Keeper Williams"; Robert Barrell, *The Spirituall Architecture* (London, 1624), p. 5; John Lawrence, *A Golden Trumpet* (London, 1624), p. 42; and Mayer, "To the King".

[63] Alexander Leighton, *Speculum Belli Sacri* (n.p., 1624), pp. 42 and 243; Wotton, *Runne from Rome*, p. 7; and Taylor, *A Heavenly Voice*, p. 30.

[64] Theophilius Higgons, *Mystical Babylon* (London, 1624), pp. 76 and 137–8.

insisted that James had overlooked a fundamental theological reality. "Have peace *from* Babylon?", Higgons asked; "you can have no peace with her in treaty with her upon sweet and amicable terms." Taylor was equally emphatic that Protestants must govern their dealings with Catholics by the same standards that the Israelites had followed with the Ameleckites; "they might never make league or peace with them all their daies, because the whole nation stood accursed before the Lord." Thomas Adams was equally emphatic: "when Religion and Superstitution meet in one bed, they commonly produce a mungrell generation." Thus Englishmen should reject the Spanish match as the sons of Jacob did a marriage with "Shichemites"; "wee cannot give our sister to a man that is uncircumcized." The Anglo-Spanish dynastic alliance therefore was a dangerous expedient, or, as Leighton termed it, a "Linciewolsie Match" which was inherently "beastly, greasie" and "lowsie-wearing."[65]

From these tracts alone, contemporaries could have deduced that a major policy shift was underway. In 1622–3 the public expression of these ideas from a pulpit, much less in print, would have earned the bold preacher considerable episcopal, if not conciliar, disapproval. Yet in 1624 the pamphlets and sermons attacking Rome and even Spain came forth in abundance. Furthermore, except those of Leighton, none of them apparently had to evade the official licensing process. Those readers anxious to pursue the reasons for this dramatic alteration would have had little trouble in satisfying their curiosity at the local booksellers; both over and under the counter they could easily have followed all the stages of the "high crisis" of 1624.

Early in the year those who hoped to break Philip's grip on James looked to Charles and the new MPs for their salvation. And to aid their deliberations, Thomas Scott produced several pamphlets. *Dignatus Dei* offered a survey of Catholics' machinations against Protestants from the time of the Waldensians. Its point was simple: the recusants had to be checked lest Englishmen share the same fate as the Parisian Huguenots in 1572. *Boarneges* hammered home the same point but more controversially confined its discussion to 1618–23. Rather than focus on the earlier Protestant heroes, Scott vividly presented the trials of the "martyrs" of the Spanish match. Although "zealous" ministers were restrained from issuing "invectives against the Antichrist," some bravely insisted on "putting the axe to the roote and applying other texts contrary to . . . [those] who affected Spains greatnesse." Meanwhile Spanish agents flourished, busily organizing the "Hispaniolized faction" and mocking all things English save the women whom they debauched. The only hope lay in the new Parliament whose resolutions, Scott prayed,

---

[65] Higgons, *Mystical Babylon*, p. 78; Taylor, *An Everlasting Record*, printed in *Two Sermons*, p. 4; and Leighton, *Speculum Belli Sacri*, p. 194.

"may extend to the glory of God . . . and the confusion of the Antichrist." In case the imminent dangers of the Spanish match may have eluded readers, Scott reiterated them in his *Aphorismes of State*. The Spaniards had consistently advanced their own political ends through the Roman Church; thus the reversal of roles between the Holy Mother Church and her most obedient son was "fit for the British nation, especially to take notice of that they may evidently see, the issue of all our treaties [with Spain]."[66]

Other authors were equally uncompromising about the treaties. The aim of *A Second Part of Spanish Practices* was simply stated in its subtitle: *A Relation of More Particular Wicked Plots and Cruell, Inhumane, Perfidious and Unnaturall Practises of the Spaniards*. The Spaniards were not merely unpleasant; they were also wildly ambitious as *The Spaniards Perpetuall Designes to an Universall Monarchie* outlined.[67] These unfortunate tendencies among Charles's prospective kinsmen made a Spanish alliance suicidal. Furthermore, as one author argued, it would not solve the Palatine problem; *A Briefe Information of the Affaires of the Palatinate* reported that Frederick's willingness to negotiate had only increased the Habsburgs' requirements for his restoration. *Certaine Reasons* presented the obvious solution with *Arguments of Policie, Why the King of England should hereafter give over all further treatie, and enter into warre with the Spaniard*. No longer could English patience and honor be abused; "how many Curriers have been sent? how many letters written? and what adoe hath been made by ordinary Ambassadors?" Philip's ministers were plainly toying with the English and in this situation only one solution remained – "Necessitie requires warre."[68]

The justice of a war, however, did not make it any easier to finance, and those who kept their eye on the bottom line had two tracts especially for them. *The Belgick Soldier* addressed the objections which "some sordide covetous Churchman, rich churlish Farmer, scurrilous fearful Lawyer or temporizing Parasite" might lodge. "I go about to prove," the author asserted, "that Warre hath been better than peace," or in the words of the subtitle, *Warre was a Blessing*. An Anglo-Spanish war would actually be a providential means to revive the depressed English economy. First, it reminded its readers how military and naval glory had gone hand-in-hand with economic prosperity in Elizabeth's reign:

Did we not search all the harbors of the world and made English Merchants and

---

66   [Thomas Scott], *Dignatus Dei* [Utrecht?, 1624]; [Scott], *Boarneges* (Edinburgh, [Utrecht?], 1624), pp. 23–4, and 33; and [Scott], *Aphorismes of State* (Utrecht, 1624), title page.
67   [Anon.], *A Second Part of Spanish Practices* (n.p., 1624); and [Anon.], *The Spaniards Perpetuall Designes to an Universall Monarchie* (n.p., 1624).
68   [Anon.], *A Briefe Information of the Affaires of the Palatinate* (n.p., 1624); and [Anon.], *Certaine Reasons* (n.p., 1624).

Adventures deserve a character of renoune? did not our inferior ships scorne the Spanish gallies and galeons, yea, thrust open the Streights to passe into the Arches? did we not visit India . . . ? did we not search the South seas and passed the Streights of Magellane? did not Michelborne and others bring Spices out of India without paying for it? Candish Silkes without bleeding for it; Drake Bullion without digging for it? . . . did not our Merchants imploy many brave sea-men who returned with great booty and prizes of all sorts?

Yet the Jacobean peace had undone the Elizabethan prosperity.

Now since our peace, what hath that done to us, or we done to ourselves? hath it not proved our sicknesse, and wrought upon our corrupt bodies like a fever . . . we are haunted with Beggars, undone in our Trades, pestered in the Prisons, the Commonwealth over-runne with poverty, the people cry out of misery, and feare and terrors make [us all amazed].[69]

Since these misfortunes were obviously "the vengeance of God" for abandoning a just war against the Spaniards, "there is no preventing of these mischiefes but warre, warre must cure this sore." *Robert, Earle of Essex, His Ghost* advocated a similar cure, but his analysis of the patient's symptoms was markedly different. All who doubted that Jacobean England was wealthier than Elizabethan England were urged to look about themselves:

if your sumptuous Buildings, your surfetting Diets, your Prodigality in Garments, your infinite Plate, and costly Furniture in your Houses, and the Pride of your Wives (especially) bee considered, England cannot be thought so poore.

Prosperity, however, had come at the expense of England's honor and Englishmen's personal virtues, which could only be recovered in a Spanish war. Such an undertaking, while expensive, would be one the wealthy England of James I could easily afford. Moreover contemporaries need not follow the Roman example of selling all their "costly Iewels and rich Ornaments" to finance a war to preserve their honor; "a free and cheerefull contribution to the Warres will serve the turne." His economic argument was coupled with reminiscences of the "flourishing State of your Faery-Land in the dayes of yore, whiles I lived on earth under the Government of that glorious Queene, of eternall memory." War in both tracts was at once an economic panacea and a nostalgic revival of "the dayes of yore . . . of that glorious Queene."[70]

These pamphlets only dimly perceived what lay beyond the dissolution of the treaties. *Certaine Reasons* pressed simply for a Spanish war without considering possible allies. *Essex's Ghost* was equally vague, apart from lodging an emphatic warning against "dis-uniting your selves from the United States

---

[69] [Thomas Scott], *The Belgick Soldier* (Dort, 1624), pp. 23 and 37–8.
[70] [Thomas Scott], *Robert Earle of Essex His Ghost* (Paradise, 1624), pp. 13–16; and *The Belgick Soldier*, p. 41.

of the Netherlands." *The Belgick Soldier* offered more detailed advice: "Let us then resolutely assist the Dutch . . . and no doubt the French will come in, and then a three-fold cable will be very strong." The author of the *Spaniards Perpetuall Designes* discussed a full-blown "common cause" in which the Venetians, Savoyards, Swiss, Germans, Danes and Swedes would join with France and the Dutch Republic to oppose the Habsburgs' "Universal Monarchie."[71] Readers in 1624 would have needed little prompting to add their own country to this confederation. Without question the strategic vision of the first wave of tracts was primitive, but it should be remembered that the main concern in these months was severing the Spanish connection, not strategy.

Once the new session convened, another group of pamphlets offered advice on issues before the House. Certainly the most influential of these was John Gee's *The Foot out of the Snare*, which explains the parliamentary insistence on a proclamation banishing the Jesuits. The reason for its impact is readily apparent. While *Boarneges* and *Dignatus Dei* voiced general apprehensions of the Catholic resurgence, Gee supplied details. He described the *modus operandi* of the Catholic proselytizers who concentrated their attentions on disgruntled scholars, the dying, and above all, women both young and old. Catholic "Printing-presses and Book-sellers almost in every corner" allowed the clerics to flood the realm with "swarmes of their bookes, which you may heere humming up and downe in every corner both of City and Countrey." Others had said as much, but Gee actually cited an extensive list of the Catholic imprints from 1623 ranging from *A New Gag for the Gospell* to *The Ingratitude of Elizabeth of England to Philip of Spain*. More importantly, he provided the names, orders, and in some cases, the addresses of Catholic clerics in London.[72] Buttressed with these facts, Gee's public plea to Archbishop Abbot and the new Parliament was almost impossible to ignore.

After Gee's spotlight on the Catholic problem, James's acceptance of the Petition on Religion became for some the climax of the session. Bishop Ussher immediately worked a glowing accolade for the royal response into a sermon, and another pamphlet promptly came out to celebrate *Englands Ioy, for Suppressing the Papists and Banishing the Priests and Iesuites.* "What?" the author asked, "the Papistrie to be suppressed? The Priests and Iesuits to be banished? And the Gospell of Iesus Christ to Flourish? My soules [*sic*] leapes for ioy . . . Oh blessed alteration: oh blessed King: oh blessed Parliament."[73]

[71] *Robert Earle of Essex*, p. 16; *The Belgick Soldier*, p. 42; and *The Spaniards Perpetuall Designes.*

[72] John Gee, *The Foot out of the Snare* (London, 1624), p. 21; and appendix, 1 and 2.

[73] [Thomas Scott], *Englands Ioy for Suppressing the Papists and Banishing the Priests and Iesuits* (n.p., 1624), p. 2; James Ussher, *An Answer to a Challenge* (London, 1624); sig. [A2v–A3].

Balladeers who normally gave a wide berth to political issues even moved to exploit the market. Martin Parker quickly issued "A scourge for the Pope" which revelled in the fact that

> Long have they looked
> To get toleration
> But God kept the heart
> Of our King in his Hand.

Not only did God stay James's heart, he also worked through "Our Parliament Royall" which

> Will give them deniall
> A meanes to destroy all
> Their causes of hope.

When the vigorous market for the ballad called for a hasty sequel, Parker brought out the prince for a bow, praying God to "with zeale Prince Charles endue / our second hope."[74]

Religious topics were not the only reason 1624 proved to be a banner year for booksellers. The open treatment of political themes was obviously less common than an indirect approach which buried political commentary amid pages of Biblical exegesis. Nevertheless the "blessed revolution" brought forth more striking examples of this rarer genre than any other period before the Civil War. A striking example occurred early in the session when John Reynolds, writing under the *nom de plume* of S.R.N.I., boldly offered his advice. Reynolds's *Votivae Angliae* implored James to abandon his unmanly fear of Spain and to make good his speech of 23 March. "Let your courage," the author advised,

but animate your Designes and your Subiects will execute them. For, give them but the worde to refetch it by Warre . . . and your Nobilitie and Gentrie . . . will flye from Thames to Rhyne as to a Fayre or Wedding.

Reynolds enthusiastically endorsed James's offer of parliamentary treasurers; he assured James that

if your Maiestie will be pleased to secure but this one doubt and feare of your Subiects, that your Souldiers may eate and not your Courtiers devoure the moneyes which a Parliament will give . . . you shall then assuredlie found out and [*sic*] Indies in your England.

James moreover should not fear the Habsburgs' power as "it seemes Heaven and Earth concurre with us in the resolution." Given the "distaste of the French, the defiance of the Hollanders, [and] the iealousie of Savoy and

---

[74] [Martin Parker], "A Scourge for the Pope"; and "The Second Part," printed in *The Pepys Ballads*, ed. H. E. Rollins (Cambridge, Mass., 1929), I, pp. 218–24.

Venice" for the Austrians, they would join James once they saw "the zeale and resolution of England."[75]

Votivae Angliae was quickly followed with the publication of *Vox Coeli*, which Reynolds had probably composed in 1623. A ghostly conference of Henry VIII, Edward VI, Mary and Elizabeth, Prince Henry and Queen Anne resolved in the end (with only Mary dissenting) that the Spanish match was unwise. But in the spring of 1624, the author added a much more timely preface, appealing to

> great Brittaines greatest Palladines and Champions . . . the Conscript fathers of our supreamest Senate . . . to tell our King that it is nothing for his Majesty to have made a brave and generous Declaration of Warres against Spaine except he speedily second it with executions.

His plea here clearly reflected the anxieties which troubled the last half of the Parliament over the question of "execution." Implementation of the Four Propositions and the banishment of the Jesuits was not enough; Parliament should urge James "to transport warre into Spaine," and if Spain or the Palatinate proved to be too far off, then "Flanders and Brabant are but the skirts and Suburbs to England." He repeated his assurance that France and the United Provinces would prove willing allies. Those filled with "feare and pusillanimitie" he urged to "thinke what a happines, what a glorie it is for England to have wars with Spaine." The goal of *Vox Coeli* was thus very straightforward: "wars, wars . . . let us prepare our selves for Warrs."[76]

Votivee Angliae and *Vox Coeli*, of all the pamphlets published and retailed during the comparative freedom of 1624, were also the only ones to attract noticeable royal displeasure. It is not surprising that James wanted to suppress these tracts and to meet the man who had depicted him as a coward terrified of Spain. Royal interest may have redoubled with the report that for having written lines such as "Our famous Elisabeth did beate Spaine, and shall our Royal and Potent King James fear it," the author earned £1,000 in sales. In July, "many of the booksellors," Woolley reported, "are now in question and in prison for selling *Votivi Anglia* [*sic*]."[77] James may also have been interested in Reynolds because he, unlike Scott, was within reach, and in August, Buckingham's nephew, Lord Fielding, curtailed his grand tour in order to present his chaplain, Mr. Reynolds, before the Privy Council. The

---

[75] [John Reynolds] S.R.N.I., *Votivae Angliae* (Utrecht, 1624), unpaginated. See also, J. H. Bryant, "John Reynolds of Exeter and His Canon: A Footnote," *The Library*, fifth series, XVIII (1963), pp. 299–303.

[76] [John Reynolds] S.R.N.I., *Vox Coeli* (Elisium, 1624), dedication to the Parliament.

[77] Locke to Carleton, 11 July 1624, SP 14/169/41; and Woolley to Trumbull, 2 July 1624, Trumbull MSS, XLVIII/130.

author ultimately spent several months in Fleet prison for his boldness.[78] Nonetheless, royal displeasure probably only further stimulated sales of both tracts.

The impact and quality of Reynolds's work can best be seen in the fact that the later collected works of Thomas Scott included *Vox Coeli* and *Votivee Angliae*.[79] But the controversialist *par excellence* of the 1620s really had no need to claim Reynolds's work since he produced three important pamphlets of his own at the end of the 1624 session. In his first, Scott returned to the form of *Vox Populi*, his notorious pamphlet of 1620 which led him into voluntary exile. *The Second Part of Vox Populi* presented further discussions of the Spanish Council where Gondomar revealed his long-term plan to subvert England. He had charmed James into suppressing loyal Protestants and encouraging disloyal Catholics; he had corrupted a host of royal officials in preparation for a Spanish invasion. But all his well-laid plans, Gondomar lamented, would certainly have met with success "had not the coming over of the Prince Charles in Person into Spaine . . . spoyled all."[80] The Spanish Council concluded its meeting after ruminating over the recent reverses in England. The priests were about to be banished; the English had accorded Mansfelt a "great entertainment"; the plot of Inijosa and Coloma against Buckingham had backfired; and the new Parliament had supplied James with the necessary funds to wage a war. The Spaniards then collectively started at the recollection of the Elizabethan war, and very conveniently outlined their own defensive weaknesses.[81]

Scott's *Vox Populi*, Part II, is important for it was the most influential in a series of tracts which lavished extravagant praise on Charles and Buckingham. Uniting the Spanish Council was the fear of Charles "upon whom and whose actions as a bright blazing Comet, Europe begins to fixe her eye, affraid and doubtfull, where the fatall effect of his discontent will light." Another Spanish councillor termed Charles "a young Lion . . . his teeth and nayles are growne to that length, that he is past iesting and playing." Scott was even more unbridled in his praise of Buckingham. One councillor voiced an explanation for the deteriorating Anglo-Spanish relations, which the Parliament of 1626 would later consider closely: it was all the result of

---

[78] Reynolds to Denbigh, 29 May 1624, Warwick County Record Office, Fielding of Newnham Paddox MSS, CR 2017/C2/187; Nethersole to [Carleton], 14 August 1624, SP 14/171/49; and Abbot to Conway, 5 November 1624, SP 14/174/20.

[79] See *The Workes of the Most Famous and Reverend Divine Mr. Thomas Scott* (Utrecht, 1624). The mistake continues even in recent scholarship; see for example Annabel Patterson, *Censorship and Interpretation* (Madison, 1984), p. 77, and M. A. Breslow, *The Mirror of England: English Puritan Views of Foreign Nations, 1618–1640* (Cambridge, Mass., 1970), pp. 167–8.

[80] [Thomas Scott], *The Second Part of Vox Populi* (Goricum, 1624), pp. 21–2.

[81] *Ibid.*, pp. 28–41.

Buckingham's personal quarrel with Olivares. Yet in Scott's account, the Archbishop of Toledo warned his colleagues against believing their own propaganda. The English duke actually "is a Noble, Wise and a Generous Prince, uppon whom the King his Maister hath deservedly conferred his grace and those transcendent Honors, yea though for no other merit else than the resolute and wise carriage of himselfe, in the businesse of this Treaty amongst us." Moreover, Toledo stated that the duke had earned "the generall love of the Common People," who earnestly prayed for Buckingham during his collapse of April–June "as if he had beene some good Landlord or great House keeper amongst them, whose losse would had beene halfe their undoinge."[82] Thus, Scott in one stroke legitimated the trip to Madrid and added two modifiers, Protestant and popular, to Buckingham's title of royal favorite.

As the successful conclusion of Parliament of 1624 seemed to surpass all Scott's expectations, he quickly produced two extraordinary tracts to commemorate how the Parliament, and Charles and Buckingham, had delivered England from certain disaster. *Vox Dei* was a highly evocative recollection of the events of 1623–4 interwoven with an anthem of praise to the Stuarts and to Buckingham. Scott based the tract on the notion that "now (that the greatest storme is over) wee behold the deliverance with more admiration." With the news of Charles's sudden departure for Madrid, Scott recalled "our hearts were filled with astonishment, doubt, despayre; wee gave them for lost, and our selves with them, and with them and us, our lawes, liberties, land, and (what was dearest) our religion." All men delighted in Charles's obedience to his father "in all respects but in this MATCH." Consequently, his docility and his "sweete nature" would make him easy prey for the Spanish nets. Even more alarming was the fact that his only adviser was Buckingham, and Scott recalled "how many curses did fill his sayles going towards Spain." The favorite then appeared "a yonge man, unfit for lack of experience, to manage great affaires or to incounter single the Grandees of Spayne, and Rome, with the Iesuites at their elbows." More importantly, Buckingham seemed "unsettled in religion ... wee knowe who was his wife, who was his mother, and all wee could then see of him made us suspect and tremble the more, the more wee saw it." Meanwhile in London,

when wee sawe the Chappell building here for Baal ... when wee saw every pocket stuft with popish pamphlets ... when wee saw *a gag for the Gospel* (like a Giant) might walke abroad with liberty in the sunneshine, when a Protestant Pismire, might scarce creepe in a darke corner, without question ... wee all seemed no other, then beasts in a market to be bought, and sould.

But in October, "on a sodaine the sunne arose," and Charles returned

---

[82] *Ibid.*, pp. 23 and 25–6.

"ALONE, o words of comfort! as choosing rather to dye a Virgine and live an Angell, then to be marryed by Antichrist."[83]

In the trip to Spain and afterwards in the Parliament, the country, Scott argued, learned the true measure of Charles and Buckingham. The prince in his actions seemed "one truly taught of God and imitating our saviour." Charles moreover performed "the greatest work of wisdome and goodness within man's power to accomplish, reconciling us to his father's favour." Since the success of the Parliament of 1624 was largely due to Charles's intercession, Scott asked, "is not he a temporall saviour, a true Josuah that doth this?" When dealing with Buckingham, Scott could not say enough. For years, the people had regarded him as

the child of Fortune only, but now [he] is found to be the favorite of vertue also. Whilst he shot up sodainely, who did not take him for a gourd, and expect his more sodaine withering againe with wishes? But now who doth not looke upon him, as upon an Oake or Cedar sound at the heart, like to last long, and be profitable for the upholding of the Church, and State, upon whose branches birdes may build with safety and under whose shadow, all distressed creatures may finde shelter against the fury of violent stormes?

From a most vocal critic of the Stuart regime, such adulation was remarkable, and these selections are only a few of the many in *Vox Dei*. Buckingham's translation from a gourd to a cedar was interesting enough, but in light of his impeachment less than two years later, the frontispiece of *Vox Dei* was indeed ironic: there Buckingham stands triumphantly over the crushed bodies of "Briberie (the bane of Commonwealth)" and "Faction." There was only one note of caution in Scott's assessment of the duke. Scott exhorted him to "goe forward . . . and prosper whilst thou doest nothing but what may justify thee and what thou maiest justify before all the world." But this was lost amid Scott's fulsome endorsements: "God will blesse thee and establish thy house forever, thy Enemies shall see it and gnash their teeth." Scott even managed to praise James, but it was largely for allowing Charles and Buckingham to lead him towards a breach with Spain. Therefore, even though *Vox Dei* was dedicated to "three mighty men," one of them, the king himself, appeared only dimly behind "Jonathan and his Armour bearer."[84]

Scott warned his readers, "after Vox Dei, expect Vox Regis to follow," and he was as good as his word. Scott's third major tract in 1624 was a popular account of the "happie Parliament . . . likely then to be the happiest Parliament that ever was." Those who had not been privy to newsletters could find in *Vox Regis* all the major parliamentary addresses and resolutions along with Scott's running commentary. Even the illiterate could find his analysis

---

[83] [Thomas Scott], *Vox Dei* (Utrecht, 1624), pp. 59, 61–2 and 68–70.
[84] *Ibid.*, pp. 58–9, 78–83, 86, 93 and 98–9.

of the session summarized in the frontispiece: there James sat enthroned holding the sword of state; the bishops at prayer on one side and the peers in arms
on the other flanked the king; before the throne, Charles on his knees
presented Elizabeth and Frederick; and the Commons in the foreground
offered up their hearts and their purses.[85] Scott repeatedly glossed over any
tensions or misunderstandings during the session. Instead he emphasized that
king and Parliament were moving towards a war and towards the reformation of the commonwealth.

Scott of course was not alone in his delight with the first "happy" Parliament of James's reign. George Webb concluded a *Protestant Kalendar* by
placing the Spanish match at the head of a long list of the English Church's
trials stretching from the Marian martyrs to the Gunpowder Plot. God, Webb
declared, "hath blessed us with an Honourable assemblie of States in the high
Court of Parliament and united hearts and minds," and until success was well
in hand, He "hath stirred up the hearts of all faithful Subiects within this
Island to pray and cry, Grace, Grace to that Parliamentarie assembly." John
Brinsley was equally delighted and relieved with the outcome. He too offered
heart-felt thanks for the "heavenly union" between James and "his faythful
Peeres and true-hearted Nobility and Commons" who had achieved "the
frustrating of the hopes and daunting the hearts of all thine and thy Churches
Adversaries: and in beginning to graunt all things according to the cryes of
they poore people, and even above our expectations." His most fervent
prayer was that God would "vouchsafe unto us such hopes for all future times
and every day to renew the same, in that heavenly union and harmony of the
Anoynted and his whole most honourable Parliament." The author of
another anonymous tract also expounded on James's new attention to "the
cryes of thy poore people"; in the recent session, "the Subiect no sooner
shewed his grievance with complaint, but the Soveraigne applied the remedie
with compassion." Thus, he concluded, "they were happie in knowing each
other."[86]

John Woolley had ample grounds for his surprise over "what privilege men
take in these days more than heretofore." Most Englishmen regarded the
Infanta Maria not simply as a foreign Catholic bride for the heir apparent but
also as a fundamental threat, in Scott's words, to "our lawes, liberties, land
and . . . our religion." Little wonder then that they followed the course of the
1624 session carefully and rejoiced in Parliament's rejection of Madrid and
Rome. But a vital question remains – were they actually interested in a
Spanish war? Russell suggested that they were not and supported his con-

---

[85] [Thomas Scott], *Vox Regis* (n.p., 1624), frontispiece and p. 39.
[86] G.S., *Sacrae Heptades* (n.p., 1625), dedication to Charles; George Webb, *Catalogus Protestantium* (London, 1624), p. 96; and Brinsley, *The Fourth Part*, pp. 402 and 311 [411].

tention with parliamentary evidence. The preceding chapters, however, have cast serious doubt on his use of this evidence. Yet there is another major category of contemporary evidence which he did not consider and which addresses this question. Therefore it is important to analyze these tracts and sermons for any indication of what contemporaries thought would follow the 1624 session. The answer overwhelmingly was war, and the authors, far from regretting this outcome, welcomed it.

This is not to say that the strategic advice became either more unified or more sophisticated. Scott, for example, remained a vigorous advocate of a "blue water" strategy; England's paramount consideration was to ensure that "our commings in . . . be answerable to our expenses," and the best, indeed the only, way to do so was to "send out our Navie . . . to fish for gould." Direct continental involvement on the other hand would quickly prove "undertakings against our selves and wee (running our selves out of breath) will soone learne to repent our forwardnes and call for peace." Pitt the Elder a century later would merely be elaborating on Scott's text. Reynolds shared much of his enthusiasm for the senior service but not Scott's aversion to continental forays. While Scott warned that "Spaine can easely charme France by the helpe of the Iesuites and pope to sit still," Reynolds had no qualms about an Anglo-French alliance. In fact such an alliance together with an Anglo-Dutch league would form the "three-fold cable" necessary to "take down the ambition and pride, and to curbe the power and malice of Spayne." These rival approaches had confounded Englishmen and would continue to do so. But aside from these two overtly political writers, the rest of the authors were blithely indifferent to these concerns in 1624. Indeed with Armageddon apparently looming nigh, some were frankly bored with traditional power politics; "however there are Monarchies and Kings against him [James]," John Brinsley was confident, "the Lambe shall overcome them." Yet the lack of sophisticated strategic thinking should not be taken as lack of interest in the Spanish war.[87]

In 1624 fairly ordinary events assumed a new meaning; in that year Thomas Barnes decided to teach Isocrates, the famous Greek orator, "to speake a little English." The work appears at first completely trivial until it becomes clear that Barnes translated Isocrates's address to the Spartan Council which was resolving whether to adopt a diplomatic or military response to Thebes's seizure of Messina. The parallel with the decision England had to make in the Palatinate could not have been more exact. "They who would enjoy their liberty," Isocrates warned, "must shun compositions tendered by command or strong hand: as tendring unto servitude." On the other hand, if Sparta resolved to contest the illegal seizure, "we shall see those

[87] [Scott], *Vox Dei*, preface; and Brinsley, *The Fourth Part*, p. 62.

that now Lord it over us and give the Lawe become our humble suppliants
and suters to receive Messina againe and to make peace with them." If the
Palatinate replaced Messina, one of the "Patriots" on the floor of the
Commons could scarcely have expressed himself better. Therefore, notwithstanding Barnes's insistence that his translation simply reflected his interest in
"words [and] construction of Phrases, not application of Histories," the
reason for his decision to publish in 1624 becomes transparent.[88] John
Brinsley's *Fourth Part of the True Watch* also seems thoroughly forgetable.
The first three parts had established Brinsley with a modest following for his
pious, if mundane, theological advice.[89] Yet in 1624 with the *Fourth Part*, he
beckoned his faithful readers into highly controversial territory; reports of
the "butchering and slaughtering of thy Saints" compelled him to plunge
into current affairs and to exhort his readers to pray for all non-Habsburg
princes and "chiefly for our dread Soveraigne" that they "may all yet, whilst
there is time now the Lord calles so lowd upon them, set themselves to enquire
wisely into the true causes of the evils already upon the Churches." Brinsley
had in mind no peace conference; in fact he consigned to "the Beasts of the
forrest" all those "blind Watchmen, crying Peace, peace and all is well and
lulling themselves and all others asleepe." For those inclined to take their
chances, he composed a short prayer: "Oh Lord Iesus, perswade my heart,
that refusing or deferring now to helpe thee, I cannot escape the curse of
Meroz." Instead of sitting still, Englishmen should always remember "that
firme bond of brotherly love" and act to "rescue, succour and protect them
[the godly] from the rage of all thine and their cruell enemies." Nor could
Englishmen argue it was already too late to save those who were dead, for
"their blood will cry for vengeance." The godly need not worry about final
victory, for God would certainly "give to us . . . the upper hand that we may
be above and not beneath." The military odds meant nothing, since "five of us
thy servants may chase a hundred . . . and a hundreds of us may put tenne
thousands to flight."[90]

The transformation of a minister interested in effective pastoral care into a
strident advocate of holy war would be remarkable in any other period of
early Stuart history; in 1624, however, it was commonplace. Thomas Taylor,
for example, followed Brinsley's logic almost step by step. Once Taylor made
the connection between Rome and the Ameleckites, the path that England
had to follow became abundantly clear. Not only must Englishmen reject any

---

[88] Isocrates, *Archidiamus* (London, 1624), translated by Thomas Barnes, Introduction and
fos. 10v and 13v.
[89] On Brinsley's career see his entry in the *DNB*, and on his earlier work see his *The True Watch*
(London, 1606), *The Second Part of the True Watch* (London, 1607), and *The Third Part of
the True Watch* (London, 1622).
[90] Brinsley, *The Fourth Part*, pp. 46, 138, 207–8, 256 and 404.

compromise with Spain, they must also "offer themselves cheerfully to the execution of this sentence [of destruction] to the utter extirpation of this hatefull people." If James was the realm's Moses, then Charles was Joshua, who "should alwaies stand out in hostility against them . . . and publiquely to execute the iudgements of God which were charged upon them." The fate of Meroz awaited those who failed to follow the new Joshua; "not onely those that warre against the Church shall fall, but those also that stand not out for it . . . Nations and Kingdoms that will not serve the Church shall perish." Finally England need not fear the constellation of Catholic states because "thou hast the hand of the highest lifted up for thee." The conflict was a holy one of retribution against the ungodly, for the Lord "will suffer no man to doe her wrong unrevenged . . . God will avenge his elect."[91]

Taylor and Brinsley were not unique; from a host of English pulpits came similar calls to arms. Robert Vase, preaching at Paul's Cross, noted "the Saints groane and cry out for the wrongs done unto them" and then observed that God had been deaf to their cries in recent years. Therefore he asked, "shall not God avenge his owne elect"? Since the four "new" regiments had just marched out to the defense of the Dutch Calvinists, the answer was obvious: "I tell you he will avenge them speedily." Gilbert Primrose agreed; the afflicted "in the Palatinate and the other parts of Germanie" can expect God "will avenge them speedily."[92] Lest such martial sermons sounded incongruous, Samuel Bachiler reminded his congregation that "Christ was not to send peace, but a sword"; thus England was simply doing what was "good and sure" in "the mysticall warre . . . against the Papacie." Ultimate victory could be assured since "God defendeth his little flock." England really had no choice about intervention, Theophilus Higgons argued; "this is no mere politicke attempt for human ends, but it is the worke of heaven . . . for you see the proclamation and ordination of this warre is from the unquestionable authoritie of God himselfe."[93] Thomas Barnes could only marvel at the audacity of the Habsburgs who, notwithstanding their initial successes, were living on borrowed time. "I tell thee tis dangerous medling against the Saints, it is fearefull." The Lord always remembered his own, and "be but a man a water-bearer to the Congregation of Israel . . . his wrongs shall be righted, his cause shall be avenged." Modern Israelites, Gilbert Primrose maintained, looked to England, because "Christs distressed members . . . have no hope, after God, but in the Churches of this island." Fortunately for them, their faith was well-placed; "what doth this whole Island desire with

[91] Taylor, *An Everlasting Record*, pp. 4, 5, 14 and 18.
[92] R[obert] V[ase], *Jonahs Contestation* (London, 1625), p. 54; and Gilbert Primrose, *The Christian Mans Teares* (London, 1625), p. 108.
[93] Samuel Bachiler, *Miles Christianus* (Amsterdam, 1625), "To the English Soldiers"; and Higgons, *Mystical Babylon*, pp. 77–8.

sighs and sobs," Primrose asked, "but to bee at warre with Christs enemies?" And this "true sympathie and fellow-feeling" in England was in itself a clear sign that "hee hath ordained that deliverie shall come from us." And to celebrate the first wave of English military support for the continental brethren, Gervase Markham published an extended paean to the four "new" regiments replete with a frontispiece showing the Earl of Oxford on horseback.[94]

There is, to be sure, an air of unreality about any predictions which cast James VI and I in the role of the champion of the faithful. After all, as Williams noted at James's funeral in the following spring, "Great Britain's Soloman" died in peace. Secondary authorities frequently quote this line, and they just as frequently overlook the fact that the preceding sentences completely alter the meaning of the sentence. "And yet towards his End," Williams recalled, "King Salomon had secret enemies, Razan, Hadad, Jeroboam, and prepared for a Warre upon his going to his Grave ... So had, and so did King James."[95] Therefore if we remember that James at his death was, like Solomon, preparing for war, these predictions seem less far-fetched. In fact a reputed prophecy of Merlin circulated in 1624 which in all seriousness depicted James as the warrior who would "great Alexanders fame out goe." After leading an invasion of the continent, "then doth men / And many princes ioyne with him" to proclaim James "Western Emperour." Eventually the new Emperor would lead his forces in a grand battle against his enemies, only to die on the field after securing a resounding victory.[96] In any other year but the last one of James's fifty-nine-year life, such a prophecy would have been wildly absurd; but in 1624 it embodied the hopes that many Englishmen felt for James as well as for Charles.

That James himself was not thrilled with his final role goes without saying, and in a sermon delivered before James at the end of the summer, Joseph Hall sought to reconcile *The True Peacemaker* to war. James had done everything humanly possible to maintain the peace of Europe; "let God and his holy Angels witnesse ... on their part [in Spain] the peace faileth; we are guiltless." Nevertheless the fact remained that "if any shall offer wrong to the Lords anointed in his person, in his seed, the worke of that iniustice shall be war; yea Bellum Domini." Thus it was that Hall prayed, "he who hath graciously said all this while, Da pacem, Domini, Give peace in our time, O Lord, may super-

[94] Thomas Barnes, *Needfull Helps* (London, 1624), pp. 6 and 7; Gilbert Primrose, *The Righteous Mans Fate* (London, 1625), pp. 67–8; and Gervase Markham, *Honour in His Perfection* (London, 1624).

[95] John Williams, *Great Britains Solomon* (London, 1625), p. 39. Set my analysis against that of Trevelyan, *England under the Stuarts* (London, 1928), pp. 130–1, and Russell, *Parliaments*, p. 203.

[96] "Merlins Prophesie," [1624], Folger Library, V. A. 275, p. 176.

scribe at the last his iust Trophees with, Blessed bee the Lord who teacheth my hand to warre and my fingers to fight."[97] And fight James could. Such was the martial atmosphere in 1624 that William Worship interrupted an ordinary visitation sermon in Boston to proclaim that *Rex Pacificus* was no man to trifle with. "When iust occasion shall be offered," Worship insisted, James

can fiercely hunt at Sea with such hounds as these, the Lyon, the Unicorne, the Beare, the Bull, the Tigre; Wooden Dogges (I confesse) but deepe mouth'd, rocking the waves, riving the aire and overthundring the thunder.[98]

When the Royal Navy made an unexpected appearance in the fens of Lincolnshire, it seems safe to say that the realm was far from indifferent, and it certainly was not lukewarm, to the prospect of a Spanish War.

The pamphlets that the curious could purchase at the booksellers reveal much about popular expectation on the eve of the war. On the simplest level the mere fact that the government was not particularly concerned about the printing and distribution of almost all of these tracts was another concrete sign that the government itself was moving into line with popular expectations. No longer did the Crown seem intent on pursuing an unpopular policy in the teeth of widespread hostility. Castle, for example, accepted with equanimity James's order that any priests who were seized after the appointed day should be imprisoned rather than executed: whatever James's intentions may have been, "one thing I am sure of, wee banishe them away every day by newe ballads and by books wee daily print wee make shewe that popery shall have no harbour in the kingdome."[99]

These tracts also served a further role in disseminating certain notions which would later prove pivotal. The early pamphlets, which highlighted the immediate danger that the Spanish match posed to England, and the later ones, celebrating the breach of the treaties, combined to convey to their readers a profound feeling of providential deliverance. In fact by Brinsley's count, the elect nation had just experienced "a third greater deliverance," greater than 1588 and 1605. Furthermore, England had not only thwarted a perilous plot of the Antichrist and Spain, but it had also embarked on a reformation of "the grievances of the commonwealth." The session early in 1624 had uprooted "briberie" and "faction" and banished the local agents of Rome and Madrid. The Michaelmas session, which in the summer appeared only weeks away, promised to continue this reformation. Hence Englishmen perceived that they were not so much progressing as they were reverting to the idealized Elizabethan type. Extended praise for "saint Elizabeth," which seemed to have been *de rigeur* in 1624, only further encouraged the sense of

[97] Joseph Hall, *The True Peacemaker* (London, 1624), pp. 31 and 39.
[98] William Worship, *Three Sermons* (London, 1625), p. 17.
[99] Castle to Trumbull, 18 June 1624, Trumbull MSS, XVIII/123.

renewal with their deliberate confusion of Elizabeth of England with Elizabeth of Bohemia, or as Scott termed her, "the most renowned and second Queene Elizabeth."[100] The return to Elizabethan practice was most pronounced in foreign policy, and although there was sharp confusion over details, England seemed on the brink of restoring that centerpiece of Elizabethan glory and prosperity – an Anglo-Spanish war. Thanks to these trends, for the first time in many years, a sizeable number of Englishmen knew where the kingdom was heading – or at least they thought they did.

The pamphlets are also representative of a striking anomaly of 1624, which may have affected Charles and Buckingham in their later approach to policy questions. Prior to October 1623, popular response to Charles can best be described as polite, and Buckingham, "the child of Fortune," had to content himself with less flattering assessments. In late 1623, however, as both men made their bid to influence royal policy more directly, their efforts met with enthusiastic popular approval. The country's jubilation over Charles's return "ALONE! O words of ioy," the parliamentary resolution on Buckingham's merits, and the Commons' compliments to the prince were only half the story. By the standards of the other tracts of 1624, Brinsley's proclamation of Charles as the new Joshua was modest; Leighton, for instance, trumped Joshua; "it shal be your greatest honour," he intoned, "to fight Gods battles . . . Charles the great made Rome great, And may not a greater Charles raze Romes greatnes?" Even the duke received lavish praise; probably the one Buckingham would have prized most was Queen Elizabeth's encomium (with a little coaching from John Reynolds) on his care of the English fleet.[101] Their metamorphosis in less than six months was nothing short of complete.

This wave of sustained applause certainly turned their heads. It may well have led these young men to concentrate too intently on the growing struggle with James and with various foreign allies and to presume that their domestic prestige would allow them much more leeway with the political nation. Had the parliamentary endorsements been less fulsome, had the pamphlets issued something less than a blanket endorsement, then Charles and Buckingham might have paid more attention to popular sentiments. As it was, they appear to have thought in the summer of 1624 that they had the country in their back pocket. Early in the Parliament of 1626, Charles remarked on the Commons' complaints that "I see you specially aim at the Duke of Buckingham. I wonder what hath so altered your affections towards him?" His question was a typical Caroline mixture of cunning and sincerity; but behind the apparent disingenuity, Charles was truly perplexed about what had happened. The meeting of Charles and Buckingham and their parliamentary allies in 1624

---

[100] [Thomas Scott], *The Second Part of Vox Populi*, p. 60; and Brinsley, *The Fourth Part*, p. 49.
[101] Leighton, *Speculum Belli Sacri*, dedication to Frederick; and [John Reynolds], *Vox Coeli*, p. 37.

may be likened, in Russell's metaphor, to that "of ships that pass in the night."[102] But it should be added that when they passed, the crews stood on deck and exchanged huzzas while blinkers spelled out the details of the planned rendezvous. The ultimate failure of the plan of 1624 cannot easily be ascribed to the blissful lack of interest of the rival parties in each other. Rather it was one of improperly deciphered signals from either side.

Admittedly the pamphleteers had trouble with James; his actions seemed unpredictable, his motives obscure, and his public pronouncements oracular. Therefore, the best approach was one Scott advocated: "Kings (like the sunne) must not be gazed upon with open eyes." Nonetheless, the problem remained of how to explain James's actions. A few hinted, and Mr. Reynolds boldly maintained, that prior to the prince's return from Spain, James had been too timorous to adopt the proper cause at home and abroad. But most others charitably argued that the Spaniards had deluded him. Given this analysis, it is hardly surprising that when Charles, Buckingham and Parliament persuaded James to cast off the Spanish toils, the popular praise should land on the sovereign in ample measure and shower on the mediators. Amid the acclamations of 1624, James increasingly slipped into the background. Scott's image of Charles as the temporal Saviour aptly described the popular conception of the situation at Court in 1624; since James, like God the Father, was too awesome to deal with directly, all popular prayers were addressed to Charles in hopes that he would intercede with his father.

The notion of Charles as the mediator between his father and the people also attributed to the prince a certain control over events. In the later pamphlets, James's celebrated talent for being contrary disappeared. *Vox Regis* presents the most striking example of this phenomenon. Scott was so insistent on presenting a united front of father, son and nation that he either glossed over or explained away James's parliamentary speeches, which at the time caused considerable confusion. James's reply of 8 March, for example, was in Scott's judgment that of "a wise Prince" which unfortunately was either "mistated" or mistaken.[103] Equally, Scott refused to see any ambiguities in James's position on Middlesex: the king had simply given up an unfaithful servant for punishment. Scott's work, although intended as propaganda for the war effort, also fostered the popular conception that Charles and Buckingham had broken the Spanish hold on James only to place their own on him. In the frontispiece to *Vox Dei*, Charles, Buckingham, Elizabeth, Frederick, the entire Palatine nursery and Christ himself shielded James from Spaniards and Catholics; but in the summer of 1624, it appeared that this formidable entourage guided as much as they protected the king.

---

[102] Lockyer, *Buckingham*, p. 313; and Russell, *Parliaments*, p. 202.
[103] [Thomas Scott], *Vox Regis*, pp. 51–2.

"CHECKMATE BY DISCOVERY"

That these tracts spread information about the "reformation" of 1624 is one thing, but that they were actually read is quite another. Even if we presume that each pamphlet had several readers, the total readership was sharply limited by the comparatively small number of printed copies. It seems safe to say that the segment of the political nation deeply concerned with the news at Court read some of the pamphlets. But, as always, the readership outside this social stratum is much harder to gauge. Nonetheless in August 1624, the illiterate and those who were less diligent in perusing the local bookseller's racks had an extraordinary service available to them. They need not have felt out of touch with current trends in the pamphlet trade for the King's Men very kindly acted out for them all the main themes of these tracts.

"All the nues I have heard since my comming to towne," Woolley reported, "is of a nue Play. It is called a game at Chess, but it may be a vox populy for by reporte it is 6 tymes worse against the Spanyard." Salvetti was even more specific; "Gondomar is dailie upon the stage."[104] Rarely, if ever, had the London stage presented such a thinly veiled political satire, and such a phenomenon obviously had a powerful attraction. The play, Chamberlain reported, attracted "an extraordinarie concourse and . . . all sorts of people, old and younge, rich and poore, master and servants, papists and puritans, wise men et ct., churchmen, and statemen." Sir Henry Wotton, Sir Albertus Morton, Sir Benjamin Rudyerd, and Sir Thomas Lake attended it; Sir Edward Gorges persuaded Lord Haughton to attend his first play in ten years; and Lady Judith Smith attempted to lure John Chamberlain, but the enormous press of people at the Globe forced him regretfully to plead an old man's infirmities.[105] Coloma indignantly noted that the play, which was staged across the river from his residence, produced "such merriment, hubbub, and applause that even if I had been many leagues away it would not have been possible for me not to have taken notice of it." Yet what was "hubbub" to Coloma was sweet music to those involved in a production which earned "great applause of the people, but greater from the plaiers that get well nigh 100 li a day."[106]

The play's well-developed hispanophobia readily accounts for the nine-day run of this *succès de scandale*, the longest on the Jacobean stage. The play is

[104] Woolley to Trumbull, 6 August 1624, Trumbull MSS, XLVIII/134; and Salvetti to Scudamore, 14 August 1624, PRO C115/N1/8488.

[105] Chamberlain to Carleton, 21 August 1624, *Letters*, II, p. 578; and Clare to Somerset, 2 August 1624, *Holles Letters*, II, p. 289.

[106] Coloma to Olivares, 10 August 1624, quoted in Edward Wilson and Olga Turner, "The Spanish Protest against 'A Game At Chess'," *Modern Language Review* (1949), pp. 476–82; and Salvetti to Scudamore, 14 August 1624, PRO C111/N1/8488.

also important for its presentation of a synthesis of the 1624 pamphlets. Thomas Middleton, the playwright, drew largely from Gee's *A Foot out of the Snare* and Scott's *Second Part of Vox Populi*, but he also drew on the general mood which the other tracts developed.[107] More importantly, Middleton's synthesis was widely disseminated; since 3,000 people a day reportedly saw the play, slightly less than 30,000 people, almost one-tenth of London's total population, saw *A Game at Chess*.

Middleton's scatological mockery of Gondomar, "the fistula of Europe," and his exposé of the hypocrisy of Catholicism were of course the main contemporary attractions of the play. But amid the recurrent gibes at the Spaniard's hemorrhoids and at priestly lasciviousness, the audience learned of the Hispano-Catholic design for England. The ambassador had so many plots and projects on foot that when one of his pawns burst in to inform him, "Sir, your plot's discovered," Gondomar had to ask which of his 20,985 plots he meant. In more expansive moments, he liked to boast to his subordinates of his more notable triumphs. He was very pleased, for example, with arranging Mansell's expedition against Algiers in 1620,

> a precious safeguard
> From the White Kingdom to secure our coasts
> 'Gainst the infidel pirates,

at the same time Spanish forces were overrunning the Palatinate. Another of his favorite accomplishments was having made "the jails fly open without miracle / And let the locusts out."[108] And once the Jesuits and priests were allowed "amongst the country-crops," they converted 38,000 Protestants in one year and became so entrenched that "the loudest tempests that authority rouses / Will hardly shake 'em off." Similarly he spent years of "summer recreation" piecing together "the state / And strength of the White Kingdom [England]." He had gathered "a catalogue of all the navy royal," of all the gentry and their disposition, and he learned "all sands / Shelves, rocks, and river for invasion proper'st." All these labors, he confessed, had been to advance "the business of the universal monarchy."[109]

The source of his extraordinary success, apart from the eager support of the English Catholics, was the ambassador's ability to charm.

> With pleasant subtlety and bewitching courtship . . .
> To many a soul, I have let in mortal poison

---

[107] Middleton's debt to Gee and Scott becomes quite clear in R. C. Bald's edition of *A Game At Chess*. For further analysis of the play and particularly the interpretation Margot Heinemann has recently advanced in *Puritanism and Theatre* (Cambridge, 1980), see Thomas Cogswell, "Thomas Middleton and the Court, 1624: *A Game At Chess* in Context," pp. 273–88.

[108] Thomas Middleton, *A Game At Chess* (London, 1966), III.i.125 and 85–96.

[109] *Ibid.*, IV.ii.75–6 and 58–74; and I.i.244.

> Whose Cheeks have cracked with laughter to receive it;
> I would so roll my pills in sugared syllables
> And strew much kindly mirth o'er all my mischiefs,
> They took their bane in way of recreation.

By this means, Gondomar and the Spaniards were able to penetrate deep into the English Court, and the ambassador casually listed "some councillors of state, some secretaries" as his double agents.[110] While Middleton merely hinted at Calvert and Cottington, Williams and Arundel, he openly described Middlesex:

> Our prime incendiary, one of these
> That promised the White Kingdom seven years since
> To our Black House.

Middlesex for his part promised to exercise his financial power on Spain's behalf:

> there shall nothing happen,
> Believe it, to extenuate your cause
> Or to oppress her friends, but I will strive
> To cross it with my counsel, purse and power,
> Keep all supplies back, both in means and men,
> That may raise strength against you.

Those at Court whom Gondomar had not corrupted, he charmed, and James as the White King provided the outstanding instance of his manipulative ability. When Gondomar revealed Middlesex as a Spanish agent, James bitterly rebuked Middlesex but not Gondomar. Later, when a maiden of the White House complained to James that one of Gondomar's clerics had attempted to ravish her, Gondomar managed to persuade James that the hysterical girl was merely attempting to traduce the honor of a clergyman.[111] The ambassador's power over the English Court seemed almost complete.

The only remaining obstacle in Gondomar's "main work . . . The hope monarchical," apart from the "Plague of those pestilent pamphlets," was Charles and Buckingham. His plan was simple: "at that White Knight [Charles], entrap him first / The Duke will follow too."[112] The trap would be to lure them to the Black Kingdom. Since Charles and Buckingham fully appreciated the desperate situation of the White Kingdom under Gondomar's spell, they resolved to place themselves in the Spaniards' power; only then could they expose the true aims of the Habsburgs and so break their hold on James. The stratagem, however, was dangerous; Buckingham pointed out to Charles at the beginning of their journey that

---

[110] *Ibid.*, I.i.258–66 and 56.
[111] *Ibid.*, I.i.249–51 and 318–23; II.ii.100–218; and III.i.253–79.
[112] *Ibid.*, III.i.247–8; II.ii.97–8; and I.i.292–3.

> all the gins, traps and alluring snares,
> The devil has been at work since '88 on
> Are laid for the great hope of this game only.

But Charles comforted the duke with the thought that "the more noble will truth's triumph be." The trip to Madrid consequently formed the denouement of Middleton's play.[113]

The Spaniards outdid themselves on the arrival of Charles and Buckingham in hopes of converting their guests. The prince and the duke responded politely, although Charles at one point remarked in an aside, "what a pain it is / For truth to fain a little." Finally, Charles coyly led Gondomar to reveal the Habsburgs' "large feast of our vast ambition."

> We count but the White Kingdom whence you came from
> The garden for our cook to pick his salads;
> The food's lean France larded with Germany,
> Before which comes the grave chaste signiory
> Of Venice, served in capon-like in whitebroth;
> From our chief oven, Italy, the bake-meats,
> Savoy, the salt, Geneva, the chipped manchet;
> Below the salt the Netherlands are placed,
> A common dish at lower end a' the table
> For meaner pride to fall to; for our second course
> A spit of Portugals served in for plovers,
> Indians and Moors for blackbirds; all this while
> Holland stands ready melted, to make sauce
> On all occasions; when the voider comes
> And with such cheer our crammed hopes we suffice,
> Zealand says grace, for fashion; then we rise.[114]

This open confession of Spanish duplicity prompted another from Charles; "I am," he announced

> an arch-dissembler, sir
> ... There you lie then
> And the game's ours — we give thee checkmate by
> Discovery, King, the noblest mate of all.

Charles then stuffed Philip, Olivares, the Catholics and Gondomar, who all bewailed their fate, into his bag of captured pieces as he rebuked them for their "Ambitious, covetous, luxurious falsehood."[115] The play ended with James welcoming home "Truth's glorious masterpiece" and "his true blessed assistant." "So now," James proclaimed

> let the bag close, the fittest womb
> For treachery, pride and malice, whilst we, winner like,

---

[113] *Ibid.*, IV.iv.5–8 and 14.
[114] *Ibid.*, IV.iv.16–17; and V.iii.83–99.   [115] *Ibid.*, V.iii.145, 159–63.

> Destroying, through heaven's power, what would destroy,
> Welcome our White Knight with loud peals of joy.[116]

The audience that packed the Globe and shouted out their delight with the play was actually reveling in a conflation of political tracts. Amid laughter over the broad farce of Gondomar and his agents, the audience learned of the Spanish designs of a universal monarchy, a design which gave a firm basis to the instinctive antipathy which many contemporaries felt toward Spain. The play also presented them with an appealing popular mythology about the trip to Madrid. Charles and Buckingham went there in a bold design to expose the Spaniards "by discovery." This conception of events, which the prince and the duke themselves encouraged, partly explains why the populace lionized them in 1624. It also explains why the Earl of Bristol, who possessed details of another, less flattering version of events in Madrid, would later in 1626 prove so disastrous to the reputation of the young king and his favorite. In 1624, however Bristol only protested his general innocence; if he had been more specific in protestations, he was so closely associated with Gondomar's party that he probably would have been discredited. The audience at the Globe and all loyal patriots of 1624 therefore cheered for their two heroes and celebrated the fact that "we, winner-like / Destroying, through heaven's power, what would destroy [us]."

The Spanish ambassador was understandably anxious to suppress the play, and Conway soon relayed to the Privy Council James's order to suppress it. The players were all duly summoned before the Council which ordered them to place bonds for their future conduct, and Middleton, after a period in hiding, was briefly imprisoned. These actions can be seen, as Ruigh remarked, as one of a king "careful . . . to avoid offense" to Spain. But other considerations modify this interpretation. *A Game at Chess* was by contemporary standards outrageous; it was in Lord Haughton's judgment a "foule iniury to Spayn, [and] no great honor to England." Yet in spite of Coloma's repeated protests against the scandal, James, who was with Charles and Buckingham only forty miles away, took his time in suppressing it. Meanwhile, the King's Men "make haye while the Sunn shyneth, acting it everyday without any intermition."[117] The *cognoscenti* of London inferred, as Woolley did, from the Court's delay and from the approval of the Master of the Revels, Sir Henry Herbert, that the play could not have been presented "with out leave from the higher powers I meane the Prince and Duke if not from the King for they were all loth to have it forbidden and by reporte laught hartely at it." And when punishment finally came, contemporaries were amazed, not

---

[116] *Ibid.*, V.iii.168–70 and 216–19.
[117] Ruigh, p. 386; Clare to Somerset, 2 August 1624, *Holles Letters*, II, p. 285; and Woolley to Trumbull, 11 August 1624, Trumbull MSS, XLVIII/135.

because James intervened, but rather because he intervened so mildly. Woolley rightly assured Trumbull that "had so much ben donne the last yeare, they had every one been hanged for it." Coloma himself certainly noted the contrast between 1623 and 1624, and, whatever James's motives in the affair may have been, the Spanish ambassador concluded from the play that "nothing else but war is to be expected from these people."[118] That indeed seems to have been the point of the play. *A Game at Chess* quite simply was a public celebration of the radical reformation, the "blessed revolution" that had taken place in England.

[118] Woolley to Trumbull, 6 and 20 August 1624, Trumbull MSS, XLVIII/134 and 136; and Coloma to Olivares, 10 August 1624, Wilson and Turner, "The Spanish Protest against 'A Game at Chess'," pp. 476–82.

CONCLUSION

The buoyant mood over the summer of 1624, unfortunately for England, was to prove all too fleeting. By the end of the year, the French marriage alliance, Mansfelt's expedition, the siege of Breda and Soubise's revolt would all vastly complicate the situation which appeared so clear-cut and promising only a few months earlier. Sounds of popular jubilation which had regularly filled the streets of London in the months after Charles's return subsequently vanished except for a brief echo on the passage of the Petition of Right in 1628. It is nevertheless important that the gloom on either side of 1623–4 is not allowed to obscure completely the euphoria and high hopes of the "blessed revolution." If we ignore this hiatus in the general pattern of the decade, we are also apt to ignore vital evidence about the eventual failure of the war and about the role of Parliament.

A broad analysis of England's road to intervention in the continental war produces results markedly different from those which Russell and Lockyer have advanced. Although a survey of contemporary views can yield only impressionistic answers, the impression that emerges from the evidence of the early 1620s is that there was widespread interest in the European war and considerable enthusiasm for English intervention. Admittedly the growing number of bellicose statements which reached a crescendo in 1624 could have been simply as another propaganda campaign orchestrated from Whitehall; thus in this view Drs. Gooch and Lushington in 1624 were martyrs for the cause of free speech just as Drs. Everard and Hall had been a year earlier. Yet while the earlier campaign for peace clearly had royal encouragement, the other in favor of war did not; University officials who rebuked Lushington were reportedly concerned about offending a sitting Parliament, not James.[1] More importantly, while aristocratic "Patriots" approved of the campaign for intervention, so too did a sizeable number of other Englishmen. In

---

[1] Thomas Lushington, *The Resurrection of our Savior Vindicated* (London, 1741), pp. vi–vii.

309

contrast neither Lushington nor Gooch ever became popular heroes, and neither of their celebrated outbursts elicited spontaneous support.

The marked lack of popular support for the continuation of the Jacobean peace in a time of continental religious war can also be clearly seen in the press. In spite of the wave of anti-war literature that washed over the realm in 1621–3, similar sentiments were practically non-existent in 1624 either over or under the counter. Of course it is possible that tight royal control of the press accounted for the sudden disappearance of meditations on the motto, *dulce bellum inexpertis*. On the other hand, as events in 1621–3 amply illustrated, the government was wholly unable to suppress arguments of which it did not approve; at the height of the Anglo-Spanish entente, Rogers's *A Strange Vineyard in Palaestrina* slipped into print, and a host of tracts and poems hostile the marriage circulated widely in the "underground" news network. There is an alternative explanation for the sudden evaporation of the anti-war position. *Dulce bellum inexpertis* was a royal adage, and those in 1624 who echoed it were dubbed, as Chaworth was, "a royalist."[2] Moreover the one constant in all contemporary anti-war literature was the rhetorical counter-attack against the apparently widespread interest in military intervention. Given these facts, it appears that the anti-war argument was a fairly artificial one which James largely foisted on his subjects. It follows therefore that once strong royal support for this unpopular position ceased, as it did in 1624, the pacifist position would suffer a swift eclipse. Furthermore it should be remembered that *the* option to neutrality was intervention; in spite of the best efforts of Gooch and Chaworth, most Englishmen saw no other alternative to a Spanish peace than a Spanish war. As Phelips's country gentleman observed, "no maryage, no peace."[3] Hence the widespread rejection of *dulce bellum inexpertis* would seem to indicate the desire for intervention, not neutrality. In short, Englishmen by and large did not have to be dragged into the middle of a continental war; rather they seemed to want to be there.

This interpretation finds support from parliamentary evidence. After the debacle of the 1621 session, MPs were understandably apt to err on the side of caution, and the inclination to caution was further reinforced in 1624 by the knowledge that another outburst of unwarranted enthusiasm would only seal the Anglo-Spanish entente and perhaps the fate of Parliament. Given this background, the MPs cannot justly be described as dragging their feet in discussing foreign policy and supply; rather they were proceeding with all deliberate speed and following the lead of royal officials. Nor can the parliamentary interest in religious matters be considered a means of avoiding

---

[2] *The Loseley Manuscripts*, p. 482.
[3] "A Discourse," Somerset RO, DD/Ph 227/16.

unpleasant financial discussions. Contemporary religious doctrine held that secular measures were likely to fail without the appropriate religious preliminaries; "strike your Covenant then with the Lord," Alexander Leighton advised the 1624 session, "and your warre shall surely prosper."[4] After all, the cry, "Jove principium," was another of James's favorite mottos, and not surprisingly the 1624 session's earlier obsession with religious questions apparently had the full support of the "Patriots," if not the king himself. To be sure, a good case can be made that the halting debates on the "war likely to ensue" are evidence of a lukewarm interest in the war. But this argument ultimately is not particularly persuasive since it ignores the fact that a well-connected and coordinated body of influential courtiers and *tribuni plebis* consistently shepherded the debates away from a full discussion. Indeed so successful was this tactic that it is now very difficult, if not impossible, to tell whether the critics of the war coalition – men such as Savile, More, Seymour and Alford – were actually against any involvement *per se* or whether they simply wanted more information on the planned war. Thus, the same logic which holds MPs to have been indifferent to the war must also regard the "Patriots," the very men responsible for the peculiar debates, as lukewarm.

When considering the question of parliamentary interest in the war, it is worth remembering that the best evidence is the 1624 subsidy bill itself. Given that MPs were addicted to precedents and given that the debates on supply flew in the face of well-established Elizabethan precedents, it is remarkable that the Commons voted any money at all. And yet the MPs approved the largest number of subsidies and fifteenths ever collected in one year. This fact alone reveals a great deal about the interest of a majority of the House. If the Parliament-men were actually lukewarm warriors, the unusual circumstances in which the subsidy bill was presented afforded them ample opportunity to reveal their true colors and to reject the bill. Yet in fact the majority ignored impassioned pleas to do so and voted the largest annual levy ever awarded. Lockyer has argued that the MPs of the decade were decidedly neurotic; if they were in fact closet admirers of the adage, *dulce bellum inexpertis*, and if they voted nonetheless for such massive taxation in support of a war, their actions in 1624 must stand as thoroughly convincing evidence of their mental ill-health.[5]

Generous though the 1624 Parliament was, the fact remains that it was not generous enough to underwrite the full expense of warfare. Thus it can be maintained that by voting inadequate funds, MPs hamstrung the war effort just as effectively as if they had flatly rejected the subsidy bill. Unfortunately

[4] Alexander Leighton, *Speculum Belli Sacri* (London, 1624), dedication to Parliament.
[5] Lockyer, *Buckingham*, p. 474.

this theory overlooks the fact that no one made a serious attempt to secure six subsidies and twelve fifteenths; if the sum voted was seriously inadequate for the tasks outlined, then no one stressed this deficiency to the House. It seems likely that this did not happen because the same Parliament-men were to re-assemble at Michaelmas to vote additional supply. In these circumstances, it is rather hard to see the Commons as actively sabotaging the war effort.

Consequently the present study suggests that scholars should react warily to the proposition that a majority of contemporaries and their parliamentary representatives were only marginally interested in the war. This is not to say that we should swing to the other extreme. Plainly there were contemporaries who had grave reservations about assailing the Habsburg colossus; at the outbreak of the Bohemian revolt, for example, one Englishman drew up a tract to illustrate that wars had always financially ruined English kings. Plainly there was in the Commons, as J. N. Ball has observed, a body of "northern men," Savile, Alford, Mallory and Ingram, who were concerned about the effect of an expanded European war on the already depressed cloth trade.[6] Yet these men were not the dominant groups in 1624; rather those in favor of intervention were. In short, it is possible to construct a case which places the blame for the abortive English war effort squarely before the door of the Chapel of St. Stephen. It should be understood, however, that such a case makes sense only if extraparliamentary evidence is largely ignored and if the parliamentary documents are subjected to only limited scrutiny.

This interpretation begs another question – if in 1624 there was widespread interest in the war, then who or what was responsible for the disasters of 1624–8 if not the fickle populace and the tightfisted provincial MPs? The answer can be given better in another book rather than a few paragraphs. Nevertheless, the central strands of an alternative explanation can be sketched out here. Well before military disasters piled up later in the decade, many of the difficulties which hobbled and eventually destroyed the war effort were visible in the "revolution" of 1624. Scott's "happie Parliament ... likely then to be the happiest Parliament that ever was" was obviously not the entry ramp onto the High Road to Civil War; it did, however, expose many of the problems which were to convulse the realm later in the decade.

The collapse of the war effort was in large part due to the disintegration of the remarkable symbiotic relationship that Charles and Buckingham had formed with Parliament in 1624. Contemporaries were understandably confused about who was controlling whom. At one point Chaworth was convinced that his ejection was an example of how "powrefull was the verie

---

[6] "The Princes Extremities," Folger Library, V.b.22; and J. N. Ball, "The Parliamentary Career of Sir John Eliot, 1624–1629" (Ph.D thesis, University of Cambridge, 1953), p. 37.

humor of the Duke in that House at that tyme." At another he noted that not even the duke's power could dissuade the Commons from insisting "beforehand to have all theyre desyres or give nothing."[7] But in actual fact, both parties worked together without one dominating the other. The drift apart occurred ironically in part because the prince got on so well with the Commons. Trying though the new Parliament undoubtedly had been, Charles can only have ended the session quite pleased with himself and Parliament. While MPs had shifted from a buoyant optimism in 1621 to a more wary caution in 1624, Charles had moved in the opposite direction; the prince, who had been deeply suspicious of parliamentary intentions in the earlier session, had eventually become more enchanted with the notion of being the parliamentary prince. Therefore, once the session broke up, and as the prince and the duke concentrated on the difficult task of guiding James into war, they understandably assumed they had Parliament under relative control. Dr. Ball rightly noted that the overall parliamentary success of Charles and Buckingham "created the illusion that Parliament would prove manageable," and this illusion developed precisely when more careful observers of Parliament would have advised the most sensitivity towards the attitude of the Commons.[8]

Inijosa and Coloma only encouraged this drift apart. Although Buckingham eventually weathered the Spanish counter-attack in May, he did so only after a great deal of anxiety. The envoys had come uncomfortably close to reality, as can be seen in a letter which the duke wrote to James during his convalescence. Although he disingenuously thanked James for having "no consete of my popularitie . . . in the upper and loer howse of parlement," Buckingham spent most of the long letter attempting to clear himself from the charge of disloyalty. In his defense he offered an unusual definition of "popularitie"; "were not onelie all your people but all the world besids sett together on one side, and you alone on the other, I should to obey and please you displease nay despise all them, and this shallbe ever my popularitie."[9] This peculiar definition in some ways accounts for Buckingham's actions in the last months of James's life and for the drift away from his close relation with parliamentary leaders. Notwithstanding his insistence that this definition had always guided his actions, Inijosa and Coloma had plainly caught him out in the public pursuit of a less flattering definition of popularity. To compensate he distanced himself a little from his "popular" relationship with Parliament.

---

[7] *The Loseley Manuscripts*, p. 482; and Chaworth to Trumbull, 8 April 1624, Trumbull Add. MSS XVIII, unfoliated.
[8] Ball, "Sir John Eliot," p. 68.
[9] Buckingham to James, [May 1624], NLS, Denmilne MSS 33.1.7, no. 88.

The assumption about Parliament's tractability and the lack of attention to parliamentary sensibilities were to cost Charles and the duke dearly in the 1625 and 1626 sessions. The Parliament of 1624 reveals a major institutional difficulty in the way of a successful war effort. The management of the session almost completely absorbed the government, and yet the Crown always had serious problems handling more than one important matter at a time. Indeed Derek Hirst concluded the government was "incapable of running a war and the country at the same time."[10] Parliament can easily be added to this list. In 1625 and 1626 Charles and Buckingham came to understand full well an awkward puzzle: in order to fight a war, parliamentary assistance was absolutely essential, and yet during a war, the government found it very difficult to dote on Parliament and so to ensure the requisite subsidies. In this situation, the relationship they had formed with parliamentary leaders in 1624 would have been invaluable in solving this puzzle – if they had not for various reasons distanced themselves from the old coalition of 1624.

Charles and the duke consequently were uncomfortably alone when they discovered that their most formidable opponent was not Spanish arms but rather popular beliefs which they had fostered in the happier days of 1624. One of the most crippling of these in which they found themselves entangled concerned Elizabeth I. When the continental crisis first developed, it was only natural that many Englishmen should search the 1580s and 1590s for answers, and what they tended to find was the epic of Gloriana, not the often somber history of Queen Elizabeth. Through the lenses of the Golden Legend, virtue and nobility seemed to have been more responsible for her victories than hard work and luck. Likewise her failures and less generous actions were politely forgotten. The Elizabethan strategy was not an inherent disadvantage for Charles and Buckingham; it was a logical and effective means of exerting English power. But the Elizabethan legend set very high, if not impossible, standards for her later admirers to equal. Prior to the French war of 1627, Charles had not done too badly when set against Elizabeth; compared with Gloriana, however, he was a pathetic failure. Even if Charles and Buckingham managed to fight clear of the myth, they would still have to disabuse the nation of these widespread notions. Instead they actively cultivated the memory of these Elizabethan glories, against which it was only natural to measure them.

Charles's father also proved as much of a liability as his celebrated cousin. One of the most "revolutionary" events of 1624 had been Charles's emergence from under James's shadow. Earlier, in spite of his pro-Palatine sympathies, the prince's "chief endeavour" reportedly had been "to disclose no other aim than to second the king . . . to stand habitually at his side . . . and

---

[10] Derek Hirst, "The Privy Council and the Problem of Enforcement in the 1620s," p. 55.

not to move except as his father does." But after the 1624 session, it was obvious to all the continent that Charles was no longer the dutifully obedient son. Indeed in 1624 the earlier situation at times appeared reversed; it seemed that the prince with Buckingham's help could eventually cajole James into doing almost anything. On the other hand, to concur with Dr. Turner in 1626 that the duke was "the causa generalissima," the "Mother" of all miseries, would to be consign James to premature burial.[11] Until his final illness he remained vigorous; late in 1624 Woolley remarked that James "lookes as well as I have seene him doe in many yeares." In fact, given Charles's crippling fall from a galloping horse in September 1624 and Buckingham's periodic relapses, it is at least arguable that any of the three men could have gone first.[12] Confirmation of James's vigor and willfulness can be easily found in the final year of his life. To cite only a few major examples, James was largely responsible for the decision to press on with the French match even after terms reached uncomfortable levels; he ensured that Mansfelt's expedition never served any useful purpose; and he publicly offered Louis XIII English ships to attack the Huguenots.[13]

Given these facts, it is safe to say that if Charles and Buckingham had had a free hand in organizing the first phase of the war, they would have been able to present Parliament in 1625 with a different variety of a war than they were in fact able to do. This is not to overlook Buckingham's talent for the mal-adroit and to say that their plans would necessarily have been more success-ful. Yet given the nature of their strategic plans earlier in 1624, they certainly would not have assumed heavy continental commitments while the fleet rotted at anchor. Moreover it should not be forgotten that King James was scarcely warm before King Charles shifted to a foreign heading more con-sistent with the implicit agreements reached in 1624.[14]

Simon Adams has maintained that Buckingham in 1624 was insincere in his dealings with Parliament; and yet Roger Lockyer has argued that Buckingham "always looked back to what in retrospect seemed to be the golden days of 1624."[15] They are both in a sense correct, and the catalyst reconciling these two irreconcilable positions is James himself. Buckingham

---

[11] Lando to the Doge and Senate, 20 January 1620, *CSPV*, XVI, p. 151; and 11 March 1626, Whitlocke Diary, Cambridge University Library, MSS, Dd, 12–20, fo. 37.
[12] Woolley to Trumbull, 25 November 1624, Trumbull MSS, XLVIII/152; and for Charles's fall, see same to same, 20 September 1624, Trumbull MSS, XLVIII/140.
[13] On the French match, see Thomas Cogswell, "Crown, Parliament and War, 1623–1625" (Ph.D. thesis, Washington University, 1983), pp. 375–535; on Mansfelt, see Conway to Carleton, 4 and 21 March 1625, SP 84/126/15 and 68; and on the loan ships, see Cogswell, "Foreign Policy and Parliament: the Case of La Rochelle, 1625–1626," *EHR* XCIX (1984), pp. 249–50.
[14] Cogswell, "Foreign Policy and Parliament," pp. 243–9.
[15] Lockyer, *Buckingham*, p. 467; and Adams, "Foreign Policy and Parliaments," pp. 170–1.

and his creatures plainly wanted what was essentially a "blue water" policy for England, and under pressure they told the Commons as much in several speeches. Yet having promised one thing in 1624, they could only present quite another in 1625. The duke's insincerity, however, was more apparent than real. It should not be forgotten that the emerging foreign conflict was not simply that of Charles and Buckingham; it was James's as well. If there was to be a war, the king understandably felt it would be on his terms. The result was Mansfelt, the Danish subsidy, the loan ships and the French match. And yet Buckingham had also given out in 1624 that he could control James; thus these policies were perceived as the exclusive responsibility of Turner's "causa generalissima." To some, the potential for disaster inherent in Buckingham's confidence about James was already apparent in 1624. After noting the sizeable discrepancy between the duke's promises and later events, Tillières warned Carlisle that such assurances could backfire and destroy the favorite's credibility. Carlisle's explanation revealed much about the tense position in which Buckingham found himself during the 1624 Parliament; the earl confessed that "l'excess de l'affection l'avoit transporte a me dire des choses pour assuree qu'il tenoir encore pour incertaines."[16] Similar assurances about uncertainties with Parliament-men ensured that he would later find it very difficult to refute Dr. Turner.

Any politician can testify to the dangers of a "credibility gap," but for Buckingham, a man whom many in 1625–6 felt they knew all too well, the danger was especially acute. Russell has proposed a model for the 1620s in which the political temperature steadily mounted under the pressure of war. Yet an analysis of the political, and not simply the parliamentary, history of the decade reveals the fundamental difficulty in seeing a progression from consensus to confrontation. Instead of one "peak" of dissatisfaction and polarization, there were two, one in 1623 and the other in 1628. Thus because Russell's model is tied to his concern about the domestic burden of warfare, he perhaps understandably underestimated the earlier crisis which the lack of warfare caused. He also underestimated the extent to which contemporaries in 1621–3 reviled Buckingham and his "kindred" as Spanish stooges. Admittedly Buckingham reversed this image in the following year by emerging as a Protestant warrior, but he remained a political leopard who had attempted to change his ideological spots. It was only natural therefore that his earlier image quickly revived as the war effort ran into difficulties. After the Cadiz misadventure, for example, one poet begged the Spaniards not to avenge the insult "since here at home doe staye, worse enemyes unto

---

[16] Tillières to Puysieux, 31 December 1623, PRO 31/3/58, fo. 2. The ambassador also discussed this problem with Charles; see his dispatch of 17 January 1624, PRO 31/3/58, fo. 15.

us." In case his audience missed the point, the poet reiterated the plea that "Spayne lett your roodes alone / Wee have enough to whip us of our one [own]."[17] Quite clearly, by 1626, some Englishmen came to perceive the old crypto-Spaniard of 1622–3 at the helm of the State.

The development of Wither's "false Patriot" might well not have wrecked the war effort if there had been more aristocratic "Patriots" alive in 1626 to separate Buckingham from the war effort. In the year after the 1624 session, the deaths of Belfast, Nottingham and Zouche depleted the ranks of Elizabethan veterans; among the "grandees" the demise of Hamilton and the brothers Lennox left Pembroke alone; and two of the more prominent warrior-earls, Southampton and Oxford died as they would have wanted, very close if not on the field of battle. Well might the Countess of Bedford lament that Pembroke was "the only honest harted man imployed that I know now left to God and his countrie."[18] After such a decimation, the remaining pro-war advocates such as Pembroke and Warwick almost had to work with hispanophiles such as Williams, Bristol and Arundel, men who would not have mourned to see the war vanish with Buckingham. Consequently it proved impossible to remove Buckingham without damaging the war effort, and the duke's "success" in remaining in power ensured that he and the war effort would die together.

How did the Parliament-men react to these changes? For Russell the answer is readily apparent; they had never been particularly interested in the war in the first place, and certainly by the summer of 1625, as the pressure of war began to be felt in the localities and in the pocketbooks, it was abundantly clear that "the House of Commons was against the war."[19] Fiscal considerations were obviously involved in the dramatic transformation of popular sentiments in 1625–6, but at this date they cannot account for a shift of this magnitude. The financial burden rested in these years with comparative ease, and apart from some coastal counties, the rest of the realm had yet to host to large military expeditions and to experience the horrors of war firsthand. Thus, while billeting and taxation explain a great deal about the mood in 1628, they cannot be pressed into service for 1625–6 with any conviction.

An alternative explanation is that Parliament-men and their constituents were distressed, not with the domestic burden of *a* war, but rather *the* war that Buckingham presented them. Although parliamentary views on the war were only fitfully articulated in 1624, an implicit understanding about a "blue water" strategy had emerged, and it was this understanding that the

---

[17] "Vox Britanniae ad Hispaniae 1626," *Trevelyan Papers* (London, 1872), III, p. 171.
[18] Bedford to Lady Cornwallis, 23 March 1625, *Cornwallis Letters*, p. 119.
[19] Russell, *Parliaments*, p. 259.

duke had allegedly disregarded. This divergence between what Buckingham said and what he did shook public confidence in his ability to manage the war. Russell's reluctance to accord this popular and parliamentary dismay its full significance represents a critical flaw in his analysis. He continually refers to the war and yet never defines this conflict. The danger of this omission can be seen in his comment that "even if Buckingham had been a commander on the scale of Gustavus Adolphus, he could not have mustered an effective military effort on the money available to him."[20] Any contemporary would have immediately spotted the problem; the duke's parliamentary addresses in 1624 and 1625 gave no indication of a desire to become the Lion of the West; rather he and many of his auditors had their eyes on the Atlantic and dreamed of equalling Drake and Essex. Without a distinction between the kind of campaigns England might pursue, Russell has understandable difficulties explaining the collapse of the war; without this distinction, the growing parliamentary turbulence can only appear as the revolt of small-minded tax-payers reluctant to shoulder the burden of war.

Aggrieved taxpayers of course were part of the problem in the troubled parliamentary sessions later in the decade, but they should not be seen merely as taxpayers simply upset with the idea of paying taxes. They also seem to have been distressed with the idea of taxes misspent. Unlike their descendants, early-seventeenth-century Englishmen did not possess a complex financial system to spread out the costs of warfare, and they simply could not afford to break their neighbors' windows with guineas. In 1621 and 1624, Parliament had offered up five subsidies and three fifteenths, nearly £400,000, to assist Frederick and Elizabeth, and justifiably MPs expected something dramatic and preferably noisy for their money. Yet in spite of their generosity, "nothing hath bene done," Seymour lamented in 1625, "wee know not our enemy." The only palpable result was that "wee have set upon and consumed our own people."[21]

The problems with the war effort of the 1620s therefore do not appear to be those "of a nation reluctantly at war." The problems instead were those of a people frustrated in their desire for war, and they with some justice blamed Charles for their frustration. For some, the scars of this disappointment ran deep. In the 1630s, knowing chaplains among the English regiments in Dutch service quietly deleted the customary prayers for the king, and those preachers who did not, risked having their congregation walk out. Col. Charles Morgan, for example, a prominent veteran of the 1620s, refused to sit through these prayers.[22] And in 1641, at the beginning of the Grand

---

[20] Russell, *Parliaments*, p. 81.
[21] 12 August 1625, *Debates in the House of Commons in 1625* (London, 1873), p. 78.
[22] K. L. Sprunger, *Dutch Puritanism* (Leiden, 1982), pp. 303–4.

Remonstrance, the MPs recalled with some considerable indignation that the government had failed to fulfill its promises of a "blue water" policy and a West Indian expedition made seventeen years earlier in the Parliament of 1624.[23] These do not sound like men who were reluctantly dragged into war in the 1620s. Hence pending further research, the blame for the disastrous war effort should be placed in Whitehall, not Westminster.

If Parliament did not stab Charles and his war in the back, what of Parliament itself? Directly related to the question of popular and parliamentary interest in the war is the question of Parliament's role in the state. Professor Russell has launched a sustained attack on the notion that "Parliament was a power in the State and that it was divided into government and opposition supporters."[24] If he meant to force us to think again about the nature of early-seventeenth-century politics, he has succeeded brilliantly. On the other hand, the speed with which his queries have been almost wholly absorbed into more general accounts of the period demands a careful re-appraisal of his theories.[25]

Early-seventeenth-century Parliaments certainly did not operate on the Gladstonian model of an organized "government" and "opposition." This is in some ways less than surprising since seventeenth-century Englishmen obviously did not organize themselves into nineteenth-century parties. Nevertheless, given the tendency of some earlier historians to employ such terms, Russell's point is well taken. Yet the evidence from the 1624 session suggests that it would be equally wrong to go to the opposite extreme and to atomize politics into its Namierian parts. In studying the 1614 session, T. L. Moir complained that courtiers and officials "should have formed a coherent group in the House"; in 1624, however, there was no need for this lament. Russell is right in saying that if the Court is taken to mean everyone who held major and minor posts across the realm, it becomes impossible to employ terms such as "court" and "country." Yet contemporaries do not seem to have used such a broad definition; much closer to contemporary usage is Christopher Thompson's model of a "political" Court, those officials and courtiers closely associated with the dominant figure at Court.[26] And in 1624,

---

[23] Article 3 of the Grand Remonstrance, printed in Rushworth, *Historical Collections*, III, pp. 439–40. See also Simon Adams, "Spain or the Netherlands?," *Before the Civil War*, pp. 79 and 101.

[24] Russell, "FH," p. 4.

[25] Compare for example the first edition (1966) of *The Stuart Constitution*, edited by J. P. Kenyon, with the second edition (1985).

[26] T. L. Moir, *The Addled Parliament of 1614* (Oxford, 1958), p. 167; Russell, "FH," p. 4; and Christopher Thompson, "The Divided Leadership of the House of Commons in 1629," *Faction and Parliament*, pp. 245–84 and especially 277.

at least on the major issues of foreign policy and supply, the "political" Court plainly operated as a recognizable group.

To be sure, the antithesis of the "Court" is a little harder to locate in 1624 – and with good reason. John Morrill's division of the "country" into two wings, the "official" and the "pure," is very useful in the 1630s when both operated together.[27] In 1624, however, the "blessed revolution" meant that most of the "official" country had just come in out of the political wilderness. Consequently with the *tribuni plebis* no longer in their customary position, the parliamentary "country" is not as easy to spot in 1624 as it is in the other sessions of the decade. And yet the "defection" of these leading MPs did not lessen the appeal of "country" ideals for many backbenchers. All it took to rivet the attention of some backwoods MPs was for the ambitious or the dedicated to voice the old "localist" concerns about taxation, the electorate and the prodigal government. The 1624 session thus reveals that the important element in the parliamentary "country" was not the leading personnel; rather it was a certain style of rhetoric. In 1624, thanks to the willingness of Savile, Alford and Seymour to attempt to equal earlier performances of Coke, Phelips and Sandys, MPs hear a good deal of "country" rhetoric. And as the intense debates over the subsidy illustrate, some Parliament-men responded to the old "localist" themes.

The frequency with which the 1624 Parliament witnessed confrontations between the "political" court and country should not be too surprising; for while faction tells much about early-seventeenth-century politics, it does not tell all. Johann Sommerville has recently reminded us that "if we distinguish too rigidly between ideas and interests we are in danger of missing the point that interests themselves are shaped by ideas."[28] His cautionary statement finds several telling illustrations in the 1624 session. Some, if not many, of those who cooperated with Buckingham had little "interest" to do so. As the favorite attempted to change ideological horses in mid-stream, the "grandees" had ample opportunity and reason to discredit him. They did not do so, however, in part because he had suddenly espoused ideas which they had consistently advocated. Yet the best example of the importance of ideas was the quarrel within the Villiers family in 1624. The strongest bound within factional politics is that of kinship. In 1623, Middlesex, as befitted one who had married into the "kindred," was villified with the rest of Buckingham's relations. Yet in the following year, the favorite ruined his own kinsmen as Cranfield later complained through "Cruell and unjust," "inhumane dealing." Historians who know all too well about Buckingham's role in Middlesex's disgrace tend to forget that the favorite had destroyed a

[27] John Morrill, *The Revolt of the Provinces* (New York, 1980), pp. 14–18.
[28] Johann Sommerville, *Politics and Ideology in England, 1603–1640* (London, 1986), p. 232.

relative; contemporaries, however, did not. Sterrell, for example, could scarcely believe that Buckingham would assail "a Creature of his owne made of nought and married to his stock."[29] And this remarkable action can really only be explained as a conflict of ideas between Middlesex and Buckingham.

Whether or not some variety of "court" and "country," however defined, describes action on the floor of the House, a much more fundamental question remains: was Parliament actually "powerless" and not "a Great power in the State"? Russell has argued as much, and he is surely right to stress that Parliament was not in continuous existence before the Civil War. It should not be forgotten, however, that in 1624 this mere "event" was perfectly capable of paralyzing the government and indeed all other political activity, and of attracting widespread international attention. Likewise this "event" could force a reversal of roles in which Privy Councillors publicly yielded to minor barristers and influential courtiers curried favor with country gentlemen. This reversal of course was quite understandable. Parliament alone proved able to break the Spanish hold on England, and it alone could lend credibility to the projects of a comparatively impotent monarch. In short the evidence from 1624 begs an obvious question; if Parliament was not a great power in the State in 1624, who or what was? While both king and Council had vast powers, both real or potential, neither was capable of resolving the diplomatic log-jam left in the wake of the abortive Anglo-Spanish dynastic alliance. Certainly neither could produce sums of money running into six figures. In these circumstances, one would like to know the definition of "great." Russell's test of greatness is the ability of Parliament to tie redress of grievances to supply. In 1624, as we have seen, Parliament had little trouble passing Russell's test with flying colors. It was painfully clear that the only legislation the Crown really wanted was the subsidy bill, and from this one overriding desire flowed a flood of concessions. As MPs returned home, they may have grumbled about the manner in which the House approved the terms of the subsidy bill, but thanks to a subsidy bill which crawled through the Commons, Parliament-men had a good deal to take their minds off this issue. They returned with pockets bulging with something for nearly everyone from the inveterate localist to the godly concerned about the foreign brethren. As a classic demonstration of the weakness of a powerless event, the Parliament of 1624 has few rivals.

In recent years, as Russell's thesis has carried almost all before it, some scholars have called for the abandonment of the traditional obsession with parliamentary history. Dr. Sharpe has called for closer attention to the Court

---

[29] Middlesex to Herman [abstracts], 29 April and 1 May 1626, Kent Archive Office, Sackville MSS, unnumbered Cranfield Papers; and Chaworth to Trumbull, 8 April 1624, Trumbull Add. MSS, XVII/unfoliated.

factions and the Council, while Sir Geoffrey Elton has wondered aloud if "the institution . . . ever really mattered all that much." The present study can only endorse such calls for further detailed studies of the political world outside Westminster; after all, the guiding maxim of this book has been Russell's observation that "Parliamentary history should be studied in context, and in proportion, with non-Parliamentary history."[30] Yet one can only wonder if further contextual studies will reveal another source of power in wartime which was greater than Parliament. It may well be that, as Dr. Sharpe has argued, "a return to the drawing board, rather than another repair of the old canvas" is in order. Yet if we do decide to begin again with a new canvas, a close study of 1624 suggests that the Palace of Westminster should be placed in the central foreground. Quite clearly, the institution was only inter-mittently in session; and it contained no organized Opposition bent on seizing power. Nevertheless, Parliament remained essential when the nearly bankrupt early Stuart monarchs wanted to do something other than amuse themselves at Court. As Secretary Conway acknowledged, "the Kinges of England having noe other sure or good wayes to ayde themselves must doe it by Parleament."[31]

---

[30] Kevin Sharpe, "Crown, Parliament and Locality: Government and Communication in Early Stuart England," *EHR* CI (1986), p. 1, and *Before the English Civil War*, p. 182; G. R. Elton, *The Parliament of England* (Cambridge, 1986), p. ix, and Conrad Russell, "The Nature of a Parliament in Early Stuart England," *Before the Civil War*, p. 152.

[31] Conway to Aston, 30 January 1624, SP 94/29/191v; and Kevin Sharpe, "Preface," *Faction and Parliament*, p.v.

A NOTE ON SOURCES

It is hoped that the goal of assembling the fullest possible portrait of the contemporary political system in a period of crisis justifies this study's comparatively narrow focus. While the present work is far from comprehensive as any tyro in the field will quickly note, it does employ a number of sources, some "canonical" and others more obscure, which deserve some comment.

The three parliamentary chapters would doubtless not have been written without the indefatigable labors of the Yale Center for Parliamentary History. I was fortunate enough to consult first the typescripts of the 1624 diaries which Hartley Simpson prepared several decades ago and then the more exact editions which Robert Ruigh and Mark Kennedy have recently produced. It is hoped that the full critical editions of these diaries will be published as soon as possible. Until that time scholars can find quite ample solace in the authoritative editions of the Holles and Rich diaries which Christopher Thompson has just published.[1] It is only to avoid the problem of citing one diary in its original language and another in a modernized text that I have not cited from Thompson's editions. Yet I must record my profound debt to his painstaking labors which have done much to guide me on the floor of the Commons.

As befits a work whose earliest form was as a diplomatic study, it began in Chancery Lane among the State Papers Foreign. The absolute mass of the contemporary documents held in this series is doubtless unequalled. Admittedly the bulk of these documents chronicle the minutiae of diplomacy; nevertheless it would be a serious error for the scholar of domestic politics to write them off as ambassadorial shoptalk. For the entire decade the chief concerns of the monarch and many of his subjects were foreign, and while Gardiner, Adams and Lockyer can offer guidance in foreign policy, there currently is no better way to understand these events than to work through the relevant State Papers Foreign. This series also provides a fascinating view

---

[1] *The Holles Account of Proceedings in the House of Commons in 1624*, transcribed by Christopher Thompson (Orsett, Essex, 1986); and *The Rich Account of Proceedings in the House of Commons in 1624*, transcribed by Christopher Thompson (Orsett, Essex, 1986).

of the government's perceptions of domestic politics. English envoys abroad frequently reacted to news from home, and they inevitably responded to parliamentary developments. Even more consistent and enthralling are the regular letters which the Secretaries of State wrote for the agents in the field. Envoys could not be expected to function without some clear idea of the larger political and diplomatic picture, and to meet this need for information the Secretaries roughly every month had to compose the latest intelligence report from Whitehall. The present study draws a great deal from these periodic *tours d'horizon*, which deserve much more attention than they have hitherto received.

Gleanings from State Papers Foreign notwithstanding, the basic source for the study of domestic politics remains the contemporary newsletters. This study relies on the "canonical" newsletter writers, Chamberlain, Kellie, Mead, and, thanks to the recent work of P. R. Seddon, the Earl of Clare. Yet it has also sought to find other underutilized sources in the British Library, country record offices, and in the case of the Sterrell letters, in the State Archives in Vienna. Although C. H. Carter discussed the Sterrell correspondence at some length over two decades ago, Dr. David Hebb deserves credit for tracking down the original documents and for discovering their relevance to the mid-1620s.[2]

As the glance at the footnotes will reveal, the most dazzling find came from tracking down a reference in Roger Lockyer's study of the duke. The path led to the Berkshire Record Office and John Castle's letters to William Trumbull, the longtime resident agent in Brussels and surely the longest serving career diplomat in early Stuart England to retire without even a knighthood. Castle's letters are remarkable enough in themselves, yet they soon led to the equally remarkable series of letters from John Beaulieu and John Woolley. The intelligence, if not the volume, of their reportage is matched by the several dozen other correspondents in the Trumbull Alphabetical and Additional series which contained letters from the likes of George Abbot, Giles Mompesson, and George Chaworth. The final tally is several hundred detailed newsletters on the early 1620s alone. Lockyer's find, although largely unheralded, must now supercede the venerable Chamberlain letters as the basic starting place for any study of Jacobean England. In fact, the collection is so rich that in terms of signal blows to scholarship, Trumbull's recall to London in 1625 must rank with the fire in the Cottonian manuscripts and the destruction of the Irish Record Office.

Newsletters are invaluable in reconstructing the events of early-seventeenth-century England because the surviving papers of the leading

---

[2] C. H. Carter, *The Secret Diplomacy of the Habsburgs* (New York, 1964), pp. 153–67. I owe the information about the letters in the HHStA to the generosity of Dr. Hebb.

figures are very sparse, if they have survived at all. One of the major exceptions are those of Sir Robert Phelips deposited in the Somerset Record Office. Given Phelips's contemporary importance, it is surprising that almost no scholar, apart from local historians, has made systematic use of this archive. Admittedly the papers may not tell as much as we might want to know about many questions, but they do reveal an extraordinary picture of a leading Parliament-man, who belatedly deserves a full-scale analysis.

Perhaps the source most neglected by early-seventeenth-century political historians are the contemporary tracts and pamphlets. Johann Sommerville had reminded us that "pamphleteering and sermonising, just as much as participation in debate on the floor of the House of Commons, were political acts." And yet thanks to what Ann Hughes and Richard Cust have recently termed the scholarly "fetish with manuscript sources," these printed materials have often been left the almost exclusive domain of ecclesiastical historians. The present work suggests that political historians need to reclaim these materials. Censorship, both formal and informal, clearly was present, but it was not able to reduce all that issued from the press to a homogeneous level of pious platitudes. As has been seen, the press was the forum for a very lively debate on royal domestic and foreign policy, and for historians to ignore this literary discourse is for them to study English politics with one eye closed. As Sommerville rightly noted, "Parliamentary debates take on a new meaning when seen in the light of the wider intellectual life of Englishmen."[3] In addition, as we come to understand "the wider intellectual life" better, the tracts, which filled gentry libraries and initially appear no more than theological soporifics, become much more controversial and worthy of closer attention.

The contemporary taste for information was far from discriminating. Indeed a passion for doggerel political verse was as much a hallmark of seventeenth-century Englishmen as a taste for theological works. Until quite recently, however, this poetry has often been overlooked.[4] To be sure, much of this verse has all of the delicacy and literary merit of modern graffiti. Yet in the seventeenth century it was nonetheless a remarkable vehicle for the dissemination of political attitudes. The present study makes considerable use of these poems not as an accurate reflection of "popular opinion" but simply as a reflection of popular interest in politics. It is hoped that the reader of the late twentieth century will find this genre's frequent descents into scatology less offensive than his Victorian predecessors did.

[3] Sommerville, *Politics and Ideology if England, 1603–1640*, p. 4; and "Introduction," *Conflict in Early Stuart England*, ed. Ann Hughes and Richard Cust (London, 1989).

[4] For two notable exceptions to this general pattern, see Richard Cust, "News and Politics in Early Seventeenth Century England," *PP* CXI (1986), pp. 60–90; and Roger Lockyer, "An English Valido? Buckingham and James I," *For Veronica Wedgwood These*, pp. 45–58.

BIBLIOGRAPHY

MANUSCRIPT SOURCES

CENTRAL ARCHIVES

British Library
Additional Manuscripts
4181	Gerbier's Relation
4276	Vere Correspondence
5832	Poetical Commonplace Book
12,528	Crowe's Accountbook
18,597	Earle Diary, 1624
28,326	"High Way to Hedelburgh"
30,646	French Diplomatic Correspondence, 1624
33,446–7	Aston Correspondence
33,452	Aston Family Correspondence
33,935	Moreton Correspondence
34,727	Miscellaneous Correspondence
46,188	Essex Correspondence
46,191	Rich Diary, 1624

Egerton Manuscripts
784	Whiteway Diary
2595	Carlisle Correspondence

Harleian Manuscripts
189	Stuteville Correspondence
6383	Holles Diary, 1624
6987	Miscellaneous Correspondence

Lansdowne Manuscripts
498	1624 Seperates

Loan Manuscripts
23	Holme Hall Correspondence
29	Portland Letters

Stowe Manuscripts
176	Edmondes Correspondence

Public Record Office
State Papers Series
14	Domestic, James I
16	Domestic, Charles I

75	Denmark
77	Flanders
78	France
81	German States
84	Holland
92	Savoy
94	Spain
99	Venice
103	Treaties and Papers
PRO 31/3	Baschet's Transcripts
PRO C115	Scudamore Correspondence
N1	Salvetti Letters
N4	Starkey Letters

LOCAL ARCHIVES

Alnwick Castle
Northumberland Correspondence

Berkshire Record Office
Downshire Deposit,
Trumbull Alphabetical Series

I	Abbot Correspondence
VII	Beaulieu Correspondence
XVII	Carleton Correspondence
XVIII	Castle Correspondence
XIX	Chandler Correspondence
XXVI	J. Hamilton Correspondence
XXIX	Locke Correspondence
XXXIII	Nethersole Correspondence
XLVIII	Woolley Correspondence

Trumbull Additional Series
XIV, XV, XVI, XX, XXIV, and XXXVIII   Miscellaneous Correspondence

Bodleian Library, Oxford University
Additional Manuscripts

D 111	Fortescue Correspondence

Carte Manuscripts

30	Irish Correspondence

Dodsworth Manuscript

79	Poetical Commonplace Book

Firth Manuscripts

C 4	Essex Lieutenancy Book

Malone Manuscripts

23	Poetical Commonplace Book

Rawlinson Manuscripts

A 346	Scott Correspondence
B 151	1624 Parliamentary Seperates
D 1100	Holland Diary, 1624

Tanner Manuscripts
72–3   Miscellaneous Correspondence

Cambridge University Library
Dd, 12–20, 21 and 22   Whitelocke Diary, 1626

Chester Record Office
CR/63/2/19   Davenport Commonplace Book

Devon Record Office
ECA/Xi–60c   Exeter Corporation Archives

Eaton Hall
Grosvenor Manuscripts

Hampshire Record Office
44M69   Jervoise of Herriard Park Manuscripts

Hull Record Office
Corporation Letters

Inner Temple Library
Petyt Manuscripts

Kent Archive Office
Sackville MSS   Cranfield Correspondence

Longleat House
Whitelocke Manuscripts

Melbourne Hall
Coke Manuscripts

Northamptonshire Record Office
Cockayne Manuscripts
Isham of Langport Manuscripts
Fitzwilliam (Milton) Manuscripts
Finch Hatton Manuscripts   Pym Diary, 1624

National Library of Scotland
33.1   Denmilne Manuscripts
3134   Melros Manuscripts
1879   Prince Charles's Account Book, 1623

National Library of Wales
9059E   Wynn of Gwydir Manuscripts

Nottingham University Library
NeC 15,406   Holles Correspondence

Scottish Record Office
GD 406   Hamilton Correspondence
GD 24/1/825   Abercairny Manuscripts

Somerset Record Office
DD/Ph   Phelips Manuscripts

Warwick County Record Office
CR 2017   Fielding of Newnham Paddox Manuscripts
CR 136   Newdegate of Newbury Manuscripts

Westminster City Library, Archives
E3 and 23   Vestry Minutes, St. Margaret's

Wiltshire Record Office
Ailesbury Manuscripts   Hawarde Diary, 1624

FOREIGN ARCHIVES

Beinecke Library, Yale University
Osborn Manuscripts
b52   Phelips Commonplace Book
b55   Strangwayes of Dublin Commonplace Book
b197   Alston Poetical Commonplace Book

Folger Shakespeare Library
V.a.223   "Vox Spiritus"
V.b.22   "The Princes Extremities"
V.a.24   "In What Lamentable State"
V.a.43, 162, 257, 345; V.b.43; and X.d.232   Poetical Commonplace Books

Haus und Hof Staatsarchiv, Vienna
Belgian PC
Fasz. 59–61

Houghton Library, Harvard University
English 980   Spring Diary, 1624

Huntington Library
Hastings Correspondence

Massachusetts Historical Society, Boston
Winthorp Papers

Trinity College Dublin
708   Roe Correspondence
E.5.17   Grosvenor Diary, 1626

TRACTS

Adams, Thomas. *Eirenopolis*. London, 1622.
  The Barren Tree. London, 1623.
  The Temple. London, 1624.
Ailesbury, Thomas. *Paganism and Papisme Parallel'd*. London, 1623.
Anagramma Regis. London, 1625.
Aphorismes of State. Utrecht, 1624.
Aylett, Robert. *Thrifts Equipage*. London, 1622.
Bachiler, Samuel. *Miles Christianus*. Amsterdam, 1625.
Barnes, Thomas. *Needfull Helps*. London, 1624.
Barrell, Robert. *The Spirituall Architecture*. London, 1624.
Beard, Thomas. *Antichrist The Pope of Rome*. London, 1625.
Bedell, William. *The Copies of Certaine Letters*. London, 1624.
Brathwaite, Richard. *Whimzies*. London, 1631.
Breton, Nicholas. *A Mother's Blessing*. London, 1621.
A Briefe Information of the Affairs of the Palatinate. n.p., 1624.
A Briefe and True Relation of the Murther of Mr Thomas Scott. London, 1628.
Brinsley, John. *The True Watch*. London, 1606.
  The Second Part of the True Watch. London, 1607.
  The Third Part of the True Watch. London, 1622.
  The Fourth Part of the True Watch. London, 1624.
Buggs, Samuel. *David's Straits*. London, 1622.
Burton, Henry. *For God and King*. n.p., 1636.
  A Censure of Simonie. London, 1624.
Carleton, George. *A Remembrance*. London, 1624.
Carolus Redux. Oxford, 1623.
Crashaw, William. *Milke for Babes, or A North Country Catechisme*. London, 1622.
Certaine Reasons. n.p., 1624.
Certaine Sermons or Homilies. London, 1623.
C[larke], T[homas]. *The Popes Deadly Wound*. London, 1621.
Cockeram, Henry. *The English Dictionarie*. London, 1623.
Davies, John. *The Scourge of Folly*. London, 1611.
Dawe, Jacke. *Vox Graculi*. London, 1623.
Denison, John. *The Christians Care*. London, 1624.
  Foure Sermons. London, 1620.
A Dolefull Evensong. London, 1623.
Donne, Daniel. *A Sub-poena from the Star-Chamber of Heaven*. London, 1623.
Drake, Sir Francis. *The World Encompassed*. London, 1628.
DuMoulin, Pierre. *A Preparation to Suffer for the Gospel*. London, 1623.
DuVal, Michael. *Rosa Hispani-Anglica*. n.p. [1623?].
Earle, John. *Microcosmographie*. London, 1628.
Everard, John. *The Gospel-Treasury Opened*. London, 1657.
The Fatal Vesper. London, 1623.
G., H. *The Mirror of Maiestie*. London, 1619.
A Gagge for the Pope and the Iesuites. London, 1624.
Gainsford, Thomas. *The Secretaries Study*. London, 1616.
Gardiner, Richard. *A Sermon Preached at St. Maries, Oxford*. London, 1622.
Garrard, Edmund. *The Countrie Gentleman Moderator*. London, 1624.

Gataker, Thomas. *The Ioy of the Iust.* London, 1623.
  A Sparke toward the Kindling of Sorrow for Sion. London, 1621.
Gee, John. *The Foot out of the Snare.* London, 1624.
Gerard, John. *The Conquest of Jerusalem.* London, 1623.
Goodwin, George. *Babels Balm.* London, 1624.
Gratulatio Academiae Cantabrigiensis. Cambridge, 1623.
Gurney, Edmund. *The Romish Chaine.* London, 1624.
Hakluyt, Richard. *The Principall Navigations . . . of the English Nation.* London, 1598.
Hall, Joseph. *Characters of Vertues and Vices.* London, 1608.
  The True Peacemaker. London, 1624.
  The Works of Joseph Hall. London, 1634.
Harris, Robert. *Gods Goodness and Mercy.* London, 1622.
  Peters Enlargement. London, 1624.
Hayward, Sir John. *Christs Prayer Upon the Crosse.* London, 1623.
Hering, Thomas. *The Triumph of the Church.* London, 1624.
Higgons, Theophilus. *Mystical Babylon.* London, 1624.
The Interpreter. 1622.
The Ioyfull Returne of . . . Charles. London, 1623.
Isocrates. *Archidamus.* Translated by Thomas Barnes. London, 1624.
Jackson, Thomas. *The Raging Tempest Stilled.* London, 1623.
  Judah Must Into Captivitie. London, 1622.
James I. *Flores Regis.* London, 1627.
James, Robert [Thomas Lushington]. *The Resurrection Rescued.* London, 1659.
Jerome, Stephen. *Irelands Iubilee.* Dublin, 1624.
King, Henry. *An Exposition upon the Lords Prayer.* London, 1628.
Lawrence, John. *A Golden Trumpet.* London, 1624.
Leighton, Alexander. *Speculum Belli Sacri.* London, 1624.
Lushington, Thomas. *The Resurrection of our Saviour Vindicated.* London, 1741.
Mainwaring, Roger. *Religion and Allegiance.* London, 1627.
Markham, Francis. *Five Decades of Epistles of Warre.* London, 1622.
Markham, Gervase. *Honour in His Perfection.* London, 1624.
Mayer, John. *An Antidote Against Popery.* London, 1625.
Minsheu, John. *Pleasant and Delightful Dialogues in Spanish and English.* London, 1623.
Myriell, Thomas. *The Christians Comfort.* London, 1623.
Nichols, P. *Drake Revived.* London, 1626.
Overbury, Sir Thomas. *A Wife now the Widow.* London, 1614.
Perceval, Richard. *A Dictionnaire in Spanish and English.* London, 1623.
Petley, Elias. *The Royal Receipt.* London, 1623.
A Pill to Purge out Poperie, or A Catechisme. London, 1624.
Pond 1629: A New Almanacke. Cambridge, 1629.
Price, Daniel. *A Heartie Prayer in a Needfull Time.* London, 1625.
Prideaux, John. *Epheseus Backsliding.* London, 1621.
  Perez-Uzzah. Oxford, 1625.
  A Sermon Preached on the Fifth Day of October 1624. Oxford, 1625.
Primrose, Gilbert. *The Christian Mans Teares.* London, 1625.
  The Righteous Mans Fate. London, 1625.
A Prophesie of the Judgement Day. London, 1620.

Prosopopeia, or a Conference held at Angelo Castle. n.p. [1620?].
Purchas, Samuel. *The Kings Towre.* London, 1622.
R[awlinson], J[ohn]. *Lex Talionis.* London, 1621.
Reeves, Thomas. *Mephiboseths Hearts Ioy.* London, 1624.
[Reynolds, John.] S.R.N.I. *Votivae Angliae.* Utrecht, 1624.
   Vox Coeli. Elisium, 1624.
Rogers, Nehemiah. *A Strange Vineyard in Palaestrina.* London, 1623.
Rogers, Timothy. *The Roman Catharist.* London, 1621.
R[owlands], S[amuel]. *Good Newes and Bad Newes.* London, 1622.
S., G. *Sacrae Heptades.* n.p., 1625.
Sarpi, Paolo. *The History of the Quarrels of Pope Paul V.* London, 1625.
Saltonstall, Wye. *Picturae Loquentes.* London, 1635.
[Scott, Thomas.] *Aphorismes of State.* Utrecht, 1624.
   The Belgick Pismire. London, 1622
   The Belgick Soldier. Dort, 1624.
   Boarneges. Edinburgh [Utrecht?], 1624.
   Dignatus Dei. [Utrecht?] 1624.
   Englands Ioy, for Suppressing the Papists and Banishing the Priests and Iesuits.
      n.p., 1624.
   Robert Earle of Essex His Ghost. Paradise, 1624.
   The Second Part of Vox Populi. Goricom, 1624.
   Symmachia. Utrecht, 1624.
   Vox Dei. 1624.
   Vox Regis. London, 1624.
   The Workes of the Most Famous and Reverend Divine Mr. Thomas Scott. Utrecht,
      1624.
A Second Part of Spanish Practices. n.p., 1624.
The Second Tome of Homelyes. London, 1623.
Sheldon, Richard. *A Sermon Preached at Paules Crosse.* London, 1625.
The Spaniards Perpetuall Designes to an Universall Monarchie. n.p., 1624.
A Spanish Grammar. London, 1623.
Squire, John. *A Sermon on the Second Commandment.* London, 1624.
Stradling, Sir John. *Beati Pacifici.* London, 1623.
Symson, Patrick. *The Historie of the Church.* London, 1625.
Taylor, John. *Taylors Travels to Prague.* London [1620?].
   Prince Charles His Welcome From Spaine. London, 1623.
Taylor, Thomas. *A Mappe of Rome.* London, 1620.
   Two Sermons. London, 1624.
Texada, Ferdinando. *Texada Retextus.* London, 1623.
   Scritaimini Scripturas. London, 1624.
Thompson, Thomas. *Antichrist Arraigned.* London, 1618.
Tisdale, Robert. *Pax Vobis.* London, 1623.
Tom Tell-Troath. London, 1809.
Udny, Alexander. *A Golde Bell and A Pomgranate.* London, 1625.
Ussher, James. *An Answer to a Challenge.* London, 1624.
V[ase], R[obert]. *Jonahs Contestation.* London, 1625.
Vicars, John. *Englands Hallelu-jah.* London, 1631.
Wall, John. *The Watering of Apollos.* Oxford, 1625.
Warburton, George. *Melchizedech.* London, 1623.
Ward, Samuel. *A Peace-Offering to God.* London, 1623.

Webb, George. *Catalogus Protestantium*. London, 1624.
Webster, John. *Monuments of Honour*. London, 1624.
Wilkinson, Robert. *The Stripping of Joseph*. London, 1625.
Williams, John. *Great Britains Salomon*. London, 1625.
Wing, John. *The Saints Advantage*. London, 1623.
Wither, George. *Britain's Remembrancer*. London, 1628.
Worship, William. *Three Sermons*. London, 1625.
Wotton, Anthony. *Runne from Rome*. London, 1624.

PRINTED PRIMARY SOURCES

Acts of the Privy Council. Ed. John Roche Dascent. London, 1890.
Ayton, Sir Robert. *The English and Latin Poems*. Edinburgh, 1963.
Ball, Thomas. *The Life of the Renowned Doctor Preston*. Oxford, 1885.
The Buller Papers. n.p., 1899.
Cabala. London, 1654.
Calderwood, David. *History of the Church of Scotland*. 8 vols. Edinburgh, 1842.
Calendar of State Papers Domestic. Ed. M. A. E. Green, John Bruce, *et al*. 81 vols. London, 1857–1947.
Calendar of State Papers Ireland. Ed. C. W. Russell, J. P. Prendergast *et al*. 13 vols. (1603–70). London, 1870–1910.
Calendar of State Papers Venetian. Ed. H. F. Brown and A. B. Hinde. 28 vols. (1603–75). London, 1900–40.
Carew, Thomas. *The Poems*. Oxford, 1949.
Chamberlain, John. *The Letters of John Chamberlain*. Ed. N. E. McClure, Philadelphia, 1939.
Clarendon, Earl of. *History of the Rebellion*. Oxford, 1843.
Commons Debates 1621. Ed. W. Notestein. New Haven, 1935.
Commons Debates 1628. Ed. R. C. Johnson *et al*. New Haven, 1978.
Corbett, Richard. *The Poems*. Ed. J. A. W. Bennett and H. R. Trevor-Roper. Oxford, 1955.
The Private Correspondence of Lady Jane Cornwallis, 1613–1644. Ed. Lord Braybrooke. London, 1842.
Corps Universel Diplomatique. Ed. J. Dumont. Amsterdam, 1728.
Cosin, John. *The Correspondence of John Cosin*. Ed. J. Samson. Durham, 1869.
The Court and Times of James I. Ed. T. Birch. London, 1848.
Coventry: Records of Early English Drama. Toronto, 1981.
Davenport, John. *The Letters of John Davenport*. Ed. I. Calder. New Haven, 1937.
Debates in the House of Commons in 1625. Ed. S. R. Gardiner. London, 1873.
D'Ewes, Simonds. *The Diary*. Ed. E. Bourchier. Paris, 1974.
 The Autobiography and Correspondence. Ed. J. O. Halliwell. London, 1845.
Dictionary of National Biography. Ed. Sir Leslie Stephen. 63 vols. London, 1885–1900.
Documentary Annals of the Reformed Church. Ed. E. Cardwell. 2 vols. Oxford, 1845.
Donne, John. *The Life and Letters*. Ed. Edmund Gosse. London, 1899.
 The Sermons. Ed. G. R. Potter and E. M. Simpson. Berkeley, 1959.
"Dr Plume's Notebook," *Essex Review* XIV (1905).
Drayton, Michael. *The Works*. Ed. J. W. Hebell. Oxford, 1961.
The Earle of Strafforde's Letters and Dispatches. Ed. W. Knowler. London, 1739.

Eliot, Sir John. *Negotium Posterorum*. London, 1881.
Evelyn, John. *The Diary*. Oxford, 1959.
Extracts from the Council Register of . . . Aberdeene, 1570–1625. 2 vols. Aberdeen, 1848.
Finnett, Sir John. *Finetti Philoxenis*. London, 1656.
Foedera. Ed. Thomas Rymer. London, 1735.
Fortescue Papers. London, 1871.
Fuller, Thomas. *The Church History of Britain*. London, 1655.
Goodman, Godfrey. *The Court of King James the First*. London, 1839.
Hacket, John. *Scrinia Reserata*. London, 1692.
Heylin, Peter. *Cyprianus Anglicus*. London, 1668.
Historical Manuscripts Commission Reports.
  8th Report, Appendix/ Wingfield-Digby MSS
  12th Report, Appendix/ Earl Cowper MSS
  Duke of Buccleuch MSS
  Marquis of Salisbury MSS
  Earl of Mar and Kellie
Holles, John, Earl of Clare. Ed. P. R. Seddon. *The Letters of John Holles*. Nottingham, 1983.
The Holles Account of Proceedings in the House of Commons in 1624. Transcribed by Christopher Thompson. Orsett, Essex, 1986.
Howell, John. *Epistolae Ho-Elianae*. Ed. J. Jacobs. London, 1890.
James I. *The Letters of King James VI and I*. Ed. G. P. V. Akrigg. Berkeley, 1984.
  The Political Works of James I. Ed. C. H. McIlwain. Cambridge, Mass., 1918.
  The Poems of King James VI. Ed. J. Craigie. Edinburgh, 1958.
Jonson, Ben. *The Complete Masques*. Ed. S. Orgel. New Haven, 1969.
  The Poems. Ed. I. Donaldson. Oxford, 1975.
Journals of the House of Commons. 17 vols. London, 1742.
Journals of the House of Lords. 19 vols. London, 1767.
Laud, William. *The Works*. 7 vols. Oxford, 1853.
Letters and Other Documents . . . between England and Germany. Ed. S. R. Gardiner. London, 1868.
The Letters and the Life of Francis Bacon. Ed. J. Spedding. 7 vols. London, 1869.
The Loseley Manuscripts. Ed. A. J. Kempe. London, 1835.
Macray, W. D. "Report on materials relating to England in Danish archives." Public Record Office, *46th Annual Report*, appendix 2, pp. 45–7. London, 1886.
Massinger, Philip. *The Plays and Poems*. Oxford, 1976.
The Memoirs of Sir Benjamin Rudyerd, Knt. London, 1881.
Middleton, Thomas. *A Game at Chess*. Ed. R. C. Bald. Cambridge, 1922.
Miscellaneous State Papers. Ed. Earl of Hardwicke. London, 1778.
Notes of the Debates in the House of Lords. Ed. S. R. Gardiner. London, 1879.
Oglander, John. *A Royalist's Notebook*. New York, 1971.
Oxford Council Acts, 1583–1626. Ed. H. E. Salter. Oxford, 1928.
Parentalia, or Memoirs of the Family of Wren. Ed. S. Wren. London, 1760.
Pett, Phineas. *The Autobiography*. London, 1918.
The Pepys Ballads. Ed. H. E. Rollins. 8 vols. Cambridge, Mass., 1929– .
A Pepysian Garland. Ed. H. E. Rollins. Cambridge, Mass., 1922.
Powell, W. S. *John Pory, 1572–1636*. Chapel Hill, 1977.
Propaganda in Germany during the Thirty Years War. Ed. E. A. Beller. Princeton, 1940.

Raleigh, Sir Walter. *The Works of Sir Walter Raleigh*. London, 1829.
Registers of the Privy Council of Scotland. Ed. J. H. Burton *et al.* 6 vols. Edinburgh, 1877– .
The Rich Account of Proceedings in the House of Commons in 1624. Transcribed by Christopher Thompson. Orsett, Essex, 1986.
The Rich Papers: Letters from Bermuda, 1615–1646. Ed. Vernon A. Ives. Toronto, 1984.
Rusdorff, J. J. von. *Mémoires et Négociations Secrètes*. Leipzig, 1719.
Rushworth, John. *Historical Collections*. 7 vols. London, 1682.
Sheppard, Samuel. *The Faerie King*. Salzburg, 1984.
Somers Tracts. Ed. Sir Walter Scott. 13 vols. London, 1809–15.
State Papers Collected by Edward, Earl of Clarendon. Ed. R. Scrope and T. Monkhouse. Oxford, 1767–86.
Stuart Constitution. Ed. J. P. Kenyon. Oxford, 1966 and 1986.
Stuart Royal Proclamations. Ed F. Larkin and P. Hughes. 2 vols. Oxford, 1973.
Tillières, Comte de. *Mémoires Inédits*. Paris, 1862.
A Transcript of the Registers of the Company of Stationers. London, 1877.
Trevelyan Papers. Ed. J. P. Collier, Sir W. C. Trevelyan *et al.* 3 vols. London, 1872.
Wallington, Nehemiah. *Historical Notes*. Ed. R. Webb. 2 vols. London, 1869.
Wilson, Arthur. *The History of Great Britain*. London, 1653.
Wood, Anthony à. *The History and Antiquities . . . of Oxford*. Oxford, 1797.
Yonge, Walter. *The Diary*. London, 1848.

SECONDARY SOURCES

Adams, S. L. "Captain Thomas Gainsford, the 'Vox Spiritus' and the 'Vox Populi'." *Bulletin of the Institute of Historical Research*, XLIX (1976), pp. 141–4.
"Foreign Policy and the Parliaments of 1621 and 1624." In *Faction and Parliament*, ed. Kevin Sharpe. Oxford, 1978, pp. 139–72.
"Spain or the Netherlands? The Dilemmas of Early Stuart Foreign Policy." In *Before the Civil War*, ed. H. Tomlinson. London, 1983, pp. 79–101.
Andrews, K. R. *Elizabethan Privateering*. Cambridge. 1964.
"Elizabethan Privateering." *Raleigh in Exeter 1985: Privateering and Colonisation in the reign of Elizabeth I*. Exeter, 1985, pp. 1–20.
Aveling, Hugh. *Northern Catholics, 1558–1790*. London, 1966.
Aylmer, G. E. *The King's Servants*. London, 1961.
Barcroft, John. "Carleton and Buckingham: The Quest for Office." *Early Stuart Studies*. Minneapolis, 1970, pp. 122–36.
Barnes, Thomas G. *Somerset, 1625–1640*. Cambridge, Mass., 1961.
Berry, H. "The Globe Bewitched and el hombre fiel." *Medieval and Renaissance Drama in England*, I (1984), pp. 211–30.
Breslow, Marvin. *The Mirror of England*. Cambridge, Mass., 1970.
Brown, Alexander. *English Politics in Early Virginia History*. Boston, 1901.
Brown, H. F. "El hombre fiel." *Somerset and Dorset Notes and Queries*, XXX (1970), pp. 238–41.
Bryant, J. H. "John Reynolds of Exeter and His Canon: A Footnote." *The Library*, Fifth Series, XVIII (1963), pp. 299–303.
Carter, Charles. *The Secret Diplomacy of the Habsburgs*. New York, 1964.
Christianson, Paul. *Reformers and Babylon*. Toronto, 1978.
Clark, J. C. D. *Revolution and Rebellion*. Cambridge, 1986.

Clark, Peter. *English Provincial Society . . . Kent, 1500–1640.* Hassocks, Sussex, 1977.
  "Thomas Scott and the Growth of Urban Opposition to the Early Stuart Regime." *Historical Journal*, XXI (1978), pp. 40–53.
Clifton, Robin. "Fear of Popery." *The Origins of the English Civil War.* New York, 1973, pp. 144–67.
Cogswell, Thomas. "Thomas Middleton and the Court, 1624: *A Game at Chess* in Context." *Huntington Library Quarterly*, XLVIII (1984), pp. 273–88.
  "Foreign Policy and Parliament: The Case of La Rochelle, 1625–1626." *English Historical Review*, XCIX (1984), pp. 241–67.
Cust, Richard. "News and Politics in Early Seventeenth Century England." *Past and Present*, CXI (1986), pp. 60–90.
Cust, Richard and Hughes, Ann. "Introduction." *Conflict in Early Stuart England.* London, 1989.
Cust, Richard and Lake, Peter. "Sir Richard Grosvenor and the Rhetoric of Magistracy." *Bulletin of the Institute of Historical Research*, LIV (1981), pp. 40–53.
Dahl, Folke. *A Bibliography of English Corantos and Periodical Newsbooke, 1620–1642.* London, 1952.
Dietz, F. G. *English Public Finance.* New York, 1932.
D'Israeli, Isaac. *Curiosities of Literature.* New York, 1865.
Edmundson, George. *Anglo-Dutch Rivalry during the First Half of the Seventeenth Century.* Oxford, 1911.
Elliott, J. H. *The Count-Duke of Olivares.* New Haven, 1986.
Elton, Sir Geoffrey. *The Parliament of England.* Cambridge, 1986.
Evans, F. M. G. *The Principal Secretary of State.* Manchester, 1926.
Evans, John T. *Seventeenth Century Norwich.* Oxford, 1979.
Fincham, K. and Lake, P. "The Ecclesiastical Policy of James I." *Journal of British Studies*, XXIV (1985), pp.169–207.
Fogel, Robert and Elton, Sir Geoffrey. *Which Road to the Past?* New Haven, 1983.
Gardiner, S. R. "The Political Element in Massinger." *New Shakespeare Society Proceedings*, First series, I (1884), pp. 314–31.
  Prince Charles and the Spanish Marriage, 1617–1623. 2 vols. London, 1869.
  A History of England under the Duke of Buckingham and Charles I, 1624–1628. 2 vols. London, 1875.
  A History of England from the Accession of James I to the Outbreak of the Civil War, 1603–1642. 10 vols. London, 1884.
Gindeley, Anton. *History of the Thirty Years' War.* 2 vols. New York, 1898.
Godfrey, R. T. *Printmaking in Britain.* New York, 1978.
Green, Mary Anne Everett. *The Lives of the Princesses of England.* 6 vols. London, 1857.
Gutman, Myron. *War and Rural Life in the Early Modern Low Countries.* Princeton, 1980.
Haigh, Christopher. "Introduction." In *The Reign of Elizabeth*, ed. C. Haigh. London, 1984, pp. 1–25.
Hawkins, E. *Medallic Illustrations of the History of Great Britain.* London, 1885.
Heinneman, Margot. *Puritanism and Theatre.* Cambridge, 1980.
Hibbard, Caroline. *Charles I and the Popish Plot.* Chapel Hill, 1982.
Hill, Christopher. "The Word 'Revolution' in Seventeenth Century England." In *For*

Veronica Wedgwood These, ed. Richard Ollard and Pamela Tudor-Craig. London, 1986 pp. 134–51.

Hirst, Derek. *The Representative of the People?* Cambridge, 1975.

Hulme, Harold. "The Winning of Freedom of Speech by the House of Commons." *American Historical Review,* LXI (1956), pp. 825–55.

Israel, Jonathan. *The Dutch Republic and the Hispanic World, 1606–1661.* Oxford, 1982.

Kenney, R. W. *Elizabeth's Admiral.* Baltimore, 1970.

Koenigsberger, H. G. "Dominium Regale and Dominium Politicum et Regale." In *Politicians and Virtuosi.* London, 1986, pp. 1–25.

Lake, Peter. "The Significance of the Elizabethan Identification of the Pope as Antichrist." *Journal of Ecclesiastical History,* XXI (1980), pp. 161–78.

"Constitutional Consensus and Puritan Opposition in the 1620s: Thomas Scott and the Spanish Match." *Historical Journal,* XXV (1982), pp. 805–26.

Lee, Maurice, Jr. *Government by Pen.* Urbana, 1980.

James I and Henri IV. Urbana, 1970.

Levy, F. J. "How Information Spread Among the Gentry, 1550–1640." *Journal of British Studies,* XXI (1982), pp. 1–24.

Lockyer, Roger. *Buckingham: The Life and Political Career of George Villiers, First Duke of Buckingham, 1592–1628.* London, 1981.

Lublinskaya, A. D. *French Absolutism: The Crucial Phase, 1620–1629.* Cambridge, 1968.

Mathew, David. *James I.* London, 1967.

Moir, Thomas. *The Addled Parliament of 1614.* Oxford, 1958.

Morgan, Irwonwy. *Prince Charles's Puritan Chaplain.* London, 1957.

Morrill, John. *The Revolt of the Provinces.* New York, 1980.

Mousnier, Roland. *L'assassinat d'Henri IV, 14 Mai 1610.* Paris, 1964.

Neale, J. E. *Elizabeth I and her Parliaments, 1584–1601.* New York, 1958.

Newman, John. *West Kent and the Weald.* London, 1969.

Pages, George. *The Thirty Years War.* New York, 1970.

Parker, Geoffrey. *The Army of Flanders and the Spanish Road.* Cambridge, 1972.

Parker, Geoffrey *et al. The Thirty Years War.* London, 1985.

Patterson, Annabel. *Censorship and Interpretation.* Madison, 1984.

Pearl, Sara. "'Sounding to Present Occasions': Jonson's Masques of 1620–5." In *The Court Masque,* ed. David Lindley. Manchester, 1984, pp. 60–77.

Polisensky, J. P. *The Thirty Years War.* London, 1971.

War and Society in Europe 1618–1648. Cambridge, 1978.

Prestwich, Menna. *Cranfield.* Oxford, 1966.

Rebholz, Ronald. *The Life of Fulke Greville, Lord Brooke.* Oxford, 1971.

Redlich, F. "Contributions in the Thirty Years War." *Economic History Review,* LXI (1959–60), pp. 247–54.

Roberts, Clayton. *Schemes and Undertakings.* Columbus, Ohio, 1985.

Roberts, Michael. *Gustavus Adolphus.* London, 1953–8.

Rose-Troup, Frances. *John White: The Patriarch of Dorchester.* New York, 1930.

Rowse, A. L. *Shakespeare's Southampton.* New York, 1965.

Ruigh, Robert E. *The Parliament of 1624.* Cambridge, Mass., 1971.

Russell, Conrad. *Parliaments and English Politics, 1621–1624.* Oxford, 1979.

"Foreign Policy Debate in the House of Commons in 1621." *Historical Journal,* XX (1977), pp. 289–309.

"The Nature of a Parliament in Early Stuart England." In *Before the Civil War*, ed. H. Tomlinson. London, 1983, pp. 123–50.

"Parliament and the King's Finances." In *The Origins of the English Civil War*, ed. Conrad Russell. New York, 1973, pp. 91–116.

"Parliamentary History in Perspective, 1604–1629." *History*, LXI (1976).

Schreiber, Roy. *The Political Career of Sir Robert Naunton*. Philadelphia, 1981.

The First Carlisle. Philadelphia, 1984.

Seaver, Paul. *The Puritan Lectureships*. Stanford, 1970.

Sharpe, Kevin. *Sir Robert Cotton*. Oxford, 1979.

"The Earl of Arundel, His Circle, and the Opposition to the Duke of Buckingham, 1618–1628." In *Faction and Parliament*, ed. Kevin Sharpe. Oxford, 1978, pp. 209–44.

"The Personal Rule of Charles I." In *Before the English Civil War*, ed. H. Tomlinson. London, 1983, pp. 58–78.

"An Unwanted Civil War?" *New York Review of Books*, XXIX (3 December 1982), pp. 43–5.

Snow, Vernon. *Essex the Rebel*. Lincoln, Nebraska, 1970.

Sommerville, Johann. *Politics and Ideology in England, 1603–1640*. London, 1986.

Stone, Lawrence. "The Revival of Narrative." *Past and Present*, LXXXV (1979).

Strong, Roy. *Van Dyck: Charles I on Horseback*. New York, 1972.

The Cult of Elizabeth. London, 1977.

Henry Prince of Wales. London, 1986.

Tanner, J. R. *Constitutional Documents of the Reign of James I, 1603–1625*. Cambridge, 1952.

Tapie, V. L. *France in the Age of Louis XIII and Richelieu*. New York, 1975.

Thompson, Christopher. "The Origins of the Politics of the Parliamentary Middle Group." *Transactions of the Royal Historical Society*, Fifth Series, XXII (1972), pp. 71–86.

Tite, Colin. *Impeachment and Parliamentary Judicature*. London, 1974.

Wernham, R. B. *After the Armada*. Oxford, 1984.

The Making of Elizabethan Foreign Policy. Berkeley, 1980.

Weyman, H. T. "Members of Parliament for Ludlow." *Transactions of the Shropshire Archaeological and Natural History Society*, Second Series, VII (1895).

White, Stephen. *Sir Edward Coke and the Grievances of the Commonwealth*. Manchester, 1979.

Willson, D. H. *King James VI and I*. New York, 1967.

The Privy Councillors in the House of Commons, 1604–1629. Minneapolis, 1940.

Wilson, Edward and Turner, Olga. "The Spanish Protest against 'A Game at Chess'." *Modern Language Review*, XXXIV (1949), pp. 476–82.

Yates, Frances. *The Rosicrucian Enlightenment*. London, 1972.

Young, Michael. *Servility and Service: The Life and Works of Sir John Coke*. London, 1986.

Zaller, Robert. *The Parliament of 1621*. Berkeley, 1971.

THESES

Adams, S. L. "The Protestant Cause: Religious Alliance with the West European Calvinist Communities as a Political Issue in England, 1585–1630." D.Phil., University of Oxford, 1973.

Ball, J. N. "The Parliamentary Career of Sir John Eliot." Ph.D, University of Cambridge, 1953.

Bonner, R. E. "Administration and Public Service under the Early Stuarts: Edward Viscount Conway as Secretary of State, 1623–1628." Ph.D, University of Minnesota, 1968.

Grayson, J. C. "From Protectorate to Partnership: Anglo-Dutch Relations, 1598–1625." Ph.D, University of London, 1978.

Levy, Jacqueline. "Perceptions and Beliefs: The Harleys of Brampton Bryan." Ph.D, University of London, 1983.

White, A. W. "Suspension of Arms: Anglo-Spanish Attempts at Mediation in the Thirty Years War, 1621–1625." Ph.D, Tulane University, 1978.

INDEX